NEAL-SCHUMAN

Guide to Recommended Children's Books and Media for Use with Every Elementary Subject

SECOND EDITION

KATHRYN I. MATTHEW and JOY L. LOWE

Neal-Schuman Publishers, Inc.
New York London

Published by Neal-Schuman Publishers, Inc.
100 William St., Suite 2004
New York, NY 10038

Printed and bound in the United States of America.

The paper used in this publication meets the minimum requirements of American National Standard for Information Sciences—Permanence of Paper for Printed Library Materials, ANSI Z39.48-1992.

Library of Congress Cataloging-in-Publication Data

Matthew, Kathryn I.
Neal-Schuman guide to recommended children's books and media for use with every elementary subject / Kathryn I. Matthew and Joy L. Lowe. — 2nd ed.
p. cm.
Includes bibliographical references and indexes.
ISBN 978-1-55570-688-3 (alk. paper)
1. Children's literature—Bibliography. 2. Children—Books and reading—United States—Bibliography. 3. Best books—United States. 4. Children's literature—Study and teaching (Elementary)—United States. 5. Content area reading—United States. 6. Children's films—United States—Catalogs. 7. Children's software—United States—Catalogs. I. Lowe, Joy L. II. Title. III. Title: Guide to recommended children's books and media for use with every elementary subject.

Z1037.M2865 2010
011.62—dc22

2010014082

Contents

Preface

The *Neal-Schuman Guide to Recommended Children's Books and Media for Use with Every Elementary Subject*, Second Edition, will help teachers and librarians integrate the best of a broad range of children's literature and media into the excitement of everyday learning. This guide is designed to lead teachers and librarians to the best resources available. In an effort to foster a love of reading in children in a range of curriculum areas, the guide recommends more than 1,000 books, videos, software, CDs, DVDs, and Internet sites that support all elementary curricular areas. Coverage spans the gamut from reprinted classics to new publications through the beginning of 2010.

Because quality materials should be an important part of the learning experience in every elementary school classroom, effective strategies for incorporating these selected resources into curricular areas are emphasized throughout. Sharing books throughout the day models the joy and importance of reading. Students delight in discovering their own feelings and experiences reflected in books. Book selections that value a variety of languages and cultures ensure that this happens for all students (Dickinson and Hinton, 2008; Ernst and Mathis, 2007; Landt, 2007). When children perceive the wonders of their world captured between the pages of a book, they are on their way to becoming lifelong readers and learners. Teachers and librarians know this and are eager to incorporate literature into classrooms in all content areas. The challenge for busy educators is to find quality media that fit naturally into core curricular topics.

How can educators make the best of the children's literature an integral part of the content area curriculum? Librarians' knowledge of current, appropriate books and media combined with teachers' knowledge of the content area curricula ensures that children have a variety of appropriate resources. Insights about curriculum content should be shared and discussed by teachers and librarians. The key is collaboration. It is essential that teachers and librarians work together with the common goal of choosing and using books and media that will expand the mind of each child.

ORGANIZATION

The *Neal-Schuman Guide to Recommended Children's Books and Media for Use with Every Elementary Subject*, Second Edition, contains annotations for contemporary children's books, videos, and related media, as well as presenting inventive ideas for exploring them. Materials cover each of the eight major subject areas: mathematics, science, language arts, social studies, physical education, health, sports, recreation, and dance, art, and music. Each chapter begins with a brief overview of the concepts included in the curricular area. Since all educators are now ever mindful of the necessity of preparing students for the inevitable rigors of testing, content area standards are included for each area.

Each of the eight chapters is subdivided into useful, smaller instructional topics (for example, math is arranged into topics, including measurement, money, problem solving, and so on). Following the subtopics are book and media annotations and suggested ideas for exploring the texts. Chapters end with teacher resources and references.

The annotations in each section are arranged by grade level with books and media for the youngest readers listed first. The grade levels are suggested with the realization that teachers and librarians must rely on their own judgments as to the appropriateness of the books and media for their children:

- P represents preschool,
- K represents kindergarten, and
- Grade levels 1 through 8 are indicated with their respective numerals.
- "And up" signifies books and media that can be used beyond eighth grade.

The annotations include bibliographic information. Following the annotations there are suggested explorations for books and media related to the particular curriculum area under discussion and general ideas for using other materials on the same topic. Each chapter concludes with teacher resources—including books, media, professional organizations, and Internet sites.

The Introduction provides critical information on meeting the needs of individual students, making personal connections, extending learning, and responding to literature through writing, discussing, questioning, and exploring. Also included is information on selecting books and media accompanied by general suggestions for using children's literature routinely as learning resources.

Chapter 1 introduces books and media that present math concepts in meaningful contexts as a part of children's everyday lives. In addition to the topics mentioned earlier, the guide explores number sense and counting; geometry; addition; subtraction; multiplication; division; fractions and decimals; and probability, statistics, and graphing. These materials provide opportunities for exploring and discussing math concepts in a natural, relaxed atmosphere.

Chapter 2 offers suggestions for interesting ways to explore pure and applied science concepts through books by a variety of noted authors and other media. The section examining life science begins with the human body. It continues with an exploration of animals including birds, mammals, reptiles, dinosaurs, insects, and fish. Life science concludes with plants, ecosystems, diversity, and adaptations. Earth and space science explores the structure of the Earth, weather, water, stars and planets, and space travel.

Light, heat, electricity, sounds, energy, machines, and liquids, solids, and gases are all part of physical science. The chapter also contains a section with biographies of scientists and inventors. Material selections exhibit the colorful graphics, enticing photographs and videos, and engaging text that enhance students' learning with intriguing scientific explorations.

Chapter 3 focuses on using books and media to enable children to identify, understand, and utilize components of the language arts. This subject is divided into alphabet, language conventions, parts of speech, figurative language, wordplay, written language, spoken language, poetry, and storytellers and writers. These materials easily lend themselves to children's exposition and expansion of concepts through listening, writing, visualizing, and speaking.

Social studies, as seen through the eyes of characters that help students experience life in other times and places, is explored in Chapter 4. This chapter is organized according to the strands of the *Curriculum Standards for Social Studies* (NCSS, 1994). These strands include culture; time, continuity, and change; people, places, and environments; individual development and identity; individuals, groups, and institutions; power, authority, and governance; production, distribution, and consumption; science, technology, and society; global connections; civic ideals and practices; and biographies. These books and media amplify information of historical and contemporary significance in lively, entertaining ways that capture the imagination and interest of children.

Chapter 5 discusses ways to use books and other media to examine the many aspects of good health. Topics include healthy behaviors, families, and growth and development. The inclusive and contemporary segment on families includes family constellations, divorce, adoption and foster care, and homelessness. Growth and development examines birth and growth, feelings, friendship, self-esteem, manners, and aging and death. These topics are presented in an informative manner that engages the attention of children and presents essential knowledge.

Recommendations for teaching students about physical fitness, sports, recreation, and dance are contained in Chapter 6. These materials are of great interest to children and help develop lifelong skills for maintaining healthy lifestyles.

Chapter 7 contains books and media that open up the world of art to children. This chapter includes art appreciation, art in children's literature, creating art, and artists. These materials enable children to explore the world of art and encourage them to create their own works of art.

Chapter 8 covers materials related to instruments, singing, and creating music. Materials are also included that help children listen and respond to music, develop an understanding of music, explore music in history and culture, and learn about musicians.

The appendix contains a comprehensive listing of teacher and librarian resources including journals, professional organizations, and Internet sites. Media sources include CDs, DVDs, audio books, and software. The subject index is complemented by full title and author/illustrator indexes.

DUAL USES, ONE PURPOSE

The *Neal-Schuman Guide to Recommended Children's Books and Media for Use with Every Elementary Subject*, Second Edition, can be used as both a collection development tool for elementary school libraries, middle school libraries, and district/regional curriculum libraries, and as a planning tool for developing or updating units, or as a quick source for materials that enhance a specific lesson. However you use this volume, its purpose is no doubt yours: successful integration of great literature into core curricular areas.

We, the authors, constructed this to be the best resource of its kind. It focuses on a great variety of subject areas, spells out the subject area content standards, displays complete and current book and media annotations, and includes innovative activities for responding to literature. We trust you will find it to be an effective, practical, and useful tool. Librarians and teachers know that the search for creative and interesting approaches to the successful integration of great literature into core curricula is rewarding. The fact that teaching and learning can become as much fun for adults as for children is simply a wonderful bonus.

REFERENCES

Dickinson, Gail, and Kaavonia Hinton. 2008. "Make the Connection: Celebrating Language Diversity to Improve Achievement." *Library Media Connection* 26, no. 7 (April/May): 5.

Ernst, Shirley B., and Janelle B. Mathis. 2007. "Multicultural Literature: Reading, Writing, and Responding Within a 'New' Literacy Context." *Journal of Children's Literature* 34, no. 1 (Spring): 10–12.

Landt, Susan. 2007. "Weaving Multicultural Literature into Middle School Curricula." *Middle School Journal* 39, no. 2 (November): 19–24.

National Council for the Social Studies. 1994. *Curriculum Standards for the Social Studies*. Washington, DC: National Council for the Social Studies. Available: www.socialstudies.org/standards/strands (accessed November 28, 2009).

Introduction

Children's early social and emotional, as well as cognitive, development is greatly enhanced by learning how to read and learning also to love to read. For many children, this love of reading begins at home when their parents and caregivers read and respond to books with them. At school, this love of reading further develops when children have teachers and library media specialists who recognize the importance of quality children's literature and who create nurturing environments where literature is shared (Williams and Bauer, 2006).

Children of all ages need opportunities to hear and to read quality literature to which they can make personal connections. They want to hear and read stories about children like themselves and they want to hear and read informational books that connect to their personal interests and their needs. Teachers and librarians recognize the uniqueness of each child by finding books appropriate to each child's interests and needs. This book provides teachers and librarians with ideas, books, media, and other resources to meet the needs of individual children.

MEETING THE NEEDS OF STUDENTS

Quality literature facilitates students' understanding because it can accommodate the different backgrounds and life experiences of the students, their prior general background knowledge, their purpose for study, and their reading levels. In literature, students encounter content area material in a variety of genres that enables the students to examine and to learn the material through different lenses. This leads to a deeper processing of the material and helps to ensure that students are learning through their preferred modalities. A selection of carefully chosen books can address individual differences, focus on a topic in great detail, and present the material in a comprehensible manner. Using quality literature in different genres helps ensure all students comprehend and learn.

Meeting the unique needs of all learners is a daunting challenge. The complex, often abstract, concepts presented in classroom textbooks are particularly daunting for English language learners (ELLs) who may not have the background knowledge, vocabulary, and/or knowledge of linguistic structures to comprehend the materials

(Weisman and Hansen, 2007). Teaching vocabulary in context, limiting the number of words introduced at any one time, using visual aids, repetition, word walls, personal dictionaries, games, and opportunities to practice ensures that all students learn the vocabulary necessary to understand content area curriculum (Weisman and Hansen, 2007). English language learners benefit from additional support and encouragement as do students with learning problems and mild disabilities. These students need to be aware of different strategies that will help them comprehend the content; they need opportunities to learn the strategies, and they need time to practice the strategies.

Upper elementary and middle school students with learning problems benefit from advance organizers, such as charts, webs, outlines, and flowcharts, to structure their learning (Steele, 2008). Students with learning disabilities also benefit from learning through stories (Dull and van Garderen, 2005). Further, they contend that stories cognitively engage learning-disabled students who may find the expository writing in textbooks, such as social studies, difficult to comprehend. Ensuring that students with special needs have opportunities to learn content from print, media, and realia enables them to use all of their senses as they learn, rather than just depending on their reading skills, which may be below grade level. Helping students make connections between the content, their personal lives, and their existing knowledge facilitates their comprehension. Working in cooperative groups that require everyone's participation to complete a task benefits students with mild disabilities (McCoy, 2005). Cooperative groups working actively to complete a task can provide the support and guidance all students need to be successful.

SELECTING BOOKS

When selecting books and media for libraries and classrooms, a place to start is the lists of award-winning books found on the websites of professional organizations. These books and media have been reviewed and voted noteworthy by committees composed of members of the organization or by committees of children. The American Library Association (ALA) presents the Randolph Caldecott Medal, the John Newbery Medal, the Coretta Scott King Book Awards, the Pura Belpré Award, the Theodor Seuss Geisel Award, and the Andrew Carnegie Medal for Excellence in Children's Video, among others. The International Reading Association (IRA) has its Children's Choices Award and its Young Adult Choices Award. The National Council of Teachers of English Language Arts awards the Notable Children's Books in the Language Arts (K–8) award and the Orbis Pictus Award for Outstanding Nonfiction for Children. The National Council for the Social Studies (NCSS) and the Children's Book Council (CBC) give the Notable Tradebooks for Young People award for books written for children in grades K–8. NCSS also gives the Carter G. Woodson Book Awards for the most distinguished social science books that depict ethnicity in the United States. The National Science Teachers

Association (NSTA) selects the Outstanding Science Trade Books for Students K–12. These award lists are just the starting place for finding books for your students. The professional organizations listed above publish journals and magazines that contain reviews of a variety of books and often publish articles with ideas for incorporating trade books into teaching. The award lists and other resources available from the professional organizations are all available on their respective websites.

GENERAL SUGGESTIONS FOR LITERATURE IN THE CLASSROOM

Reading aloud books in the classroom, no matter the grade level, is a great way to activate students' prior knowledge and to build an inviting classroom environment that is conducive to learning. The shared knowledge that comes from reading books together helps to establish strong ties between librarians and students, teachers and students, and between students.

1. First, share the books for pleasure and encourage the students to offer their personal responses to the books. Some books are for reading aloud to the children and others should be introduced to the students prior to their independent reading and exploration of the books.
2. Children enjoy opportunities to read and reread books. Younger students want the teacher to read certain books again and again. Older students want to read the books themselves once the teacher has read them aloud. Once read, these books can be placed in the classroom collection, many of which can be on long-term loan from the school library for the students to explore independently.
3. Students enjoy responding to books in a variety of creative, open-ended ways. They like having choices as to how they respond to the books, and to be given opportunities to suggest ways to respond to the books.
4. Students need assistance in making connections between the books, the content area material, and their lives. Activating children's prior knowledge or filling in some gaps in general background knowledge before reading and encouraging them to discuss the book after reading helps ensure that the book becomes personally meaningful to them.
5. Literature presented in this book is suitable to a variety of ages, interests, abilities, and reading levels. When selecting books for children, remember that children who are very interested in a topic are often able to read books above their normal reading level.
6. Many of the books discussed in these chapters can be integrated across content areas. If you encounter a book in one chapter that you think might be misplaced, consider how it can be used to connect two or more content areas. Connecting books across content areas enhances children's comprehension and fosters retention of the concepts presented.

REFERENCES

Dull, Laura J., and Delinda van Garderen. 2005. "Bringing the Story Back into History: Teaching Social Studies to Children with Learning Disabilities." *Preventing School Failure* 49, no. 3 (Spring): 27–31.

McCoy, Kathleen. 2005. "Strategies for Teaching Social Studies." *Focus on Exceptional Children* 38, no. 3 (November): 1–16.

Steele, Marcee M. 2008. "Teaching Social Studies to Middle School Students with Learning Problems." *Clearing House* 81, no. 5 (May/June): 197–200.

Weisman, Evelyn Marino, and Laurie E. Hansen. 2007. "Strategies for Teaching Social Studies to English-Language Learners at the Elementary Level." *The Social Studies* 98, no. 5 (September/October): 180–184.

Williams, Nancy L., and Patricia T. Bauer. 2006. "Pathways to Affective Accountability: Selecting, Locating, and Using Children's Books in Elementary School Classrooms." *The Reading Teacher* 60, no. 1 (September): 14–22.

Chapter 1

Mathematics

Children's literature presents mathematics concepts in a natural way that makes sense to children. Literature enables them to see the connections between mathematics and their everyday lives as they discover mathematics concepts all around them. Through literature children can be exposed to mathematics in natural everyday occurrences in meaningful contexts. Shatzer (2008) emphasizes that first students need to enjoy the stories and the illustrations then students need to revisit the books to make connections to their lives. Helping children make connections to their lives facilitates their understanding of the mathematics concepts found in the books. Sharing a variety of children's literature with them, including fiction and nonfiction books, provides opportunities for explorations and discussions of these concepts in a natural, relaxed atmosphere.

The National Council of Teachers of Mathematics' *Principles and Standards for School Mathematics* (NCTM, 2000) establishes a foundation for and goals for teaching mathematics. The principles encompass these themes: equity, curriculum, teaching, learning, assessment, and technology. The standards focus on content and process. The first five standards are the content standards students should learn including:

1. Number and operations
2. Algebra
3. Geometry
4. Measurement
5. Data analysis and probability

Standards six through ten are process standards including:

6. Problem solving
7. Reasoning and proof
8. Communication
9. Connections
10. Representations

The standards provide guideposts to help determine students' progress as they develop the mathematical knowledge they need to be productive members of society. NCTM recognizes the societal need for mathematical knowledge: mathematical literacy, cultural literacy, workplace mathematics, and active mathematics users. NCTM realizes that students need multiple opportunities to discover mathematical concepts in a variety of contexts, to analyze, solve, and reflect on mathematical problems in addition to opportunities to create their own mathematical problems. Students' mathematical knowledge is expressed through discussing, visualizing, writing, communicating, illustrating, and dramatizing. Making daily entries in mathematics journals give students opportunities to reflect, illustrate, write, and communicate their understanding of the mathematical concepts they explored in class. Carter (2009) found that her students' journal entries provided her with insight as to their thinking and understanding of mathematics and helped the students monitor their learning.

Literature is a resource for mathematics teachers as they seek a variety of ways to present mathematics concepts to students to ensure that each student understands the mysterious, ordered world of mathematics and can communicate mathematically. The books in this chapter demonstrate mathematics as a natural part of life and provide the background knowledge children need to recognize mathematics all around them. Sections in this chapter include number and operations, algebra, geometry, measurement, money, time, data analysis and probability, problem solving, mathematicians, and teacher resources.

NUMBER AND OPERATIONS

Young children's introduction to mathematics begins with counting, comparing, and sorting concrete objects they can hold in their hands and explore. Content standard one focuses on students' development of an understanding of numbers, an understanding of operations, and the ability to compute fluently (NCTM, 2000). From the concrete, they move to the abstract through natural experiences with numeration at home and then at school. Situating numbers in natural contexts makes the learning personally meaningful to the children, which allows them to make connections, communicate mathematically, and problem solve (Cotti and Schiro, 2004). Children need to count objects in their surroundings, such as oranges in a basket; next they need opportunities to draw pictures of the oranges and to count the number of oranges in the pictures. Comparing, sorting, and counting familiar objects helps children develop their number sense. Simple everyday objects like silverware being moved from the dishwasher to its proper place in the drawer provide explorations of comparing, sorting, and counting. In addition, children need opportunities to discover that numbers can be decomposed; for example, four can be two sets of two, or one set of one and one set of three. Books and media in this section explore addition, subtraction, multiplication, division, and fractions.

Counting

The largest category of books available for use in the mathematics classroom is counting books. Animals, children, and food are just some of the objects available to count in these books, which may be children's first introduction to the number system. Effective counting books have the numeral, the number, distinct objects to count, and only the objects to be counted on the page. Understanding the concept of counting requires that students have extensive opportunities to manipulate a wide variety of common objects. They need to have their own sets of objects to count again and again. Providing students with counters to use while a book is being shared enables them to more fully understand the concept of counting. Counting helps students develop a sense of number and operations, which is reflected in content standard one.

Book and Media Choices

Falwell, Cathryn. *Turtle Splash! Countdown at the Pond.* New York: HarperCollins, 2001. Unp. ISBN 978-0-06-029463-2. Grades: P–1.

Ten turtles basking in the sunlight, lounging on a log, slip from the log one by one as passing animals startle them. The rhythm, suspense, and descriptive text in this reverse counting book holds students' attention as they count down from ten to one. The book concludes with information about each of the animals depicted in the book and instructions for making the leaf prints that appear in the collage illustrations. ALA Notable Children's Book, 2002.

Cotten, Cynthia. *At the Edge of the Woods: A Counting Book.* Illustrated by Reg Cartwright. New York: Henry Holt, 2002. Unp. ISBN 978-0-8050-6354-7. Grades: P–2.

Counting, rhyming, and repeating combine to make this a book for counting aloud as the teacher reads. The browns and greens in the illustrations offer a peaceful woodland scene complete with a collection of charming animals just waiting to be counted. A two-page spread near the end of the book shows all of the groups of animals just before they scurry into the woods as a large bear lumbers from his den. Center for Children's Books "Best Books" List, 2002.

Gorbachev, Valeri. *Christopher Counting.* New York: Penguin, 2008. Unp. ISBN 978-0-399-24629-6. Grades: P–2.

Christopher Rabbit learns to count in school and his exuberant passion for this new skill has him counting everything. The pen, ink, and watercolor illustrations offer young readers opportunities to count along with Christopher.

Knick Knack Paddy Whack. Illustrated by Christiane Engel. Cambridge, MA: Barefoot Books, 2008. 24p. ISBN 978-1-84686-144-4. Grades P–2.

This traditional counting song with its new interpretation has youngsters singing along as they learn to count. Bright, colorful acrylics and digital collage illustrations of multiethnic children and a variety of musical instruments invite students to clap, to count, and to sing along. At the end of the book there is information about instrument families, words for a sing-along, and a CD with the song sung by SteveSongs.

Seeger, Laura Vaccaro. *One Boy*. New York: Roaring Brook, 2008. Unp. ISBN 978-1-59643-274-1. Grades: P–3.

Readers count along as one boy paints a series of pictures just perfect for counting from one to ten. On the left side of the two-page spread is simple text describing what is to be counted. On the right side a die cut frames the objects to count. Turn the page and the die cut frames a word within a word that is part of a new phrase describing the painting. On the last two-page spread the paintings are all taped on the wall as the boy, his work done, walks off. The counting and the wordplay make this a book for both the mathematics class and the language arts class. Theodor Seuss Geisel Award Honor Book, 2008.

Cuyler, Margery. *100th Day Worries*. Illustrated by Arthur Howard. New York: Simon and Schuster, 2005. Unp. ISBN 978-1-41690-789-3. Grades: K–2.

The looming class assignment to bring in 100 items on the 100th day of school has Jessica worrying. Nothing she thinks of will quite do—ice cubes, marshmallows. On the morning of the big day, her family comes to her rescue and provides her with nine collections of ten items each. The resourceful Jessica collects ten more items in time to present her 100 items to her classmates. Pastel cartoon illustrations accurately show Jessica's collections, allowing readers to easily count them. This book is also available on DVD.

Math Missions: *The Race to Spectacle City Arcade*. Mac/Win. New York: Tom Snyder, 2003. Grades K–2.

Mathematics challenges await students who venture into the stores in Spectacle City. The mathematics activities in this software reinforce a variety of skills including counting, place value, sorting, classifying, addition, and subtraction. ALSC Notable Children's Software Award, 2004.

Denise, Anika. *Pigs Love Potatoes*. Illustrated by Christopher Denise. New York: Penguin, 2007. Unp. ISBN 978-0-399-24036-2. Grades: K–3.

Rich acrylic and charcoal pictures, rhyming text, and a charming pig family peeling and cooking potatoes entice young readers into counting. As more pigs arrive and more potatoes are added to the pot, the counting continues until ten potatoes are boiling for dinner.

Markle, Sandra. *How Many Pandas?* New York: Walker, 2009. 23p. ISBN 978-0-8027-9783-4. Grades: K–3.

Photographs of the pandas at the Woolong Giant Panda Breeding Center in China introduce children to these fascinating animals and introduce children to counting from one to eight. The crisp, clear pictures make it easy to count the pandas and the numerals and the words help students understand the concept of counting. Back matter includes additional facts about pandas, a glossary/index, and a map of the panda's habitat.

Adler, David. A. *Fun with Roman Numerals.* Illustrated by Edward Miller III. New York: Holiday House, 2008. Unp. ISBN 978-0-8234-2060-5. Grades: 2–5.

Bright bold graphics and succinct text explain Roman numerals by building on students' knowledge of Arabic numerals. Toward the end of the book students are challenged to use Roman numerals written on dots stuck on familiar coins. A collection of photographs of Roman numerals in everyday settings concludes the book.

Ekeland, Ivar. *The Cat in Numberland.* Illustrated by John O'Brien. Chicago, IL: Cricket Books, 2006. 60p. ISBN 978-0-8126-2744-2. Grades: 5–8.

The Hotel Infinity is home to Mr. and Mrs. Hilbert, their cat, and their number guests. There are just enough rooms for all of the numbers, but confusion reigns when zero arrives looking for a room, the letters come for a visit, the odd numbers leave for a visit and return, the even numbers leave for a visit and return, and then just when things seem to be settling down the fractions arrive looking for rooms. As the numbers move from room to room to accommodate the new guests, the hotel always has just enough rooms for everyone. As guests arrive and leave the mathematical problem changes and continues to challenge readers. An author's note about the origin of infinity concludes the book.

One Million Things: A Visual Encyclopedia. New York: Dorling Kindersley, 2008. 297p. ISBN 978-0-7566-3843-6. Grades: 5–8.

Eight chapters of spectacular images and photographs draw readers into exploring the concept of one million. Each chapter focuses on a different subject area: nature, human body, science and technology, space, Earth, people and places, history, and lastly art and culture. A reference section and an index conclude the book.

Explorations

1. As you are reading *Turtle Splash! Countdown at the Pond* (Falwell, 2001) pause and let the students look at the pictures and name the next animal that will startle the turtles.
2. After reading *Turtle Splash! Countdown at the Pond* (Falwell, 2001) first graders can create their own reverse counting book using animals such as sleeping puppies or curious cats.
3. Give each child ten counting cubes so they can count along as you read *At the Edge of the Woods: A Counting Book* (Cotten, 2002). Then, have the students use the cubes to help them retell the story to a partner.
4. *Christopher Counting* (Gorbachev, 2008) contains many ideas for items to count. Provide the students time to work with partners to create a list of things in the classroom they can count such as, pencils, crayons, desks, chairs, toys, or shoes. Then, let each pair select one item on their list that they will count and report back to the class how many of the items there are in the classroom. Create a class chart on the board to record their results.

5. Prior to reading *Knick Knack Paddy Whack* play the CD for students so they can become familiar with the words and the tune. Then, encourage them to sing along as the book is read. Additional songs can be accessed on the SteveSongs website at www.stevesongs.com.
6. After reading *Knick Knack Paddy Whack* talk to the students about the different instruments the children in the story are playing and have them mimic playing the instruments. Select students to represent each of the children in the book. As you read the book have the students come to the front of the room and act out playing the instruments as their number is read.
7. Before reading *Fun with Roman Numerals* (Adler, 2008) have the students study the list of Roman and Arabic numerals on the back cover of the book. Ask them to talk about any patterns they see and what they might be able to deduce about Roman numerals.
8. *One Million Things: A Visual Encyclopedia* provides students with opportunities to explore the concept of one million. Use the photographs in the book to provide students with familiar contexts for learning about large numbers and for making connections to their own lives. David Whitin (2008) found that allowing students to explore the concept of one million in familiar contexts facilitated their understanding and involved them in solving challenging problems.

Addition

Stories have the power to involve students in thinking about mathematics (Clark, 2007). Listening and responding to stories imbedded with mathematical concepts helps students understand and remember them. Further, students need opportunities to model and act out the operations described in these books using a variety of mathematics manipulatives. These manipulatives should be kept in an easily accessible place so the students can use them to practice adding. Learning addition requires that students be given practice sorting and classifying a variety of objects. In addition, students' understanding of mathematical concepts is enhanced when they share conversations with their peers about their learning and when they write about their learning in mathematics journals. As students discuss and write about their learning they develop communication skills described in process standard eight. Books and media included in this chapter enhance children's understanding of addition.

Book and Media Choices

Miller, Amanda. *Let's Add to Ten, Again and Again!* New York: Children's Press, 2007. 24p. ISBN 978-0-531-14869-3. Grades P–1.

Bright, colorful photographs, cheerful rhymes, and simple addition problems introduce young readers to the concept of addition. Once introduced to this book, young readers will be able to return to the book again and again to enjoy it on their own.

Schubert, Ingrid, and Dieter Schubert. *There's Always Room for One More.* Asheville, NC: Front Street, 2002. Unp. ISBN 978-1-886910-77-5. Grades: P–1.

One by one beaver's friends climb aboard his raft as he floats down the river. As the animals climb aboard, the raft sinks lower and lower into the water, finally capsizing when Butterfly joins them. Muted watercolors and a menagerie of animated creatures make this picture book one to savor.

Tang, Greg. *Math Fables.* Illustrated by Heather Calhoon. New York: Scholastic, 2004. Unp. ISBN 978-0-439-45399-8. Grades: P–1.

Not only do the rhymes in this book have children counting to ten, they also show children how numbers can be seen as combinations of smaller numbers. For example, six otters can also be seen as five otters plus one otter or as three otters plus three otters. Colorful, computer-generated animals are grouped on the pages to facilitate students' counting. An author's note at the beginning of the book explains to adults that early experiences with mathematics develop children's fluency with numbers. The book concludes with challenges for students to extend their learning.

Ochiltree, Dianne. *Ten Monkey Jamboree.* Illustrated by Anne-Sophie Lanquetin. New York: Simon and Schuster, 2001. Unp. ISBN 978-0-689-83402-8. Grades: P–2.

Ten cavorting monkeys in colorful shorts are having a jungle jamboree. Action words describe the monkeys' antics as they group themselves in different number combinations all adding up to ten. While young readers will not be able to follow the addition problems that spread across several pages, older readers enjoy learning addition facts with this lively bunch of monkeys. This book is available on audiotape.

Slade, Suzanne. *What's New at the Zoo? An Animal Adding Adventure.* Mount Pleasant, SC: Sylvan Dell, 2009. Unp. ISBN 978-1-934359-93-8. Grades: K–2.

Watercolor paintings of zoo animals, rhyming text, objects to add, and equations to complete make this picture book visit to the zoo an opportunity to learn about addition. As readers accompany a young boy through the zoo they learn about the animals as they practice adding. Back matter includes resources and ideas for reinforcing students' learning.

Tang, Greg. *Math Fables Too: Making Science Count.* Illustrated by Taia Morley. New York: Scholastic, 2007. 40p. ISBN 978-0-439-78351-4. Grades: K–2.

Rhymes, science, and counting combined with computer-generated graphics in bright colors lead to learning fun. Not only does the book offer opportunities for counting but there are also opportunities to learn new words. An author's note at the beginning of the book explains the concept of the book to adults. Additional information about each of the animals highlighted in the rhymes concludes the book.

Sayre, April Pulley, and Jeff Sayre. *One Is a Snail, Ten Is a Crab: A Counting by Feet Book.* Illustrated by Randy Cecil. Cambridge, MA: Candlewick, 2003. Unp. ISBN 978-0-7636-2631-0. Grades: K–3.

Counting by feet at the beach leads to addition as the animals group themselves. An agreeable snail and his one foot join the fun and make the odd numbers. Once the creatures reach ten they group themselves in a variety of ways to count by tens to 100. ALA Notable Children's Book, 2004.

Explorations

1. While reading *There's Always Room for One More* (Schubert and Schubert, 2002) place tally marks on chart paper to count the animals as they climb aboard the raft. As each animal climbs aboard have the students predict if that animal is going to be the one to sink the raft.
2. After reading *There's Always Room for One More* (Schubert and Schubert, 2002) have the students create Popsicle stick rafts to float in a pan of water. Have the students predict how many pennies their rafts will hold and write their predictions in their mathematics journals. Next, have them carefully place pennies on their rafts to see how many pennies they will hold. Then, have them write about their results in their mathematics journals and compare their results with their classmates' results.
3. Before reading *Math Fables* (Tang, 2004) review the fact families for numbers to ten.
4. While reading *Math Fables* (Tang, 2004) to small groups of children give them time to count the animals on the page and then give them time to use manipulatives to create the fact families.
5. Prior to reading *Ten Monkey Jamboree* (Ochiltree, 2001) have the students mix up some "Ten Monkey Crunch Snack Mix" to eat while you read the book aloud. The recipe is on Ochiltree's website at www.ochiltreebooks.com/For-Librarians~61.aspx.
6. Students can group manipulatives to create fact families as *Ten Monkey Jamboree* (Ochiltree, 2001) is read aloud. After each fact family is created have the students write the addition problem in their mathematics journals. For younger children, you can write the fact families on the board as you read and they can draw pictures to represent the fact families.
7. After reading *Ten Monkey Jamboree* (Ochiltree, 2001) return to the book to look for action words such as "flip," "hop," "run," and "scramble." Write the words on the board. Challenge the students to write the fact families for another number such as eight. Then, have them write sentences using the action words.
8. As they read *Math Fables Too: Making Science Count* (Tang, 2007) have the students record unfamiliar words in their mathematics notebooks. After reading the book have the students share the unfamiliar words and then work in small groups to determine the meanings of the words.
9. After reading *Math Fables Too: Making Science Count* (Tang, 2007) have the students create mathematic tales about animals they are learning about in science using the fables in the book as a model. To get the students started on this activity read aloud "The Sound and the Furry" fable in the book. As you read stop and

record all the information about bats that is in the fable, such as their night flights, insect eating, and echolocation. Remind the children that as they write their fables, they want to include the different fact families and information about the animals.

Subtraction

To understand the concept of subtraction, students need opportunities to manipulate concrete objects as they learn to classify and group. As they work with manipulatives, help them discover, compare, and reflect on the four models of subtraction including take away, missing addend, comparison, and set within a set. Using manipulatives to re-create problems found in books read in the classroom fosters students' understanding and retention of subtraction facts. As students develop their understanding of subtraction they are addressing content standard one, which focuses on developing a sense of number and operations.

Book and Media Choices

Fuller, Jill. *Toy Box Subtraction.* New York: Scholastic, 2004. 31p. ISBN 978-0-516-24423-5. Grades: P–K.

Colorful photographs, large font, and a brimming toy box lead to lessons in subtraction as the children decide how to share the toys. The subtraction problems are shown in both words and Arabic numerals. A picture glossary concludes the book. From the Rookie Read-About Math series.

Olson, K. C. *Construction Countdown.* New York: Henry Holt, 2004. 24p. ISBN 978-0-8050-6920-4. Grades: P–1.

Computer-enhanced illustrations of construction vehicles introduce children to the concept of subtraction as they count down from ten to one. The surprise ending reveals that these mighty construction vehicles are rolling through a sandbox with a group of smiling children.

Helakoski, Leslie. *The Smushy Bus.* Illustrated by Salvatore Murdocca. Brookfield, CT: Millbrook Press, 2002. Unp. ISBN 978-0-7613-1398-4. Grades: K–3.

With the regular school bus in the shop for repairs, a clever driver uses subtraction to figure out how to get seventy-six children on and off the four-seat substitute bus. Slid onto overhead bookshelves in pairs, tied in four stacks of three, crunched into seats, slipped in sideways, and stacked like dominoes, the children are transported home. Smiling round-faced children and a calm, cool bus driver add up to a fun mathematics problem that will have young readers subtracting as the story is read.

Ribke, Simone T. *Pet Store Subtraction.* New York: Scholastic, 2006. 32p. ISBN 978-0-516-29673-9. Grades: K–3.

A familiar setting, a pet store, is transformed into a series of subtraction problems as a friendly clerk sells items and orders more. Colorful photographs accompany the simple subtraction word problems found throughout the book. A picture glossary and an index conclude the book. From the Rookie Read-About Math series.

Cleary, Brian P. *The Action of Subtraction*. Illustrated by Brian Gable. Brookfield, CT: Millbrook Press, 2006. 31p. ISBN 978-0-7613-9461-7. Grades: K–4.

Rhyming text and silly cartoons convey that with subtraction you end up with less. Angry bulldogs, toothy hornets, crashing bowling pins, flying shoes, and a collection of stuffed animals are all familiar objects that help students make connections between the subtraction problems in the book and their own lives. The number problems appear in both text and numerals.

Explorations

1. A collection of miniature vehicles and a shoebox will enable students to create their own toy box subtraction problems. The students can record their problems in their mathematics journals. Older students can write story problems about the toy collection.
2. With a collection of miniature toys or unifix cubes the students can reenact the subtraction countdown in *Construction Countdown* (Olson, 2004).
3. Read aloud *The Smushy Bus* (Helakoski, 2002). Then, read it again and work out the subtraction problem on the board as you read. Also, as you write the problem on the board talk aloud about your thoughts and actions to help the students understand the problem.
4. After reading *The Smushy Bus* (Helakoski, 2002) have the students work with base ten blocks to determine other combinations that add up to seventy-six. Ask them to write their solutions in their mathematics journals or have the students create displays on poster board showing their solutions.
5. As you read *Pet Store Subtraction* (Ribke, 2007), use a document camera to show the word problem to the students. Then, think aloud as you work to solve the problem, pointing out the keywords in the problem that helped you decide what you will do to solve the problem. You might also have the students predict what the number sentence will look like before you turn the page and reveal it.
6. The text in *The Action of Subtraction* (Cleary, 2006) is a rap that groups of students can memorize and perform. After reading and performing the rap give the students an opportunity to work in groups in order to write and perform their own subtraction raps.

Multiplication

Memorizing multiplication tables in order to complete a worksheet of multiplication problems is not much of an incentive to learn them. However, needing to memorize them in order to play games and to complete activities might be just the incentive students need. Manipulatives, such as base ten blocks, provide students hands-on opportunities to portray multiplication problems using different groupings (P. Whitin, 2008). Books on skip counting are included in this section because learning to skip count helps students master the multiplications facts. As students create row-by-row displays using base ten blocks they come to see multiplication as repeated addition and they develop an understanding of numbers and number operations that addresses content standard one.

Book and Media Choices

Dahl, Michael. *Pie for Piglets: Counting by 2s.* Illustrated by Todd Ouren. Mankato, MN: Capstone, 2005. 24p. ISBN 978-1-4048-0943-7. Grades: P–2.

Bright, colorful illustrations draw young readers into the book as the piglets count by twos. "Fun Facts" sections provide interesting trivia. From the Know Your Numbers series.

Ochiltree, Dianne. *Sixteen Runaway Pumpkins.* Illustrated by Anne-Sophie Lanquetin. New York: Simon and Schuster, 2001. Unp. ISBN 978-0-689-85090-5. Grades: P–2.

Searching the pumpkin patch reveals one, then two, then four, then eight, then sixteen rambunctious pumpkins. As the colorful pumpkins double and fill the wagon, students learn about multiplying by two. Descriptive words, rhyming text, and the cumulative tale make this a book for the language arts classroom as well as the mathematics classroom. This book is available on audiotape.

DeFelice, Cynthia C. *One Potato, Two Potato.* Illustrated by Anrea U'Ren. New York: Farrar, Straus and Giroux, 2006. Unp. ISBN 978-0-374-35640-8. Grades: K–3.

Mr. and Mrs. O'Grady live all alone and they share one chair, one bed, one coat, and one blanket. Each day they share one potato until Mr. O'Grady digs up a magic pot that doubles everything that goes into it and so they have two potatoes. Two potatoes is just the beginning! A magic pot is just the ticket to introduce students to multiplication. Imagine if the magic pot tripled everything that went in to it.

Pallotta, Jerry. *Ocean Counting: Odd Numbers.* Illustrated by Shennen Bersani. Watertown, MA: Charlesbridge, 2004. Unp. ISBN 978-0-88106-151-2. Grades: 2–4.

This book offers a twist on counting by twos as it starts with one and so the counting is done in odd numbers. The book ends with even numbers fifty and zero. Counting by twos all the way to fifty and showing the numbers in both words and numerals gives older students still struggling with mathematical concepts the additional support they need to make sense of numbers. Colored-pencil illustrations of the sea creatures accompany the text that contains some interesting facts about the creatures.

Mills, Claudia. *7 x 9 = Trouble.* Illustrated by G. Brian Karas. New York: Farrar, Straus and Giroux, 2004. 112p. ISBN 978-0-374-46452-3. Grades: 2–5.

Passing timed multiplication tests is a common elementary school challenge and students relate to third grader Wilson Williams' worries. Others in the class have passed the tests. Poor Wilson! Even his kindergarten brother is better in mathematics, but Wilson's talent is not in mathematics: it is in art. This chapter book includes humorous pictures that help readers relate to Wilson's predicament. ALA 2003 Notable Children's Book, 2003.

Explorations

1. While reading *Pie for Piglets: Counting by 2s* (Dahl, 2005) have the students follow along using calculators to multiply by two.
2. After reading *Pie for Piglets: Counting by 2s* (Dahl, 2005) have the students illustrate and write their own counting by twos books.
3. As you read *Sixteen Runaway Pumpkins* (Ochiltree, 2001) use number cubes to show the students how the number of pumpkins doubles as the story progresses.
4. *Sixteen Runaway Pumpkins* (Ochiltree, 2001) is not only a mathematics book; it is also an introduction to autumn. Check craft stores for small pumpkins that students can use to reenact the story. Then, have the students create their own stories having the pumpkins multiply by three, then four, then five.
5. As you read *Ocean Counting: Odd Numbers* (Pallotta, 2004) have students count along on number lines or with calculators.
6. After reading *Ocean Counting: Odd Numbers* (Pallotta, 2004) take the students on a field trip through the school in search of items they can put in the form of multiplication problems. Then, have them illustrate and write multiplication problems using the items they saw on the field trip. Compile their work into a class multiplication book (Cotti and Schiro, 2004).
7. After reading *7 x 9 = Trouble* (Mills, 2004) engage the students in a discussion about how they all have different talents and that for some of them mathematics may not be their strength. However, they can learn mathematics by learning strategies to help them understand the concepts.

Division

Division may present problems for children who have not fully grasped their addition, subtraction, and multiplication facts. Explorations with manipulatives and opportunities to write out the algorithms enhances students' understanding of division. Grouping and regrouping manipulatives enhances their understanding of division as repeated subtraction, fair sharing, and distribution. Exploring division in literature provides students with a deeper understanding and a chance to practice what they have learned. As students come to an understanding of division they are addressing content standard one, focusing on number and operations.

Book and Media Choices

McElligott, Matthew. *Bean Thirteen.* New York: G.P. Putnam's Sons, 2007. Unp. ISBN 978-0-3992-4535-0. Grades: K–3.

How can two bugs evenly share thirteen beans? The bugs, Flora and Ralph, invite friends to dinner and try out different ways to divide the beans evenly, although

Ralph is determined not to be the unlucky person eating bean thirteen. This perplexing division problem introduces prime numbers and the solution shows how creative thinking can be used to solve mathematics problems. This book is also available as an audiobook.

McElligott, Matthew. *The Lion's Share*. New York: Walker, 2009. Unp. ISBN 978-0-8027-9768-1. Grades: K–3.

As the host of the dinner party, lion offers dessert to his guests first. Unfortunately, his guests have poor manners and as the cake is passed around each guest takes half of what is on the plate. By the time the cake gets back to the lion there is only a crumb left. The ant realizes that the crumb on the plate is too small to divide in half to share with the lion, so she offers to bake him a cake. The other guests decide to bake the lion a cake and each doubles the number of cakes they plan to bake. The lively story deftly weaves in division, multiplication, and fractions. To reinforce the division of the cake many pages of the book are divided into panels that are also divided.

Wingard Nelson, Rebecca. *Division Made Easy*. Illustrated by Tom LaBaff. Berkeley Heights, NJ: Enslow, 2005. 48p. ISBN 978-0-7660-2511-0. Grades: 2–4.

Starting with the definition of division, the author offers a simple-to-understand look at the properties of division. The book can be used to introduce the concept of division or to review division skills. The book concludes with resources for learning more, websites, and an index. From the Making Math Easy series.

Long, Lynette. *Dazzling Division: Games and Activities That Make Math Easy and Fun*. New York: Wiley, 2000. 122p. ISBN 978-0-471-36983-7. Grades: 2–5.

The hands-on activities in this book involve students in exploring division with a variety of materials in different ways. Students struggling to learn division benefit from trying to understand it using manipulatives and by approaching it from different angles. An index concludes the book. From the Magical Math series.

Explorations

1. Before reading *Bean Thirteen* (McElligott, 2007), give each student a small bag with thirteen dried beans. Put the students in groups of two, three, or four students and have them divide up the beans. As they work, have one student in the group record the different ways they decide to divide up the beans. Then, share the groups' answers before reading the story.
2. While reading *The Lion's Share* (McElligott, 2009), have the students divide squares of paper as the cake is cut. You might stop periodically to ask the children to show their neighbor what they have done. This will help make sure that all of the students understand the concept.
3. After reading *The Lion's Share* (McElligott, 2009) or *Bean Thirteen* (McElligott, 2007) encourage older students to visit McElligott's website at matthewmcelligott .com to explore the mathematics concepts presented in the books.

Fractions

Fractions are befuddling. Children learn that 1 + 1 = 2. Then, they discover that with fractions one whole equals two parts, or four parts, or even thirty-two parts. Through literature children discover that fractions are all around them and a natural part of their lives. For example, they have all had experiences sharing food with siblings or friends, so they understand the importance of having things divided equally in order to get their fair share. These experiences form the basis of their understanding of fractions. Literature provides teachers with a way of presenting fraction concepts to students by using realistic activities, such as cooking, to explore fractions. The books below provide a way to extend the fraction concepts presented in textbooks and make them meaningful to students. Many activities used to teach fractions involve measurement as for example, in cooking. This helps to address content standard four, measurement.

Book and Media Choices

Townsend, Donna. *Apple Fractions.* New York: Scholastic, 2004. Unp. ISBN 978-0-5162-4419-1. Grades: K–2.

Everyday objects depicted in color photographs and simple sentences introduce young readers to fractions. A glossary and an index conclude the book. From the Rookie Read-About Math series.

Adler, David A. *Working with Fractions.* Illustrated by Edward Miller. New York: Holiday House, 2007. Unp. ISBN 978-0-8234-2010-0. Grades: 1–3.

Bold, bright computer graphics, a smiling clown, repetitive vocabulary, and hands-on activities involve students in exploring and understanding fractions.

Dodds, Dayle Ann. *Full House: An Invitation to Fractions.* Illustrated by Abby Carter. Cambridge, MA: Candlewick Press, 2007. Unp. ISBN 978-0-7636-2468-2. Grades: 1–3.

Rhyming couplets accompanied by charming watercolor illustrations introduce fraction concepts as the Strawberry Inn fills with guests. The repeated refrain ensures that students will be chiming in as this book is read aloud.

Napoli, Donna Jo. *The Wishing Club: A Story about Fractions.* Illustrated by Anna Currey. New York: Henry Holt, 2007. Unp. ISBN 978-0-8050-7665-3. Grades: 1–4.

Watercolor and ink illustrations depicting warm summer evenings and star-filled nights set the stage for four siblings wishing on a star. However, the children get only a fraction of what they wish for, such as a quarter instead of a dollar. They solve the problem of why they are only getting a fraction of what they wish for and figure out that by working together they can wish for a whole. The book concludes with questions to extend students' fraction explorations.

Stamper, Judith Bauer. *Go, Fractions!* Illustrated by Chris Demarest. New York: Penguin, 2003. 48p. ISBN 978-0-4484-3139-4. Grades: 2–4.

Sixteen kids with a mathematics teacher for a coach find themselves immersed in soccer and fractions. Throughout this easy-to-read chapter book the players encounter mathematics problems all related to fractions. From the All Aboard Math Reader series.

Gifford, Scott. *Piece=Part=Portion: Fractions=Decimals=Percents.* Photographs by Shmuel Thaler. Berkeley, CA: Ten Speed Press, 2003. 32p. ISBN 978-1-58246-102-1. Grades: 3–5.

Large, eye-catching color photographs of familiar objects on the right side of each two-page spread depict piece=part=portion. On the left side are a few descriptive words about the objects and the numeral equivalents expressed as fractions, decimals, and percentages. For example, one page shows two stocking-clad feet with one large toe sticking out of a hole, depicting one-tenth.

Equivalent Fractions and Mixed Numbers. DVD. Wynnewood, PA: Schlessinger Media, 2004. 15 min. ISBN 978-1-41710-454-3. Grades: 3–6.

Students join secret agent Matt Mattics and his team as they attempt to foil Dr. Strangeglove's plan to cause a mathematical catastrophe. Since the video was filmed in England there are some words to watch for such as "naught" for "zero." The soundtrack includes an English and a Spanish version. A teacher's guide is included. From the Math Challenge DVD series.

Long, Lynette. *Fabulous Fractions: Games and Activities That Make Math Easy and Fun.* New York: Wiley, 2001. 122p. ISBN 978-0-471-36981-3. Grades: 3–6.

Forty hands-on activities involve students in learning fractions while having fun. One activity involves cutting a sandwich into fourths six different ways. Each activity has clear instructions, a list of needed materials, and helpful tips. Also available as an eBook.

Wingard-Nelson, Rebecca. *Decimals and Fractions.* Berkeley Heights, NJ: Enslow, 2008. 64p. ISBN 978-0-7660-2877-7. Grades: 5 and up.

Concise, easy-to-understand text explains decimals and fractions. The book can be used to introduce the concepts or to review them. Resources for learning more and an index conclude the book. From the Math Busters series.

Math Mysteries: Fractions. Mac/Win. New York: Tom Snyder, 2000. Grades: 4–7.

The town folks in Balancing Rock have heard rumors about gold in the nearby hills. Students add and subtract fractions and multiply whole numbers as they solve word problems to discover the story behind the rumors.

Math Mysteries: Advanced Fractions. Mac/Win. New York: Tom Snyder, 2000. Grades: 4–7.

In order to escape from a remote island before the volcano erupts students have to use their knowledge of fractions to solve fourteen word problems. These complex word problems require students to multiply and divide fractions. Media clips and onscreen guides provide assistance as students work to solve the problems. A teacher's guide is included.

Explorations

1. After reading *The Wishing Club: A Story about Fractions* (Napoli, 2007), have the students use fraction tiles to help them understand why the children's wishing resulted in only part of what they wanted. Then, have the students use the fraction tiles to help them understand how all of the children wishing together resulted in them getting a whole pig.
2. After reading *The Wishing Club: A Story about Fractions* (Napoli, 2007), challenge the students to use the fraction cubes and play money to solve the questions at the end of the book.
3. While reading *Go, Fractions!* (Stamper, 2003) cut oranges in halves and then fourths just as Coach Curtis does. Talk to the students about which is larger—one-half or one-fourth. Then, let them munch on the orange sections as you finish reading the book. Reinforce this concept by dividing another orange into halves and thirds. At the end of the lesson have the students write their reflections on fractions in their mathematics journals. Their writings can be used to assess their understanding of fractions.
4. Using *Piece=Part=Portion: Fractions=Decimals=Percents* (Gifford, 2003) as a model have students create their own piece=part=portion scenes. Next, let them use a digital camera to capture their work. Then, have the students write a description to accompany their photograph. Writing helps clarify students' thinking and enhances their understanding.
5. While sharing games and activities from *Fabulous Fractions: Games and Activities That Make Math Easy and Fun* (Long, 2001) challenge the students to think up solutions before sharing the solution with them. For example, one activity has them figuring out as many ways as they can to cut the sandwich six different ways. Give the students squares of paper and let them work in groups to devise as many ways as they can to cut the sandwich.
6. To check for students' understanding of fraction word problems have them use the word problems in *Decimals and Fractions* (Wingard-Nelson, 2008) as models as they write word problems for their classmates to solve.

ALGEBRA

In order for students to develop an understanding of algebra they need experiences using algebra throughout their school years. For younger students this includes discovering patterns as well as sorting and classifying objects. As students progress through the grades they build on their knowledge of patterns, sorting, and classifying by using algebraic expressions to describe the patterns they observe. To facilitate their understanding of algebra students need to understand the concept of equality, which is explored in *Equal, Shmequal* (Kroll, 2005) annotated below. Content standard two focuses on students' development of an understanding of algebra, noting that it is a skill to be developed over time rather than waiting until high school algebra classes (NCTM, 2000).

Book and Media Choices

Roy, Jennifer Rozines and Gregory Roy. *Patterns in Nature.* Tarrytown, NY: Marshall Cavendish, 2006. 31p. ISBN 97978-0-7614-1999-0. Grades: K–3.

Colorful photographs highlight patterns found in nature such as the symmetry in butterflies' wings. Large print and short sentences make these books accessible to early readers. A glossary, an index, and resources for learning more conclude the book. From the Math All Around series.

Kroll, Virginia L. *Equal, Shmequal.* Illustrated by Philomena O'Neill. Watertown, MA: Charlesbridge, 2005. 32p. ISBN 978-1-57091-891-9. Grades: K–3.

When schoolchildren leave behind their tug-of-war rope a charming group of forest animals decide to play tug-of-war. This sets in motion a lively exercise in determining what equal means so that they can balance their teams. They settle on using a seesaw to determine what combination of animals will make equal sides. Includes nonfiction mathematics notes for the meaning of equal.

Tang, Greg. *Math Appeal.* Illustrated by Harry Briggs. New York: Scholastic, 2003. Unp. ISBN 978-0-4392-1046-1. Grades: 1–3.

Bright, colorful illustrations and riddles entice readers to discover the patterns in mathematics and how to use the patterns to solve the riddles. The solutions require students to use critical thinking skills and just in case they cannot solve the riddles, the book concludes with a detailed answer key.

Number Patterns. DVD. Wynnewood, PA: Schlessinger Media, 2004. 15 min. ISBN 978-1-57225-875-4. Grades: 3–6.

Agent Matt Mattics explores the secrets of number patterns to solve a puzzling case. Since the video was filmed in England there are some words to watch for such as "naught" for "zero." The soundtrack includes an English and a Spanish version. A teacher's guide is included. From the Math Challenge DVD series.

Algebraic Thinking. DVD. Wynnewood, PA: Schlessinger Media, 2006. 23 min. ISBN 978-1-41710-599-1. Grades: 4–7.

Multiethnic children involved in realistic problems use algebraic thinking to find their answers. As with other films in this series students are shown how to use multiple ways to get the correct answer. Includes a teacher's guide that is available online. From the Math for Students series.

McKellar, Danica. *Kiss My Math: Showing Pre-algebra Who's Boss.* New York: Hudson Street Press, 2008. 335p. ISBN 978-1-59463-049-1. Grades: 7–8.

Aimed at female teens, this book makes mathematics fun; even students who are not struggling will learn something. This book has five sections: Number Stuff, Variable Stuff, Solving for X, All About Exponents, and Intro to Functions and Graphing Lines. Real-life examples of practical examples of using algebra and testimonials from women who use mathematics in their jobs are included. Voice of Youth Advocates (V.O.Y.A.) Award.

Explorations

1. Outdoor explorations on the playground can reinforce the concepts presented in *Patterns in Nature* (Roy and Roy, 2006).
2. Bring into class a collection of nonfiction books about animals and plants. Model for the students how to look through the books searching for patterns. Ask them to mark their discoveries with sticky notes describing the patterns they see. Then, provide them time to share their findings with their classmates.
3. Students can practice creating patterns by visiting the National Library of Virtual Manipulatives algebra website at nlvm.usu.edu/en/nav/topic_t_2.html and clicking on color patterns or pattern blocks.
4. Show *Algebraic Thinking* in segments, periodically stopping the film to have the students discuss what they have learned and write down their reflections. At the end of the film have the students share their reflections in small groups and then involve them in a class discussion about the film.

GEOMETRY

Active explorations with two- and three-dimensional shapes enhance students' understanding of geometric objects. Content standard three addresses the importance of students developing their spatial sense and understanding of geometry. In order to do this, students need to analyze, describe, draw, classify, and create shapes. Students who struggle with numerical skills may find it easier to understand geometric concepts. The books and materials in this section provide students with examples of geometric principles in the environment. Students need a strong foundation in order to succeed in the more formal geometric applications they will encounter in later years.

Book and Media Choices

Ross, Kathy. *Crafts: Triangles, Rectangles, Circles, and Squares!* Illustrated by Jan Barger. Brookfield, CT: Millbrook Press, 2002. 48p. ISBN 978-0-7613-2104-0. Grades: P–1.

Young children benefit from hands-on activities that allow them to explore shapes and this book involves them in a variety of craft activities using different shapes.

Step-by-step illustrated instructions and easy-to-obtain materials have students creating games, puppets, and collages as they learn about shapes.

Olson, Nathan. *Cubes.* Mankato, MN: Capstone, 2008. 32p. ISBN 978-1-4296-0049-1. Grades: P–2.

Cubes can be played with (dice) and eaten (croutons) as illustrated in the colorful photographs in this introductory book. The book includes a table of contents, a glossary, a resource guide, a hands-on activity, and an index. This is from the 3-D Shapes series.

Hanson, Anders. *What in the World Is a Cylinder?* Edina, MN: ABDO, 2008. 24p. ISBN 978-1-59928-888-8. Grades: K–3.

Color photographs, line drawings, and short, simple sentences describe cylinders and show everyday examples. The book ends with an activity that sends readers looking for cylinders. From the 3-D Shapes series.

Roy, Jennifer Rozines, and Gregory Roy. *Shapes in Transportation.* Tarrytown, NY: Marshall Cavendish, 2007. 31p. ISBN 978-0-7614-2265-5. Grades: K–3.

On a trip to visit friends two giggling girls find polygons, trapezoids, triangles, and rectangles in the traffic signs, construction zones, and the wheels of vehicles. Color photographs and illustrations accompanied by simple sentences introduce a variety of shapes and the concept of lines and segments. The book concludes with a glossary, resources for learning more, and an index. From the Math All Around series. This book is available as an e-book.

Murphy, Stuart J. *Hamster Champs.* Illustrated by Pedro Martin. New York: HarperCollins, 2005. 33p. ISBN 978-0-06-055772-0. Grades: 1–4.

When the humans leave, three feisty hamsters escape from their cage and keep the family cat entertained as their toy car flies through the air on a ramp placed at different angles. The lively conversation between the hamsters and the cat helps to explain concept of angles. From the MathStart series.

Explorations

1. After creating the rectangle pussycat puppet in *Crafts: Triangles, Rectangles, Circles, and Squares!* (Ross, 2002), have the students work with a partner to tell stories with their puppets.
2. Geometric shapes are hidden everywhere. A field trip through the school halls can become a hide-and-seek adventure as children look for triangles, circles, squares, and rectangles. Take along a digital camera to record the students' discoveries or have them sketch their findings in their mathematics journals. Parents can be encouraged to extend this activity at home by having students discover shapes in their homes.
3. Students and parents can work together to create a journal of common shapes they encounter in their neighborhood, such as stop signs and yield signs. Giving students opportunities to illustrate the shapes fosters retention.

4. *Hamster Champs* (Murphy, 2005) introduces angles and measuring with a protractor. To fully understand the concepts presented in the book students need opportunities to create and measure angles. Place the children in small groups and provide each group with a small car, a protractor, and a short one-inch by two-inch board. As they create slopes for their cars to race down have them record their findings and reflections in their mathematics journals.

MEASUREMENT

Developing an understanding of measurement requires students to be actively involved in using both standard and nonstandard units of measure. Measurement involves counting, estimating, or using tools, such as, clocks, scales, rulers, and containers. Literature can enhance children's motivation to engage in measurement activities on their own (Castle and Needham, 2007). Students enjoy measuring with nonstandard units of measure, as there seems to be something special about getting to measure objects with other objects. Content standard four addresses understanding of measurement and its everyday uses.

Book and Media Choices

Pelley, Kathleen T. *Magnus Maximus, A Marvelous Measurer.* Illustrated by S. D. Schindler. New York: Farrar, Straus and Giroux, 2010. Unp. ISBN 978-0-374-34725-3. Grades: K–3.

Magnus Maximum spends so much time measuring and counting extraordinary things that the town declares him their official measurer. He counts the fleas in a lion's mane and he measures the stinkiness of socks. In fact, he spends so much time measuring and counting that he forgets to appreciate life until one day a small boy reminds him to take time to enjoy living.

Scott, Janine. *Take a Guess: A Look at Estimation.* Minneapolis, MN: Compass Point Books, 2003. 24p. ISBN 978-0-7565-0446-5. Grades: K–3.

Color photographs of familiar events such as heading down a slide, watching the weather, and cooking introduce young readers to guessing how much and how many. Back matter includes fun facts, a glossary, resources for learning more, and an index. From the Spyglass Books series.

Reisberg, Joanne. *Zachary Zormer: Shape Transformer.* Illustrated by David Hohn. Watertown, MA: Charlesbridge, 2006. 32p. ISBN 978-1-57091-875-9. Grades: 2–4.

On Fridays in Zachary's mathematics class, show-and-tell involves bringing in something to measure. Each week Zachary forgets but at the last minute he comes up with measurement activities demonstrating length, width, perimeter, and area. The book concludes with instructions and illustrations for creating the measurement tricks Zachary shares with his classmates including how to make a Möbius strip and an expanding frame.

Roy, Jennifer Rozines, and Gregory Roy. ***Measuring at Home.*** **Tarrytown, NY: Marshall Cavendish, 2007. 31p. ISBN 978-0-7614-2263-1. Grades: 2–4.**

With standard measuring tools such as a measuring cup, a tape measure, a stopwatch, a bathroom scale, and a thermometer, a journey through the house reveals lots of items to measure. Colorful photographs of everyday household objects and simple sentences introduce students to the concept of measurement. Back matter includes a glossary, resources for learning more, and an index. From the Math All Around series.

Goldstone, Bruce. ***Great Estimations.*** **New York: Henry Holt, 2006. 32p. ISBN 978-0-8050-7446-8. Grades: 2–5.**

Readers are introduced to different methods of estimating such as "clump counting" and "box and count" as they explore the multitude of items in the colorful photographs of everyday objects. Once the concepts are explained readers get to practice these estimating techniques that are used every day by professionals. Hint boxes are included to help readers as they estimate. Bank Street Best Children's Book of the Year.

Goldstone, Bruce. ***Greater Estimations.*** **New York: Henry Holt, 2008. 32p. ISBN 978-0-8050-8315-6. Grades: 2–5.**

Colorful photographs of ducks, plastic flies and spiders, dandelion seeds, and a domino maze offer opportunities to learn and practice estimating skills. Hints at the bottom of the page provide the information needed to estimate the number of items in the picture. From simple objects to aerial views of crowds at a concert, the estimations skills needed to determine the number of objects in the pictures require increasingly harder skills. The book concludes with an author's note on the everyday uses of estimating.

Long, Lynette. ***Measurement Mania: Games and Activities That Make Math Easy and Fun.*** **New York: Wiley, 2001. 122p. ISBN 978-0-471-36980-6. Grades: 3–6.**

Chapters include five different forms of measurement using the English and the metric systems: (1) length and distance, (2) volume, (3) weight, (4) temperature, and (5) time. Brain stretchers along with tips and tricks extend the hands-on activities in the book. This book is also available as an e-book. From the Magical Math series.

Neuschwander, Cindy. ***Sir Cumference and the Isle of Immeter: A Math Adventure.*** **Watertown, MA: Charlesbridge, 2006. 32p. ISBN 978-1-57091-680-9. Grades: 3–6.**

Perimeter and area are used to solve the mystery and tame the sea serpent lurking within the pages of the book. Diagrams help students understand the geometric concepts and additional information at the end of the book helps the students understand geometry. From the Sir Cumference series.

Zanzarella, Marianne, compiler. ***The Good Housekeeping Illustrated Children's Cookbook.*** **Photographs by Tom Eckerle. New York: Hearst, 2004. 166p. ISBN 978-1-58816-424-7. Grades: 3–6.**

Cooking is a delicious way to practice measurement in a real-life activity that yields yummy meals. Detailed instructions in an accessible format complete with safety cautions involve young chefs in cooking meals for their families and friends. Photographs accompany some of the recipes.

Explorations

1. Use *Magnus Maximus, A Marvelous Measurer* (Pelley, 2010) to introduce students to using nonstandard units of measure. For example, lead students through a discussion of how they might measure the scratchiness of a sweater or the softness of a towel.
2. *Zachary Zormer: Shape Transformer* (Reisberg, 2006) concludes with the instructions for making a Möbius strip, creating an expanding frame, and using a flashlight and graph paper to examine area. Gather the needed materials and have the students work with partners to complete the activities.
3. After reading *Take a Guess: A Look at Estimation* (Scott, 2003) and *Measuring at Home* (Roy and Roy, 2007) students are eager to set out on measurement excursions at home and at school. Provide the students with a variety of measurement tools and a variety of objects to measure. Have them first estimate what they think the measurement will be and record their estimate in their mathematics journals. Then, have the students measure the object and record the measurement next to their estimate. Encourage the students to reflect on their estimates and their actual measurements.
4. Activity 26 "The Price Is Right" in *Measurement Mania: Games and Activities That Make Math Easy and Fun* (Long, 2001) involves a real-life activity that shoppers face regularly in the grocery store. Bring into the classroom several grocery items in different sizes and have the students compare prices and sizes to determine which one is the best value.
5. Prior to actually measuring objects, encourage students to estimate the length of the object being measured and record the measurement in their mathematics journal. Once the object is measured have them record the actual measurement and then make comparisons between their estimate and the actual length.
6. Have the students create collections or locate collections in the classroom for their classmates to practice their estimation skills. For example, a container of crayons or paper clips could be used to practice estimation skills. Give the students a clear, plastic jar to take home and fill with objects for their classmates to estimate (Callan, 2004).
7. As you read *Sir Cumference and the Isle of Immeter: A Math Adventure* (Neuschwander, 2006) aloud have the students take notes in their journals about any mathematics concepts they notice (Clark, 2007). Pause periodically for the students to share their ideas about how to solve the mystery. At the end of the story have students write down their reflections on what they learned from the story.

MONEY

Students' interest in money begins when they realize it is needed to buy the toys, electronic gadgets, and clothes they see in advertisements. As cash is replaced by checks, checks by credit cards, and credit cards by online electronic banking, concrete coins and bills are not as available to help students grasp the concept of money. Reading books such as the ones in this section expands students' opportunities to comprehend the value of money.

Book and Media Choices

Robinson, Elizabeth Keeler. *Making Cents.* Illustrated by Bob McMahon. Berkeley: Ten Speed, 2008. Unp. ISBN 978-1-58246-214-1. Grades: K–2.

Dreams of a clubhouse set the neighborhood children on a quest to make money to buy the materials they need to build clubhouse. As their money accumulates the denominations grow and the materials for the clubhouse appear. The book concludes with an author's note containing information about the half-dollar, dollar coin, and two-dollar bill, which are not mentioned in the book.

Adler, David A. *Money Madness.* Illustrated by Edward Miller. New York: Holiday House, 2009. Unp. ISBN 978-0-8234-1474-1. Grades: K–3.

Currency is not limited to paper and coins. It can be rocks, feathers, fishhooks, purple beads, and animals. From bartering objects to spending coins and currency, this thought-provoking book explains how money is used. Uncle Sam guides readers through the text. The back cover of the book depicts the men found on our money.

Doudna, Kelly. *Let's Add Bills.* Edina, MN: Abdo, 2003. 24p. ISBN 978-1-57765-898-1. Grades: K–3.

Full-color photographs depict various denominations of bills and simple sentences explain how to add the bills together to pay for different items. The repetitive text helps students remember the addition concepts presented in the book. The book concludes with a picture glossary and a word list. From the Dollars and Cents series.

Harris, Trudy. *Jenny Found a Penny.* Illustrated by John Howell. Minneapolis, MN: Millbrook Press, 2008. Unp. ISBN 978-0-8225-6725-7. Grades: K–3.

This lively cumulative tale has readers counting along as Jenny saves her money to buy something special. To help readers track how much money Jenny has in her glass jar the coins are displayed in a separate column. When she has just enough money, with glass jar in hand she goes to the store only to discover she does not have money for the sales tax. Just when things could not get any worse she drops her glass jar and her coins scatter across the sidewalk. There is a happy ending and her purchase is not revealed until the last page.

Williams, Vera. *A Chair for My Mother* (25th Anniversary Edition). New York: HarperCollins, 2007. Unp.ISBN 978-0-688-04074-1. Grades: K–3.

When a fire destroys their home three generations of women, a grandmother, a mother, and a young girl, decide to save their change in a large jar in order to buy an upholstered chair for them to share at the end of the workday. When the jar is filled they buy a big, comfortable chair to share. Caldecott Medal Honor Book, 1983.

Seuling, Barbara. *There Are Millions of Millionaires: And Other Freaky Facts about Earning, Saving, and Spending*. Illustrated by Ryan Haugen. Minneapolis, MN: Picture Window Books, 2009. 40p. ISBN 978-1-4048-4115-4. Grades: 3–5.

Children love reading and sharing interesting facts with anyone who will listen and this book is filled with tantalizing facts about money. Imagine using feathers as currency or clay tablets for checks. This book is from the Freaky Facts series.

Rancic, Bill with Karen Soenen. *Beyond the Lemonade Stand: Starting Small to Make It Big*. New York: Penguin, 2005. 160p. ISBN 978-1-5951-4103-3. Grades: 3–6.

Rancic, winner of *The Apprentice* television show, shares his own childhood business adventures as he explains how to start a business. Included are twenty ideas for starting a kid business with lessons learned from other youthful entrepreneurs. The book also contains information on building a business, money management, and investing profits. A glossary concludes the book.

Hall, Alvin. *Show Me the Money*. New York: DK, 2008. 96p. ISBN 978-0-7566-3762-0. Grades: 4–6.

The book is divided into four sections: (1) history of money, (2) expenses and income, (3) economics, and (4) work and business. Real-life examples explain the concepts and information on wealthy entrepreneurs and noted economists are included. Credit, the stock market, cash flow, and taxes are some of the topics covered in this informative text.

Greenwald, Lisa. *My Life in Pink and Green*. New York: Abrams, 2009. 267p. ISBN 978-0-8109-8352-6. Grades: 4–7.

A foreclosure warning on the family pharmacy has twelve-year-old Lucy devising plans to attract customers by offering makeup advice. She builds on her initial success at offering makeup advice by opening an eco-spa and applying for the town's Going Green grant. Young adults relate to this upbeat story that shows that they can help out and make a difference.

Thomas, Keltie. *The Kids Guide to Money Cent$*. Illustrated by Steve MacEachern. Tonawanda, NY: Kids Can Press, 2004. 56p. ISBN 978-1-5533-7389-6. Grades: 4–7.

A social studies assignment brings three students together to learn about money—why we need it, how to make it, and how to budget it. The students have three different perspectives on money, which is a powerful lesson for students as they learn about the impact of money on their lives. Cartoon characters in comic strip format explain difficult concepts using realistic examples.

Sid Meier's Railroads. Win. Hunt Valley, MD: Firaxis, 2007. Grades: 4 and up.
This real-life business simulation with railroads and railroad barons and real locomotion sounds entices students to build their own railroad and become a railroad baron. Along the way students learn lessons in supply and demand as their railroad empire grows. Multiple children can play this game over the Internet. ALA Great Interactive Software for Kids Winner, Fall 2007.

Explorations

1. After reading *Let's Add Bills* (Doudna, 2003), return to the book and give the students play money to use as they work out the problems in the book with a partner.
2. After reading *A Chair for My Mother* (Williams, 2007) have the students consult furniture ads and select a comfortable-looking one. Record the price on the board and figure out the sales tax on the chair using the local sales tax rate. As you figure out the sales tax explain to the children what you are doing. Have the students work with you as you add the sales tax to the price of the chair. Decide with the students the amount of money to save each week and then figure out how many weeks it will take before they can purchase the chair.
3. After reading about stocks in *Show Me the Money* (Hall, 2008) discuss stocks with the students. Then, have them brainstorm a list of products that they use such as cell phones, iPods, shampoo, and snacks. Explain to the students that stock market investors often buy stocks in companies whose products they use. Help the students research the companies that make the products they use and find their stock market symbols. Then, assign each student $500 to buy stock in the company of their choice. Show the students how to set up an Excel spreadsheet to track the progress of their stock over several weeks.
4. As students play *Sid Meier's Railroads* have them record their decisions in their mathematics journals. As the game progresses ask them to reflect on the impact of their decisions. Then, have the students work in groups to examine each others' decisions and make suggestions about what they can do to expand their empires.

TIME

Young children's introduction to time may first come when they are told that dinner will be ready in half an hour. When the child asks how long a half-hour is, the parent responds by explaining time in relation to the length of the child's favorite television show. Children mark time in holidays, birthdays, and summer vacations. Time is an abstract concept that is not readily explained with manipulatives. Students need a variety of opportunities to explore the concept of time in order to develop their understanding. The materials in this section provide students with opportunities for exploring time.

Book and Media Choices

Fraser, Mary Ann. *I.Q., It's Time.* New York: Walker, 2005. Unp. ISBN 978-0-8027-8980-8. Grades: P–K.

The classroom is filled with last-minute preparations for Parent's Night and I.Q., the class pet mouse, is intent on creating a surprise for the parents. A digital clock tucked into the corner of each page marks the passing of the school day. Interwoven into the story are facts about time such as the twenty-four hours in a day and sixty minutes in an hour. At the end of the book I.Q.'s surprise is revealed: a paper plate clock with a small drawing of the children's hour-by-hour activities.

Gleick, Beth Youman. *Time Is When.* Illustrated by Marthe Jocelyn. Toronto, ON: Tundra Books, 2008. 32p. ISBN 978-0-88776-870-5. Grades: P–1.

Originally published in 1960, this easy reader explains the difficult-to-grasp concept of time using familiar activities. Multiethnic children, digital clocks, and poetic text explore how long it takes to paint a picture and how long between birthdays. Anchoring the concept of the passage of different lengths of time in familiar activities helps students make connections to their own lives, which enhances understanding.

Baker, Keith. *Hickory Dickory Dock.* Orlando, FL: Harcourt, 2007. Unp. ISBN 978-0-15-205818-0. Grades: P–2.

This expanded version of the nursery rhyme "Hickory Dickory Dock" starts off with a mouse scurrying up a large grandfather clock. As the hours pass, different animals interact with the clock and a careful look at the illustrations reveals the mouse is mimicking each animal's actions. For example, when the hare hops over, the mouse hops along on a pogo stick. The large uncluttered face of the clock makes it easy for students to see the hours ticking away.

Omololu, Cynthia Jaynes. *When It's Six O'clock in San Francisco: A Trip through Time Zones.* Illustrated by Randy DuBurke. Boston: Houghton Mifflin Harcourt, 2009. 31p. ISBN 978-0-618-76827-1. Grades: 2–4.

Readers make their way around the globe as they travel through the time zones. Warm, colorful acrylic illustrations depict children's everyday lives and help readers understand that while they are eating breakfast, elsewhere in the world other children are already in school or are sleeping. The string of numerical clocks across the bottom of the pages grows as each time zone is visited. Back matter includes a map depicting the time zones and a brief explanation of time zones.

Lasky, Kathryn. *The Man Who Made Time Travel.* Illustrated by Kevin Hawkes. New York: Farrar, Straus and Giroux, 2003. 40p. ISBN 978-0-374-34788-8. Grades: 3–5.

John Harrison's life work was the building of seagoing clocks to enable sailors to determine their ships' longitude in order to avoid getting lost at sea. Harrison's pursuit of the Longitude Prize involved years of work creating the clocks and then years of struggle to get the prize money. Hawke's detailed illustrations capture the period and the endpapers showcase one of Harrison's timepieces. An author's note, an illustrator's note, and a bibliography offer resources for learning more. NCTE Orbis Pictus Honor Book, 2004.

Mass, Wendy. *11 Birthdays.* New York: Scholastic, 2009. 267p. 978-0-545-05239-9. Grades: 4–6.

Caught in a time warp, feuding friends Amanda and Leo are doomed to spend their shared eleventh birthday over and over again. Each day they awaken to find that it is once again their eleventh birthday. They realize that in order to escape the time trap they need to forget their differences and work together.

Collier, James Lincoln. *Clocks.* Tarrytown, New York: Marshall Cavendish, 2004. 126p. ISBN 978-0-7614-1538-1. Grades: 5–8.

Sundials, water clocks, hourglasses, and turret clocks have all been used to measure time through the ages. The book includes chapters on the evolution of the calendar, navigation time, the development of affordable clocks and watches, and atomic clocks. The book concludes with websites, a bibliography, and an index. From the Great Inventions series.

TimeLiner XE. Mac/Win. New York: Tom Snyder, 2002. Grades: 6 and up.

Students can create timelines, sequences, and cycles using templates or they can design their own with this interactive organizational software. Text and media can be combined to create timelines or to show a sequence. Sequences can be transformed into slideshows or saved in PDF format so that students can communicate what they have learned to their classmates or their parents. *Instructor* Teachers' Pick Best of 2009.

Explorations

1. Prior to reading *I.Q., It's Time* (Fraser, 2005) go over the class schedule with the students. Then, as you read the book help the students make comparisons between their class schedule and the students in the book's class schedule.
2. After reading *Time Is When* (Gleick, 2008) have the children brainstorm a list of things they can do in thirty minutes. Then, have them illustrate the activities and write about them. Compile their text and drawings into a class book.
3. While reading *Hickory Dickory Dock* (Baker, 2007) have the students use paper plate clocks to show the passing of the hours. As students move the hands of their clocks their neighbors can check to make sure that the hands are in the correct place.
4. After reading *When It's Six O'clock in San Francisco: A Trip through Time Zones* (Jaynes, 2009), use a document camera to project the time zone map at the end of the book to help students understand how the world is divided into twenty-four

time zones. To reinforce the concept of time zones share the Greenwich Mean Time website at wwp.greenwichmeantime.com.

5. Before reading *11 Birthdays* (Mass, 2009) briefly explain that two children in the story end up reliving their eleventh birthday over and over again. Then, have the students make predictions about what caused the time trap and how the children will escape.
6. After reading *Clocks* (Collier, 2004) have the students use *TimeLiner XE* to create a timeline of the development of clocks through the years.
7. After examining the pictures of sundials in *Clocks* (Collier, 2004) have the students design and create their own sundials. Then, take them outside to try out their sundials.

DATA ANALYSIS AND PROBABILITY

Data analysis involves students in collecting data and determining how to use the data to solve problems and answer questions. The problems and questions must be ones that are personally interesting to the students and they must be given ownership of the data collection and analysis (Whitin and Whitin, 2008). Data may be organized into charts, tables, and graphs from which students make inferences and draw conclusions. As students analyze data they are introduced to statistics to help them understand the data. Understanding probability begins with encounters of chance and randomness. As students' understanding grows they recognize the connections between statistics and probability. Standard five encompasses data analysis and probability. Books in this section show students how data analysis and probability are embedded in their daily lives.

Book and Media Choices

Harris, Robie H. *Maybe a Bear Ate It!* Illustrated by Michael Emberley. New York: Scholastic, 2008. Unp. ISBN 978-0-439-92961-5. Grades: P–1.

Tucked into bed with his favorite stuffed animals and his favorite book, a little critter is settling in for the night, when a wide yawn and a stretch send the book sliding to the floor buried under the bedclothes. The animals in the bedclothes come to life as the critter imagines that each one of them probably ate his book. This wonderful bedtime story can also be used to introduce probability to the youngest students. An ALA Notable Children's Book, 2009.

Bodach, Vijaya Khristy. *Pie Graphs*. Mankato, MN: Capstone, 2008. 24p. ISBN 978-1-4048-0943-7. Grades: P–2.

Simple, easy-to-understand text and brightly colored photographs explain pie graphs to young readers. Short chapters define pie graphs and explain how to use them to depict data such as favorite foods and how much time is spent in school each week.

A table of contents, a glossary, resources for learning more, and an index are included. This book is from the Making Graphs series.

Bodach, Vijaya Khristy. *Tally Charts.* Mankato, MN: Capstone, 2008. 32p. ISBN 978-1-42960-043-9. Grades: P–2.

Photographs of familiar objects and step-by-step instructions for creating tally charts ensure that young mathematicians are ready to create their own tally charts. The book concludes with questions to answer with a tally chart, bibliographic references, a glossary, websites, and an index. From the A Plus Books: Making Graphs series.

Leedy, Loreen. *It's Probably Penny.* New York: Henry Holt, 2007. 32p. ISBN 978-0-8050-7389-8. Grades: K–3.

Certainly, probably, possibly are explained as Lisa makes predictions about her dog Penny's actions over the weekend. Lively, imaginative illustrations accompany the clear understandable text ensuring that young readers will grasp these important mathematics concepts. This book is a follow up to two other successful mathematics books featuring Penny: *Measuring Penny* (Leedy, 1998) and *Mapping Penny's World* (Leedy, 2000). Bank Street Best Children's Book of the Year.

The Graph Club 2.0. Mac/Win. New York: Tom Snyder, 2004. Grades: K–4.

This software helps students transition from graphing with objects to graphing with abstract representations. The program allows students to create four types of graphs: picture, bar, line, and circle. After creating graphs students can write about what they did in an onscreen notebook that includes an audio recorder. The program includes cross-curricular activities. Macworld Editors' Choice Award.

Roy, Jennifer Rozines, and Gregory Roy. *Graphing in the Desert.* Tarrytown, NY: Marshall Cavendish, 2007. 31p. ISBN 978-0-7614-2262-4. Grades: 2–4.

The Sonoran Desert is showcased in colorful photographs that depict the animals and the plants inhabiting this harsh environment. Graphs interspersed throughout the text and pictures provide another way of learning about the animals and plants. A glossary, resources for learning more, and an index conclude the book. From the Math All Around series. This book is also available as an e-book.

Einhorn, Edward. *A Very Improbable Story.* Illustrated by Adam Gustavson. Watertown, MA: Charlesbridge, 2008. Unp. ISBN 978-1-57091-871-1. Grades: 2–5.

Ethan awakens one morning with a talking cat perched on his head. Odds, the cat, sets out to teach Ethan about probability and as Ethan learns so do young readers. In order to get the cat off his head Ethan has to play games of odds and win. Throughout the story, Ethan plays a series of games of probability and in the end not only does he get Odds off his head, he also uses probability to figure out how to score in his soccer game. Oil illustrations depict the humorous antics of Ethan and his living headgear.

Kline, Suzy. *Horrible Harry Cracks the Code.* Illustrated by Frank Remkiewicz. New York: Viking, 2007. 66p. ISBN 978-0-670-06200-3. Grades: 3–6.

With help from the Fibonacci sequence, Harry figures out how Mrs. Funderburke awards prizes in the cafeteria contest. The realistic portrayal of life in the third grade draws readers in as it teaches them the secrets to the Fibonacci sequence. From the Horrible Harry series.

Graph Master. Mac/Win. New York: Tom Snyder, 2001. Grades: 4–8.

This software involves students in analyzing data and interpreting the results in order to solve problems. Data sets and cross-curricular activities are included. Data tables are provided for students to record their own data sets that they can transform into nine different graphs. Technology and Learning Award of Excellence.

Shea, Therese. *The Great Barrier Reef: Using Graphs and Charts to Solve Word Problems.* New York: Rosen, 2007. 32p. ISBN 978-1-40423-359-1. Grades: 4–8.

Readers discover the importance of the reefs hidden beneath the ocean as they learn to read graphs and charts of the species inhabiting the reefs and the number of visitors to the watery paradise. From the Math for the Real World series.

Explorations

1. While reading *Maybe a Bear Ate It!* (Harris, 2008) pause after the picture of the elephant sleeping on the book and talk to the students about the probability of each of the animals having the book. Then, ask them to predict where they think the book will be found.
2. After reading *Pie Graphs* (Bodach, 2008) help students survey their classmates about favorite foods and create pie graphs to depict the preferences. They could create pie graphs of favorite ice cream, cookies, or vegetables.
3. After reading *It's Probably Penny* (Leedy, 2007) model how to complete the probability homework assignment by having students construct charts like the one in the book and make predictions about things that might happen in school that day. Go over the results with the students and then have them make predictions about what might happen in their home over the weekend. Provide the students with time to share their results the following Monday.
4. After reading *It's Probably Penny* (Leedy, 2007) and *A Very Improbable Story* (Einhorn, 2008) re-create some of the probability problems presented in the books using collections of familiar items such as socks and jellybeans. Then, have the students bring collections of objects from home to create their own probability problems. Provide the students with tally charts or have them create their own to record their results.
5. After reading *Graphing in the Desert* (Roy and Roy, 2007) or *The Great Barrier Reef: Using Graphs and Charts to Solve Word Problems* (Shea, 2007) have the students collect data about a habitat they are studying in science. Once they have

created data sets they can access the National Center for Educational Statistics Kids' Zone Create a Graph webpage at www.nces.ed.gov/nceskids/createagraph/default.aspx to use the online software to create graphs. The website includes examples of graphs and an online tutorial.

PROBLEM SOLVING

Content standard six focuses on students' developing problem-solving skills. Children's literature contains real-world mathematics problems to solve, set in familiar contexts (Moyer, 2000). These problems are likely to spark students' interest and challenge their perceptions and organizational skills as they work to find solutions. Books in this section involve students in examining problems from different perspectives and in using their critical thinking skills to solve the problems.

Book and Media Choices

Leedy, Loreen. *Missing Math: A Number Mystery.* Tarrytown, NY: Marshall Cavendish Children, 2008. Unp. ISBN 978-0-7614-5385-7. Grades: K–2.

The townsfolk are in a tizzy when all the numbers disappear. This imaginative look at how much we depend on numbers will have students pondering the problems caused by their disappearance. Essential vocabulary words are defined in text boxes interspersed in the colorful, lively illustrations.

Adler, David A. *You Can, Toucan, Math: Word Problem-Solving Fun.* Illustrated by Edward Miller. New York: Holiday House, 2006. Unp. ISBN 978-0-8234-1919-7. Grades: 1–3.

Rhyming word problems about birds have readers adding, subtracting, multiplying, and dividing as they discover the answers. The illustrations and the endpapers contain resources to help the students solve the problems.

Bowen, Anne. *The Great Math Tattle Battle.* Illustrated by Jaime Zollars. Morton Grove, IL: Albert Whitman, 2006. Unp. ISBN 978-0-8075-3163-1. Grades: 1–3.

Harley uses his mathematics journal to tally and report on his classmates' transgressions, such as the number of erasers Erwin chewed off his pencil. He meets his match with the new kid, Emma Jean, who begins to tally and report on Harley's transgressions. Tally marks and reports generated by Harley and Emma Jean on their lined paper are included in the full-page illustrations. The book concludes with "Math Tattle Battle Teasers" for students to practice problem solving and the answers are included.

Horvath, Polly. *The Pepins and Their Problems.* New York: Farrar, Straus and Giroux, 2004. 179p. ISBN 978-0-374-35817-4. Grades: 4–7.

How would you get down if you were trapped on your roof? Perplexing problems such as this keep the Pepins stumped. But the story narrator calls on readers to offer solutions to get the Pepins out of their predicaments. Readers offer a variety of solutions to help the Pepins; however, the readers are just as confused as the Pepins.

Math Mysteries: Advanced Whole Numbers. Mac/Win. New York: Tom Snyder, 2000. Grades: 4–7.

Challenging word problems set in a virtual environment require students to practice their problem-solving skills in order to discover the secrets of the mansion, Casa Loca. Students use basic operations to complete the multi-step problems they encounter. Includes a teacher's guide.

Leech, Bonnie Coulter. *Mesopotamia: Creating and Solving Word Problems*. New York: Rosen, 2007. 32p. ISBN 978-1-40423-357-7. Grades: 4–8.

While learning about the "cradle of civilization" students solve mathematical problems involving the content they are learning. For example, they learn how to find the surface area of a ziggurat or temple tower. Throughout the book they are challenged to write their own word problems using the ones in the book as models. A glossary and an index conclude the book. From the Math for the Real World series.

Explorations

1. Prior to reading *Missing Math: A Number Mystery* (Leedy, 2008) have the students brainstorm a list of ways they use numbers every day, such as the numbers on the clock, the numbers on the classroom, and the numbers on the school buses. Then, engage the students in a discussion of the problems that might happen if the numbers all disappeared for a day.
2. Prior to reading *Missing Math: A Number Mystery* (Leedy, 2008) discuss the vocabulary words defined in the book with the students and then add them to the class word wall.
3. The illustrations in *The Great Math Tattle Battle* (Bowen, 2006) can be used as models for students as they determine what to write in their mathematics journals.
4. While reading aloud *The Pepins and Their Problems* (Horvath, 2004) pause after some of the Pepins' predicaments are introduced and have the students pretend they are the readers who are sending in solutions. They can use the readers' suggestions in the books as models for their own writing.
5. While reading *Mesopotamia: Creating and Solving Word Problems* (Leech, 2007) have the students create mathematics word problems using the ones in the book as models. Then, as the students study other topics in social studies have them create mathematics word problems using the new material they are learning.

MATHEMATICIANS

Books in this section explore the lives of great mathematical thinkers, whose contributions continue to impact our daily lives. Some of them were persecuted for their beliefs and the feminine mathematicians encountered gender bias when they tried to study mathematics. Learning about their contributions and their interesting lives helps students develop an appreciation for mathematics and helps them make connections between their lives and the lives of the mathematicians. As students read these biographies they develop an understanding of how natural occurrences in their lives can have profound impacts. For example, when the remodelers ran out of wallpaper in Sonya Kovalevsky's bedroom, they finished the job by covering the wall with copies of lecture notes from one of her father's old calculus textbooks (Bradley, 2006). Kovalevsky spent hours staring at the notes and memorizing the formulas and symbols. This was the beginning of her mathematical studies.

Book and Media Choices

D'Agnese, Joseph. *Blockhead–The Life of Fibonacci.* Illustrated by John O'Brien. New York: Macmillan, 2010. Unp. ISBN 978-0-8050-6305-9. Grades: K–5.

As a young boy, Leonardo Fibonnacci was so fascinated by numbers that he daydreamed about them and his daydreaming earned him the nickname "Blockhead." His daydreams led him to the realization that natural objects often followed a particular pattern; that pattern is known as the Fibonacci Sequence.

Hakim, Joy. *Aristotle Leads the Way.* Washington, DC: Smithsonian Books, 2004. 282p. ISBN 978-1-58834-160-0. Grades: 5 and up.

The connections between mathematics and science are evident in this book that could be used in either content area. Lively chapter titles including "Aristarchus Got It Right—Well, Almost!" and "No Joke—the Earth Is Pancake Flat" entice readers into the book, and they are not disappointed. Color photographs, illustrations, diagrams, and textboxes contain additional information that enhances understanding of the complex ideas presented in the text. The book includes a table of contents, resources for learning more, and an index. From the Story of Science series.

Bradley, Michael J. *The Birth of Mathematics: Ancient Times to 1300.* New York: Facts on File, 2006. 148p. ISBN 978-0-8160-5423-7. Grades: 6 and up.

Ten early mathematicians are profiled in this volume of the series. Each entry includes a brief biography and details of their mathematical discoveries. Hypatia, the first woman of mathematics, is included. The book contains a multimedia resource list, resources for learning more, a glossary, and an index. From the Pioneers in Mathematics series.

Bradley, Michael J. *The Foundations of Mathematics: 1800 to 1900.* New York: Chelsea House, 2006. 162p. ISBN 978-0-8160-5425-1. Grades: 6 and up.

Explore the lives of ten mathematicians in this collection of short biographies that include in-depth information on their mathematics' contributions. This book includes Marie-Sophie Germain, Carl Friedrich Gauss, Mary Fairfax Somerville, Niels Henrik Abel, Évariste Galois, Augusta Ada Lovelace, Florence Nightingale,

Georg Cantor, Sonya Kovalevsky, and Henri Poincaré. A glossary, a bibliography, resources for learning more, and an index conclude the book. From the Pioneers in Mathematics series.

Staeger, Rob. *Ancient Mathematicians.* Greensboro, NC: Morgan Reynolds, 2008. 112p. ISBN 978-1-59935-065-3. Grades: 6 and up.

An exploration of mathematics in ancient Greece introduces the four mathematicians whose lives are profiled in the book. Brief biographies of Pythagoras, Euclid, Archimedes, and Hypatia examine their contributions to mathematics. Maps, artifacts, sidebars, diagrams, timelines, and mathematical explanations are included. Back matter includes a bibliography, websites, and an index. From the Profiles in Mathematics series.

Explorations

1. Prior to reading *Blockhead—The Life of Fibonacci* (D'Agnese, 2010) visit the book's website at www.blockhead.com to read the author's blog and discover ways to use this book in both mathematics and science.
2. When introducing *Aristotle Leads the Way* (Hakim, 2004) point out the diagrams and mathematical problems in the sidebars. Remind the students that the sidebars are there to help them understand the content. Encourage the students to try out the activities and solve the mathematics problems as they read.
3. The women profiled in *The Foundations of Mathematics: 1800 to 1900* (Bradley, 2006) lived at a time when women were not given the same access to schooling as men. Have the students examine the brief biographies of Marie-Sophie Germain, Mary Fairfax Somerville, and Augusta Ada Lovelace to determine how these mathematicians overcame the limitations placed on them because of their gender.
4. Before reading *The Foundations of Mathematics: 1800 to 1900* (Bradley, 2006) have the students begin a timeline in TimeLiner XE. As the students read have them add the mathematicians' birth dates, death dates, and dates of their contributions to the timeline. When it is completed print it out and have the students make inferences about the connections between the mathematicians and their contributions.
5. After reading *The Foundations of Mathematics: 1800 to 1900* (Bradley, 2006) have the students select a mathematician to research to learn more about that mathematician's contributions and their continuing impact on society.

TEACHER RESOURCES

Materials in this section contain useful resources for teaching mathematics concepts across the content area curriculum. Some of the professional books noted below are devoted entirely to using children's literature to teach mathematics and some contain ideas for linking mathematics to other content areas. Included in this section are a collection of websites for both teachers and students. Many of the sites have sections just for teachers and some include links for parents with ideas for working with their children to enhance their understanding of the mathematics concepts they are learning in school.

Book and Media Choices

Bay-Williams, Jenny, and Karen Karp, editors. *Growing Professionally.* Reston, VA: National Council of Teachers of Mathematics, 2008. 311p. ISBN 978-0-87353-605-9. Grades: P–8.

This edited collection of mathematics teachers' and mathematics educators' favorite articles include ideas for professional development and ideas for classroom teaching. The articles are grouped into three sections: Ideas for Using Articles for Professional Development, Strategies for Growing as a Professional, and Topics for Growing as a Professional.

Thiessen, Diane, editor. *Exploring Mathematics through Literature: Articles and Lessons for Prekindergarten through Grade 8.* Reston, VA: National Council of Teachers of Mathematics, 2004. 304p. ISBN 978-0-87353-553-7. Grades: P–8.

Discover more ways to integrate children's literature into the mathematics curriculum to ensure that students understand the five mathematics content strands. The book contains articles and lessons with black line masters of recording sheets that are used in the lessons.

Leinwand, Steve. *Accessible Mathematics: 10 Instructional Shifts That Raise Student Achievement.* Portsmouth, NH: Heinemann, 2009. 128p. ISBN 978-0-325-02656-5. Grades: P–12.

Discover how to make small changes in your teaching that will increase your students' mathematics achievement. The book also includes ideas for teacher professional development.

National Council of Teachers of Mathematics. *Principles and Standards for School Mathematics.* Reston, VA: National Council of Teachers of Mathematics, 2000. 402p. ISBN 978-0-87353-480-2. Grades: P–12.

The NCTM standards, information on the progression of students' learning through the grade levels, and ways to incorporate technology in the mathematics classroom make this a very useful book for teachers.Included with the book is a CD with a hypertext version of the book, pages from the Illuminations website, and interactive tools.

Barnett-Clarke, Carne, Alma Ramirez, Debra Coggins, and Susie Alldredge. *Number Sense and Operations in the Primary Grades: Hard to Teach and Hard to Learn?* Portsmouth, NH: Heinemann, 2003. 185p. ISBN 978-0-325-00546-1. Grades: K–2.

This book contains cases for teachers to analyze in order to deepen their understanding of how to teach mathematics, to understand mathematics from their students' perspectives, to examine different teaching strategies, and to understand the impact of communication on learning. A facilitator's guide is included as this is a book to explore with other teachers.

Ward, Robin A. *Activities for Integrating Mathematics with Other Content Areas, Grades K–2*. Upper Saddle River, NJ: Pearson, 2009. 240p. ISBN 978-0-205-53040-3. Grades: K–2.

This is a compilation of literature-based activities appropriate for grades kindergarten to second that integrate mathematics with science, social studies, and visual arts. The National Content Standards for each content area are incorporated into the activities. An appendix contains assessment tools and rubrics.

Lake, Jo-Anne. *Math Memories You Can Count On: A Literature-Based Approach to Teaching Mathematics in Primary Classrooms*. Portland, ME: Stenhouse, 2008. 128p. ISBN 978-155138-227-2. Grades: K–6.

Children's literature enables students to make connections between their lives and real-world applications of mathematics, which enhance their understanding of essential mathematical concepts. Appendixes include useful resources such as reproducible graphic organizers and a literature/mathematics manipulative organizer.

Mastering Elementary and Middle School Math. Win/Mac. Weekly Readers Learning Systems. Grades: 1–8.

The lessons in this software combine audio and video that enhance the students' understanding of complex mathematics concepts. The program explains the Rapid Calculation Method, which provides students with problem-solving strategies. Struggling students and those in need of enrichment activities benefit from working the mathematics problems. This software also works on iPods. ALA Great Interactive Software for Kids, Fall/Winter, 2008.

Ward, Robin A. *Literature-Based Activities for Integrating Mathematics with Other Content Areas, Grades 3–5*. Upper Saddle River, NJ: Pearson, 2009. 240p. ISBN 978-0-205-51409-0. Grades: 3–5.

This is a compilation of literature-based activities appropriate for grades three to five that integrates mathematics with science, social studies, and visual arts. The National Content Standards for each content area are incorporated into the activities. An appendix contains assessment tools and rubrics.

Whitin, David J., and Robin Cox. *A Mathematical Passage: Strategies for Promoting Inquiry in Grades 4–6*. Portsmouth, NH: Heinemann, 2003. 160p. ISBN 978-0-325-00506-5. Grades: 4–6.

Discover how to turn your students into a community of mathematical inquirers. Whitin and Cox share activities that foster curriculum connections, writing ideas for mathematics journals, connections to children's literature, strategies for incorporating a mathematics workshop, as well as other classroom-tested ideas for promoting inquiry in the mathematics curriculum.

Hyde, Arthur, Susan Friedlander, Cheryl Heck, and Lynn Pittner. *Understanding Middle School Math: Cool Problems to Get Students Thinking and Connecting.* Portsmouth, NH: Heinemann, 2009. 280p. ISBN 978-0-325-01386-2. Grades: 6–8.

Combining research and classroom experience the authors developed intriguing, thought-provoking real-world problems for students to solve. These problems use students' prior knowledge and their present lives to involve them in solving problems that help them see the connections between their classroom learning and their life experiences.

National Council of Teachers of Mathematics. *Cartoon Corner.* Reston, VA: National Council of Teachers of Mathematics, 2007. 99p. ISBN 978-0-87353-600-4. Grades: 6–8.

Get your students thinking and laughing as you use the cartoons in this book to introduce mathematical concepts including algebra, fractions, decimals, geometry, and probability. The cartoons were gathered from the "Cartoon Corner" in the journal, *Mathematics Teaching in the Middle School.*

Wallace, Faith H., and Jill Shivertaker. *Teaching Mathematics through Reading: Methods and Materials for Grades 6–8.* Columbus, OH: Linworth, 2008. 95p. ISBN 978-1-58683-324-4. Grades: 6–8.

Explore ideas for teaching mathematics using trade books, children's literature, and environmental print in this teacher resource book. It contains annotations for books in a variety of genres and activities for incorporating books into the mathematics curriculum.

Ward, Robin A. *Literature-Based Activities for Integrating Mathematics with other Content Areas, Grades 6–8.* Upper Saddle River, NJ: Pearson, 2009. 240p. ISBN 978-0-205-52916-2. Grades: 6–8.

This is a compilation of literature-based activities appropriate for grades six to eight that integrate mathematics with science, social studies, and visual arts. The National Content Standards for each content area are incorporated into the activities. An appendix contains assessment tools and rubrics.

Professional Organizations

National Council of Teachers of Mathematics
1906 Association Drive
Reston, VA 20191-1502
703-620-9840 (Phone)
703-476-2970 (Fax)
mctm@nctm.org
www.nctm.org

Journals: *Teaching Children Mathematics, Mathematics Teaching in the Middle School, Mathematics Teacher, Journal for Research in Mathematics Education, ON-Math: Online Journal of School Mathematics*

Internet Sites

Bureau of Printing and Engraving
www.moneyfactory.gov

Youth Education is one of the links on the site and it reveals a variety of interactive resources for learning about money. There are materials to download, information on the redesigned currency, and games to help students learn about money.

Illuminations: Resources for Teaching Mathematics
illuminations.nctm.org

Activities, lessons, standards, and web links for teaching mathematics are available on this website. The National Council of Teachers of Mathematics and Thinkfinity.org sponsor this site. Grade level bands organize the activities, lessons, and standards: P–2, 3–5, 6–8, and 9–12. Web links are grouped according to the standards including number and operations, algebra, geometry, measurement, and data analysis and probability.

The Math Forum
mathforum.org

Featured on the site are mathematics problems and puzzles, opportunities for online professional development, links to websites, and mathematics tools. "Ask Dr. Math" contains an archive of answers to mathematics questions and if students do not find answers to their questions in the archives they can post their questions. The Drexel School of Education sponsors this site.

Math Slice
www.mathslice.com

Math Slice has a collection of interactive onscreen activities and games to sharpen students' mathematics skills. For example, Roman Math challenges users to convert Arabic numerals to Roman numerals and Roman numerals to Arabic numerals. In addition to mathematics games there are games related to science and social studies.

National Center for Education Statistics Kids' Zone
nces.ed.gov/nceskids/

This site houses online games, activities, and quizzes for students to try their skills at graphing and probability. The "Create a Graph" page includes examples of graphs and an online tutorial. Students can also compare their knowledge of civics, economics, geography, history, mathematics, and science with other students in the nation and the world.

National Library of Virtual Manipulatives
nlvm.usu.edu

This is an online collection of manipulatives that is free to teachers for use in their classrooms. Students become actively involved in practicing and reinforcing the mathematics concepts they learn in the classroom. Grade levels group the manipulatives.

Public Broadcasting Service (PBS) Teachers
www.pbs.org/teachers/math/

This resource for teachers has a searchable database of lesson plans, activities, and multimedia resources that are organized by grade range and topic.

U. S. Mint
www.usmint.gov

Click on the Kids and Teachers link to discover games, coin news, mint history, collectors club and other resources for children to learn about money. The Teachers' corner has lesson plans, a resource room, a collection of projects, and other useful resources.

REFERENCES

Callan, Richard. 2004. "Reading + Math = A Perfect Match." Available: www.teachingk-8.com/ archives/table_of_contents/january_2004.html (accessed January 19, 2010).

Carter, Susan. 2009. "Connecting Mathematics and Writing Workshop: It's Kinda Like Ice Skating." *The Reading Teacher* 62, no. 7 (April): 606–610.

Castle, Kathryn, and Jackie Needham. 2007. "First Graders' Understanding of Measurement." *Early Childhood Education* 35, no. 3 (December): 215–221.

Clark, Julie. 2007. "Mathematics saves the day." *Australian Primary Mathematics Classroom* 12, no. 2 (June): 21–24.

Cotti, Rainy, and Michael Schiro. 2004. "Connecting Teacher Beliefs to the Use of Children's Literature in the Teaching of Mathematics." *Journal of Mathematics Teacher Education* 7, no. 4 (December): 329–356.

Leedy, Loreen. 1997. *Measuring Penny*. New York: Henry Holt.

Moyer, Patricia S. 2000. "Communicating Mathematically: Children's Literature as a Natural Connection." *The Reading Teacher* 54, no. 3 (November): 246–255.

National Council of Teachers of Mathematics. 2000. *Principles and Standards for School Mathematics*. Reston, VA: National Council of Teachers of Mathematics. NCTM STANDARDS by NCTM, Copyright 2000 by National Council of Teachers of Mathematics, Reproduced with permission of National Council of Teachers of Mathematics via Copyright Clearance Center.

Shatzer, Joyce. 2008. "Picture Book Power: Connecting Children's Literature and Mathematics." *The Reading Teacher* 61, no. 8 (May): 649–653.

Whitin, David. J. 2008. "Learning Our Way to One Million." *Teaching Children Mathematics* 14, no. 8 (April): 448–453.

Whitin, Phyllis. 2008. "Exploring a 'Wonder' about Multiplication." *Connect* 62, no. 5 (September/ October): 1–3.

Whitin, Phyllis, and David J. Whitin. 2008. "Learning to Read the Numbers: A Critical Orientation toward Statistics." *Language Arts* 85, no. 6 (July): 432–441.

Chapter 2

Science

Children's natural curiosity motivates them to question their environment and the science classroom furnishes opportunities for them to find answers to their questions. Many of the answers they seek can be found in the pages of science information books that encourage them to use the inquiry process. Reading several books on the same topic furnishes them with opportunities to note consistencies and discrepancies between the books and engages the students in using higher order thinking skills as they ponder their discoveries. As students read and experiment, recording their discoveries in science notebooks provides them with opportunities to think about their learning and to enhance their understanding and achievement (Gilbert and Kotelman, 2005; Klentschy, 2005).

The National Research Council (NRC, 1996) released the National Science Education Standards (NSES) to enable students to achieve scientific literacy. These standards are divided into the following eight categories:

1. Unifying concepts and processes in science
2. Science as inquiry
3. Physical science
4. Life science
5. Earth and space science
6. Science and technology
7. Science in personal and social perspectives
8. History and nature of science

These standards provide teachers insights into teaching science as inquiry where students pose a question and then seek possible answers to their questions (Alberts, 2000). Further, Alberts contends science education should include learning science principles and concepts, acquiring scientific reasoning and procedural skills, and understanding the nature of science as a human endeavor.

Major sections in this chapter include science as inquiry, physical science, life science, earth and space science, science and technology, science in personal and social perspectives, history and nature of science. The unifying concepts and processes in the science standards connect science learning across grade levels and with other content standards. The science as inquiry standard focuses on books that help students develop an understanding of the processes of science. Physical science includes sections on electricity, sound, energy, machines, and properties of matter. Life science includes sections on the human body, animals, plants, ecosystems, and diversity. In the earth and space science section books can be found on landforms, natural disasters, solar systems, and space travel. The science and technology section contains books that explore how science is linked to technology. In the science in personal and social perspectives section, books focus on helping students make informed decisions as citizens from a global perspective. The history and nature of science section includes books on scientists and inventors. Reference materials and teacher resources conclude the chapter. The National Science Teachers Association (NSTA) recognizes many of the books in this chapter as Outstanding Science Trade Books for Students K–12.

UNIFYING CONCEPTS AND PROCESSES IN SCIENCE

The unifying concepts and processes in the science standards connect science learning across grade levels and with other content standards. Included in this standard are (1) systems, order, and organization; (2) evidence, models, and explanation; (3) change, constancy, and measurement; (4) evolution and equilibrium; and (5) form and function. For example, evidence is important in science, but also in mathematics and in history. A book such as *Health Science Projects about Nutrition* (Gardner, 2002) helps students make connections between science and health as they work through experiments that help them understand the importance of proper nutrition.

Book and Media Choices

Scieszka, Jon. *Science Verse*. Illustrated by Lane Smith. New York: Viking, 2004. Unp. ISBN 978-0-670-91057-1. Grades: 2–5.

Mr. Newton has zapped a science verse curse on a hapless student who takes readers along on a journey to discover the poetry of science. The scientific method gets its very own poem based on "Casey at the Bat." At the end of the book the classic poems used as models for the book's poems are noted. The CD version of the book has commentary by Scieszka and Smith and includes poems that did not make it into the book.

Cleary, Brian P. *"Mrs. Riley Bought Five Itchy Aardvarks" and Other Painless Tricks for Memorizing Science Facts*. Illustrated by J. P. Sandy. Minneapolis, MN: Millbrook Press, 2008. 48p. ISBN 978-0-8225-7819-2. Grades: 3–6.

After a brief introduction to mnemonics, readers are ready to use mnemonics to help them memorize science facts. Cartoon illustrations and lively colorful text add to the fun of learning and remembering science facts. Back matter includes information on the scientific method, a glossary, resources for learning more, and an index.

Gardner, Robert. ***Health Science Projects about Nutrition.*** **Berkeley Heights, NJ: Enslow, 2002. 112p. ISBN 978-0-7660-1442-8. Grades: 5–10.**

The book contains chapters on the energy in food, components of food, math and food, digestion, and weight. Throughout the book asterisks identify experiments that can lead to science fair projects. The introduction cautions students that rather than replicate the experiment, they need to extend or modify the experiment for their science fair projects. Back matter includes a list of suppliers, books for further reading, Internet sites, and an index. From the Science Projects series.

Explorations

1. After reading *Science Verse* (Scieszka, 2004) or listening to the poems on the CD, discuss how Scieszka used famous poems as models for the poems he included in the book. Using one of the poems as a model, have the students help you write a poem using information from their mathematics or social studies class. Then, have the students share ideas and write poems of their own using one of the poems in the book as a model.
2. After sharing *"Mrs. Riley Bought Five Itchy Aardvarks" and Other Painless Tricks for Memorizing Science Facts* (Cleary, 2008) have the students work in groups to create mnemonics to help them remember important facts in another subject area.
3. *Health Science Projects about Nutrition* (Gardner, 2002) does not include a glossary; however, key vocabulary words are explained in the text. For example, on pages 85–87 diffusion and osmosis are defined and explained. Use a document camera to project the text and point out the definitions in the text on page 85 and then show the students how the meanings of the words are explained on pages 86 and 87. The students can write the definitions and illustrate them in their science notebooks to demonstrate their understanding of the processes.

SCIENCE AS INQUIRY

Questions based on observations, investigations, and experiences launch students into scientific inquiry. Starting with a question, they plan and then conduct an experiment to gather data. Based on their data collection they formulate explanations and then share their results. Scientific inquiry includes examining other scientists' findings and comparing their results. This section focuses on books that help students develop an understanding of the processes of science. Middle school students should have their current understanding of science concepts challenged and should be able to express their understanding in written reports, labeled drawings, concept maps, and computer graphics (NRC, 1996). For some students a written report can be a daunting challenge, so Holbrook (2005) suggests having students write poems about the processes of science to demonstrate their understanding. To do this students create a list of short phrases containing keywords about the process. Then, they move the phrases around and play with the words to find the poem hidden in the words.

Book and Media Choices

Plourde, Lynn. *Science Fair Day*. Illustrated by Thor Wickstrom. New York: Dutton, 2008. Unp. ISBN 978-0-525-47878-2. Grades: P–4.

Mrs. Shepherd's class is in the midst of putting the final touches on their science fair projects, when classmate Ima Kindanozee begins asking them questions about their projects. While she interviews her classmates, she sets off a rocket and destroys a dinosaur skeleton. Ima's own project is a pile of papers, which she crafts into a newspaper describing her classmates' projects. This is a great way to introduce science fairs and help students see that they all have different talents.

Hopwood, James. *Cool Gravity Activities: Fun Science Projects about Balance*. Edina, MN: ABDO Publishing, 2008. 32p. ISBN 978-1-59928-908-3. Grades: K–6.

An explanation of the scientific method and instructions on writing down observations launch students into fun and challenging experiments. Detailed step-by-step instructions and color photographs provide students the support they need to be successful. Each activity includes text boxes titled think like a scientist, the science behind the fun, and science at work. Across from the table of contents is a note for adult helpers with ideas for supporting the students as they experiment. A glossary and an index complete the book. From the Cool Science series.

Farndon, John. *The Human Body*. Tarrytown, NY: Marshall Cavendish, 2001. 32p. ISBN 978-0-7614-1339-4. Grades: 3–5.

Organs and body systems are first explained and then readers are able to explore what is happening in their bodies by conducting simple experiments. For example, with plastic tubing and a funnel they can listen to their hearts pumping. Back matter includes information on scientific rigor that will be useful for students working on science fair projects. A glossary and an index conclude the book.

Tocci, Salvadore. *Space Experiments*. New York: Scholastic, 2001. 48p. ISBN 978-0-516-22509-8. Grades: 3–5.

The book uses a question/answer format and the answers to the questions are revealed in simple experiments, which help students explore blasting off, floating in space, and reentry. Back matter includes resources for learning more, a glossary, and an index. From A True Book series.

Ross, Michael Elsohn. *Toy Lab*. Minneapolis, MN: Carolrhoda Books, 2003. 48p. ISBN 978-0-87614-456-5. Grades: 4–6.

Introducing the scientific method as a recipe using toys for the main ingredients is a wonderful way to get students asking questions and conducting experiments as they search for answers. Scattered throughout the book are the histories of famous toys including the Slinky and the Frisbee. From the You are the Scientist series.

Explorations

1. After trying one of the activities in *Cool Gravity Activities: Fun Science Projects about Balance* (Hopwood, 2008), work with the whole class to create a haiku using their written observations as the basis of the poem. Once students have created a whole class haiku, have them work in groups to write one (Holbrook, 2005).
2. Prior to reading *Space Experiments* (Tocci, 2001) give the students an opportunity to play with a gyroscope. Introduce the gyroscope to the students and then place it on a table in the room with a tablet of paper and a pencil. Invite the students to play with the gyroscope and record their observations. As they explore encourage them to record their answers to the question "How does a gyroscope help astronauts navigate in space?
3. Before reading *The Human Body* (Farndon, 2001) use a document camera to project the pages in the book to call students' attention to the diagrams, photographs, and text boxes scattered through the text. Show them how these aids can help them understand and remember what they read.
4. After reading *The Human Body* (Farndon, 2001) provide the students with the materials they need to conduct the simple experiments in the book.
5. After reading *Toy Lab* (Ross, 2003), have the students work in small groups to decide which experiment they are going to try. Then, have them bring their toys to class to conduct the experiments. As the students work, you can talk to them about how to expand their experiments into science fair projects.

PHYSICAL SCIENCE

Physical science includes studying the properties of matter, motions, forces, and energy transfer. This section includes books on electricity, sound, energy, and properties of matter. The books offer a wide array of activities for the hands-on exploration of physical science, which is science category three. While hands-on activities are the best way to learn these concepts, virtual labs offer an exciting alternative. Learningscience.org offers physical science virtual labs arranged by grade level groups and framed by the National Science Education Standards.

Electricity

Spending even a few minutes without electricity makes us realize how important it is in our lives. Students who wonder where the electricity in their schools and homes comes from and how it gets there will find the answers in Suen's (2007) *Wired*. Older students' questions about electricity can be answered as they read the books in this section and try the experiments, some of which can lead to science fair projects. As students try the experiments, they can record their observations in learning logs, which can be used to assess their understanding of the concepts (Heuser, 2005; Knipper and Duggan, 2006).

Book and Media Choices

Suen, Anastasia. *Wired.* Illustrated by Paul Carrick. Watertown, MA: Charlesbridge, 2007. 32p. ISBN 978-1-57091-599-4. Grades: 2–4.

This nonfiction picture book explains how electricity moves from a power plant to a house. The bold black rhyming text tells the basic story and then text boxes on each page contain detailed explanations. Back matter includes power safety tips, resources for learning more, and a glossary/index.

Mullins, Lisa. *Inventing the Electric Light.* New York: Crabtree, 2007. 32p. ISBN 978-0-7787-2818-4. Grades: 3–6.

This brief history of the invention of the light bulb includes fascinating information on its impact on society. There is a detailed labeled illustration of the inner workings of the light bulb. Colorful illustrations and text boxes supplement the information provided in the text. The book concludes with a section on the future of light, a glossary, and an index. From the Breakthrough Inventions series.

Gardner, Robert. *Dazzling Science Projects with Light and Color.* Illustrated by Tom Labaff. Berkeley Heights, NJ: Enslow, 2006. 48p. ISBN 978-0-7660-2587-5. Grades: 4–6.

This is a collection of step-by-step experiments for students to conduct as they discover the wonders of light and color. Following each experiment is an explanation, and many include ideas for extending the experiment into a science fair project. Back matter includes a glossary, resources for further reading, and an index. From the Fantastic Physical Science Experiments series.

Woodford, Chris. *Electricity.* San Diego: Thomson Gale, 2004. 40p. ISBN 978-1-4103-0165-6. Grades: 4–6.

Photographs, diagrams, and experiments draw readers into this fascinating book. Starting with static electricity, Woodford explains the discovery of electricity and the development of uses for electricity. Included are pictures and information on the contributions of noted scientists. A glossary, resources for learning more, and an index conclude the book. From the Routes of Science series.

Explorations

1. After reading *Wired* (Suen, 2007) return to the text and show the students how the bold text summarizes the details in the text boxes. Using the bold text, students can create flowcharts showing the path electricity takes to get to their homes.
2. Using *Dazzling Science Projects with Light and Color* (Gardner, 2006) have the students work in groups to discuss ways to extend the experiments in the book into science fair projects.

3. Prior to having students read *Electricity* (Woodford, 2004) explain how keywords in the text are circled, written in bold, and have lines drawn from them to text boxes that contain additional information.

Sounds

Sounds are all around us, some loud, some soft, some jarring, and some pleasant. The third standard, physical science, includes the study of sound. Books in this section contain experiments and activities for hands-on explorations of sound. Gather the everyday materials used in the projects in the books and allow the students time to explore sound and write about their observations and experiences in their science notebooks. With software such as Audacity or GarageBand students can create podcasts to record their explorations and to share them with their classmates.

Book and Media Choices

Goldsmith, Mike. *Light and Sound.* Boston, MA: Kingfisher, 2007. 48p. ISBN 978-0-7534-6036-8. Grades: 1–3.

Glossy photographs and vibrant diagrams accompany the brief fact-filled paragraphs in this introductory text. Rather than a glossary at the end of the book, keywords are defined at the bottom of the page on which they appear. The book concludes with projects to enhance understanding of some of the concepts presented in the book. The projects involve making shadow puppets, a shadow clock, a xylophone, and plastic-cup telephone. From the Kingfisher Young Knowledge series.

Parker, Steve. *The Science of Sound: Projects with Experiments with Music and Sound Waves.* Chicago, IL: Heinemann, 2005. 32p. ISBN 978-1-40347-281-6. Grades: 4–7.

The two-page chapters briefly explain concepts about sound followed by experiments for students to explore the concepts. Colorful photographs of children and diagrams show how to conduct the experiments. A timeline of the history of sound, a glossary, and an index conclude the book.

Sayre, April Pulley. *Secrets of Sound: Studying the Calls and Songs of Whales, Elephants, and Birds.* Boston, MA: Houghton Mifflin, 2002. 64p. ISBN 978-0-618-01514-6. Grades: 5–9.

From Uzbekistan to Africa to Texas to Hawaii, scientists are recording animals' sounds to learn more about them. Recording the animals' sounds is one way to count animals and to record the migration patterns of animals that cannot easily be seen, such as whales deep in the ocean and birds flying at night. Back matter includes resources for learning more, suggestions for getting involved in research and conservation, a glossary, and an index. Outstanding Science Trade Book for Students K–12, 2003.

Explorations

1. Help students explore light and shadow by having them make shadow puppets using the instructions at the end of *Light and Sound* (Goldsmith, 2007). Students can make shadow puppets of the characters in one of their favorite storybooks. Then, they can use the shadow puppets to retell the story.
2. Check out the Bill Evans Bird Tracking Site at www.oldbird.org for instructions for building a microphone to record bird sounds and to purchase a CD of flight calls. This website is also available in Spanish.
3. Prior to reading *Secrets of Sound: Studying the Calls and Songs of Whales, Elephants, and Birds* (Sayre, 2002) model for the students how to skim the text to look for key concepts to focus on as they read.
4. What better way to study sound than to record it, manipulate it, and play it back? Audacity, an open-source software available from www.sourceforge.com is an easy way to experiment with sound and to create podcasts. GarageBand comes installed on Macintosh computers and is another great way to create podcasts.

Energy

Bradley's book title *Energy Makes Things Happen* (2003) summarizes why energy is such an important part of our daily lives. Flags waving, tops spinning, and kites flying are all using energy, and when framed in the context of familiar events students have a solid basis for understanding energy. In addition, the books in this section contain activities and experiments that help students understand how energy makes things happen.

Book and Media Choices

Manolis, Kay. *Energy*. Minneapolis, MN: Bellwether Media, 2008. 24p. ISBN 978-1-60014-096-9. Grades: P–2.

Bright colorful photographs and large text introduce beginning readers to the energy around them. Keywords found in the glossary are in bold in the text. Books for further reading, a link to websites, and an index conclude the book. From the Blastoff! Readers series.

Murphy, Patricia J. *Back and Forth*. New York: Scholastic, 2003. 32p. ISBN 978-0-516-22552-4. Grades: K–2.

This easy-to-read introduction to force depicts everyday activities such as swinging, frosting a cake, wagging tails, and waving flags. A photo glossary and index concludes the book. From the Rookie Read-About Science series.

Holland, Gini. *Hot and Cold*. Pleasantville, NY: Weekly Reader Books, 2008. 16p. ISBN 978-0-8368-8294-0. Grades: K–2.

Each two-page spread has a photograph of something hot on the left and something cold on the right. A simple repetitive sentence under each photograph names the object and tells if it is hot or cold. While young readers will need support to read the book at first, they will quickly be able to read the book on their own. From the I Know Opposites series.

Bradley, Kimberly Brubaker. *Energy Makes Things Happen.* Illustrated by Paul Meisel. New York: HarperCollins, 2003. 33p. ISBN 978-0-06-445213-7. Grades: 1–3.

Energy is explored through familiar everyday activities such as flying a kite, roasting hot dogs, lighting a fire, and growing carrots. The book concludes with questions and answers that help children apply the concepts presented in the book. From the Let's Read and Find-Out Science series.

Cobb, Vicki. *Whirlers and Twirlers: Science Fun with Spinning.* Illustrated by Steve Haefele. Brookfield, CT: Millbrook Press, 2001. Unp. ISBN 978-0-8225-7025-7. Grades: 2–5.

On playgrounds everywhere children are spinning in circles until they fall, and Cobb explains to them why they fall. Through simple experiments and fascinating facts, students learn how and why objects spin. Chapter titles include: (1) Simply spinning, (2) Whirl on a string, (3) Wind whirlers, yo-yos, (4) Tops, and (5) Gyroscopes. The experiments use readily available materials and have easy-to-understand instructions. From the Science Fun with Vicki Cobb series.

Snedden, Robert. *Forces and Motion.* Milwaukee, WI: Gareth Stevens, 2007. 48p. ISBN 978-0-8368-8087-8. Grades: 4–6.

The introduction defines the terms "force" and "motion" and makes the distinction between force and energy. Throughout the book, in the text and in the pictures, readers find familiar objects and events that help them make connections between the concepts in the book and their prior experiences. The last chapter explores simple machines. Terms that are in the glossary appear in bold throughout the text. Back matter includes a glossary, resources for learning more, and an index. From the Gareth Stevens Vital Science series.

Hammond, Richard. *Can You Feel the Force?* New York: DK, 2006. 96p. ISBN 978-0-7566-2033-2. Grades: 5–8.

Explore physics through text, experiments, photographs, and graphics. Readers step back in time to explore the origins of physics in the first chapter. Force, matter, and light are explored in the next three chapters. A who's who of scientists, a glossary, and an index conclude the book.

Explorations

1. Prior to reading *Energy* (Manolis, 2008), visit the Fact Surfer website at www.factsurfer.com to locate websites that contain additional information on your students' grade levels.
2. After reading *Back and Forth* (Murphy, 2003) create a simple chart for students to use to record observations of objects they observe going back and forth. Younger

students can draw pictures rather than write. You might have students start their observations at school and then continue them at home.

3. After reading *Energy Makes Things Happen* (Bradley, 2003) have students answer and discuss the questions at the end of the book. Then, have them create a flowchart depicting where the energy in a cheese sandwich comes from.
4. While studying energy have the students visit the Energy Kid's Page at www.eia.doe.gov/kids/. The site features links to games, energy history, classroom activities, a glossary, an energy calculator, and other resources to help students understand energy.
5. When you introduce students to *Forces and Motion* (Snedden, 2007) show them the paragraph in bold text at the beginning of each chapter. Reading and thinking about these paragraphs before reading the chapter will help to activate students' prior knowledge and to focus their attention on the key concepts presented in the text.

Solids, Liquids, and Gases

Science standard three is physical science, which includes states of matter. Solids, liquids, and gases are the three states of matter and all are made from small particles called atoms and molecules. Students know that ice cubes melt when taken out of the freezer but they may not recognize this as a solid changing to a liquid nor realize that the liquid will eventually become a gas. Books in this section help students understand the general properties of matter by conducting simple experiments.

Book and Media Choices

Boothroyd, Jennifer. *What Is a Liquid?* New York: Scholastic, 2007. 23p. ISBN 978-0-8225-6838-4. Grades: K–2.

Color photographs with short sentences in large font introduce students to the properties of liquids. Back matter includes fun facts, a glossary, and an index. This book is available as an e-book. From the First Step Nonfiction series.

Tocci, Salvatore. *Hydrogen and the Noble Gases.* New York: Scholastic, 2004. 47p. ISBN 978-0-516-22830-3. Grades: 2–3.

Basic facts and illustrations of the Hindenburg and the Goodyear blimp introduce readers to hydrogen, one of the noble gases. The other noble gases explored in the book are neon, argon, krypton, xenon, and radon. Back matter includes resources for learning more, a glossary, and an index. From A True Book series.

Stille, Darlene R. *Solids, Liquids, and Gases.* Chanhassen, MN: The Child's World, 2005. 32p. ISBN 978-1-59296-225-9. Grades: 3–8.

Filling a glass with water, blowing up a balloon, and grilling hamburgers are all familiar activities used to introduce students to the states of matter. Colorful photographs and diagrams enhance the double-spaced text. Keywords are in bold and are defined in the glossary. At the end of the book are a glossary, interesting facts, a timeline, resources for learning more, and an index. From the Science Around Us series.

Oxlade, Chris. *States of Matter.* Chicago, IL: Heinemann Library, 2007. 48p. ISBN 978-1-4329-0055-7. Grades: 6–8.

Illustrations, photographs, and diagrams help explain the actions of solids, liquids, and gases. Experiments in the book challenge students to explore the states of matter and the experiment results are explained in the "Further Reading" section at the end of the book. The periodic table, a glossary, resources for further reading, and an index conclude the book. From the Chemicals in Action series.

Fleisher, Paul. *Liquids and Gases: Principles of Fluid Mechanics.* Minneapolis, MN: Lerner, 2002. 55p. ISBN 978-0-8225-2988-0. Grades: 6 and up.

Chapters in this book focus on Archimedes' Principle, Pascal's Law, Boyle's and Charles's Laws, and Bernoulli's Principle. The well-organized text is enhanced with line drawings and diagrams. Back matter includes a timeline, brief scientists' biographies, resources for learning more, a glossary, and an index. This book is also available as an e-book. From the Secrets of the Universe series.

Explorations

1. Before reading *Hydrogen and the Noble Gases* (Tocci, 2004) demonstrate the activity on page 24 of the book. A slightly deflated shiny foil balloon containing helium and a lamp with a bare light bulb are the materials used. Put the balloon near the warm light bulb, so that heat from the bulb warms the helium, causing it to rise. Have the students record what is happening in their science notebooks, and then have them discuss why they think the balloon went up and down.
2. The Child's World publisher of *Solids, Liquids, and Gases* (Stille, 2005) maintains a website with child safe links for learning more. The address is www.childsworld.com/links.html and the password is given in the book. After reading the book, have the students generate a list of questions to research using the links on the website.
3. Before reading *States of Matter* (Oxlade, 2007) have the students visit www.chem.purdue.edu/gchelp/liquids/character.html to view simulations of microscopic views of a gas, a liquid, and a solid.
4. After reading *States of Matter* (Oxlade, 2007) have the students visit the Matter section of Chem4kids.com at www.chem4kids.com/files/matter_intro.html. The site contains additional information, illustrations, and diagrams. There are also quizzes to test their knowledge.
5. After reading the book *Solids, Liquids, and Gases* (Stille, 2005) divide the students into six groups. Assign each group one of the six experiments in the book. Have each group share the results of their experiment with their classmates.

LIFE SCIENCE

As students study science it is important for them to make connections between the concepts they are studying and their own life experiences. Life science is perhaps the easiest for them to make connections to since this standard examines the characteristics of living organisms, their life cycles, and their environments. For grades five to eight this also includes the structure and function in living systems and heredity. This section of the chapter includes subsections on the human body, animals, plants, ecosystems, and diversity.

Human Body

Curious children have questions about their bodies and how they work, and the books in this section contain answers to their questions. These books take students on journeys of discovery inside their own bodies. Two of noted science writer Seymour Simon's books are annotated in this section and the large, color photographs will intrigue students of all ages. *What Makes Me Me?* (Winston, 2004) introduces students to the fascinating concept of heredity, which helps them understand why they look and act as they do.

Book and Media Choices

Powell, Judith. *Moving.* North Mankato, MN: Smart Apple Media, 2004. 32p. ISBN 978-1-58340-437-9. Grades: K–3.

Moving requires that bones, joints, muscles, nerves, lungs, and heart all work together. Diagrams, photographs, and cross-sections help explain what moving the human body involves. Did You Know? text boxes provide additional fascinating facts sure to catch young readers' attention. Back matter includes a glossary, resources for learning more, and an index. From the Body in Action series.

Schoenberg, Jane F. *My Bodyworks: Songs about Your Bones, Muscles, Heart, and More!* Illustrations by Cynthia Fisher. Northampton, MA: Interlink, 2005. 32p. ISBN 978-1-56656-583-7. Grades: K–2.

This book serves as a printed version of the lyrics to the twelve songs featured on the accompanying CD. Singing about bones, teeth, skin, senses, and other information about the human body ensures that students remember the concepts. Outstanding Science Trade Book for Students K–12, 2006.

Winston, Robert M. L. *What Makes Me Me?* New York: DK, 2004. 96p. ISBN 978-0-7566-0325-0. Grades: 3–6.

From body parts to genes to the brain to personality, readers discover who they are and why they are unique. They can determine if they have a hitchhiker's thumb or a Darwin's ear point. There is a test of spatial intelligence and numerical intelligence. The book has so many fascinating facts and interesting concepts to explore it is one to buy and keep in the classroom for students to explore again and again. Back matter includes a glossary, an index, and answers to the book's tests.

Simon, Seymour. *Guts*. New York: HarperCollins, 2005. Unp. ISBN 978-0-06-054652-6. Grades: 4–6.

Take a journey through the digestive system and discover how food is digested. Each two-page spread features straightforward text and a large color photograph or illustration depicting the insides of the organs of the digestive system. It is a fascinating book that is just gross enough to capture readers. Outstanding Science Trade Book for Students K–12, 2006.

Simon, Seymour. *The Human Body*. New York: HarperCollins, 2008. 64p. ISBN 978-0-06-055541-2. Grades: 4–7.

This collaboration between Simon and the Smithsonian Institution resulted in a stunning look at the systems of the human body. Color photographs of magnified body parts, labeled cross-sections, and detailed diagrams accompanied by explanatory text allow readers to peer inside the human body. A glossary, index, and resource for learning more conclude the book.

Kim, Melissa L. *The Endocrine and Reproductive Systems*. Berkeley Heights, NJ: 2003. 48p. ISBN 978-0-7660-2020-7. Grades: 5 and up.

This book provides basic information on the endocrine and reproductive systems, how they work, and disorders that affect them. Simple labeled diagrams accompany the text on the glands and organs that make up the two systems. A glossary, resources for learning more, and an index conclude the book. From the Human Body Library series.

Macaulay, David, with Richard Walker. *The Way We Work: Getting to Know the Amazing Human Body*. Boston, MA: Houghton Mifflin, 2008. 336p. ISBN 978-0-618-23378-6. Grades: 6 and up.

With headings like "down the hatch," "crossing the border," "drain and defend," and "clean and clone," readers know that they are set for a humorous journey inside the human body. Watercolor and colored-pencil illustrations across two-page spreads depict labeled cross-sections of the inner workings of the body. Technical, detailed text is interspersed throughout the illustrations. Back matter includes a glossary, an index, and not the typical appendix. *Boston Globe*–Horn Book Award for Excellence in Children's Literature Honor Book, 2009.

Explorations

1. Before reading *What Makes Me Me?* (Winston, 2004) ask the students about characteristics they share with their relatives, such as hair color, height, or personality. For younger students the discussion might start with the question, "Has anyone ever told you that you look like someone in your family?"
2. After reading Seymour Simon's books have the students visit his blog at www.seymoursimon.com to learn more about this prolific science author and to

contact him. On the website are videos related to his books, contests to enter, and a video interview with Simon.

3. The Nemours Foundation website at www.kidshealth.org contains information about keeping the human body healthy and is divided into sections for parents, children, and teens. Bookmark the parts of the site appropriate for your students.

Animals

The life science standard focuses on the characteristics of organisms, their life cycles, and their environments. For older students, books in this section such as *The Case of the Monkeys That Fell from the Trees and Other Mysteries in Tropical Nature* (Quinlan, 2003) contain intriguing stories that hold their interests. Books in the adaptations and diversity section also contain books on animals.

Book and Media Choices

Jenkins, Steve. *Actual Size*. Boston: Houghton Mifflin, 2004. Unp. ISBN 978-0-618-37594-3. Grades: P–5.

Life-size, collage representations of animals show how big and how small animals or parts of animals actually are. Few words and artful layouts draw readers into this book that is perfect for making comparisons, measuring, and observing. The last four pages are devoted to small pictures of the animals in the book with detailed information about the animals.

Somervill, Barbara A. *Leeches: Waiting in the Water*. New York: The Rosen Publishing Group, 2008. 24p. ISBN 978-1-4042-3801-5. Grades: K–5.

Members of the worm family, leeches make their homes in water and most but not all survive on blood from other animals. Blood splotches frame the text and capture readers' attention. Two-page spreads feature text on the left side with small text boxes and bright, colorful photographs on the right side. A glossary, index, and a link to other resources conclude the book. From the Bloodsuckers series.

Williams, Brian. *Amazing Reptiles and Amphibians*. Pleasantville, NY: Gareth Stevens, 2008. 32p. ISBN 978-0-8368-8898-0. Grades: 3–5.

Two-page chapters contain brief paragraphs, color photographs, and amazing facts about reptiles and amphibians. This is just the book to pique students' interest in learning about these colorful, intriguing animals. The life cycle charts feature color photographs of different stages of their lives. An index and a glossary conclude the book. From the Amazing Life Cycles series.

McLimans, David. 2006. *Gone Wild: An Endangered Animal Alphabet*. New York: Walker, 2006. Unp. ISBN 978-0-8027-9563-2. Grades: 3 and up.

From the letters of the alphabet emerge black-and-white representations of 26 endangered animals. Each page includes a box of information about the animals' habitats, range, threats to their existence, and status. Back matter has additional information on the animals. Caldecott Medal Honor Book, 2007.

Keenan, Sheila. *Animals in the House: A History of Pets and People.* New York: Scholastic, 2007. 122p. ISBN 978-0-439-69286-1. Grades: 4–6.

Feathers, fur, fins, and four feet make up the pets that find their way into our homes. Color photographs enhance the text that provides knowledge about pets and interesting tidbits about famous pets and their owners. How a Dog Works is a two-page spread featuring a full-color photograph of a bulldog surrounded by text boxes filled with fascinating information about dogs. For example, there's a block of text explaining how to read the motions of a dog's tail. The book concludes with a selected bibliography and an index. NCTE Orbis Pictus Recommended Book, 2008.

Rodriguez, Ana Maria. *Secret of the Puking Penguins... and More!* Berkeley Heights, NJ: Enslow, 2009. 48p. ISBN 978-0-7660-2955-2. Grades: 4–8.

Join scientists as they uncover animal secrets including the chameleon's powerful gripping tongue, the alligator's facial pressure sensors, the puking penguins, the cuckoo chick's imitative calls, and the secret of the peacock's colors. Included is an experiment to explore how chameleon's tongues grip their prey. Back matter includes chapter notes, a glossary, resources for learning more, and an index.

Quinlan, Susan E. *The Case of the Monkeys That Fell from the Trees and Other Mysteries in Tropical Nature.* Honesdale, PA: Boyds Mills, 2003. 171p. ISBN 978-1-56397-902-6. Grades: 6–9.

Young scientists not only discover the answers to perplexing questions faced by real scientists, they also learn how the scientists painstakingly research the mysteries to find the answers. As students read each mystery, they see the scientific process in action and discover the interconnectedness of the complex relationships between the creatures. A reference list of the original reports the author researched and an index conclude the book. Outstanding Science Trade Book for Students K–12, 2004.

Explorations

1. On the pbskids website at pbskids.org/itsmylife/family/pets/, students can learn about the responsibilities of pet ownership and gather information about which pet is right for them. Students who own pets can write about their pets and post the information on this website.
2. Prior to beginning a unit on reptiles and amphibians introduce students to *Amazing Reptiles and Amphibians* (Williams, 2008) and then put the book in an accessible spot for students to examine on their own. This book is a wonderful way to activate their prior knowledge and to get them interested in learning more.
3. After reading *The Case of the Monkeys That Fell from the Trees and Other Mysteries in Tropical Nature* (Quinlan, 2003) let the students select the mysteries to revisit and chart the process the scientists used to find their answers. In the

chart the students should include what the scientists observed and the steps they used to solve the mystery.

Birds

In addition to basic information about birds, books in this section contain information about caring for injured birds and about taking care of pet birds. There are also books containing information about usual birds such as the turkey vulture, the Great Bustard, and the Andean condor. These are the books that students will be reading more than once.

Book and Media Choices

Sayre, April Pulley. *Vulture View.* Illustrated by Steve Jenkins. New York: Henry Holt, 2007. Unp. ISBN 978-0-8050-7557-1. Grades: P–2.

Scavenging turkey vultures clean up the environment by eating dead, stinky animals, which is a fact just gross enough to appeal to young readers. The poetic text is filled with questions and answers as well as colorful collage illustrations. Additional information about turkey vultures and a list of turkey vulture festivals concludes the book. ALSC Notable Children's Book, 2008.

Graham, Bob. *How to Heal a Broken Wing.* Cambridge, MA: Candlewick, 2008. Unp. ISBN 978-0-7636-3903-7. Grades: K–2.

On a busy, crowded city street only small Will notices a bird on the sidewalk with a broken wing. With help from his parents, Will tenderly cares for the injured bird and then releases it into the wild once it heals. The details of the story are in the watercolor illustrations of assorted sizes, on some pages small panels and on others two-page spreads. The text is sparse and some pages are wordless. ALSC Notable Children's Book, 2009.

Hall, Kirsten. *Great Bustard: The World's Heaviest Flying Bird.* New York: Bearport Publishing, 2007. 24p. ISBN 978-1-59716-390-3. Grades: K–3.

Children's fascination with the biggest and best will be satisfied with this fact-filled book about a bird weighing up to forty-six pounds. Short sentences and bright colorful pictures will draw young readers into this book. The book concludes with brief information on three other heavy birds, a picture glossary, an index, and books for learning more. From the SuperSized! series.

Gibbons, Gail. *Chicks & Chickens.* New York: Holiday House, 2003. Unp. ISBN 978-0-8234-1700-1. Grades: 1–3.

Colorful detailed illustrations and succinct text introduce readers to the life cycle of chickens as they develop from eggs to adults. There is information on large and small chicken farms. The labeled cross-sections of chickens and eggs explain how chickens digest food, lay eggs, and develop from eggs. The book concludes with additional fun facts about chickens and eggs.

Burstein, John. ***Birds.*** **Pleasantville, NY: Gareth Stevens, 2008. 32p. ISBN 978-0-8368-8953-6. Grades: 3–5.**

Have you ever wondered how birds can sleep while perched on a tree branch? Filled with fascinating bird facts and information on caring for pet birds, this book teaches young bird owners all about their pets. Throughout the text there are comparisons between birds and humans such as the fact that humans can smell and birds cannot. Birds' nostrils are only used for breathing. Back matter includes amazing facts about birds, a glossary, resources for learning more, and an index. From the Slim Goodbody's Inside Guide to Pets series.

Couzens, Dominic. ***Extreme Birds: The World's Most Extraordinary and Bizarre Birds.*** **Tonawanda, NY: Firefly Books, 2008. 287p. ISBN 978-1-55407-423-5. Grades: 6–8.**

The bird extremes explored in the book are divided into four categories—form, ability, behavior, and families—and each is filled with fascinating facts. For example, in the extreme ability category is the most vicious kicker, secretary bird; the best flock coordination, European starling; and the biggest binge eater, Andean condor. Each two-page spread has a full-page color photograph of the bird on the left and information about what makes them extreme on the right. Details about the Andean condor's eating binges include the fact that after an eating binge the birds cannot take off. The book includes a table of contents and an index.

Explorations

1. Before reading *Vulture View* (Sayre, 2007) visit the Turkey Vulture Society at vulturesociety.homestead.com/ for photographs of turkey vultures to share with your students.
2. As you read *Vulture View* (Sayre, 2007) explain to the students that the author uses a question/answer format to structure the text. Pause as you read each question and ask the students to predict the answers. While the book is written for younger readers, this book can also be used with older readers to teach them how the structure of the text facilitates their comprehending the material.
3. Before reading *Chicks & Chickens* (Gibbons, 2003) have the class create a Venn diagram showing the differences and similarities between hens and roosters using the labeled illustrations on the first two-page spread. After reading the book, show the students how to create a Venn diagram showing the similarities and differences between small and large chicken farms.
4. While reading *Birds* (Burstein, 2008) have students complete a comparison chart showing how birds and humans are alike and different. For example, birds and humans both have nostrils; however, birds use their nostrils only for breathing, while humans use theirs for both breathing and smelling.
5. After completing the comparison chart the students can use what they have learned to write and illustrate a nonfiction text about birds for younger students

in the school. Writing about birds helps students recognize their understanding of the content and creating texts for younger students provides an authentic audience and purpose for writing (Tower, 2005).

Bugs

Successful learning experiences include opportunities for students to connect what they are learning with their everyday life experiences. Students come to school knowing about bugs and hence have a background to build on as they learn about bugs' life cycles and habitats, especially if the habitat is their own body. In *Bugs That Live on Us* (Perritano, 2009) and *What's Eating You: Parasites—The Inside Story* (Davies, 2007) students learn that bugs are on them and inside of them.

Book and Media Choices

Barner, Bob. *Bugs! Bugs! Bugs!* DVD. New York: Weston Woods Studios, 2008. 8 min. ISBN 978-0-545-09211-1. Grades: P–1.

Based on Barner's book by the same name, this rollicking animated film has children singing along. Included are a bonus segment of bug facts and an interview with Barner. ALSC Notable Children's Video, 2009.

Ehlert, Lois. *Waiting for Wings*. New York: Harcourt, 2001. ISBN 978-0-15-202608-0. Grades: K–2.

Beautiful, bright cut-paper collages of flowers rival the colorful butterflies. In rhyming text, Ehlert describes how caterpillars are transformed into butterflies. The book concludes with additional information on butterflies, a visual glossary, and information on growing a butterfly garden. This book is also available on CD and DVD.

Gran, Julia. *Big Bug Surprise*. New York: Scholastic, 2007. Unp. ISBN 978-0-439-67609-0. Grades: K–3.

Prunella is obsessed with bugs and the adults in her life have little patience for listening to the bug facts she spouts. Just as she begins her show-and-tell presentation a queen bee flies into the classroom followed by a horde of bees. Prunella's knowledge of bees saves the day and her entranced classmates eagerly listen as she shares her wealth of bug knowledge. Bug facts conclude the book.

Luxbacher, Irene. *123 I Can Make Prints!* Tonowanda, NY: Kids Can, 2008. 23p. ISBN 978-1-55453-040-3. Grades: 1–3.

With inexpensive materials children can learn about bugs as they create prints of them. Thumb and fingerprints can be transformed into bees and a design scratched into a Styrofoam tray can be transformed into an anthill. The instructions are easy to follow and step-by-step images are included. From the Starting Art series.

Perritano, John. *Bugs That Live on Us*. New York: Marshall Cavendish, 2009. 32p. ISBN 978-0-7614-3187-9. Grades: 2–4.

Head lice, tapeworms, threadworms, human botflies, bedbugs, dust mites, ticks, mosquitoes, and fleas fill the pages of the book. The creatures are shown in magnified photographs that invite young readers to learn more. There are diagrams, text boxes, and fascinating facts about their life cycles and where they thrive. The book concludes with resources for learning more, a glossary, and an index. From the Bug Alert series.

Siy, Alexandra. *Mosquito Bite*. Photographs by Dennis Kunkel and Alan Siy. Watertown, MA: Charlesbridge, 2005. 32p. ISBN 978-1-57091-591-8. Grades: 2–4.

A summer evening game of hide-and-seek includes not only humans seeking humans but a mosquito seeking humans. Black-and-white photographs depict the human game of hide-and-seek while colored photomicrographs provide an up-close look at the female mosquito seeking her prey. Detailed information on the life cycle of a mosquito is included. A glossary, resources for learning more, and an index conclude the book. Outstanding Science Trade Book for Students K–12, 2006. NCTE Orbis Pictus Honor Book, 2006.

Petrie, Kristin. *Fleas*. Edina, MN: ABDO, 2009. 32p. ISBN 978-1-60453-067-4. Grades: 3–5.

This brief chapter book explores the life cycle of fleas, where they live, what they eat, and ways to avoid getting bitten. Labeled enlarged photographs of a flea and its life cycle make this a book sure to capture readers' attention and keep them reading and rereading. Back matter includes a glossary, a pronunciation guide, websites, and an index. From the Bugs! series.

Davies, Nicola. *What's Eating You: Parasites—The Inside Story*. Illustrated by Neal Layton. Cambridge, MA: Candlewick, 2007. 60p. ISBN 978-0-7636-3460-5. Grades: 4–6.

This is a humorous look at the parasites on and in the human body. The cartoon illustrations and the pun-filled text tell what parasites are, where they live, and how they reproduce. The book concludes with a glossary and an index.

Camper, Cathy. *Bugs before Time: Prehistoric Insects and Their Relatives*. Illustrated by Steve Kirk. New York: Simon and Schuster, 2002. Unp. ISBN 978-0-689-82092-2. Grades: 4–7.

With an introduction proclaiming that bugs rule the earth, readers immediately realize they need to know more about insects, and more important, they want to know more. The evolution of prehistoric insects to their present-day relatives reveals fascinating facts and intriguing unanswered questions. A geologic timeline, resources for learning more, and a glossary conclude the book.

Solway, Andrew. *Classifying Insects.* Chicago, IL: Heinemann Library, 2003. 32p. ISBN 978-1-40343-346-6. Grades: 4–8.

A ladybug in flight and leaf-cutter ants transporting chunks of leaves draw readers into this informative text that explains how to classify ants and is filled with intriguing information on the earth's insects. Color photographs, charts, and a diagram accompany the text. A glossary, more books to read, and an index conclude the book.

Stewart, Melissa. *Maggots, Grubs, and More: The Secret Lives of Young Insects.* Brookfield, CT: Millbrook Press, 2003. 62p. ISBN 978-0-7613-2658-8. Grades: 4–8.

The book is divided into two sections with the first one devoted to nymphs and the second one devoted to larvae. The critters' life cycles are explained in just enough detail, so as not to overwhelm the readers. Close-up color photographs and text boxes enhance the information presented in the text. Back matter includes a glossary, resources for learning more, and an index.

Explorations

1. Before reading *Waiting for Wings* (Ehlert, 2001) visit the Carolina Biological Supply Company website at www.carolina.com to purchase a "Butterflies in the Classroom Kit," so that after you read the book to the students, they can observe the life cycle of butterflies.
2. After reading *Big Bug Surprise* (Gran, 2007) return to the illustrations and have the students focus on how Gran drew Prunella. They should notice that Prunella looks remarkably like her beloved bugs. Ask them to identify Prunella's bug parts and then give them an opportunity to create their own bug self-portraits.
3. Science learning includes opportunities to draw and label the things they study, and what better way to learn about bugs than to make prints of them using the instructions in *123 I Can Make Prints!* (Luxbacher, 2008). After students make the prints have them label the parts of the insects and their habitats.
4. *Bugs That Live on Us* (Perritano, 2009) includes information on the life cycles of the bugs. Help students use their knowledge of story sequencing to understand the how bugs' life cycles follow a set sequence. Students can also compare and contrast the life cycles of two of the bugs in the book.

Mammals

Mammals come in all shapes and sizes and live in a variety of habitats. The books in this section provide students with information on how to identify mammals (*Why Am I a Mammal*; Pyers, 2006), and how to classify them (*Classifying Mammals*; Solway, 2003). From the heartwarming story of a baby hippopotamus' rescue to the heart-wrenching book on whale strandings, the books in this section help students understand the characteristics of organisms that are part of the life science standard.

Book and Media Choices

Bauer, Marion Dane. *A Mama for Owen.* Illustrated by John Butler. DVD. Guilford, CT: Nutmeg Media, 2008. 9 min. ISBN 978-1-933938-53-0. Grades: P–3.

Bauer narrates the iconographic rendering of her book chronicling baby hippopotamus Owen's loss of his mother and his adoption by a tortoise, Mzee. ALSC Notable Children's Video, 2009.

Hall, Kirsten. *African Elephant: The World's Biggest Land Mammal.* New York: Bearport, 2007. 24p. ISBN 978-1-59716-387-3. Grades: K–3.

Did you know that an elephant dies when its teeth wear out and it can no longer chew food? Fascinating facts and color photographs in their native habitats entrance readers as they learn about elephants. Back matter includes a chart comparing the elephant to other large mammals, a glossary with pictures, an index, and resources for learning more. From the Supersized! Series.

Batten, Mary. *Who Has a Belly Button?* Illustrated by Higgins Bond. Atlanta, GA: Peachtree, 2004. Unp. ISBN 978-1-56145-235-4. Grades: K–4.

Students are sure to be examining their own belly buttons after reading this book. Colorful, realistic illustrations depict a wide variety of mammals in their natural habitats. Cross-sections help students understand how umbilical cords attach mother to baby. Italicized words in the text are defined in the glossary.

Hatkoff, Craig, Isabella Hatkoff, and Paula Kahumbu. *Owen & Mzee: The True Story of a Remarkable Friendship.* Photographs by Peter Greste. New York: Scholastic, 2006. 40p. ISBN 978-0-439-82973-1. Grades: K–5.

Orphaned by the December 2004 tsunami, Owen, a baby hippopotamus, was rescued and taken to the Haller Park sanctuary. There he bonded with a 130-year-old Aldabra tortoise named Mzee. Moved by a photo of the unlikely pair, father and daughter, Craig and Isabella, teamed with the director of the sanctuary Paula Kahumbu to tell the remarkable story. ALSC Notable Children's Book, 2007. NCTE Orbis Pictus Recommended Book, 2007.

Pyers, Greg. *Why Am I a Mammal?* Chicago, IL: Raintree, 2006. 32p. ISBN 978-1-41092-016-4. Grades: 3–5.

Photographs, fact boxes, diagrams, and short chapters help students make their way through this book filled with easy-to-understand information about what makes a mammal. Glossary words are identified in bold text and a checkmark in the text indicates facts that describe mammals. Back matter includes resources for learning more, a glossary, and an index. From the Classifying Animals series.

Solway, Andrew. *Classifying Mammals.* Chicago, IL: Heinemann, 2003. 32p. ISBN 978-1-40343-347-3. Grades: 3–6.

Mammals are explored from top to bottom and nose to tail. Characteristics of mammals are explained and explored through a variety of different mammals that share common characteristics. At the end of the book, readers are challenged to think about fishy mammals, flying mammals, and scaly mammals. Back matter includes a glossary, more books to read, and an index. From the Classifying Living Things series.

Jane Goodall's Wild Chimpanzees. DVD. Sherman Oaks, CA: Slingshot Entertainment, 2002. 40 min. ISBN 978-1-58448-311-3. Grades: 3 and up.

This IMAX documentary explores the forty-year career of Dr. Jane Goodall and her research on chimpanzees living in Tanzania's Gombe National Park. Dr. Goodall narrates the film and the soundtrack is recorded in both English and French. The film was produced in collaboration with the Science Museum of Minnesota.

Montgomery, Sy. *Quest for the Tree Kangaroo: An Expedition to the Cloud Forest of New Guinea.* Photographs by Nic Bishop. Boston, MA: Houghton Mifflin, 2006. 7pp. ISBN 978-0-618-49641-9. Grades: 4–9.

Readers travel with scientists on an expedition to a remote forest in Papua New Guinea to capture and tag tree kangaroos, so that they can be tracked and studied. Not only do readers learn about tree kangaroos, they learn about science field work, the people and culture of Papua New Guinea, and the importance of conservation. web resources, notes about conservation, a glossary of words from the local language, and an index are included. From the Scientists in the Field series. Orbis Pictus Award, 2007.

Hodgkins, Fran. *The Whale Scientists: Solving the Mystery of Whale Strandings.* Boston: Houghton Mifflin, 2007. 64p. ISBN 978-0-618-55673-1. Grades: 5–8.

Worldwide research is underway to discover why whales strand themselves on beaches. Book chapters include (1) A transformed mammal; (2) Why do whales strand? (3) Getting answers to strandings; and (4) A tragedy and a triumph. Gripping color photographs and illustrations enhance the informative text. Back matter includes sources, a glossary, an index, and a list of other books in the series. From the Scientists in the Field series.

Explorations

1. After reading *African Elephant: The World's Biggest Land Mammal* (Hall, 2007) visit the Bearport website (www.bearportpublishing.com/SuperSized) to learn more about African elephants and other animals featured in the SuperSized series. The site has links to other websites that have video and audio resources for learning about animals.
2. After reading *Owen & Mzee: The True Story of a Remarkable Friendship* (Hatkoff, Hatkoff, and Kahumbu, 2006) show the students the documentary of their story on the website at www.owenandmzee.com/omweb/.
3. After reading *Owen & Mzee: The True Story of a Remarkable Friendship* (Hatkoff, Hatkoff, and Kahumbu, 2006) students can visit www.owenandmzee.com/omweb/ to view a slideshow of pictures of these two faithful companions

and to create their own video of Owen and Mzee with sound and text. Remind the children to return to the book for ideas as they write the script for their video.

4. Before reading *African Elephant: The World's Biggest Land Mammal* (Hall, 2007) visit the Defenders of Wildlife website at www.defenders.org/wildlife_and_habitat/wildlife/elephant.php to learn about how your class can adopt an elephant. There is also an audio file of an elephant sound and more information about elephants.
5. Before reading *Why Am I a Mammal?* (Pyers, 2006) explain to the students how the author has put in markers, such as words in bold and checkmarks, to help them understand the text.
6. Students who are interested in learning more about whales and whaling after reading *The Whale Scientists: Solving the Mystery of Whale Strandings* (Hodgkins, 2007) can view exhibits from the New Bedford Whaling Museum at www.whalingmuseum.org/exhibits/index_ex.html.

Reptiles

Frogs, chameleons, snakes, alligators, and crocodiles are all explored within the pages of the books in this section. A not-to-be-missed DVD in this section introduces Timothy the Tortoise, who has been in an English family since 1892. The life science standard includes studying animals in their habitats and exploring the adaptations that enable them to live in their particular habitat. Color photographs in *Nic Bishop Frogs* put readers directly into the frogs' habitats.

Book and Media Choices

Arnosky, Jim. *All about Frogs*. New York: Scholastic, 2002. Unp. ISBN 978-0-590-48164-9. Grades: K–2.

Colorful, detailed, acrylic paint illustrations fill the pages of this book. Interspersed in the informational text are Arnosky's reflections on personal encounters with frogs. The book includes a comparison of frogs and toads as well as a diagram of the life cycle of a frog.

Stewart, Melissa. *How Do Chameleons Change Color?* Tarrytown, NY: Marshall Cavendish, 2009. 32p. ISBN 978-0-7614-2922-7. Grades: 1–4.

Five brief chapters provide the answer in understandable text accompanied by up-close color photographs of chameleons. "Now I Know" questions in the chapters help to focus students' attention as they read. The book concludes with an activity for learning why chameleons change color, a glossary, resources for learning more, and an index. From the Tell Me Why, Tell Me How series.

Thomson, Sarah L. *Amazing Snakes!* Photographs by the Wildlife Conservation Society. New York: HarperCollins, 2006. 32p. ISBN 978-0-06-054462-1. Grades: 2–3.

Basic and fascinating facts about snakes and their importance to humans are written in an easy-to-read format superimposed on color photographs and colorful pages.

Pronunciation keys for important vocabulary words are included in the text. From the I Can Read series.

Bishop, Nic. *Nic Bishop Frogs.* New York: Scholastic, 2008. 48p. ISBN 978-0-439-87755-8. Grades: 3–5.

Spectacular color photographs put readers eyeball to eyeball with frogs in their natural environments. The text provides fascinating facts about frogs with highlighted sentences that may be all students read, as it will be hard for them to stop looking at the pictures long enough to read the text. An author's note, a glossary, and an index conclude the book. Outstanding Science Book for Students K–12, 2008. ALSC Notable Children's Book, 2009.

Nature Reptiles: Alligators and Crocodiles; Nature Reptiles: Turtles and Tortoises. DVD. Chicago, IL: Questar, 2003. 112 min. ISBN 9781594640094. Grades: 3 and up.

On this videodisc are two programs exploring these ancient reptiles. The movies show the reptiles in their natural habitats, which for alligators includes Florida suburbs. There is a clip showing employees of Pesky Critters at work as they relocate an alligator, which has moved to the suburbs. The second film starts by introducing viewers to Timothy the Tortoise, who has been in an English family since 1892. The videos are both entertaining and educational. Additional resources for using these films with students can be found by doing a search on "Nature Reptiles" at www.pbs.org.

Singer, Marilyn. *Venom.* Plain City, OH: Darby Creek, 2007. 96p. ISBN 978-1-58196-043-3. Grades: 4–8.

Snakes are not the only venomous creatures on earth. There are venomous spiders, insects, frogs, toads, fish, and other toxic creatures to learn about. Short quizzes focus readers' attention throughout the chapters. A concluding chapter explains the importance of protecting these creatures. The book concludes with a bibliography/webliography, a glossary, and an index. NCTE Orbis Pictus Honor Book, 2008.

Explorations

1. *All About Frogs* (Arnosky, 2002) starts with six questions that are answered in the book. Share the questions with the students and ask them to listen for the answers as you read the book. As the questions are answered, stop reading, and discuss the answers with the children.
2. The photographs in *Amazing Snakes!* (Thomson, 2006) were provided by the Wildlife Conservation Society. After reading the book show the students the website at www.wcs.org to show them how this organization works to take care of wildlife around the world.
3. Before sharing the DVD *Nature Reptiles: Alligators and Crocodiles* or *Nature Reptiles: Turtles and Tortoises* with the students, look at the chapter selections in the main menu to decide which parts of the films to show the students. For

example you may want to focus on conservation, feeding habits, or how they lay eggs and care for their young.

4. When introducing *Venom* (Singer, 2007) show students how the questions in the book help them focus on the most important concepts in the book.

Dinosaurs

Dinosaurs fascinate readers of all ages. These giant, mysterious, fearsome creatures, however, hold particular fascination for young readers who relish pronouncing their strange names and trying to fathom their size. Students also enjoy drawing dinosaurs and *Drawing Manga Dinosaurs* (Nishida, 2008) provides them with step-by-step instructions. Books in this section, *Dinosaur Teeth* (Gray, 2007) and *Bringing Dinosaur Bones to Life: How Do We Know What Dinosaurs Were Like?* (Farlow, 2001) explain how scientists conduct investigations to answer questions.

Book and Media Choices

Barner, Bob. *Dinosaur Bones.* DVD. New York: Weston Woods, 2006. 12 min. ISBN 978-0-439-90580-0. Grades: P–2.

Rhyming text, collage illustrations, and lively music introduce young readers to basic dinosaur facts. The video is based on Barner's book. ALSC Notable Children's Video, 2008.

Gray, Susan H. *Dinosaur Teeth.* New York: Scholastic, 2007. 24p. ISBN 978-0-531-17484-5. Grades: K–2.

Large print and color illustrations explain how scientists learn about dinosaurs by examining their teeth. A word hunt with pictures and pronunciation keys introduces readers to important vocabulary words they will encounter while reading this book. An index and resources for learning more conclude the book.

Birch, Robin. *Meat-Eating Dinosaurs.* New York: Chelsea House, 2009. 32p. ISBN 978-1-60413-407-0. Grades: K–3.

This introduction to meat-eating dinosaurs includes Tyrannosaurus, Deinonychus, Compsognathus, Gallimimus, and Baryonyx. Photographs, labeled colorful illustrations, and large font on a white background make this a book that students are eager to return to on their own as they discover the mysteries of dinosaurs. The book ends with a list of the meanings of the dinosaurs' names, a glossary, and an index.

Gibbons, Gail. *Dinosaur Discoveries.* New York: Holiday House, 2005. 34p. ISBN 978-0-8234-1971-5. Grades: 1–3.

A timeline of the age of dinosaurs, how fossils are formed, discovered, and displayed form the introduction to this study of dinosaurs. Framed pages set off the detailed illustrations of the dinosaurs. The illustrations incorporate the dinosaurs' names, pronunciation keys for the names, and information on how the names were selected.

The book includes an author's note, a section on more dinosaur discoveries, an index, and a map of the world indicating where dinosaurs have been found.

Lessem, Don. *Flying Giants of Dinosaur Time.* Illustrated by John Bindon. Minneapolis, MN: Lerner, 2005. 32p. ISBN 978-0-8225-1424-4. Grades: 2–4.

The book begins with an introduction to the flying reptiles, which includes illustrations of their heads, pronunciation guides to their names, wingspans, and when they lived. A graphic timeline, maps, illustrations, and photographs reveal intriguing details about these ancient winged creatures. A glossary and an index conclude the book. From the Meet the Dinosaurs series.

Arnold, Caroline. *Giant Sea Reptiles of the Dinosaur Age.* Illustrated by Laurie Caple. New York: Clarion Books, 2007. 40p. ISBN 978-0-618-50449-7. Grades: 3–5.

Step back in time and under the sea to learn about ancient giant reptiles. Watercolor illustrations in blues, greens, and browns form the backdrop for the informative text that is filled with facts.

There is also a chapter on Fossil Girl, Mary Anning. Back matter includes a list of places to go in the United States and Canada to view sea reptile fossils and an index.

Nishida, Masaki. *Drawing Manga Dinosaurs.* New York: Rosen, 2008. 24p. ISBN 978-1-40423-845-9. Grades: 3–5.

A brief history of manga introduces young artists to this unique Japanese art form. Each two-page spread features directions for drawing a different dinosaur and a story that includes the dinosaur. A glossary of comic book terms, very brief information about the dinosaurs in the book, and an index conclude the book.

Farlow, James O. *Bringing Dinosaur Bones to Life: How Do We Know What Dinosaurs Were Like?* New York: Scholastic, 2001. 60p. ISBN 978-0-531-11403-2. Grades: 5–8.

What did they look like? What did they eat? How did they fight, grow, and reproduce? Within the pages of this book readers learn how scientists examine dinosaur fossils to find their answers. Photographs, diagrams, illustrations, and computer-generated models help tell the story of how scientists learn about dinosaurs. The book concludes with a glossary, resources for learning more, and an index.

Gray, Susan Heinrichs. *Compsognathus.* Chanhassen, MN: The Child's World, 2005. 32p. ISBN 978-1-60253-237-3. Grades: 4–8.

Compsognathus was one of the smallest dinosaurs that ever lived, standing only about twenty-eight inches tall. The text explores how this tiny dinosaur lived and how it was discovered. There is also a section on why it was advantageous to be small. The book concludes with a glossary, resources for learning more, a geologic time scale, and an index. From the Exploring Dinosaurs series. This book is also available as an e-book.

Explorations

1. Before reading *Dinosaur Discoveries* (Gibbons, 2005) visit Gail Gibbons' website at www.gailgibbons.com to explore the teacher resources.
2. *Flying Giants of Dinosaur Time* (Lessem, 2005) contains information about the dinosaurs' wingspans. Mark off a few of the wingspans on the playground and have the students estimate the size of the wingspans. Then, have them use a yardstick or tape measure to determine the actual length.
3. Drawing is one form of prewriting. Have students use the instructions in *Drawing Manga Dinosaurs* (Nishida, 2008) to create their favorite dinosaur and then to write about their dinosaur.
4. The comic book structure of *Drawing Manga Dinosaurs* (Nishida, 2008) appeals to students, and as they draw the dinosaurs they are learning about them. Scan the students' drawings into a computer and allow the students to create digital stories about their dinosaurs.
5. After reading *Bringing Dinosaur Bones to Life: How Do We Know What Dinosaurs Were Like?* (Farlow, 2001) share the Smithsonian's dinosaur tracking blog at blogs.smithsonianmag.com/dinosaur/2009/02/11/how-to-bring-dinosaurs-back-to-life/ with the students. On the right side of the webpage is a listing of other Smithsonian blogs that contain useful resources for teaching science.

Fish

From goldfish to sharks the books in this section introduce students to fish, their life cycles, and their habitats. An aquarium in the library or in the classroom provides students with opportunities for hands-on observations. Young children enjoy feeding the fish and take delight in watching the fish swim to the top of the aquarium to eat. In addition, observations of the fish can lead to the development of observation skills, questioning skills, and writing skills as students study the fish and record their observations.

Book and Media Choices

Tourville, Amanda Doering. *Flutter and Float: Bringing Home Goldfish.* Illustrated by Andi Carter. Minneapolis, MN: Picture Window Books, 2009. 24p. ISBN 978-1-40484-853-5. Grades: K–3.

This informative text covers the selection and the care of goldfish using a picture-book format complete with tip boxes of helpful hints on ensuring that the goldfish have long and healthy lives. The book includes a table of contents, labeled diagram of a goldfish, life cycle, glossary, resources for learning more, and an index. From the Get a Pet series.

Bradley, Timothy J. *Paleo Sharks: Survival of the Strangest.* San Francisco, CA: Chronicle Books, 2007. 46p. ISBN 978-0-8118-4878-7. Grades: 4–7.

While the focus of the book is on paleo sharks, connections are made to present-day sharks. A timeline and a description of sharks introduce the three chapters on

Paleozoic sharks and their relatives, Mesozoic sharks and their relatives, and the Senozoic shark. A timeline and size-comparison charts provide additional at-a-glance information about the sharks. The book concludes with additional information about sharks today, a glossary, further reading, and a bibliography.

Stacey, Pamela. *Sharks at Risk and Gray Whale Obstacle Course*. DVD. Alexandria, VA: PBS Home Video, 2006. 120 min. ISBN 978-0-7936-9234-7. Grades: 5–8.

The importance of sharks is evident in this gripping video that dispels myths about sharks and shows viewers why they are essential to the to ocean ecosystems. The video is narrated by Pierce Brosnan and produced by Jean-Michel Cousteau. From the Ocean Adventures series. Educator resources, including podcasts, can be found by conducting a search on "Ocean Adventures" at www.pbs.org.

Explorations

1. Tourville's *Flutter and Float: Bringing Home Goldfish* (2009) contains all the information needed to set up an aquarium and keep fish healthy. Once the aquarium is set up, the students can observe the fish and record their observations. This hands-on exploration of fish provides students with the background knowledge they need to learn more about fish.
2. Before sharing *Sharks at Risk and Gray Whale Obstacle Course* (Stacey, 2006) with your students download the Shark Encounter pdf at www.pbs.org/kqed/oceanadventures/educators/sharks/. The file contains ideas for activating students' background knowledge about sharks.

Plants

Planting seeds and watching them grow helps students understand the life cycle of plants, which addresses the life science standard. The books in this section help students understand the interdependence of plants and animals. *Monarch and Milkweed* (Frost, 2008) explains how the life cycles of the monarch butterfly and the milkweed are beautifully interwoven. *Bread Comes to Life: A Garden of Wheat and a Loaf to Eat* (Levenson, 2004) explains how wheat grains become bread, and while written for younger students, the book could also be used with older students to reinforce their understanding of the interdependence of plants and animals.

Book and Media Choices

Levenson, George. *Bread Comes to Life: A Garden of Wheat and a Loaf to Eat*. Photographs by Shmuel Thaler. New York: Ten Speed, 2004. Unp. ISBN 978-1-58246-114-4. Grades: P–1.

Rhyming text and color photographs show how wheat seeds become bread in the hands of a charming baker. The book concludes with additional information about wheat and a recipe for bread. NCTE Orbis Pictus Recommended Book, 2005.

Williams, Karen Lynn. *Circles of Hope*. Illustrated by Linda Saport. Grand Rapids, MI, 2005. Unp. ISBN 978-0-8028-5276-2. Grades: P–2.

When his sister is born, Facile decides to plant a mango tree in her honor. A hungry goat, a rainstorm, and a fire thwart his attempts. When clearing stones from the garden, he realizes they can be used to create a circle of hope around a mango seed. Protected by the circle of stones and Facile's tender care, a mango tree grows to honor his sister. A glossary of Haitian Creole words found in the book and an author's note on the trees Haitians are planting to reforest their mountainsides concludes the book. Green Earth Book Award Honor Book, 2006.

Wallace, Nancy Elizabeth. *Seeds! Seeds! Seeds!* Tarrytown, NY: Marshall Cavendish, 2004. Unp. ISBN 978-0-7614-5159-4. Grades: P–3.

A surprise package from Gramps gets Buddy started on a seed collection. Gramps sent five bags each with a collection of seeds and activities to complete with them. Cut-paper collages and photographs of real seeds illustrate this entertaining story that will encourage students to start their own seed collections.

Aliki. *Quiet in the Garden*. New York: HarperCollins, 2009. Unp. ISBN 978-0-06-155208-3. Grades: K–2.

The beauty and wonders of the garden are revealed as a small boy quietly observes, explores, and discovers the animals and the plants. The cumulative tale follows animals and insects as they nibble their way through the garden. At the end of the tale, the boy prepares a feast for his new friends. The book ends with illustrated instructions for constructing a quiet garden.

Frost, Helen. *Monarch and Milkweed*. Illustrated by Leonid Gore. New York: Simon and Schuster, 2008. Unp. ISBN 978-1-41690-085-6. Grades: 1–4.

The life cycles of the monarch butterfly and the milkweed plant are perfectly intertwined in this poetic text accompanied by acrylic and pastel illustrations. The book concludes with an author's note including additional information on the butterflies' migration and the importance of the milkweed plant. The endpapers contain maps of the monarch's migration patterns. Outstanding Science Trade Book for Students K–12, 2009.

Blaxland, Beth. *Mangroves*. Broomall, PA: Chelsea House, 2000. 32p. ISBN 978-0-7910-6565-5. Grades: 3–5.

Colorful photographs of tree roots growing above ground and salt crystals clinging to leaves show readers that mangroves are very different from other plants. These plants survive even though they are flooded with seawater as the tide rises. Diagrams and "Did you know?" fact boxes contain additional fascinating facts about these unusual plants. Back matter includes an environment watch with information on why mangroves are important, a glossary, and an index. From the Water Worlds series.

Goodman, Susan E. *Seeds, Stems, and Stamens: The Ways Plants Fit into Their World.* Photographs by Michael Doolittle. Brookfield, CT: Millbrook Press, 2001. 48p. ISBN 978-0-7613-1874-3. Grades: 3–5.

The question-and-answer format of the book actively involves students in learning about plants' adaptations to their environments. Clear, concise text and colorful photographs hold students' attention as they predict the answers to the questions. Outstanding Science Trade Book for Students K–12, 2002.

Patent, Dorothy Hinshaw. *Plants on the Trail with Lewis and Clark.* Photographs by William Munoz. New York: Clarion, 2003. 104p. ISBN 978-0-618-06776-3. Grades: 4–8.

Lewis and Clark traveled over 2,000 miles across North America and along the way they collected plant specimens. Lewis carefully recorded details of the plants he found and how they used them. Back matter includes a list of the plants they collected, resources for learning more, and an index. Outstanding Science Trade Book for Students K–12, 2004.

Explorations

1. Put the students in small groups and give each group a copy of *Seeds! Seeds! Seeds!* (Wallace, 2004). Then, distribute small bags of a variety of seeds for students to identify using the pictures in the book. Ask the students to sort the seeds and then ask them to explain how they sorted the seeds.
2. As students read *Monarch and Milkweed* (Frost, 2008) have them record the changes in the butterfly and the plant over time in their science notebooks.
3. After reading *Seeds, Stems, and Stamens: The Ways Plants Fit into Their World* (Goodman, 2001) take the students on a nature walk with their science notebooks to look for plant adaptations.
4. Students reading *Plants on the Trail with Lewis and Clark* (Patent, 2003) might also be interested in *Animals on the Trail with Lewis and Clark* (Patent, 2002.)

EARTH AND SPACE SCIENCE

This standard explores the properties of the earth and the objects in our universe. It includes the study of changes in the earth and in the sky. There are books on landforms, natural disasters, the solar system, and space travel in this part of the chapter.

Structure of the Earth

Books in this section take readers from the tops of mountains to the floor of the ocean to examine the structure of the earth. Readers may be surprised to learn that volcanoes are found not only on the tops of mountains, but also deep in the sea. Books on rocks and minerals encourage students to explore the rocks and minerals in their own backyards and in their kitchen pantries. To pique students' interest in learning about new science concepts and to involve them in writing activities, Straits (2005) suggests using a "Mystery Box." For example, when starting a study of rocks he would put a rock in a box and then have the students ask him questions about the rock. Using his answers, the students would make inferences to determine which rock is in the box. As students ask questions, they periodically stop, reflect, and write about their predictions.

Book and Media Choices

Tocci, Salvatore. *Experiments with Rocks and Minerals.* New York: Scholastic, 2002. 48p. ISBN 978-0-516-22507-4. Grades: 1–2.

Eight experiments set students off on inquiry adventures that ensure they retain what they learn about rocks and minerals. Colorful photographs, illustrations, and step-by-step instructions accompany the easy-to-read text. The book concludes with resources for learning more, a glossary, and an index.

Harrison, David L. *Mountains: The Tops of the World.* Illustrated by Cheryl Nathan. Honesdale, PA: Boyds Mills, 2005. Unp. ISBN 978-1-59078-326-9. Grades: 1–3.

Plate tectonics, mountain building, and erosion are explored in this introductory text. Colorful illustrations and diagrams help to explain how fish fossils end up on mountaintops. An author's note and books for further reading conclude the book. From the Earthworks series.

Branley, Franklyn Mansfield. *Volcanoes.* Illustrated by Megan Lloyd. New York: HarperCollins, 2008. 30p. ISBN 978-0-06-028011-6. Grades: 3–4.

Originally published in 1985, this text has been updated with vibrant, colorful illustrations and diagrams. The book concludes with facts about volcanoes and the baking soda erupting volcano experiment. From the Let's Read and Find Out Science – Stage 2 series.

Stewart, Melissa. *Extreme Rocks and Minerals.* Washington, DC: Smithsonian and New York: HarperCollins, 2007. 48p. ISBN 978-0-06-089982-0. Grades: 3–6.

Color photographs of rocks and minerals fill the pages and draw readers into this intriguing book that reveals the wonders of rocks and minerals. Descriptions and examples of the three different kinds of rocks include how to identify the rocks, where they can be found, and how people use the rocks. The book concludes with an interview with a geologist, a glossary, resources for learning more, and an index.

Faulkner, Rebecca. *Sedimentary Rock.* Chicago, IL: Raintree, 2007. 48p. ISBN 978-1-4109-2748-4. Grades: 4–6.

Beautiful color photographs, diagrams, flowcharts, a map, and text boxes complement the succinct text that provides basic information about sedimentary rocks. The book concludes with resources for learning more, a glossary, and an index. From the Geology Rocks! series.

Mallory, Kenneth. *Diving to a Deep-Sea Volcano.* New York: Houghton Mifflin, 2006. 60p. ISBN 978-0-618-33205-2. Grades: 4–8.

Readers follow along as marine biologist, Rich Lutz, climbs aboard his deep-sea submarine and discovers a volcanic eruption. Photographs, illustrations, maps, and diagrams reveal the mysterious world beneath the sea. The book concludes with a glossary, suggestions for further reading, and an index. Outstanding Science Trade Book for Students K–12, 2007.

McCollum, Sean. *Volcanic Eruptions, Earthquakes, and Tsunamis.* New York: Chelsea House, 2007. 80p. ISBN 978-0-7910-9047-3. Grades: 5–7.

Following the introductory chapter are chapters on volcanoes, earthquakes, tsunamis, changes in construction codes, and information on predicting disasters. Photographs, charts, and diagrams extend and enhance the ideas presented in the text. Back matter includes a glossary, bibliography, resources for learning more, and an index. From the Scientific American series.

Kelly, Erica, and Richard Kissel. *Evolving Planet: Four Billion Years of Life on Earth.* New York: Abrams, 2008. 136p. ISBN 978-0-8109-9486-7. Grades: 5–8.

A geologic time scale in the introduction and repeated throughout the book helps guide readers on this journey through time and evolution. Photographs and illustrations depicting unusual creatures add to the intrigue of this exciting story. This book was published in association with the Field Museum, Chicago. Back matter includes a pronunciation key, a glossary, illustration credits, a bibliography, and an index.

Explorations

1. As students work with partners to complete the experiments in *Experiments with Rocks and Minerals* (Tocci, 2002) provide them with time to talk about the experiments and to write about what they learned.
2. After reading *Volcanoes* (Branley, 2008) have the students visit Volcano World at volcano.oregonstate.edu/ to search for the closest volcano to their homes. The site contains images and live video feeds of volcanoes around the world.
3. As students read *Extreme Rocks and Minerals* (Stewart, 2007) have them create a chart to record what they learn about the three types of rocks and to note examples of each of the types.
4. While studying *Extreme Rocks and Minerals* (Stewart, 2007) have the students visit Harvard University's Mineralogical Museum online at www.fas.harvard.edu/~geomus/index.htm. The site has information on the museum's collections and links to other sites about rocks and minerals.
5. As students study *Sedimentary Rock* (Faulkner, 2007) take them on a geology field trip in their schoolyard using the materials provided by the Learning Web at the U.S. Geological Survey at education.usgs.gov/schoolyard/index.html.

6. After reading *Volcanic Eruptions, Earthquakes, and Tsunamis* (McCollum, 2007) students wanting to learn more can visit the Savage Earth website at www.pbs.org/wnet/savageearth/. Animations on the site demonstrate the actions of volcanic eruptions, earthquakes, and tsunamis.

Weather

Weather is part of standard five focusing on earth and space science. As the seasons change so does the weather, and books in this section provide students with hands-on explorations of the weather in their area and the weather around the world. Books in this section also contain information about the earth's changing climate and the impact of global warming.

Book and Media Choices

Cobb, Vicki. *I Face the Wind.* Illustrated by Julia Gordon. New York: HarperCollins, 2003. Unp. ISBN 978-0-688-17840-6. Grades: P–2.

A note to the reader addressed to adults explains that easy-to-obtain objects such as balloons, a wire coat hanger, tape, and a ball are needed to complete the activities in the book. The question-and-answer format combined with the activities allow budding scientists to explore the concept of air. From the Vicki Cobb Science Play series. ALA Robert F. Sibert Honor Book, 2004.

Gershator, Phillis. *Listen, Listen.* Illustrated by Allison Jay. Cambridge, MA: Barefoot Books, 2007. Unp. ISBN 978-1-84686-084-3. Grades: P–3.

Listening to the sounds of the seasons in this delightful rhyming text encourages students to listen to the sounds of the seasons in their own surroundings. At the end of the story readers are challenged to explore the illustrations for signs of the seasons.

Wright, Betty Ren. *The Blizzard.* Illustrated by Ronald Himler. New York: Holiday House, 2003. Unp. ISBN 978-0-8234-1656-1. Grades: P–3.

With a snowstorm on the way, Billy's cousins will not be coming to help celebrate his birthday. The blinding blizzard closes the roads, so the teacher gathers the class and holding hands they walk to the closest home to spend the night—Billy's house. There is an abundance of children to help with the farm chores and to help celebrate Billy's birthday. Blue and gray watercolor illustrations depict the old-fashioned rural life and set just the right tone for this heartwarming story.

Manolis, Kay. *Temperature*. Minneapolis, MN: Bellwether Media, 2008. 25p. ISBN 978-1-60014-100-3. Grades: K–2.

Colorful photographs and easy-to-read text introduce young readers to facts about temperature with chapters on how to measure temperature and the effects of temperature. Back matter includes a glossary, resources for learning more, and an index. From the First Science series.

Singer, Marilyn. *On the Same Day in March: A Tour of the World's Weather*. Illustrated by Frané Lessac. New York: HarperCollins, 2000. 33p. ISBN 978-0-0644-3528-4. Grades: K–3.

Lyrical verse and colorful illustrations show readers how geography and weather are interrelated. Top Ten Science Books for Children, 2000. Notable Children's Trade Book in the Field of Social Studies, 2001.

Gardner, Robert. *Stellar Science Projects about Earth's Sky*. Illustrated by Tom Labaff. Berkeley Heights, NJ: Enslow Publishers, 2006. 48p. ISBN 978-0-7660-2732-9. Grades: 4–6.

This is a collection of step-by-step experiments for students to conduct as they explore the air, the sky, the clouds, and the stars. Following each experiment is an explanation, and many include ideas for extending the experiment into a science fair project. Back matter includes a glossary, resources for further reading, and an index. From the Rockin' Earth Science Experiments series.

Gardner, Robert. *Wild Science Projects about Earth's Weather*. Illustrated by Tom Labaff. Berkeley Heights, NJ: Enslow Publishers, 2006. 48p. ISBN 978-0-7660-2734-3. Grades: 4–6.

This is a collection of step-by-step experiments for students to conduct as they explore weather. Following each experiment is an explanation, and many include ideas for extending the experiment into a science fair project. Back matter includes a glossary, resources for further reading, and an index. From the Rockin' Earth Science Experiments series.

Cherry, Lynne. *How We Know What We Know about Our Changing Climate*. Photographs by Gary Braasch. Nevada City, CA: Dawn, 2008. 66p. ISBN 978-1584-691037. Grades: 4–8.

Scientists around the world are studying global warming and this book provides the background knowledge students need to begin explorations into what they can do to stem global warming. Color photographs show children involved in projects that require them to make personal choices and to advocate for changing public policy. From A Sharing Nature with Children series.

Mordhorst, Heidi. *Pumpkin Butterfly: Poems for the other Side of Nature*. Illustrated by Jenny Reynish. Honesdale, PA: Boyds Mills Press, 2009. 32p. ISBN 978-1-59078-620-8. Grades: 4 and up.

This celebration of nature reflects the changing seasons in poetry filled with metaphors and sensory delights. Watercolor illustrations enhance the poems and spark discussions about these tantalizing verses.

Gore, Albert. *An Inconvenient Truth: The Crisis of Global Warming*. New York: Viking, 2007. 191p. ISBN 1-4157-2478-4. Grades: 5–8.

Based on Gore's adult book and Oscar-winning documentary, this book is written for young adults. The book explains the effects of global warming and the dire predictions for its future impact. Steps for taking action now to save the Earth are included. Notable Social Studies Trade Book for Young People, 2008.

Pringle, Laurence P. *Global Warming: The Threat of Earth's Changing Climate.* New York: Sea Star Books, 2003. 48p. ISBN 978-1-58717-228-1. Grades: 5–8.

Noted science writer Pringle describes global warming and its devastating consequences, as well as what has been done to slow down global warming. Clear, crisp color photographs, diagrams, and graphs accompany the short readable chapters. This concise book is just the starting place for students' explorations of global warming. The book concludes with a glossary, resources for learning more, and an index.

Johnson, Rebecca L. *Investigating Climate Change: Scientists' Search for Answers in a Warming World.* Minneapolis, MN: 2009. 112p. ISBN 978-0-8225-6792-9. Grades: 6–10.

This is an overview of global warming starting with historical background and ending with the challenges the world faces. Photographs, diagrams, charts, and maps help readers grasp the major issues and develop an appreciation for the need to take action. The book concludes with a glossary, source notes, resources for learning more, and an index. From the Discovery! series.

Explorations

1. Start the school year by reading *Listen, Listen* (Gershator, 2007). After reading the book, create a large chart of the seasons and record the sounds of autumn on the chart. As the seasons change, have the students revisit the chart and record not only the visible changes to the earth, but also the unique sounds of the seasons.
2. While studying *Temperature* (Manolis, 2008) share the Weather Wiz Kids site with your students at www.weatherwizkids.com/temperature.htm. The site features a temperature conversion calculator, a windchill calculator, and a heat index calculator. The site also has lesson plans and experiments.
3. After reading *On the Same Day in March: A Tour of the World's Weather* (Singer, 2000) go to www.weather.com to show the children the day's weather in different countries.
4. Additional resources to accompany *Global Warming: The Threat of Earth's Changing Climate* (Pringle, 2003) can be found on the U.S. Environmental Protection Agency Climate Change website at www.epa.gov/Climatechange/. The sidebar has a link to webpages on "What You Can Do" with activities for involving students in hands-on learning about climate change. Resources for younger students studying global warming can be found at www.epa.gov/Climatechange/kids/.

Water

From rivers to oceans to water wells, books in this section explore the importance of water in our daily lives. Water conservation and water pollution are explored in the following books and websites. *One Well: The Story of Water on Earth* (Strauss, 2007) and *Tracking Trash: Flotsam, Jetsam, and the Science of Ocean Motion* (Burns, 2007) contain suggestions for taking action to preserve water resources. Also included below is a book of water science experiments that can be extended into science fair projects, *Water Science Fair Projects: Using Ice Cubes, Super Soakers, and Other Wet Stuff* (Goodstein, 2004).

Book and Media Choices

Karwoksi, Gail Langer. *River Beds: Sleeping in the World's Rivers.* Illustrated by Connie McLennan. Mt. Pleasant, SC: Sylvan Dell, 2008. Unp. ISBN 978-0-9777423-4-9. Grades: P–2.

On a soothing float down a river a sleepy boy encounters mammals curling up for a restful snooze. Action verbs and rich descriptions accompany the colorful illustrations. The back matter includes activities for reinforcing the book's information.

Wallace, Nancy Elizabeth. *Shells! Shells! Shells!* Tarrytown, NY: Marshall Cavendish, 2006. Unp. ISBN 978-0-7614-5332-1. Grades: P–2.

Cut-paper illustrations complete with photographs of real shells tell the story of Buddy Bear's trip to the beach, where his mother teaches him about shells. The text is filled with facts about shells and there are more shell facts in the back matter. Step-by-step instructions are included for creating a bookmark. This is an excellent introduction to beach marine life.

Hodgkins, Fran. *Between the Tides.* Illustrated by Jim Sollers. Camden, MA: Down East Books, 2007. Unp. ISBN 978-0-89272-727-8. Grades: P–3.

A repeated refrain gives the book a predictable pattern as the sea appears and disappears with the tides alternately revealing and concealing the sea creatures. The animals' adaptations to the coming and going of the sea are briefly explained. The book concludes with the scientific explanation of the tides.

Sidman, Joyce. *Song of the Water Boatman and Other Pond Poems.* Illustrated by Beckie Prange. New York: Houghton Mifflin, 2005. Unp. ISBN 978-0-618-13547-9. Grades: P–5.

Bold woodcut prints accompany the vivid poetry filled with scientific facts about plants, insects, and animals thriving in a pond through the seasons. The book includes a glossary. An Outstanding Science Trade Book for Students K–12, 2006.

Wiesner, David. *Flotsam.* Boston, MA: Houghton Mifflin, 2006. Unp. ISBN 978-0-618-19457-5. Grades: K–4.

A curious boy at the seashore discovers a boxy, barnacle-encrusted camera washed up in the flotsam in this wordless picture book. When he has the film in the camera developed, the photographs reveal an astonishing undersea world and children from different lands and different times. The boy takes his own picture and returns the camera to the sea for another child to find. Caldecott Medal Winner, 2007.

O'Neill, Michael Patrick. *Ocean Magic*. Palm Beach Gardens, FL: Batfish Books, 2008. Unp. ISBN 978-0-9728653-5-7. Grades: 1–4.

An author's note introduces the book and explains that its purpose is to introduce readers to the diversity and complexity of the inhabitants of the oceans of the world. Stunning, large color photographs and informative text reveal the wonders beneath the ocean. A two-page glossary concludes the book.

Chambers, Catherine, and Nicholas Lapthorn. *Rivers*. Chicago, IL: Heinemann Library, 2008. 32p. ISBN 978-1-4034-9604-1. Grades: 3–5.

Charts, maps, diagrams, photographs, and illustrations help readers understand how rivers are formed and how vital rivers are to humans around the world. Three map activities spaced throughout the text challenge students to apply what they are learning. Glossary words are in bold in the text and this is noted on the table of contents page. Back matter includes resources for learning more, a glossary, and an index. From the Mapping Landforms series.

Strauss, Rochelle. *One Well: The Story of Water on Earth*. Illustrated by Rosemary Woods. Tonawonda, NY: Kids Can Press, 2007. 32p. ISBN 978-1-55337-954-6. Grades: 4–8.

Information on the importance of water to survival is followed by information on how to protect and conserve water. The text explains water conservation in easy-to-understand language that inspires students to conserve water. Colorful pages and detailed illustrations enhance students' understanding of the text. The book concludes with information about what children can do to conserve water, with notes to parents, guardians and teachers, and an index.

Burns, Loree Griffin. *Tracking Trash: Flotsam, Jetsam, and the Science of Ocean Motion*. Boston: Houghton Mifflin, 2007. 58p. ISBN 978-0-618-58131-3. Grades: 5–8.

Oceanographers study ocean currents using sophisticated equipment, but Curt Ebbesmeyer studies them by examining the trash he finds washed up on ocean beaches. Ocean trash is polluting the water and endangering marine life and this book explores the harm being done and provides resources for learning how to protect the ocean. A glossary, resources for learning more, and an index conclude the book. ALSC Notable Children's Book, 2008. NCTE Orbis Pictus Recommended Book, 2008. *Boston Globe*–Horn Book Award for Excellence in Children's Literature Honor Book, 2007.

The Great Ocean Rescue. Mac/Win. New York: Tom Snyder Productions. Grades: 5–8.

This software presents students with four rescue missions that require them to investigate ocean ecosystems to solve the problems. The CD-ROM includes a teacher's guide and student activity sheets. Teacher's Choice Award Winner.

Song of the Salish Sea: A Natural History of Northwest Waters. DVD. Poulsbo, WA: Earthwise Media, 2006. 45 min. Grades: 5–8.

Explore Puget Sound, the Strait of Georgia, and the Strait of Juan de Fuca known as the Salish Sea in this video. A wide range of habitats and life forms are showcased. The DVD includes a printable teacher's guide, tidal pool curriculum, and additional short films. ALSC Notable Children's Video, 2007.

Goodstein, Madeline. *Water Science Fair Projects: Using Ice Cubes, Super Soakers, and Other Wet Stuff.* Berkeley Heights, NJ: Enslow, 2004. 128p. ISBN 978-0-7660-2124-2. Grades: 7 and up.

The science experiments are grouped into four sections: (1) structure of water; (2) three states of matter of water; (3) surface tension, adhesion, and cohesion of liquid water: and (4) chemical properties of water. Easy-to-locate materials, step-by-step instructions, black-and-white figures, and experiments that build on the previous ones ensure that students can successfully conduct the experiments. Following the experiments are ideas and questions to develop the experiments into science fair projects. Back matter includes a glossary, resources for learning more, and an index. From the Chemistry! Best Science Projects series.

Explorations

1. After reading *River Beds: Sleeping in the World's Rivers* (Karwoksi, 2008) share the activities at the end of the book with the students. Then, have them locate the animals' homes on the class globe or map.
2. Before reading *Shells! Shells! Shells!* (Wallace, 2006) pass around some real shells for the students to hold and explore.
3. After reading *One Well: The Story of Water on Earth* (Strauss, 2007) have the students visit Ryan's Well Foundation at www.ryanswell.ca/ to learn about Ryan Hreljac's work to provide clean water to children around the world. There is a link on the site to their Youth in Action Program that teaches students about what they can do to help.
4. After reading *Tracking Trash: Flotsam, Jetsam, and the Science of Ocean Motion* (Burns, 2007) have the students visit Curt Ebbesmeyer's website at oceanmotion.org/html/research/ebbesmeyer.htm to find out what he is tracking and to report interesting beach finds.
5. Have the students visit the Ocean Conservancy website at www.oceanconservancy.org/ to learn more about conserving the world's oceans and to find ways to take action. Even if students do not live near the ocean, the website contains ideas they can follow to live responsibly and protect the environment.

Stars and Planets

The sun, the stars, and the planets shine and seem to twinkle in the sky. The closest heavenly body to the Earth is the moon, whose shape seems to change as it waxes and wanes. Studying these heavenly bodies is encompassed in science standard five, which includes developing an understanding of the earth's place in the solar system. The books and DVDs in this section reveal some of the wonders of these magnificent objects in the sky.

Book and Media Choices

Barner, Bob. *Stars! Stars! Stars!* San Francisco, CA: Chronicle Books, 2002. Unp. ISBN 978-0-8118-3159-8. Grades: K–2.

Gazing at the night sky, a child marvels at the planets and stars overhead. Rhyming phrases swirl across cut and torn paper collages depicting the wonders of the universe. The book concludes with four pages of information about the planets and other heavenly bodies.

Lundebrek, Amy. *Under the Night Sky*. Illustrated by Anna Rich. Gardiner, ME: Tilbury House, 2008. Unp. ISBN 978-0-88448-297-0. Grades: 1–3.

The nightly routine of a mother quickly slipping into her dark apartment after working at a factory is suddenly altered as she bursts into the house and rouses her son from his warm bed. Hurriedly he dons warm clothes and is rushed outside to the parking lot where he joins the neighbors to celebrate the magic of the aurora borealis. Surrounded by the magical lights his mother reminds him that no matter what happens in their lives they will always have this special moment and she will always be on his side.

Lenglen, Jean-Marc. *The Moon and Other Objects in the Sky*. DVD. Wynnewood, PA: Schlessinger, 2006. 20 min. ISBN 978-1-41710-669-1. Grades 2–5.

Animated characters Adi and Woops answer questions about the moon and other objects in the sky. Chapter titles include: How did the moon get where it is? Why does the moon seem to change? How does an eclipse work? Why do comets have tails, and What are artificial satellites? Activities have students exploring: (1) the moon's place in the solar system; (2) the moon's surface; (3) phases of the moon; (4) the tides; and (5) eclipse. Chapter selections, discussion questions and activities, and a Spanish soundtrack are included on the DVD. From the Space Exploration Adi in Space series.

Landau, Elaine. *Pluto: From Planet to Dwarf*. New York: Scholastic, 2008. 48p. ISBN 978-0-531-12566-3. Grades: 3–5.

In easy-to-understand language, Landau explains why Pluto is no longer considered a planet. Interesting information that will appeal to children such as the fact that the name "Pluto" was suggested by an eleven-year-old girl accompany the colorful illustrations and diagrams. The book concludes with statistics, resources, a glossary, and an index. From A True Book series.

Scherer, Glenn, and Marty Fletcher. *Uranus*. Berkeley Heights, NJ: Enslow, 2005. 48p. ISBN 978-0-7660-5307-6. Grades: 4–10.

Amateur astronomer William Herschel's discovery of Uranus in 1781 continues to provide inspiration for other amateur astronomers as they comb the heavens with their telescopes in search of new finds. Concise text, color photographs, diagrams, and screenshots of webpages reveal the wonders of this gas giant. A glossary, chapter notes, books for further reading, and an index conclude the book. The book comes with a password that grants the readers access to www.myreportlinks.com, which provides links to additional resources about Uranus. From the Solar System series.

Pearson, Scott. *Exploring Space: The Quest for Life.* DVD. Arlington, VA: PBS Home Video, 2006. 120 min. ISBN 978-0-7936-9199-9. Grades: 6–8.

This quest to explore the possibility of life on other planets includes interviews with scientists, as well as videos and animations. Scene selections include early solar system, Pangea, 250 million years ago, Galileo, solar system and moons of Jupiter, MIR space station, comparing Earth to Mars, looking and listening for aliens, manned mission to Mars, and the atmosphere of Earth.

Explorations

1. The National Aeronautics and Space Administration (NASA) Solar System Exploration website at solarsystem.nasa.gov/planets/index.cfm includes multimedia resources and activities to help students learn about the stars and the planets.
2. Students who are interested in learning more about the Kuiper Belt Objects discussed in *Pluto: from Planet to Dwarf* (Landau, 2008) can visit pluto.jhuapl.edu. This website is tracking NASA's New Horizons spacecraft as it heads toward Pluto and the Kuiper Belt. Resources on the site include podcasts, photographs, and a link to Twitter for up-to-date postings.
3. Before viewing *The Moon and Other Objects in the Sky* (Lenglen, 2006) have the students observe the moon for a few weeks and draw the shape of the moon as it changes in the night sky.

Space Travel

Journeys into space capture the imaginations and interests of students. Books and media in this section provide information about space travel as well as cause students to wonder and formulate questions. Their questions will lead them on searches to find answers, just as scientists seek answers to their questions about space travel. But scientists and astronauts are just a few of the people involved in space travel. In *Team Moon: How 400,000 People Landed Apollo 11 on the Moon* (Thimmesh, 2006) students discover behind-the-scenes work that makes space travel possible.

Book and Media Choices

Kortenkamp, Steve. *Space Stations.* Mankato, MN: Capstone, 2008. 24p. ISBN 978-1-4296-0064-4. Grades: K–2.

From Salyut, to Skylab, to Mir, to the International Space Station, this is a brief introduction to how humans live and work in space. Information on building the space station is also included. A glossary, resources for learning more, and an index conclude the book. From the First Facts: The Solar System series.

Leedy, Loreen, and Andrew Schuerger. *Messages from Mars.* New York: Holiday House, 2006. 40p. ISBN 978-0-8234-1954-8. Grades: 2–4.

Take a field trip to Mars in this informative picture book that combines actual photographs of Mars and drawings of characters making the trip in 2016. There are diagrams, a timeline, and resources for learning more. Leedy's coauthor is her husband, an astrobiologist.

Lenglen, Jean-Marc. *Space Travel.* DVD. Wynnewood, PA: Schlessinger, 2003. 20 min. ISBN 978-1-41710-671-4. Grades 3–6.

Space travelers Adi and Woops answer questions about space travel, such as how rockets work and what it takes to survive in space. Images from space and animations help to explain the duo's answers. A teacher's guide is available and the soundtrack is in both English and Spanish. From the Space Exploration: Adi in Space DVD series.

Vogt, Gregory L. *Space Mission Patches.* Brookfield, CT: Millbrook Press, 2001. 78p. ISBN 978-0-7613-1613-8. Grades: 4–6.

Accompanying each space patch is the purpose of the space mission and information on the astronauts who designed the patch. Twenty space missions are included in the book. Over the years the designing of the patches has evolved as designers and graphic artists work with the astronauts to create a unique patch for each mission. A glossary, resources for learning more, and an index are included.

Thimmesh, Catherine. *Team Moon: How 400,000 People Landed Apollo 11 on the Moon.* New York: Houghton Mifflin, 2006. 80p. ISBN 978-0-618-50757-3. Grades: 4 and up.

Discover all the people, and their various jobs, involved in the first moon landing. Direct quotes interspersed throughout the text immerse readers directly into the experience. NASA photographs and materials showcase the work of these dedicated, ingenious individuals, whose behind-the-scenes work is often unrecognized by the general public. The book includes a glossary, sources, chapter notes, and an index. Outstanding Science Trade Book for Students K–12, 2007. ALA Robert F. Sibert Medal Winner, 2007.

Spangenburg, Ray, and Kit Moser. *Onboard the Space Shuttle.* New York: Scholastic, 2002. 112p. ISBN 978-0-531-11896-2. Grades: 5–9.

In seven chapters the authors provide a brief history of the space shuttle and its impact on the space program. The book includes information on living in the space station, the repair of the Hubble, and the Challenger tragedy. Photographs, diagrams, and sidebars showcase interesting highlights. Back matter includes a list of key shuttle flights, a timeline, a glossary, resources for learning more, and an index. From the Out of this World series.

Ackroyd, Peter. *Escape from Earth: Voyages through Time*. New York: DK, 2003. 144p. ISBN 978-0-7566-0171-3. Grades: 6 and up.

Informative text, diagrams, photographs, and brief biographies provide the details of humans' travels in space. Stunning photographs draw readers into the book and the well-written text will keep them interested in learning more. The reference section includes landmark space explorations, moon landings, spacecraft, space facts, a glossary, and an index.

Explorations

1. After reading *Space Stations* (Kortenkamp, 2008) have the students visit the FactHound website to learn more about space stations. The book includes an ID number for access to the website.
2. For the latest information on the International Space Station including images, video, and audio files visit www.nasa.gov/mission_pages/station/main/index.html.
3. After reading *Messages from Mars* (Leedy and Schuerger, 2006) visit Leedy's website at www.loreenleedy.com to learn more about Mars and to learn more about Schuerger's work.
4. After reading *Space Mission Patches* (Vogt, 2001) have the students examine the patches noting the symbols embodied in them and discuss the meaning behind the symbols. For example, among the symbols on the Apollo 17 patch is an eagle whose wings have stars and stripes representing the American flag. Not all of the patches' symbols are explained in the book. Using the resources at the end of the book, students can find out the meanings behind those symbols.
5. After reading *Team Moon: How 400,000 People Landed Apollo 11 on the Moon* (Thimmesh, 2006) have the students generate a list of questions about the Apollo 11 mission. Then, direct the students to the Apollo Lunar Surface Journal at www.hq.nasa.gov/Alsj/frame.html to find answers to their questions. There are actual video and audio clips from the mission on the site. This website also houses information on the other Apollo missions.

SCIENCE AND TECHNOLOGY

The emphasis of this standard is on designing solutions to problems in order to understand the relationship between science and technology. In addition, students learn about the characteristics that distinguish natural objects from objects made by humans. Books in this section explore the reasons familiar objects such as zippers, buttons, and airplanes were created and the problems they were expected to solve. Students also learn about the far-reaching impact of science and technology on daily lives by reading about the invention of the sewing machine and the atom bomb.

Book and Media Choices

Priceman, Marjorie. *Hot Air: The Mostly True Story of the First Hot-Air Balloon Ride*. New York: Antheneum, 2005. Unp. ISBN 978-0-689-82642-9. Grades: P–3.

Readers are introduced to French history as they travel to Versailles in 1783 for the Montgolfier brothers' hot-air balloon experiment. High above the ground a duck, a sheep, and a rooster sail through the air. Watercolor illustrations capture the excitement and adventure of this historic event. The book concludes with additional information about the flight. Caldecott Medal Honor Book, 2006.

Hopkins, Lee Bennett, Selector. *Incredible Inventions*. Illustrated by Julia Sarcone-Roach. New York: HarperCollins, 2009. 32p. ISBN 978-0-06-087245-8. Grades: K–3.

This poetic celebration of familiar inventions from the drinking straw to the Ferris wheel to the hairbrush was written for reading aloud and sharing. Lively mixed media illustrations capture the styles of the poems and add to the excitement. The last four pages of the book have a timeline and additional information about the inventions.

Thales, Sharon. *Screws to the Rescue*. Mankato, MN: Capstone, 2007. 24p. ISBN 978-0-7368-6749-8. Grades: K–3.

Did you ever think of a spiral staircase as a screw? Young readers discover that screws are everywhere and are essential to our everyday lives. Back matter includes an experiment, a glossary, resources for learning more, and an index. From the First Facts: Simple Machines to the Rescue series.

Dahl, Michael. *Scoop, Seesaw, and Raise: A Book about Levers*. Illustrated by Denise Shea. Minneapolis, MN: Picture Window Books, 2005. 24p. ISBN 978-1-40481-303-8. Grades: 1–4.

Children find that simple machines are all around them and that they use them every day. Basic pictures and text explain how levers work. The back matter includes an experiment with marshmallows, fun facts, a glossary, resources for learning more, and an index. A special code enables students to access additional information at www.facthound.com. This book is also available as an e-book. From the Amazing Science series.

Hudson, Cheryl Willis. *Construction Zone*. Photographs by Richard Sobol. Cambridge, MA: Candlewick, 2006. Unp. ISBN 978-0-7636-2684-6. Grades: 2–6.

Over the course of three years, photographer Richard Sobol chronicled the construction of the Massachusetts Institute of Technology's State Center designed by Frank O. Ghery. The construction is likened to a giant puzzle that goes together piece by piece. Throughout the text bold words are defined at the bottom of the page beneath gold- and black-striped ribbons. The book concludes with a note from the photographer. NCTE Orbis Pictus Recommended Book, 2007.

Walker, Sally M., and Roseann Feldmann. *Inclined Planes and Wedges.* Minneapolis, MN: Lerner, 2002. 47p. ISBN 978-0-8225-2221-8. Grades: 2–4.

The book begins by challenging readers to be word detectives and to discover the meanings of a list of keywords as they read. Colorful photographs of children exploring planes and wedges accompanied by directions and questions make this a book for students to use to explore these simple machines on their own. There are chapters on work, machines, inclined planes, gravity and friction, and wedges. Back matter includes resources for learning more, a glossary, and an index. From the Early Bird Physics Books.

Tocci, Salvadore. *Experiments with Simple Machines.* New York: Scholastic, 2003. 48p. ISBN 978-0-516-22604-0. Grades: 3–5.

Students explore simple machines by conducting experiments using household objects. The step-by-step instructions and colorful photographs and illustrations ensure that curious students will be able to complete the experiments with adult help. The back matter includes resources for learning more, websites, a glossary, and an index. From A True Book series.

Carlson, Laurie M. *Queen of Inventions: How the Sewing Machine Changed the World.* Minneapolis, MN: Lerner, 2003. 47p. ISBN 978-0-7613-2706-6. Grades: 3–6.

Isaac Singer not only invented the sewing machine, he was also a shrewd businessperson. Realizing that not everyone could afford to buy a sewing machine, he allowed purchasers to pay for the machines as they earned money with their sewing. This machine revolutionized sewing because clothing and other fabric goods could now be mass-produced. Black-and-white photographs and reproductions help to tell the story. The book concludes with a song excerpt and resources for further learning.

Crazy Machines II. Win. New York: Viva Media, 2009. Grades: 4–8.

What better way to learn about simple machines than to use them? The challenge is to create a crazy contraption to solve a puzzle. As students progress through the game the puzzles get harder, but they get more tools to work with. ALA Great Interactive Software for Kids, Spring 2009.

Sullivan, George. *Built to Last: Building America's Amazing Bridges, Dams, Tunnels, and Skyscrapers.* New York: Scholastic, 2005. 128p. ISBN 978-0-439-51737-9. Grades: 5–8.

The architectural masterpieces featured in this book are grouped by four time frames and include wonders such as the Transcontinental Railroad, the Golden Gate Bridge, and the Sears Tower. Back matter includes resources for learning more and an index. Outstanding Science Trade Book for Students K–12, 2006.

The Best of Modern Marvels. DVD. New York: A & E Television Networks, 2008. 35 hr 25 min. ISBN 978-1-42290-351-3. Grades: 6 and up.

Learn the stories behind modern marvels such as vacuums, adhesives, the Manhattan Project, the world's longest bridge, the Hoover Dam, and the Empire State Building.

This set includes the History Channel documentaries featuring engineering disasters, technology marvels, architectural wonders, and weird, wonderful everyday marvels. From the Modern Marvels series.

Explorations

1. Read selected phrases from *Incredible Inventions* (Hopkins, 2009) and have the students guess the invention before reading the entire poem.
2. Older students can use the poems in *Incredible Inventions* (Hopkins, 2009) as models for writing their own poems about inventions not included in the book.
3. After reading *Screws to the Rescue* (Thales, 2007) have the students search the classroom and record on the board all the places they find screws. This could also be a fun parent and child activity.
4. Provide the students with the materials they need to try the experiments in *Experiments with Simple Machines* (Tocci, 2003). After they complete the experiments have them talk about and then write about their results.
5. The Franklin Institute Online has a webpage (www.fi.edu/qa97/spotlight3/) that has explorations and animations that provide students with additional information on simple machines.

SCIENCE IN PERSONAL AND SOCIAL PERSPECTIVES

While personal health is included in this section, books on this subject are found in the health chapter and in the physical education and dance chapter. This section focuses on the impact of changes in environments and changes brought about by technology. In the science in personal and social perspectives section, books focus on helping students make informed decisions from a global perspective.

Ecosystems

From a single tree to an entire forest from the North Pole to the South Pole the earth contains an abundance of ecosystems each sustaining unique plants and animals. Books in this section explore ecosystems and the impact of humans on ecosystems. As students learn about these fragile systems, they develop understanding of the ecosystems' importance and recognize their responsibilities as global citizens to protect the ecosystems. To enable their third grade students to showcase and to share their understanding of ecosystems Robertson and Mahlin (2005) had them create newspapers that were published using a word-processing program.

Book and Media Choices

Gibbons, Gail. *Coral Reefs*. New York: Holiday House, 2007. 32p. ISBN 978-0-8234-2080-3. Grades: P–3.

Coral reefs are found in tropical waters close to the equator as shown on the map on the first two-page spread. Colorful labeled illustrations accompanied by brief text boxes explore the wonders of these fragile undersea ecosystems. The book concludes with additional information about coral reefs and the Papahanaumokuakea Marine National Monument, which is a coral reef surrounding the Northwestern Hawaiian Islands.

Brenner, Barbara. *One Small Place in a Tree.* Illustrated by Tom Leonard. New York: HarperCollins, 2004. Unp. ISBN 978-0-688-17181-0. Grades: K–3.

Realistic, detailed full-page illustrations and lyrical text reveal that a tree in the woods is home to a changing collection of organisms. From beetles living under its bark to birds raising their young in its hole, as the tree lives and dies it provides shelter and food to forest animals. The companion book is One Small Place by the Sea (Brenner, 2004).

Bishop, Nic. *Forest Explorer: A Life-Size Field Guide.* New York: Scholastic, 2004. 48p. ISBN 978-0-439-17480-0. Grades: K–4.

Life-size photographs of animals, plants, and insects and field notes allow young explorers to journey through the forest discovering its wonders. Following the two-page spreads are field notes giving the names and information about the featured critters. The book concludes with tips for forest explorations and season-by-season information on what might be seen. A picture index concludes the book and encourages readers to revisit the text.

Yolen, Jane. *Welcome to the River of Grass.* Illustrated by Laura Regan. New York: Putnam, 2001. Unp. ISBN 978-0-399-23221-3. Grades: K–4.

Concealed in the river of grass is an astonishing ecosystem waiting to be discovered. Lyrical verse and haunting illustrations are filled with factual information about the plants and animals that call the Florida Everglades home. The book concludes with information about the destruction of the Florida Everglades and websites for learning more.

Levinson, Nancy Smiler. *North Pole, South Pole.* Illustrated by Diane Dawson Hearn. New York: Holiday House, 2002. 40p. ISBN 978-0-8234-1737-7. Grades: 1–2.

Maps, illustrations, and diagrams accompany this concise text that explains the differences between the North and the South Poles. After focusing on the differences between the North and South Poles Levinson then goes into more details first about the North Pole and then the South Pole. Short sentences with keywords defined in context explore the geography, climate, and inhabitants of these frigid expanses.

Cherry, Lynne. *The Sea, the Storm, and the Mangrove Tangle.* New York: Farrar, Straus and Giroux, 2004. ISBN 978-0-374-36482-3. Grades 1–3.

During hurricanes mangroves offer shelter and safety to birds, sea creatures, and other animals. Cherry describes the life cycle of a mangrove tree and offers a cautionary environmental tale about how these safe havens are being destroyed. Shrimp farms and tourist sites are taking over the mangrove islands. Green Earth Book Award Book, 2005.

Earth Matters: An Encyclopedia of Ecology. New York: DK, 2008. 256p. ISBN 978-0-7566-3435-3. Grades: 5 and up.

The earth's biomes including polar regions, temperate forests, deserts, grasslands, tropical forests, mountains, freshwater, and oceans each have their own chapter. Readers learn of the impact of humans on each of the biomes and how the threats posed by humans can be overcome. The book includes a chapter on helping the earth and includes suggestions for making changes in our lives that will impact our environment. Maps, websites, and stunning color photographs help explain how each of the biomes work and the threats to each of them.

Warhol, Tom. *Chaparral and Scrub*. Tarrytown, NY: Marshall Cavendish, 2007. 80p. ISBN 978-0-7614-2195-5. Grades: 5 and up.

The delicate balance between the Mediterranean scrub and human civilization is explored around the world from North America, to South America, to Europe, to Africa, and on to Australia. The impact and importance of fires to the scrub provides thought-provoking information for classroom discussions. Back matter includes a glossary, resources for learning more, a bibliography, and an index. From the Earth's Biomes series.

Walker, Sally M. *Life in an Estuary*. Minneapolis, MN: Lerner, 2003. 72p. ISBN 978-0-8225-2137-2. Grades: 6 and up.

Discover the Chesapeake Bay estuary and its plants and animals in this informative text. In the last chapter, the human impact on the estuary is discussed. The book concludes with information on what needs to be done to protect estuaries, websites for learning more, books for further reading, a glossary, and an index. From the Ecosystems in Action series.

Explorations

1. After reading *Coral Reefs* (Gibbons, 2007) visit the website of the Papahanaumokuakea Marine National Monument at hawaiireef.noaa.gov/welcome.html. Under the education link on this site is a slideshow of stunning color photographs of the plants and animals inhabiting this national monument.
2. Before reading *One Small Place in a Tree* (Brenner, 2004) ask the students to predict which animals will use the tree as their home and record their responses on chart paper or the chalkboard. After reading the book, return to the students' list of animals and add and delete based on the information in the book.
3. In *Welcome to the River of Grass* (Yolen, 2001) each page features a lush illustration focusing on plants or inhabitants of the Florida Everglades accompanied by a poem. After reading the poems, have the students use the poems as

models to write poems about plants and inhabitants of other ecosystems they have studied.

4. To learn more about plant and animal adaptations specific to the world biomes introduce students to the website World Biomes at www.blueplanetbiomes.org/world_biomes.htm. Students can work in groups to prepare multimedia presentations to share with their classmates about plant and animal adaptations in one of the biomes.
5. Prior to studying biomes with your students visit the Global Learning and Observations to Benefit the Environment Seasons and Biomes webpage at www.globe.gov/projects/seasons to learn about current scientific investigations that you and your students can consider joining.
6. Before studying estuaries explore the website of the National Estuary Program to find out if there is an estuary nearby that students can learn more about. The website provides links to the homepages of estuaries around the United States at www.epa.gov/nep/kids/about/index.htm.

Diversity and Adaptations

From teeth to eggs to eyes to feet, the diversity of the creatures of the earth is apparent. By studying this diversity students learn about the adaptations that allow the creatures to survive in their particular locales. Books in this section like *I Feel a Foot!* (Maranke and van der Linden, 2008), *How Many Ways Can You Catch a Fly?* (Jenkins and Page, 2008), and *All Kinds of Feet* (Miller, 2008) help students learn about animals by comparing and contrasting them.

Book and Media Choices

Rinck, Maranke, and Martijn van der Linden. *I Feel a Foot!* Honesdale, PA: Boyds Mills, 2008. Unp. ISBN 978-1-59078-638-3. Grades: P–1.

The familiar tale of a blind man's encounter with an elephant is retold in this animal guessing game. A turtle, a bat, an octopus, a bird, and a goat are all awakened by a sound in the night and each sets out to explore the animal making the noise. Glimpses of the mysterious animal's various parts are shown as each explorer determines that the creature is a larger version of itself. The animals are kaleidoscopes of color against black pages and young readers will be kept guessing along with the animals.

Collard, Sneed B, III. *Teeth.* Illustrated by Phyllis V. Saroff. Watertown, MA: Charlesbridge, 2008. Unp. ISBN 978-1-58089-120-2. Grades: P–3.

Not only do teeth slash, stab, slice, mash, and munch, they also come in a variety of shapes and sizes. For example, an elephant's molar can weigh as much as nine pounds. Realistic illustrations focus on the animal's teeth with some close-ups of unique teeth such as the tongue teeth of the cutthroat trout. Resources for learning more and a glossary conclude the book.

Aston, Dianna. *An Egg Is Quiet.* Illustrated by Sylvia Long. San Francisco, CA: Chronicle Books, 2006. Unp. ISBN 978-0-8118-4428-4. Grades: K–5.

Shapely, artistic, textured, and fossilized all describe the eggs explored in this evocative text with colorful illustrations. Children and adults are sure to learn something interesting about eggs and their inhabitants as they share this book together. It is filled with fascinating facts that answer children's questions and spark more questions. NCTE Orbis Pictus Recommended Book, 2007.

Jenkins, Steve, and Robin Page. *How Many Ways Can You Catch a Fly?* Boston, MA: Houghton Mifflin, 2008. Unp. ISBN 978-0-616-96634-9. Grades: K–5.

Catching flies, hatching eggs, using leaves, digging holes, and eating clams can all be done in different ways and this book explores how different animals accomplish the same task in a variety of ways. The paper collage illustrations are scattered across the pages with the text hugging the outer edges of the illustrations. The book concludes with additional information about the animals in the book.

Strauss, Rochelle. *Tree of Life: The Incredible Biodiversity of Life on Earth.* Illustrated by Margot Thompson. Toronto, ON: Kids Can Press, 2004. 40p. ISBN 978-1-55337-669-9. Grades: 3–7.

Strauss pictorially introduces readers to the five kingdoms of living things and explains how living things are classified and related. The book concludes with ideas for children on becoming guardians of the tree of life, notes for parents, teachers and guardians, and an index. Green Earth Book Award Honor Book, 2005.

Singer, Marilyn. *Eggs.* Illustrated by Emma Stevenson. New York: Holiday House, 2003. 32p. ISBN 978-0-8234-1727-8. Grades: 3–8.

A short descriptive poem sets the stage for this wondrous look at eggs. Gouache paintings reveal the variety and beauty of the eggs of reptiles, insects, spiders, and birds. It is fascinating to read about all of the different ways that parents guard the precious eggs. The book includes a peek inside of an egg to view a developing chick. Back matter includes information on protecting eggs, a glossary, source notes, a list of wildlife organizations, and an index. Outstanding Science Trade Book for Students K–12, 2009.

Miller, Sara Swan. *Eyes.* Tarrytown, NY: Marshall Cavendish, 2008. 48p. ISBN 978-0-7614-2519-9. Grades: 3 and up.

Insect eyes, fish eyes, amphibian eyes, reptile eyes, bird eyes, and mammal eyes are examined from inside out in this informative text. Intriguing animal eyes peer out at readers from colorful photographs, such as the shot of a gecko cleaning its eye with its tongue. Fact boxes and diagrams and an index are also included. From the All kinds of . . . series.

Davies, Nicola. *Extreme Animals: The Toughest Creatures on Earth.* Illustrated by Neal Layton. Cambridge, MA: Candlewick, 2006. ISBN 978-0-7636-3067-6. Grades: 4–8.

Discover the adaptations animals have that enable them to live in extremely inhospitable environments in this intriguing text accompanied by cartoon illustrations.

Lack of food, extreme temperatures, and the squash factor of the deep sea are some of the extreme conditions that animals have adapted to in order to survive.

Miller, Sara Swan. *All Kinds of Feet*. Tarrytown, NY: Marshall Cavendish, 2008. 48p. ISBN 978-0-7614-2520-5. Grades: 4–8.

This is a fascinating exploration of animals' feet, which come in all sizes and shapes and numbers. The chapters include insects, amphibians and reptiles, bird feet and wings, and mammals. The fact-filled text is accompanied by bright colorful photographs that focus on the animals and their feet, and text boxes contain additional intriguing tidbits of information. A glossary, resources for learning more, and an index conclude the book.

Silverstein, Alvin, Virginia Silverstein, and Laura Silverstein Nunn. *Adaptation*. Minneapolis, MN: Twenty-First Century Books, 2008. 112p. ISBN 978-0-8225-3434-1. Grades: 6–8.

Following the introduction is a chapter on Darwin and evolution. The next four chapters examine animal adaptations and the last chapter is on human adaptations. Photographs, maps, diagrams, and fact-filled sidebars included on every page help to clarify and enhance the narrative. The book provides an accessible introduction to a complex topic and students are sure to use the resources at the end of the book in their quests to learn more. Back matter includes a glossary, a selected bibliography, a list of resources for further information, and an index. From the Science Concepts series. Outstanding Science Trade Book for Students K–12, 2009.

Hiaasen, Carl. *Hoot*. New York: Alfred A. Knopf, 2002. 292p. ISBN 78-0-375-82181-3. Grades: 6–9.

Discovering that the habitat of some tiny burrowing owls is going to be destroyed so a pancake restaurant can be built, a quirky band of middle school students set out to halt the construction. This book was made into a movie and is available on DVD. An audio version of this book is available on CD. Newbery Medal Honor Book, 2003.

Explorations

1. As you read *I Feel a Foot!* (Maranke and van der Linden, 2008) stop and have the students predict what animal will be revealed at the end of the book. Write their predictions on chart paper as you read.
2. *How Many Ways Can You Catch a Fly?* (Jenkins and Page, 2008) encourages divergent thinking in students. Before reading the book, have them brainstorm the different ways they think animals complete the task. Also, encourage them to think of the different ways they might do the same tasks.
3. As students read *Tree of Life: The Incredible Biodiversity of Life on Earth* (Strauss, 2004) have them record the oddest or most intriguing fact they discover and post it on the class bulletin board.

4. While reading *Eyes* (Miller, 2008) have students create a chart on the location of animals' eyes and the reason for the location.
5. As students read *Hoot* (Hiaasen, 2002) have the students visit websites to learn more about the habitats and habits of the Burrowing Owl. The Defenders of Wildlife website at www.defenders.org/wildlife_and_habitat/wildlife/burrowing_owl.php is a great place to start.

HISTORY AND NATURE OF SCIENCE

Science standard eight focuses on the history and nature of science and includes studying about the lives and work of scientists and inventors. As students read about the individuals profiled in the books in this section they develop an appreciation and understanding of these individuals' contributions to society. They also learn that their own scientific interests may one day lead them to a career as a scientist or an inventor.

Book and Media Choices

Yaccarino, Dan. *The Fantastic Undersea Life of Jacques Cousteau.* New York: Alfred A. Knopf, 2009. ISBN 987-0-375-85573-3. Grades: K–4.

Oceanographer Jacques Cousteau's research, inventions, filmmaking, and lifelong interest in the sea are examined in this picture book biography filled with colorful illustrations that submerge readers in Cousteau's underwater world. Included in the text is information on his efforts to make the world aware of the effects of pollution. The book includes a timeline and resources for learning more.

Bardoe, Cheryl. *Gregor Mendel: The Friar Who Grew Peas.* Illustrated by Joseph A. Smith. New York: Abrams, 2006. Unp. ISBN 978-0-8109-5475-5. Grades: 2–5.

A curious child eager to learn about nature goes without food in order to study and eventually becomes a friar so that he can surround himself by books and scholars in order to continue his studies. This curious child, Gregor Mendel, becomes the first geneticist and his work continues to form the basis of genetic research today. An author's note with additional information about Mendel and a selected bibliography conclude the book. ALSC Notable Children's Book, 2007. NCTE Orbis Pictus Honor Book, 2007.

Barretta, Gene. *Now & Ben: The Modern Inventions of Benjamin Franklin.* DVD. New Rochelle, NY: Spoken Arts, 2007. 13 min. ISBN 978-0-8045-8055-7. Grades: 2–5.

Barretta's book by the same title was the inspiration for this video, which includes additional watercolor cartoon illustrations that were created just for the film. Juxtaposing present and past causes readers to pause and reflect on how Benjamin Franklin's inventions are still in use today. From bifocals to odometers to chairs, his inventions continue to impact our lives and Barretta challenges readers to think about how his inventions will be used in the future. He appears briefly in the film and talks about his fascination with Benjamin Franklin, statesman and inventor. ALSC Notable Children's Video, 2008.

Brown, Don. *Odd Boy Out: Young Albert Einstein.* New York: Houghton Mifflin, 2004. Unp. ISBN 978-0-618-49298-5. Grades: 2–5.

As a child Einstein did not begin talking when others his age did, he did not like sports, soldiers parading disturbed rather than excited him, and he was the only Jewish child in his school. Gifted in mathematics, science, and music, he focused intently on those subjects and ignored his other school subjects. This picture book biography introduces Einstein and his brilliant scientific discoveries. An author's note and a bibliography conclude the book. ALSC Notable Children's Book, 2005. Notable Children's Trade Book in the Field of Social Studies, 2005.

Krull, Kathleen. *The Boy Who Invented TV: The Story of Philo Farnsworth.* Illustrated by Greg Couch. New York: Alfred A. Knopf, 2009. Unp. ISBN 978-0-375-84561-1. Grades: 2–5.

Krull invites readers into this biography by asking them to imagine life without television. As a young boy on his family's farm, Philo Farnsworth was always fixing things and as a teenager while plowing a field had an idea about how to transmit pictures over the air. Over the years he developed his ideas into patents that eventually led to the invention of the television. An author's note provides additional details on his life and his unsuccessful battle with the Radio Corporation of America for the rights to his invention.

Tanaka, Shelley. *Amelia Earhart: The Legend of the Lost Aviator.* Illustrated by David Craig. New York: Abrams, 2008. 48p. ISBN 978-0-8109-7095-3. Grades: 3–6.

The focus of this well-written picture book biography is on Amelia's flying adventures. Vivid paintings, historical photographs, quotes, and sidebars capture Amelia's spirit and help to tell her story. The book concludes with a bibliography and an index. NCTE Orbis Pictus Award Winner, 2009.

Wyckoff, Edwin Brit. *The Teen Who Invented Television: Philo T. Farnsworth and His Awesome Invention.* Berkeley Heights, NJ: Enslow, 2008. 32p. ISBN 978-0-7660-2845-6. Grades: 4–6.

Plowing rows in the fields on a farm gave teenager Philo an idea about how to transmit pictures through the air, ideas that eventually led him to invent television. Readers learn how his high school science teacher, Justin Tolman, helped Philo establish his claim to be first to invent television. The brief well-written biography will have students searching for more information on this boy genius. Back matter includes a timeline, a glossary, resources for learning more, and an index. From the Genius at Work! Great Inventor Biographies series.

Stone, Tanya Lee. *Almost Astronauts: Thirteen Women Who Dared to Dream.* Cambridge, MA: Candlewick, 2009. 133p. ISBN 978-0-7636-3611-1. Grades: 5–7.

Through interviews, photographs, and documents, Stone tells the story of thirteen women pilots whose attempts to become astronauts were thwarted by gender prejudice in the early 1960s. It was not until 1978 that NASA began to accept women and people of color as astronauts. The book concludes with a bibliography, endnotes, and an index. This book is available on CD. *Boston Globe*–Horn Book Honor, 2009.

Fortey, Jacqueline. *Great Scientists.* New York: DK, 2007. 72p. ISBN 978-0-7566-2974-8. Grades: 5–8.

Thirty scientists are showcased in the book; only two of them are women. For each scientist there is a brief paragraph introduction, a small photograph, and a timeline. The pages are filled with photographs and diagrams accompanied by captions in very small type. It is sure to pique students' interest in the scientists. A CD of clip art is included.

Graham, Amy. *Thomas Edison: Wizard of Light and Sound.* Berkeley Heights, NJ: Enslow, 2008. 128p. ISBN 978-1-59845-052-1. Grades: 5–8.

A timeline of important dates in Edison's life positioned at the front of the book provides students with an overview that helps to focus their reading. Edison's persistence and intelligence resulted in inventions that made life easier. Readers discover the stories behind his successes and they get a glimpse into ideas that were not successful. Back matter contains a glossary, resources for learning more, and an index. From the Inventors Who Changed the World series.

Nelson, Marilyn. *Carver: A Life in Poems.* Asheville, NC: Front Street, 2000. 103p. ISBN 978-1-886910-53-9. Grades: 5–8.

The life's work of scholar, scientist, and inventor George Washington Carver is portrayed in powerful, moving poems told through his eyes and through the eyes of those who knew him. Historical black-and-white photographs interspersed throughout the poems confirm for readers the political and cultural context of the times. Newbery Medal Honor Book, 2000. Coretta Scott King Author Award Honor Book, 2000.

Thimmesh, Catherine. *Girls Think of Everything: Stories of Ingenious Inventions by Women.* Illustrated by Melissa Sweet. Boston: Houghton Mifflin, 2000. 59p. ISBN 978-0-395-93744-0. Grades: 5–8.

Women inventors have long been ignored and overlooked. Setting out to correct that oversight Thimmesh shares the stories of selected women inventors. These women found unique solutions to everyday problems. Included are the stories of selected women inventors who responded to everyday problems with their own unique solutions. Back matter includes resources for young inventors, books for further reading, a list of sources, and an index. The sequel to this book is *The Sky's the Limit: Stories of Discovery by Women and Girls* (Thimmesh, 2002). Outstanding Science Trade Book for Students K–12, 2001.

Fleming, Candace. *Ben Franklin's Almanac: Being a True Account of the Good Gentlemen's Life.* New York: Simon and Schuster, 2003. 120p. ISBN 978-0-689-83549-0. Grades: 5–9.

Designed to mimic Franklin's almanac this multigenre biography portrays the depth and complexity of this noted statesman, author, and inventor. Maps, illustrations, and cartoons accompany the text, which includes Franklin's own writings. A bibliography, resources for learning more, and an extensive index conclude the book. ALA Notable Book, 2004.

Krull, Kathleen. *Isaac Newton.* Illustrated by Boris Kulikov. New York: Viking, 2006. 126p. ISBN 978-0-670-05921-8. Grades: 5 and up.

Imagine inventing a new branch of mathematics. Isaac Newton did; he invented calculus. His lifelong feud with fellow scientist Robert Hooke, his three laws of motion, his quest to turn metals into gold, and his mental imbalance are all explored in this fascinating look at a genius. A bibliography and an index conclude the book. From the Giants of Science series. Outstanding Science Trade Book for Students K–12, 2008.

McClafferty, Carla Killough. *Something Out of Nothing: Marie Curie and Radium.* New York: Farrar, Straus and Giroux, 2006. 144p. ISBN 978-0-374-38036-6. Grades: 6–8.

Radium, for which Marie Curie won two Nobel Prizes and spent her life studying, ultimately led to her death. Throughout her life she struggled to be educated as a scientist and to be recognized as one. Quotes from her diary and notebooks as well as photographs help readers know and appreciate this remarkable scientist. Source notes, a selected bibliography, recommended websites, and an index conclude the book. Notable Social Studies Trade Book for Young People, 2007.

Explorations

1. After viewing *Now & Ben: The Modern Inventions of Benjamin Franklin* (Barretta, 2007) challenge the students to decide how one of Franklin's inventions will be used in the future. Allow the students to work in groups to design a presentation to share their ideas with their classmates.
2. Students who enjoyed *The Teen Who Invented Television: Philo T. Farnsworth and His Awesome Invention* (Wyckoff, 2008) will be interested in the By Kids for Kids website at www.bkfk.com/, which showcases the work of innovative teens and provides tips on inventing. There is also a blog and inspirational videos on the website.
3. After reading *Thomas Edison: Wizard of Light and Sound* (Graham, 2008) students can access the MyReportLinks.com website with the password included in the book in order to learn more about Edison and his inventions.

4. Students interested in learning more about Isaac Newton can be referred to the Isaac Newton Resources Page of the Isaac Newton Institute for Mathematical Sciences at www.newton.ac.uk/newton.html.
5. In *Carver: A Life in Poems* (Nelson, 2000) students will find many poems that can be used for dramatic interpretations that will enhance students' oral language skills.

TEACHER RESOURCES

This section contains books and Internet sites to enhance the science curriculum. Contact information is also given for the National Science Teachers Association.

Book and Media Choices

Ansberry, Karen, and Emily Morgan. *More Picture-Perfect Science Lessons: Using Children's Books to Guide Inquiry, K-4.* Arlington, VA: National Science Teachers Association, 2007. 238p. ISBN 978-1-93353-112-0. Grades: K–4.

Discover ideas for using picture books to teach science concepts and reading in this book. Lesson plans in the book incorporate children's fiction and nonfiction books into science lessons. Bibliographic references and an index conclude the book.

Ansberry, Karen, and Emily Morgan. *Picture-Perfect Science Lessons: Using Children's Books to Guide Inquiry.* Arlington, VA: National Science Teachers Association, 2005. 304p. ISBN 978-0-87355-243-1. Grades: 3–6.

In this collection of fifteen lesson plans, the authors present practical ideas for using children's literature to develop students' interest in science. Bibliographic references and an index conclude the book.

Klentschy, Michael P. *Using Science Notebooks in Elementary Classrooms.* Arlington, VA: National Science Teachers Association, 2008. 125p. ISBN 978-1-93353-103-8. Grades: K–6.

Discover how writing in science notebooks encourages students to observe, record, and think about their classroom science activities. Writing about science helps students understand and remember what they have learned.

Stebbins, Robert, David Ipsen, Gretchen L. Gillfillan, Judy Diamond, and Judy Scotchmoor. *Animal Coloration: Activities on the Evolution of Concealment* (Revised New Edition). Arlington, VA: National Science Teachers Association, 2008. 175p. ISBN 978-1-93353-129-8. Grades: K–6.

The activities in this book lead elementary and middle school students through explorations of how animals adapt to their environments. The activities are based on National Science Education Content Standards. The book includes a glossary and an index.

Abruscato, Joseph. *Whizbangers and Wonderments: Science Activities for Children.* Boston, MA: Allyn and Bacon, 2000. 312p. ISBN 978-0-205-28409-2. Grades: K–8.

This book takes an interdisciplinary approach to science, integrating it into the language arts, math, and arts curriculums for upper elementary and middle school students.

Duschl, Richard A., Heidi A. Schweingruber, and Andrew W. Shouse, editors. *Taking Science to School: Learning and Teaching Science in Grades K–8.* Washington, DC: National Academy Press, 2007. 387p. ISBN 978-0-309-10205-6. Grades: K–8.

This is a comprehensive guide for teachers, administrators, and policymakers who want to understand how children learn about science and what is necessary to facilitate their understanding of science concepts.

National Science Teachers Association. *Mixing It Up: Integrated, Interdisciplinary, Intriguing Science in the Elementary Classroom.* Arlington, VA: National Science Teachers Association, 2003. 184p. ISBN 978-0-87355-231-8. Grades: K–8.

Included in this book is a collection of twenty-five articles from the National Science Teachers Association journal, *Science and Children.* All of the articles focus on how to integrate science into other content areas. At the beginning of the book is a quick reference chart to help locate just the right article. Many of the articles in the book have SciLinks code numbers that give readers access to a list of websites for teachers and for students that contain additional information related to the article.

Alderfer, Jonathan K., and Jon L. Dunn. *National Geographic Birding Essentials.* Washington, DC: National Geographic, 2007. 224p. ISBN 978-1-4262-0135-6. Grades: K and up.

Birding gives students opportunities to connect with nature, and also helps to develop their observation skills. While binoculars and scopes are helpful, they are not required. All the essentials you need to know to get started birding are included. A glossary, books for additional reading, websites, and an index are included.

Elphick, Jonathan, editor. *Atlas of Bird Migration: Tracing the Great Journeys of the World's Birds.* Buffalo, NY: Firefly Books, 2007. 176p. ISBN 978-1-55407-248-4. Grades: 4–8.

Stunning color photographs, charts, diagrams, illustrations, maps, calendars, and fact files entice readers to peruse the pages and enhance readers' understanding of this complex subject. The chapter headings make it easy to focus on migratory birds in different parts of the world, such as North American migrants and migratory sea birds. An index and books for further reading conclude the book.

Swango, C. Jill, and Sally Boles Steward. *Help! I'm Teaching Middle School Science.* Arlington, VA: National Science Teachers Association, 2003. 133p. ISBN 978-0-87355-225-7. Grades: 6–8.

Everything you need to get started teaching science in the middle school from safety, to writing, to adapting labs, to classroom management and more can be found in this book. The National Science Education Standards, resources, recipes, and references are included. The book concludes with an index.

Professional Organizations

National Science Teachers Association
1840 Wilson Boulevard
Arlington, VA 22201-3000
703-243-7100 (Phone)
703-243-7177 (Fax)
nsta.org

Journal: *Science and Children*, *Science Scope*

The NSTA Learning Center
learningcenter.nsta.org/default.aspx

This is an e-professional development portal for teachers from elementary school to college. There are do-it-yourself learning activities and online learning events.

National Space Society
The society's vision is to have humans living and working in space. It includes a link with information on space tourism.
1620 I (Eye) Street NW, Suite 615
Washington, DC 20006
202-429-1600 (Phone)
202-463-8497 (Fax)
www.nss.org

Internet Sites

American Museum of Natural History
www.amnh.org

Download and subscribe to podcasts by renowned scientists on a wide variety of topics at this website. The information on the website changes as the museum exhibits change. The site has a search engine for locating information on topics including anthropology, astronomy, biology, and earth science.

Audubon Society
www.audubon.org

There are resources for teachers, parents, and students including information on bird watching and backyard bird feeding. The site includes activities for becoming involved in caring for birds by writing to congressional representatives and through innovation grants.

Boston Museum of Science
www.mos.org
Download podcasts and videocasts on the latest developments in science and technology at this website. Subscribe to them through iTunes and get them automatically delivered to your classroom computer.

Carolina Biological Supply Company
www.carolina.com
Check out the Teacher Resources tab for classroom activities, workshop downloads, teaching tips, care guides, and safety information. Also under Teacher Resources is a link to educational standards that can be searched by state and grade level. There are links to materials that correlate to state science standards.

Cool Science for Curious Kids
www.hhmi.org/coolscience/
Links on this site include: For Educators, Biointeractive, For Curious Kids, Science Education Alliance, Ask a Scientist, and Becoming a Scientist. The For Curious Kids link has interactive activities and projects to involve students in exploring biology.

The Exploratorium
www.exploratorium.edu/learning_studio/index.html
Exploratorium: The Museum of Science, Art, and Human Perception is located at the Palace of Fine Arts in San Francisco, California. The Educate link houses a digital library, hands-on activities, webcasts, podcasts, video clips, websites, and publications sure to engage young scientists. Search their collection of resources and activities for students, which can be browsed by these topics: earth and space science, life sciences, mathematics, physical sciences, and the nature of science.

The Franklin Institute Science Museum
www2.fi.edu
Case files to examine, videos to view, and interactive games are just some of the science resources available on this website. There are links for students and links for teachers. Sign up for Braindrops and have science tidbits delivered to your e-mail through an RSS feed.

Geological Society of America
www.geosociety.org/educate/index.htm
There are sections of their website for teachers and for students including links to information on fellowships and scholarships for teachers and for students.

The GLOBE Program
www.globe.gov
GLOBE stands for the Global Learning and Observations to Benefit the Environment, which is an international science and education program for primary and secondary

students and their teachers. Students, teachers, and scientists collaborate to investigate the Earth's environment through Earth System Science Projects (ESSPs).

How Stuff Works
videos.howstuffworks.com/science

On this website there are links for earth science, engineering, everyday science, life science, military, physical science, space, and supernatural science. Students can access games, experiments, activities, and videos that explain how things work.

Insect Lore
www.insectlore.com

Play, learn, and shop at this one-stop website for resources for teaching and learning about insects. Silly jokes, insect activities, and an insectlorepedia are sure to appeal to elementary students.

Lab Out Loud: Science for the Classroom and Beyond
laboutloud.com

Science teachers Dale Basler and Brian Bartel post science news podcasts, which include interviews with leading scientists, researchers, and writers. Brian Bartel also has a blog on the site. There are notes and websites to extend each podcast. The National Science Teachers Association sponsors the podcasts.

Museum of Science and Industry
msichicago.org

Under the online link on the homepage there are videos, hands-on activities, and podcasts. The education link includes resources for teachers including classroom activities.

National Aeronautics and Space Administration (NASA) Education
education.nasa.gov

There are links for kids, for students, for teachers, and for education news on this website. The resources under the links are organized by grade level bands to make it easier to find exactly what you need. Under the For Students link, the Grades K–4 section has games for playing and learning. Under the link for Grades 5–8, there are multimedia presentations for space and earth science explorations.

National Aeronautics and Space Administration (NASA) Human Spaceflight
spaceflight.nasa.gov/home/index.html

Find the latest news about human space flight including coverage of the space shuttle missions and the international space station crews.

National Geographic
www.nationalgeographic.com

The links on the left side of the screen labeled animals, environment, kids, and science and space have multimedia activities, blogs, videos, and other resources for teaching science. Click the animal link to view videos and to create a video using Wildlife Filmmaker.

National Oceanic and Atmospheric Administration Education Resources
www.education.noaa.gov/index.html

On this website there are resources for teaching about weather, climate, oceans, and space. Under the students' link there is information on opportunities for students to participate in research about science, math, and engineering.

National Wildlife Federation
www.nwf.org

Magazines published by the National Wildlife Federation include: *National Wildlife*, *Ranger Rick*, *Just for Fun*, *Your Big Backyard*, and *Wild Animal Baby*. Click the Wildlife tab to discover information on endangered animals and consider having your class adopt one. Check out the Outside in Nature link to find ideas for getting your students and their parents involved in the Wildlife Watch Program.

The Nine Planets
www.nineplanets.org

This site houses an extensive collection of information about the solar system, including history, mythology, and scientific knowledge. Images, sounds, and movies from NASA are included.

Savage Earth Online
www.pbs.org/wnet/savageearth/

Animations and articles on this website explore the science behind the earth's crust, earthquakes, volcanoes, and tsunamis. The animations explain the science behind these savage natural disasters. This is a companion website to the PBS series.

Science Learning Network
www.sln.org

In this online community, educators, students, museums, and other institutions collaborate to create resources for science learning. The National Science Foundation and Unisys Corporation provide funding for this international project. Every month, ten cool websites are featured and there are educational hotlists of links to online resources. Explore the links to the member museums for even more resources.

Science NetLinks
www.sciencenetlinks.com

Explore the interactive learning activities for ideas to incorporate in your classes, sign up to download podcasts, and explore the blogs available on this website. The

American Association for the Advancement of Science and Thinkfinity.org sponsor this site.

Science News for Kids
www.sciencenewsforkids.org
PuzzleZone, GameZone, SciFiZone, SciFairZone, and LabZone are interactive resources designed to engage students in hands-on science activities including information on agriculture, finding the past, food, and nutrition. The Society for Science and the Public sponsors this website.

Solar System Exploration
solarsystem.nasa.gov/index.cfm
Sponsored by National Aeronautics and Space Administration this website includes stunning photographs, and multimedia explorations, such as recordings of spooky sounds from Saturn. The sidebar on the left side of the screen has a link to activities for kids and an education link with resources for, among others, Girl Scouts, educators, students, and scientists.

Spacecraft Sightings
spaceflight1.nasa.gov/realdata/sightings/
Find out when spacecraft can be viewed in your area. There are also links to real-time data about spacecrafts and satellites orbiting the earth.

United States Department of Energy
fossil.energy.gov/education/
This site has information for students, teachers, and parents. The link to Online Energy Lessons contains information appropriate for students of all ages. The Teachers and Parents' link has study guides and classroom activities. There are also links to other resources.

United States Geological Survey and Science Education
education.usgs.gov
On this site there is a searchable multimedia gallery with videos and animations on climate change, geology, earthquakes, plate tectonics, hurricanes, and other phenomena. There are also podcasts and online lectures. The animations help students understand complex topics.

Wildlife Conservation Society
www.wcs.org
Learn about threats to wildlife and wild places across the globe. The site houses multimedia explorations and has a link to teacher resources.

World Wildlife Fund
www.worldwildlife.org
The site has videos, photo galleries, and games to help students learn more about preserving the earth. Expedition diaries posted on the site allow visitors to follow

along as scientists travel to remote locations gathering data to help in the organization's conservation work.

REFERENCES

Alberts, Bruce. 2000. "Preface." *Inquiry and the National Science Education Standards: A Guide for Teaching and Learning*. Washington, DC: National Academy.

Brenner, Barbara. 2004. *One Small Place by the Sea*. New York: Harper Collins.

Gilbert, Joan, and Marleen Kotelman. 2005. "Five Good Reasons to Use Science Notebooks." *Science and Children* 43, no. 3 (November/December): 28–32.

Heuser, Daniel. 2005. "Learning Logs: Writing to Learn, Reading to Assess." *Science and Children* 43, no. 3 (November/December): 46–49.

Holbrook, Sara. 2005. *Practical Poetry: A Nonstandard Approach to Meeting Content-Area Standards*. Portsmouth, NH: Heinemann.

Klentschy, Michael. 2005. "Science Notebook Essentials." *Science and Children* 43, no. 3 (November/December): 24–27.

Knipper, Kathy J., and Timothy J. Duggan. 2006. "Writing to Learn Across the Curriculum: Tools for Comprehension in Content Area Classes." *The Reading Teacher* 59, no. 5 (February): 462–470.

National Research Council. 1996. *National Science Education Standards*. Available: www.nap.edu/readingroom/books/nses/html/ (accessed October 30, 2000). Reprinted with permission from National Science Education Standards (c) 1996 by the National Academy of Sciences, Courtesy of the National Academies Press, Washington, DC.

Patent, Dorothy Hinshaw. 2003. *Plants on the Trail with Lewis and Clark*. Photographs by William Munoz. New York: Clarion.

Robertson, Amy, and Kathryn Mahlin. 2005. "Ecosystem Journalism." *Science and Children* 43, no. 3 (November/December): 42–45.

Straits, William. 2005. "Mystery Box Writing." *Science and Children* 43, no. 3 (November/December): 33–37.

Thimmesh, Catherine. 2002. *The Sky's the Limit: Stories of Discovery by Women and Girls*. Boston, MA: Houghton Mifflin.

Tower, Cathy. 2005. "What's the Purpose? Students Talk about Writing in Science." *Language Arts* 82, no. 6 (July): 472–483.

Chapter 3

English Language Arts

The language arts, reading, writing, speaking, listening, viewing, and representing, are interconnected and learned simultaneously. Children's literature serves as a model for student writing and, when read aloud, serves as a model for speaking and listening. Through literature students grasp the conventions of language and learn to use language for communication and to think.

The *Standards for English Language Arts* as prepared jointly by the National Council of Teachers of English (NCTE, 1986) and the International Reading Association give evidence of the interconnectedness of reading and writing. These organizations recognize that all students need both opportunities and resources to learn to use language effectively. They also note the importance of building on the emerging literacy skills that children bring to school. The standards are as follows:

1. Students read a wide range of print and nonprint texts to build an understanding of texts, of themselves, and of the cultures of the United States and the world; to acquire new information; to respond to the needs and demands of society and the workplace; and for personal fulfillment. Among these texts are fiction and nonfiction, classic, and contemporary works.
2. Students read a wide range of literature from many periods in many genres to build an understanding of the many dimensions (e.g., philosophical, ethical, aesthetic) of human experience.
3. Students apply a wide range of strategies to comprehend, interpret, evaluate, and appreciate texts. They draw on their prior experience, their interactions with other readers and writers, their knowledge of word meaning and of other texts, their word identification strategies, and their understanding of textual features (e.g., sound-letter correspondence, sentence structure, context, and graphics).
4. Students adjust their use of spoken, written, and visual language (e.g., conventions, style, and vocabulary) to communicate effectively with a variety of audiences and for different purposes.
5. Students employ a wide range of strategies as they write and use different writing process elements appropriately to communicate with different audiences for a variety of purposes.

6. Students apply knowledge of language structure, language conventions (e.g., spelling and punctuation), media techniques, figurative language, and genre to create, critique, and discuss print and nonprint texts.
7. Students conduct research on issues and interests generating ideas and questions, and by posing problems. They gather, evaluate, and synthesize data from a variety of sources (e.g., print and nonprint texts, artifacts and people) to communicate their discoveries in ways that suit their purpose and audience.
8. Students use a variety of technological and information resources (e.g., libraries, databases, computer networks, and video) to gather and synthesize information and to create and communicate knowledge.
9. Students develop an understanding of and respect for diversity in language use, patterns, and dialects across cultures, ethnic groups, geographic regions, and social roles.
10. Students whose first language is not English make use of their first language to develop competency in the English language arts and to develop understanding of content across the curriculum.
11. Students participate as knowledgeable, reflective, creative, and critical members of a variety of literacy communities.
12. Students use spoken, written, and visual language to accomplish their own purposes (e.g., for learning, enjoyment, persuasion, and the exchange of information).

As teachers and librarians integrate children's literature throughout the curriculum they address many of these standards. The activities they use to extend the literature selections ensure that these standards are met, as well as the appropriate content area standards.

Literature written expressly for children located in the English language arts classroom motivates students to learn to write, speak, and listen in ways that textbooks cannot. Informational trade books that look like narrative picture books facilitate children's transition to learning from textbooks (Headley and Dunston, 2000). Further, students soon learn that the informational books' style of writing is different from the narrative found in picture books and they discover that informational books do not have to be read from beginning to end. Instead students can read just the parts that are of interest. Books and media in this chapter stimulate children to think, to play, and to respond as they explore and experiment with the alphabet, parts of speech, wordplay, writing, speaking, and poetry. The chapter concludes with reference materials for the English language arts classroom and teacher resources.

THE ALPHABET

Alphabet books and songs introduce young readers to the letters of the alphabet and their sounds. They also provide for many children their first introduction to reading and teach children about the fundamentals of reading. Young readers learn about the placement of words and pictures in books and come to learn the relationship between the two. Readers both young and old derive hours of pleasure from alphabet books such as the ones in this section. Books and media in this section address content standard three regarding students' understanding of letter and word identification.

Book and Media Choices

Fleming, Denise. *Alphabet under Construction.* New York: Henry Holt, 2006. 32p. ISBN 978-0-8050-8112-7. Grades: P–1.

Mouse constructs the twenty-six letters of the alphabet using scaffolds, ladders, and a variety of materials. Mouse's construction projects not only introduce readers to the letters of the alphabet, they also introduce readers to words that stretch their vocabularies. However, as the detailed illustrations show, the construction project can be quite messy.

Wood, Audrey. *Alphabet Rescue.* Illustrated by Bruce Wood. New York: Blue Sky Press, 2006. 40p. ISBN 978–0-439-85316-3. Grades: P–1.

The Wood mother-son team's series of alphabet books with charming alphabet letters characters are a fun way for students to learn the alphabet. In this book, the lowercase letters come to the rescue and work with the capital letters to save the factory where the letters are made. This is a terrific resource for helping young learners understand the distinction between upper- and lowercase letters.

Cleary, Brian P. *Peanut Butter and Jellyfishes: A Very Silly Alphabet Book.* Illustrated by Betsy E. Snyder. Minneapolis, MN: Millbrook Press, 2006. 32p. ISBN 978-0-8225-6188-0. Grades: P–2.

Colorful collages, hidden letters, word pictures, and alphabet sentences presented in rhyme make this a delightful book for teaching the ABCs. Nonsensical sentences that are as wacky as the illustrations enchant children as they learn. This book is also available as an e-book.

Elting, Mary, and Michael Folsom. *Q Is for Duck: An Alphabet Guessing Game.* Illustrated by Jack Kent. New York: Houghton Mifflin, 2005. 64p. ISBN 978-0-61857412-4. Grades: K–2.

Originally published in 1980, this alphabet book, with its creative associations between the letters and words they represent, encourages readers to use higher-order thinking skills to solve the riddles.

Stewig, John Warren. *The Animals Watched: An Alphabet Book.* Illustrated by Roseanne Litzinger. New York: Holiday House, 2007. Unp. ISBN 978-0-8234-1906-7. Grades: K–2.

Beginning with aardvarks and ending with zebras, the animals tell the story of Noah's Ark. Each animal pair contributes the next event in the story, hence, the zebras tell how the story ends. The book concludes with a glossary containing information about the animals and the pronunciation of their names.

Gerstein, Mordicai. *The Absolutely Awful Alphabet*. New York: Voyager Books, 2001. 32p. ISBN 978-0-15-216343-3. Grades: 1–4.

Ghoulish and creepy letters of the alphabet have arrived and each letter is nastier than the one before with plans to attack one of its neighbors. Alphabet lessons have never been so slimy, ugly, nasty, or just plain weird. The illustrations are just "gross" enough to thrill and entertain older students.

Gaiman, Neil. *The Dangerous Alphabet*. Illustrated by Gris Grimly. New York: HarperCollins, 2008. Unp. ISBN 978-0-06-078334-1. Grades: 2–4.

Rhyming couplets, wordplay, ghoulish characters, and a suspenseful treasure hunt lead older readers through the alphabet. A brother, a sister, and their faithful gazelle travel through the underworld depicted in sepia tones and faded watercolor washes. While not for the faint of heart, older English language learners enjoy learning the alphabet with this spine-tingling adventure.

Sanders, Nancy I. *D Is for Drinking Gourd: An African American Alphabet*. Illustrated by E. B. Lewis. Farmington Hills, MI: Sleeping Bear, 2007. Unp. ISBN 978-1-58536-293-6. Grades: 2–5.

Watercolor illustrations help to tell the history of African Americans in a poetic alphabet format. The inspirational struggles, triumphs, and contributions of African Americans are showcased in this historical treat. Notable Social Studies Trade Book for Young People, 2008.

Explorations

1. After reading aloud *Alphabet under Construction* (Fleming, 2006), have the children work in small groups to see if they can think of any other ways that the letters can be constructed. Then, let them share their findings with the entire class.
2. After reading *Peanut Butter and Jellyfishes: A Very Silly Alphabet Book* (Cleary, 2006), have students think of other words for each letter and then find the letter hidden on each page.
3. While reading *Q Is for Duck: An Alphabet Guessing Game* (Elting and Folsom, 2005), ask students to guess why the sounds are related to the letters. Finish reading the book and have the class suggest other sounds they can use for each letter.
4. After reading *The Animals Watched: An Alphabet Book* (Stewig, 2007), revisit the book to talk about the different animals on the ark.
5. After reading aloud *The Absolutely Awful Alphabet* (Gerstein, 2001), divide the class into two teams to see if they can produce alphabetical characters that are "absolutely awful." Have them share the results with their classmates.

LANGUAGE CONVENTIONS

Standard six encompasses language conventions, which includes spelling and punctuation. Wilde (2008) offers ideas for busy teachers who recognize that some of their middle school students have difficulty spelling words correctly. For whole class instruction she suggests techniques that call students' attention to the importance of spelling and that have them set goals for their spelling. She also offers ideas for working with individual students, and these techniques work well in upper elementary classrooms.

Book and Media Choices

The Best of the Best of Electric Company. DVD. Los Angeles, CA: Shout Factory Theatre Studio, 2006. 10 hr 30 min. ISBN 978-0-7389-3356-6. Grades: P–3.

This nostalgic favorite from the 1970s and early 1980s teaches children basic grammar information and basic reading skills. The lively programs feature an impressive list of actors, who capture students' attention and make learning fun.

Pulver, Robin. *Silent Letters Loud and Clear*. Illustrated by Lynn Rowe Reed. New York: Holiday House, 2008. Unp. ISBN 978-0-8234-2127-5. Grades: K–3.

When the students in Mr. Wright's class send a letter to the newspaper complaining about the problems the silent letters are causing them in their spelling lessons, the silent letters disappear from the letter. The resulting uproar shows the children just how important the silent letters are to their spelling.

Carr, Jan. *Greedy Apostrophe: A Cautionary Tale*. Illustrated by Ethan Long. New York: Holiday House, 2007. Unp. ISBN 978-0-8234-2006-3. Grades: 1–3.

This story demonstrates how important apostrophes are to the English language and the havoc they can cause when used incorrectly. Lively colors and cartoon characters draw readers in and add to the fun as the punctuation marks go to the Hiring Hall to get their jobs for the day. Greedy Apostrophe is given instructions on his possessive assignment; however, he disregards his instructions and begins inserting apostrophes into plurals.

Pulver, Robin. *Punctuation Takes a Vacation*. Illustrated by Lynn Rowe Reed. New York: Holiday House, 2003. Unp. ISBN 978-0-8234-1687-5. Grades: 1–3.

In Mr. Wright's classroom punctuation is on vacation and sending postcards back to the class showing off their particular punctuation skills. After borrowing some punctuation marks from the class next door, the students write postcards to their vacationing friends begging them to come back. As students laugh at the antics, they learn about how to use punctuation and why it is important. This book is also available on CD.

Truss, Lynne. *Eats, Shoots and Leaves: Why Commas Really Do Make a Difference!* Illustrated by Bonnie Timmons. New York: Putnam, 2006. Unp. ISBN 978-0-399-24491-9. Grades: 1–3.

This attractive and entertaining book is filled with humorous comma-related goofs. Fourteen sentence pairs aptly demonstrate the importance of correctly placing commas in sentences. The accompanying cartoon illustrations add to the hilarity and ensure that the lessons stay with students.

Truss, Lynne. *The Girl's Like Spaghetti: Why, You Can't Manage Without Apostrophes!* Illustrated by Bonnie Timmons. New York: Putnam, 2007. Unp. ISBN 978-0-399-24706-4. Grades: 2–4.

With humorous sentence groups and cartoon-like illustrations, Truss and Timmons keep readers giggling as they learn about why apostrophes are so important in their writing. Endnotes explain the differences in the sentences.

Frasier, Debra. *Miss Alaineus: A Vocabulary Disaster*. New York: Voyager Books, 2007. 40p. ISBN 978-0-15-206053-4. Grades: 3–5.

Being homesick and having to obtain vocabulary words over the telephone from a classmate leads to a comical misunderstanding of the spelling and definition of "miscellaneous" for a fifth grade student. However, she manages to turn the disaster into an opportunity to poke fun at herself by appearing in the school's vocabulary parade as "Miss Alaineus, Queen of All Miscellaneous Things."

Truss, Lynne. *Twenty-Odd Ducks: Why, Every Punctuation Mark Counts!* Illustrated by Bonnie Timmons. New York: Putnam, 2009. Unp. ISBN 978-0-399-25058-3. Grades: 3–6.

Using the wrong punctuation mark can dramatically change the meaning of a sentence as Truss demonstrates in the sentences in this lively book. Watercolor illustrations help to ensure that readers recognize the impact of the punctuation marks on the sentences. Endnotes provide additional details to help students understand the punctuation choices for each sentence.

Explorations

1. After reading *Greedy Apostrophe: A Cautionary Tale* (Carr, 2007), divide the class into small groups of four or five and using the examples in the book as models ask the groups to think of other words whose meaning can be changed with the addition of an apostrophe.
2. After reading *Greedy Apostrophe: A Cautionary Tale* (Carr, 2007) have the students create a class chart of examples of correct apostrophe use. Place the chart where the students can reach it and encourage them to add to the chart when they encounter words with apostrophes in their reading.
3. After reading *Eats, Shoots and Leaves: Why Commas Really Do Make a Difference!* (Truss, 2006), have the students look through the work in their writing folder and check for the correct placement of commas in their writing.
4. At the beginning of *Miss Alaineus: A Vocabulary Disaster* (Fraiser, 2007), the author has the students examining a dictionary to select three words that all begin with the same letter and then writing a sentence using the three words. Challenge

the students to find three words all beginning with the same letter that can be used one right after the other in their sentences.

PARTS OF SPEECH

Learning the parts of speech is fun with this collection of interesting, intriguing books. Vibrant, colorful illustrations, rhyming text, humor, and nonsense encourage students to read these books again and again. The books contain a great deal of information about the parts of speech, and the information is presented in such a way that students learn and remember what they read. In this second edition we have included only books published after 2000, so Ruth Heller's beloved books are not included in this section, but we highly recommend them. *Behind the Mask: A Book about Prepositions* (Heller, 1998), *Many Luscious Lollipops: A Book about Adjectives* (Heller, 1998), and *Kites Sail High: A Book about Verbs* (Heller, 1991) are a few of the colorful, informative books that she wrote about the parts of speech.

Book and Media Choices

Pulver, Robin. *Nouns and Verbs Have a Field Day.* Illustrated by Lynn Rowe Reed. New York: Holiday House, 2006. Unp. ISBN 978-0-8234-1982-1. Grades: K–3.

When the kids leave the classroom for a field day the nouns and verbs decide to have their own field day. The nouns form one team and the verbs another, but it is not long before they figure out that they have to work together. Bright, colorful illustrations crowded with nouns and verbs create a lively, entertaining opportunity for learning.

Fisher, Doris. *Hole-in-One Adverbs.* Illustrated by Scott Angle. Strongsville, OH: Gareth Stevens, 2008. Unp. ISBN 978-0-8368-8902-4. Grades: 1–4.

This short chapter book teaches adverbs in the context of a golf game and it concludes with a concise summary of the grammar rules for using adverbs. While non-sports fans may not appreciate the book, reluctant readers who are sports fans clamor for this book and others from this series. From the Grammar All Stars: The Parts of Speech series.

Cleary, Brian P. *A Lime, a Mime, a Pool of Slime: More about Nouns.* Illustrated by Brian Gable. Minneapolis, MN: Millbrook Press, 2006. 31p. ISBN 978-1-58013-934-2. Grades: 2–4.

From concrete to abstract to proper nouns, students remember the zany words and the brightly colored cartoon illustrations. This entertaining book makes learning about nouns fun and the lively writing is sure to inspire students to write their own rhymes with nouns. From the Words Are Categorical series.

Cleary, Brian P. *Slide and Slurp, Scratch and Burp: More about Verbs.* Illustrated by Brian Gable. Minneapolis, MN: Millbrook Press, 2007. Unp. ISBN 978-1-58013-935-9. Grades: 2–4.

Cleary makes learning about verbs fun and exciting with his clever rhymes and Gable's zany illustrations add to the fun. This is a great book to read aloud with the students chiming in as a chorus. From the Words Are Categorical series.

Walker, Sally M. *The Vowel Family: A Tale of Lost Letters.* Illustrated by Kevin Luthardt. Minneapolis, MN: Lerner, 2008. Unp. ISBN 978-0-8225-7982-3. Grades: 2–4.

Life is devoid of vowels for Pm and Sm until their children, Alan, Ellen, Iris, Otto, and Ursula, are born. As each child joins the family, another vowel is added to the text. While the storyline might get lost as children try to pronounce the words without vowels, the book is a fun way to introduce vowels. It can also be used for spelling and vocabulary lessons.

Cleary, Brian P. *I and You and Don't Forget Who: What Is a Pronoun?* Illustrated by Brian Gable. Minneapolis, MN: Millbrook Press, 2004. Unp. ISBN 978-1-57505-596-1. Grades: 2–5.

Humorous illustrations accompany the child-friendly text in this introduction to pronouns. The text is both rhythmic and rhyming and gives good explanations and examples of types of pronouns and their uses. This title is available as an e-book. From the Words Are Categorical series.

Schoolhouse Rock! Thirtieth Anniversary Edition. DVD. FL: Disney DVD, 2002. 283 min. ISBN 978-0-7888-2925-3. Grades: 2–6.

Parts of speech, grammar, multiplication, finance, history, and government are covered in the two discs that contain delightful animated characters and rousing songs whose lyrics replay in your head long after the video ends. These animated shorts were first seen on television from 1972 to 1986 and this DVD attests to their lasting impact on generations of students.

Explorations

1. While reading *Slide and Slurp, Scratch and Burp: More about Verbs* (Cleary, 2007) pause to let the student pantomime the action verbs.
2. A fun way to share *The Vowel Family: A Tale of Lost Letters* (Walker, 2008) with students is to use a document camera to project the text and invite the students to help you pronounce the vowel-less words.
3. After reading *I and You and Don't Forget Who: What Is a Pronoun?* (Cleary, 2004) ask students to write one or two paragraphs without using pronouns. Then have them rewrite the same paragraphs using the correct pronouns.
4. The short animations on *Schoolhouse Rock! Thirtieth Anniversary Edition* are a lively way to review parts of speech and can be easily slipped in at the beginning

of class as students are settling down to work or at the end of class as students are packing to leave.

FIGURATIVE LANGUAGE

Figurative language can be a word or a phrase that creates an image in the mind that is different from the literal meaning of the words. Examples of figurative language include metaphor, simile, hyperbole, alliteration, onomatopoeia, and personification. Used appropriately they add interest and clarity to writing. The following books help students understand what figurative language is, and as they encounter figurative language in books they are reading they will begin to recognize it. Exploring figurative language helps students to master it, so they can use it in their writing and speaking. Using metaphors and similes in their writing enables students to expand their thought processes and makes their writing more interesting. With modeling from their teacher or librarian, students learn to incorporate figurative language in their writing. Content standard six has students applying their knowledge of figurative language to create, critique, and discuss a variety of texts.

Book and Media Choices

Singer, Marilyn. *City Lullaby.* Illustrated by Carll Cneut. New York: Houghton Mifflin, 2007. Unp. ISBN 978-0-618-60703-7. Grades: P–2.

Counting, rhymes, action verbs, and a cacophony of sights and sounds combine to make this book a joyful celebration. The book closes with groups of objects for counting. While targeted at younger students, elementary teachers find it an excellent choice for teaching figurative language, such as onomatopoeia.

Shaskan, Trisha Speed. *If You Were Alliteration.* Illustrated by Sara Gray. Minneapolis, MN: Picture Window Books, 2008. Unp. ISBN 978-1-40484-097-3. Grades: K–4.

The title page has the definition of alliteration and then the pages are filled with additional information about alliteration and many examples to ensure that students understand the concept. Back matter includes a glossary, resources for learning more, and an index. This book is also available as an e-book. From the Word Fun series.

Shaskan, Trisha Speed. *If You Were Onomatopoeia.* Illustrated by Sara Gray. Minneapolis, MN: Picture Window Books, 2008. Unp. ISBN 978-1-40484-098-0. Grades: K–4.

The repeating refrain "If you were . . ." draws readers along as they discover that onomatopoeia allow them to make loud, lively sounds. Back matter includes a glossary, resources for learning more, and an index. This book is also available as an e-book. From the Word Fun series.

Leedy, Loreen. *Crazy Like a Fox: A Simile Story.* New York: Holiday House, 2008. Unp. ISBN 978-0-8234-1719-3. Grades: 1-4.

When Rufus, a fox, scares his friend, Babette, a lamb, the merry chase begins, as do the similes that narrate the story. While not all of the similes fit together well, it is a clever way to tell a story. The book includes a definition of a simile and Leedy invites readers to write their own.

Alley, Zoe B. *There's a Wolf at the Door.* Illustrated by R. W. Alley. New York: Macmillan, 2008. Unp. ISBN 978-1-59643-275-8. Grades: 2–4.

In this collection of retold tales, the wolf's attempts to find a meal are met with disaster. The oversized comic book replete with detailed pen-and-ink and water-color illustrations and humorous tales filled with puns and alliteration elicits giggles and chuckles as it is read aloud.

Cleary, Brian P. *Skin Like Milk, Hair of Silk: What Are Similes and Metaphors?* Illustrated by Brian Gable. Minneapolis, MN: Millbrook Press, 2009. Unp. ISBN 978-0-8225-9151-1. Grades: 4–6.

Silly rhymes and clever illustrations teach students about similes and metaphors in a humorous, quirky way that makes learning fun. From the Words Are Categorical series.

Explorations

1. After reading *If You Were Alliteration* (Shaskan, 2008), model writing an acrostic poem for the students as demonstrated in the activity at the end of the book. The activity involves writing acrostic poems with their names—each line filled with alliteration. For example,

   Sam saw a shooting star.
   Anxiously awaiting another.
   Moonbeams moved magically.
2. While writing an entire story in similes would be daunting, students can use the similes in *Crazy Like a Fox: A Simile Story* (Leedy, 2008) as models to write their own similes. Put the students in small groups so they can work and talk out loud as they think up and write their similes. When they are finished have them store the similes in their writing folders so they can try to incorporate them into their writing.
3. After reading *There's a Wolf at the Door* (Alley, 2008) revisit the text and share the puns and alliteration with the students.

WORDPLAY

Wordplay furnishes students opportunities to play and explore the English language in order to understand how language works. The knowledge of words gained from wordplay enables students to enhance their writing and speaking skills. Wordplay shows students that words can have more than one meaning and hence, sentences that contain the words can have more than one meaning. As students participate in the explorations of the books in this section they are developing the language skills addressed in content standard five, which focuses on the development of a range of strategies for written communication.

Book and Media Choices

My First Word Play: Interactive Book and CD-ROM. New York: DK Publishing, 2008. 12p. ISBN 978-0-7566-3756-9. Grade: P.

The games in this interactive board book help kids develop early language and thinking skills. The CD-ROM perfectly complements the material in the book, which actively involves young readers in learning.

Barretta, Gene. *Dear Deer: A Book of Homophones.* New York: Henry Holt, 2007. Unp. ISBN 978-0-8050-8104-6. Grades: K–3.

The book begins with a note about the difference between homophones and homonyms. Animals in the zoo provide the perfect backdrop for the tale filled with homophones and accompanied by colorful illustrations that help explain the differences between the words. Notable Children's Book in the Language Arts, 2008.

Doyen, Denise. *Once Upon a Twice.* Illustrated by Barry Moser. New York: Random House, 2009. Unp. ISBN 978-0-375-85612-9. Grades: K–3.

Reminiscent of "Jabberwocky," this narrative poem filled with nonsense words and phrases offers a cautionary tale about being overconfident. A mouse named Jam defies the "eldermice" by staying alone by the pond, during a dark, scary night. His encounter with a menacing snake makes for a suspenseful tale that is a delight to read aloud.

Arnold, Ted. *Even More Parts: Idioms for Head to Toe.* New York: Penguin, 2004. Unp. ISBN 978-0-8037-2938-4. Grades: 1–3.

Chaos reigns when idioms are literally interpreted and illustrated, as a young boy gets ready for school. A lost head and a tied tongue are showcased in hilarious illustrations that ensure students remember the idioms in the book. The character is the same small boy who appeared in *Parts* (Arnold, 1997) and *More Parts* (Arnold, 2001).

Moses, Will. *Raining Cats and Dogs.* New York: Penguin, 2008. 37p. ISBN 978-0-399-24233-5. Grades: 1–5.

Moses explains forty-eight of the most common idioms with definitions and sentences accompanied by folk-art paintings. These tricky phrases cause problems for youngsters and for English language learners, so share this book in small chunks over several weeks.

Rayevsky, Kim. *Antonyms, Synonyms and Homonyms.* Illustrated by Robert Rayevsky. New York: Holiday House, 2006. Unp. ISBN 978-0-8234-1889-3. Grades: 2–5.

An alien lands and tries to figure out the English language as he encounters antonyms, synonyms, and homonyms. Wordplay and puns add to the fun. Each term is defined and accompanied by small, labeled drawings that help students understand the terms.

Leedy, Loreen, and Pat Street. *There's a Frog in My Throat: 440 Animal Sayings a Little Bird Told Me.* New York: Holiday House, 2003. Unp. ISBN 978-0-8234-1774-2. Grades: 2–6.

Students confronted by idioms they do not understand are likely to find their answers here. Animals' sayings such as "My goose is cooked!" are explained in words and illustrations. An index is included.

Cleary, Brian P. *Rhyme and Punishment: Adventures with Wordplay.* Illustrated by J. P. Sandy. Minneapolis, MN: Millbrook Press, 2006. 48p. ISBN 978- 1-57505-849-8. Grades: 4–6.

As Cleary shows in this entertaining book, puns are everywhere. The book begins by defining puns and explaining how to decode them. His division of the puns into four chapters—music, animals, food, and geography—makes it easy to integrate them into content area learning. Each chapter contains four-line poems, and difficult words are defined at the bottom of the page. Cartoon illustrations add to the fun.

Explorations

1. Read only portions of *Raining Cats and Dogs* (Moses, 2008) at a time and then let the students create their own illustrations of the idioms. Creating their own illustrations allows students to demonstrate their understanding of the idioms.
2. As students read *Antonyms, Synonyms and Homonyms* (Rayevsky, 2006) have them create word maps to help them grasp the connections between the words. For example, the map might have a word and its definition in the center. Then, radiating out from the center are spokes for writing down antonyms and synonyms for the words. Inspiration software can also be used for creating word maps as the software contains templates for word maps.
3. Add the geography section of *Rhyme and Punishment: Adventures with Wordplay* (Cleary, 2006) to a geography lesson and give students time to work with partners to write and to illustrate their own geography puns.
4. Have students work in small groups to explore the idioms in *There's a Frog in My Throat: 440 Animal Sayings a Little Bird Told Me* (Leedy and Street, 2003). Then, have them create their own collages of the idioms to display on a bulletin board. During writing workshop the students can refer to the idioms and try to include them in their writing.

WRITTEN LANGUAGE

Books and media in this section look at writing from different perspectives, but all focus on writing for authentic purposes. In these materials are ideas for writing and models that show students how to write. Students may dread writing, but books, videos, and software programs make writing fun. Publishing students' writing and placing it in the school or class library gives students both a purpose and an audience for their writing. Teachers who save student-created books from year to year find that these books continue to be favorites with each new class of students. Having a writing center in the classroom near a reading center encourages young authors to write and to model their writing after the writing of their favorite authors.

Incorporating a writing workshop into the classroom provides students with opportunities to practice their writing and hence develop their writing skills. Conferencing with their peers and with their teacher gives them the support and encouragement they need to hone their skills. When they are ready to edit their work, Kissel and Wood (2008) suggest working with a peer editor using an editing checklist. Throughout the year the checklist is changed to include the writing skills being taught in the classroom. Peer conferences allow students to help one another with their writing, which means that the teacher is not the only one reading and correcting their writing.

As students develop their writing skills they meet content standards four, five, seven, eight, and twelve. Standards four and five address using the writing process for effective communication to a variety of audiences for a variety of purposes and in a variety of genres. Standards seven and eight concern using both print and electronic formats for research and communicating their findings to an audience.

Book and Media Choices

Dotlich, Rebecca Kai. *Bella and Bean.* Illustrated by Aileen Leiften. New York: Simon and Schuster, 2009. Unp. ISBN 978-0-689-85616-7. Grades: P–1.

Bella is a poet who needs time alone to write; however, her best friend Bean is an energetic creature who craves adventure and attention. So, they compromise and collaborate on a poem about themselves. While written for the very young, this book about friendship and writing resonates with writers of every age.

Cronin, Doreen. *Diary of a Worm.* Illustrated by Harry Bliss. DVD. New York: Weston Woods, 2004. 8 min. ISBN 978-0-7882-0531-6. Grades: P–3.

The worm's diary reveals that he has adventures similar to those faced by most young people—a bothersome sibling, eating too much, and staying out of the way of large people. Looking at the world from the worm's vantage point provides a new and different perspective for students to observe their own world. The video is based on the book by the same name. Other books in diary format by this talented duo include *Diary of a Spider* (Cronin, 2005) and *Diary of a Fly* (Cronin, 2007). ALA Notable Children's Video, 2005.

Darbyshire, Kristen. *Put It on the List.* New York: Penguin, 2009. Unp. ISBN 978-0-525-47906-2. Grades: P–3.

"Put it on the list!" is a familiar household refrain. In this family of chickens, just as in other families, inevitably something does not get put on the list and soon after a trip to the grocery store the family discovers they are out of essential household items—diapers, syrup, milk. Bold colorful pages, thick black text, and yellow, stick-legged chickens are a delight to behold.

Bottner, Barbara, and Gerald Kruglik. *Wallace's Lists.* Illustrated by Olof Landström. DVD. New York: Weston Woods, 2007. 15 min. ISBN 978-0-545-04271-0. Grades: K–3.

Wallace has an amazing collection of lists; however, Wallace can only do things that are on his list. Envious of his new neighbor Albert's freewheeling lifestyle, Wallace eventually takes a chance and discovers that having an adventure is more fun than living by a list. This animated video is based on the book by the same title. ALA Notable Video, 2008.

Teague, Mark. *Dear Mrs. Larue: Letters from Obedience School.* New York: Scholastic, 2002. Unp. ISBN 978-0-439-20663-1. Grades: K–3.

Stealing food, chasing cats, and tearing clothing land Ike in obedience school. He pens dramatic, exaggerated letters home to his owner, Mrs. LaRue, trying to convince her to spring him from his prison. In reality, the prison is a doggy spa; however, Ike is anxious to be home and as foreshadowed on the jacket he has just the book, *50 Great Escapes*. Ike's letter-writing adventures continue in *Detective LaRue: Letters from the Investigation* (Teague, 2004) and in *LaRue for Mayor: Letters from the Campaign Trail* (Teague, 2008). Christopher Award Winner, 2003.

Christelo, Eileen. *Letters from a Desperate Dog.* New York: Houghton Mifflin, 2006. Unp. ISBN 978-0-618-51003-0. Grades: K–4.

Emma is a misunderstood pooch whose failed attempts to please her owner, George, land her in trouble. Desperate for help, she e-mails the advice columnist, Queenie, who writes for the *Weekly Bone*. Queenie's sage advice backfires and Emma joins a traveling acting troupe. Eventually reunited, George and Emma continue to misunderstand each other and the correspondence with Queenie continues.

McNaughton, Colin. *Once Upon an Ordinary School Day.* Illustrated by Staoshi Kitamura. New York: Farrar, Straus and Giroux, 2004. Unp. ISBN 978-0-374-35634-7. Grades: K–4.

From music to pictures to words to writing, an ordinary school day becomes an extraordinary day as daydreams turn into adventures. The story provides inspiration for writers of all ages as they first let their imaginations wander and then they write.

Stearns, Peggy Healy. *Stationary Studio: The Irresistible Tool to Encourage Writing.* Illustrated by Peter Reynolds. Mac/Win. Boston, MA: Fablevision, 2006. Grades: K and up.

This writing tool allows children to create stationary and shape books. Combined with an interactive whiteboard it is perfect for interactive writing activities. The software comes with curriculum-based activities. A free demo is available. ALA 2007 Notable Computer Software for Children Award Winner, 2007.

Johnson, Crockett. *Magic Beach.* Ashville, NC: Front Street, 2005. Unp. ISBN 978-1-932425-27-7. Grades: 1–3.

A boy and a girl discover that when they write nouns in the sand, the waves wash away the words and leave the objects in the sand. As they write, their story envelops them and transports them to a magic kingdom. Originally published in 1965 as *Castles in the Sand*, this new edition features Johnson's original artwork found in the Smithsonian archives. It also contains an appreciation by Maurice Sendak and an afterword by Philip Nel that recounts the history of the story.

Allen, Susan, and Jane Lindaman. *Written Anything Good Lately?* Illustrated by Vicky Enright. New York: Lerner, 2006. Unp. ISBN 978-0-7613-2426-3. Grades: 1–4.

Each letter of the alphabet represents a different kind of writing, making this more than just an alphabet book. It is a compendium of ideas for multigenre writing, including driving directions, a myth, a play, and a sensational speech. The detailed illustrations show children writing and include samples of their writing.

Hershenhorn, Esther. *S Is for Story: A Writer's Alphabet.* Illustrated by Zachary Pullen. Farmington Hills, MI: Sleeping Bear, 2009. ISBN 978-1-58536-439-8. Grades: 3–6.

Reluctant writers who encounter this book just might decide to try some of the writing techniques explored in this clever alphabet book. Poems, quotes from famous authors, and writing tips fill the colorful pages.

Goodinson, Clive. *Pixton Interactive Web Comics.* Software. Vancouver, BC, Canada: 2009. Grades: 3 and up.

In this virtual classroom, students create and share their very own comics. This interactive website motivates students to think creatively and to write in a genre they enjoy reading. A free fourteen-day trial version is available for downloading at pixton.com/schools/overview. ALA Great Interactive Software for Kids Winner, 2009. Top 20 Web 2.0: Pick 20 Award, 2009.

Avi. *A Beginning, a Muddle, and an End: The Right Way to Write Writing.* Illustrated by Tricia Tusa. New York: Harcourt, 2008. 164p. ISBN 978-0-15-205555-4. Grades: 4–6.

Avon, a snail, and Edward, an ant, muddle along as Edward offers advice to Avon on how to overcome his writer's block. As the book explores the complexity of the writing process the friends' devotion to each other becomes evident. The wordplay included throughout the book makes it fun to read and the content of the book will open class discussions of the writing process. This is a book for reading aloud.

Caudle, Melissa, Brad Caudle, and Michelle Chandler. *Rock 'N Learn: Writing Strategies.* DVD. Conroe, TX: Rock 'N Learn Studio, 2007. 50 min. ISBN 978-1-934312-02-5 Grades: 4–6.

Marko the Pencil breaks the writing process down to simple sequential steps and encourages reluctant writers to get started. Story elements on the DVD include transitions, creating a hook, colorful words, similes, onomatopoeia, and others.

Fletcher, Ralph. *How to Write Your Life Story.* New York: HarperCollins, 2007. 102p. ISBN 978-0-06-050769-5. Grades: 4–7.

Filled with practical tips and exercises, this book is sure to get students interested in writing their life stories. Interviews with authors including Kathy Appelt and Jack Gantos and passages from their memoirs provide models for students as they write. Notable Children's Book in the Language Arts, 2008.

Sturtevant, Katherine. *A True and Faithful Narrative.* New York: Farrar, Straus and Giroux, 2006. 250p. ISBN 978-0-374-37809-7. Grades: 6–9.

In this first-person narrative, sixteen-year-old Meg Moore is forbidden to write by her bookseller father and by seventeenth-century mores. However, her writing cannot be stopped and so she secretly writes. Readers were first introduced to this heroine in Sturtevant's (2000) historical novel *At the Sign of the Star.*

Todd, Mark, and Esther Pearl Watson. *Whatcha Mean, What's a Zine? The Art of Making Zines and Mini-Comics.* New York: Houghton Mifflin, 2006. 110p. ISBN 978-0-618-56315-9. Grades: 6 and up.

Zines are self-published mini-magazines and when combined with mini-comics they make two enticing choices for reluctant writers. This how-to book provides all the details they need and numerous models for students to use as they create their own zines and mini-comics. ALSC Notable Children's Book, 2007.

Explorations

1. One simple form of authentic writing is making lists, and *Put It on the List* (Darbyshire, 2009) is a wonderful model text for students to use as they create their own lists.
2. After reading *Dear Mrs. Larue: Letters from Obedience School* (Teague, 2002), project the pages on a document camera and have the students note the format for writing letters. Then, have them write letters to Ike from Mrs. Larue explaining why he has to stay.
3. While reading *Letters from a Desperate Dog* (Christelo, 2006), call students' attention to the misunderstandings that arise. This book is an excellent choice for discussing point of view and helps explain why Emma's actions are misunderstood.

4. After reading *Letters from a Desperate Dog* (Christelo, 2006), ask students to share their reflections on when a sibling or friend's actions caused them to be misunderstood.
5. *Written Anything Good Lately?* (Allen and Lindaman, 2006) and *S is for Story: A Writer's Alphabet* (Hershenhorn, 2009) are filled with examples of multigenre writing. Share the books with the students during a writing workshop and encourage them to write in different genres.
6. While reading *A True and Faithful Narrative* (Sturtevant, 2006), have students record the cause-and-effect events that happen as a result of Meg writing.
7. Use *Whatcha Mean, What's a Zine? The Art of Making Zines and Mini-Comics* (Todd and Watson, 2006) and model for students how they can develop their writing skills as they create their own zines. Bott (2002) and Cohen (2004) explain how a zine project can be implemented within the writing workshop.

SPOKEN LANGUAGE

Speaking and listening take up a large part of each day in classrooms; however, not much time is devoted to practicing speaking and listening. Students need direct instruction, guided practice, and independent practice to fully develop these skills. Discussions, readers' theater, puppet shows, storytelling, choral reading, oral reports, and dramatic readings are all ways to practice speaking and listening. This practice ensures that students develop their listening and speaking vocabularies. The materials in this section contain practical ideas and suggestions for developing speaking and listening skills. Wheeler and Swords (2006) focus on the importance of accepting and valuing students' native language while helping them develop Standard English. One suggestion they have for doing this is to have students use their home language when they write dialogue for characters in their stories.

Providing students opportunities to develop their speaking and listening skills ensures that they are working toward the guidelines established by content standards four and twelve. These standards encompass using spoken language for effective communication with a variety of audiences for different purposes.

Book and Media Choices

Cleary, Brian P. *Stop, Drop, and Flop in the Slop: A Short Vowels Sound Book with Consonant Blends.* Illustrated by Jason Miskimins. Minneapolis, MN: Millbrook Press, 2009. 30p. ISBN 978-0-8225-7635-8. Grades: 2–5.

The humorous words and illustrations go a long way toward encouraging youngsters as they speak and learn in language arts classrooms. From the Sounds Like Reading series.

Somervill, Barbara A. *Oral Reports.* Portsmouth, NH: Heinemann Library, 2009. 32p. ISBN 978-1-43291-172-0. Grades: 3–6.

From planning to performance this is a practical guide to oral reports. With support and guidance from their teacher or librarian, students will be able to successfully complete their oral reports. A glossary and an index conclude the book. From the School Projects Survival Guide series.

Blackwell, Angela, and Therese Naber. *Open Forum: Academic Listening and Speaking (Student Book 1).* New York: Oxford University Press, 2006. 105p. ISBN 978-0-19-436109-5. Grades: 4–8.

Open Forum is a three-level comprehensive series for the development of essential listening and speaking skills. The diverse listening selections—including lectures, radio interviews, news reports, and monologues—ensure a high level of engagement and discussion.

Schlitz, Laura Amy. *Good Masters! Sweet Ladies! Voices from a Medieval Village.* Illustrated by Robert Byrd. CD. Prince Frederick, MD: Recorded Books, 2008. 1 hr 30 min. ISBN 978-1-43611-963-4. Grades: 4–8.

Based on the Newbery Medal–winning book by the same title, this recording presents the monologues as models for students' performances. The book is comprised of monologues Schlitz wrote for students at her school to perform to help them understand and appreciate medieval life.

Shuster, Kate. *Speak Out! Debate and Public Speaking in the Middle Grades.* International Debate Association, 2005. 191p. ISBN 978-1-932716-02-3. Grades: 6–8.

Whether preparing for class debates or contest debates, this handbook contains details on how to prepare for and participate in debates. The book includes information on how to conduct research, develop debate strategies, and how to conduct debates.

Haney, Johannah, and Jennifer Rozines Roy. *You Can Write Speeches and Debates.* Berkeley Heights, NJ: Enslow, 2003. 64p. ISBN 978-0-7660-2087-0. Grades: 6 and up.

From selecting a topic to persuading an audience, this is a step-by-step guide to writing speeches and debates. Bibliographic references and an index conclude the book. From the You Can Write series.

Explorations

1. The nonsense sentences in *Stop, Drop, and Flop in the Slop: A Short Vowels Sound Book with Consonant Blends* (Cleary, 2009) coupled with zany illustrations help students remember the rules for pronouncing short vowels and consonant blends. These sentences are terrific tongue twisters for students to practice their oral speaking skills.
2. Use *Open Forum: Academic Listening and Speaking* (Blackwell and Naber, 2006) as a resource for students who are interested in recording podcasts. Audacity

(audacity.sourceforge.net/), is a free, open source software available for creating podcasts for both Macintosh and Windows operating systems. GarageBand is another software for creating podcasts and is available on Macintosh computers.

3. Debates are not just for speech class; they can be used across the content areas to teach students how to think critically about topics they are studying. Use *Speak Out! Debate and Public Speaking in the Middle Grades* (Shuster, 2005) to teach students how to debate.

POETRY

Poetry activates the senses as it draws images, rekindles smells, creates sounds, triggers the sense of touch, and makes readers feel. The figurative language in poetry evokes the senses and causes readers to stop and feel the words. Imagery, personification, metaphor, simile, rhyme, rhythm, repetition, alliteration, consonance, assonance, and onomatopoeia provide the lyrical, musical sounds of poetry. Poetry creates a mood; a feeling that evokes responses in the reader in ways that prose does not. Poetry can be shared through choral readings, dramatizations, and read-alouds.

Poetry is affirming; it connects to students' lives, and hence they are motivated to read and enjoy poetry (Grimes, 2000). Further, Grimes contends that poetry is portable. It can be memorized and carried with children in their minds. Students need exposure to a wide variety of poetry, so that they learn that it does not all rhyme, it is not all humorous, but that it can all be enjoyed.

Book and Media Choices

Mannis, Celeste Davidson. *One Leaf Rides the Wind: Counting in a Japanese Garden.* Illustrated by Susan Kathleen Hartung. New York: Viking, 2002. ISBN 978-0-316-48889-1. Grades: P–2.

Easily understood haiku introduces young children to the delights of a Japanese garden. The verses are engaging and shed light on various aspects of ancient Japanese culture. The book can also be used as a counting book. IRA Children's Book Award, 2003.

Thomas, Jan. *Rhyming Dust Bunnies.* New York: Simon and Schuster, 2009. Unp. ISBN 978-1-41697-976-0. Grades: P–2.

Four brightly colored dust bunnies huddled under the furniture greet readers on the title page. Close inspection shows the fourth has a forlorn expression and droopy ears as opposed to his companions with cheery smiles and perky ears. His name does not rhyme with the others' names, and when they call out rhyming words he calls out words that do not rhyme, but instead portend disaster. The others are too busy rhyming to notice the danger, but younger readers will catch on and along the way learn about rhyming words.

Wilbur, Richard. *The Disappearing Alphabet.* Illustrated by David Diaz. New York: Voyager Books, 2001. 32p. ISBN 978-0-15-216362-4. Grades: P–4.

While this book does have "alphabet" in its title, it is also a fine book of poetry. Each of these delightful poems, one for each letter of the alphabet, speculates on the disasters that would occur should that letter suddenly disappear. Diaz's computer-generated illustrations are lush and playful.

Montes, Maria. *Los Gatos Black on Halloween.* Illustrated by Yuyi Morales. New York: Henry Holt, 2006. Unp. ISBN 978-0-8050-7429-1. Grades: K–3.

Halloween trick-or-treaters meet Day of the Dead ghouls in the surreal, glowing illustrations and the rhyming quatrains that blend Spanish and English. Spanish words woven through the text are defined in context; however, they are also included in a glossary at the end of the book. This book is also available on CD and DVD. Pura Belpré Award Book for Illustration, 2008. ALA Notable Children's Book, 2008.

George, Kristine O'Connell. *Hummingbird Nest: A Journal of Poems.* Illustrated by Barry Moser. San Diego: Harcourt, 2004. 48p. ISBN 978-0-15-202325-9. Grades: K–12.

When Anna's hummingbird built a nest in George's potted ficus tree and then raised her young, she provided inspiration for this wonderful collection of poems. Moser's translucent watercolors depict the family from different perspectives just as the poems report on the avian family from different viewpoints. Children's Literature Assembly Notable Children's Books in the Language Arts, 2005.

Prelutsky, Jack. *Pizza, Pigs, and Poetry: How to Write a Poem.* New York: HarperCollins, 2008. 191p. ISBN 978-0-06-143449-5. Grades: 3–6.

Ordinary objects like pizza and pigs offer inspiration for writing poems when viewed through Prelutsky's eyes. He shares his poetry-writing techniques with young poets in an easy-to-understand format that engages even the most reluctant writers. The book concludes with "poemstarts" and an index.

Prelutsky, Jack, selector. *Read a Rhyme, Write a Rhyme.* Illustrated by Meilo So. New York: Alfred A. Knopf, 2005. 23p. ISBN 978-0-375-82286-5. Grades: 3–6.

Each two-page spread contains a collection of poems grouped by topics, bright colorful illustrations, and "poemstarts." A letter from Prelutsky invites readers to read each group of poems and then to use the "poemstarts" to write their own poems. An index of titles and an index of authors conclude the book.

Grimes, Nikki. *What Is Goodbye?* Illustrated by Raul Colón. New York: Hyperion, 2004. 64p. ISBN 978-0-7868-0778-9. Grades: 3–8.

The impact of the sudden death of an older brother is explored through the feelings of a brother and sister grieving the untimely death. The paired poems of siblings, Jerilyn and Jesse, capture their grieving process. The last poem is one for two voices and shows that the siblings are ready to move on with one piece missing.

Janeczko, Paul B. *A Kick in the Head: An Everyday Guide to Poetic Forms.* Illustrated by Chris Raschka. Cambridge, MA: Candlewick, 2005. 61p. ISBN 978-0-7636-0662-6. Grades: 3–9.

Janeczko explains in the introduction that poetic forms make it more fun and more challenging to write poems, but that poets do not always follow the rules for writing poems. Across the two-page spreads are poems in a different form accompanied by an illustration that includes useful clues about the form. At the bottom of the page in tiny print is a sentence about the form featured on that page, and the book concludes with expanded notes on each poetic form.

Weston, Robert Paul. *Zorgamazoo.* New York: Penguin, 2008. 281p. ISBN 978-1-59514-199-6. Grades: 4–6.

Rhyming couplets that beg to be read aloud tell the magical, mysterious tale of Katrina and Mortimer Yorgle's journey to find the missing Zorgles of Zorgamazoo. Imaginative black-and-white illustrations and text in different fonts careen across the pages, transporting readers into an imaginative world. Children's Choices, 2009.

Creech, Sharon. *Heartbeat.* New York: HarperCollins, 2004. 180p. ISBN 978-0-06-054023-4. Grades: 4–7.

In this free-verse novel, Creech explores the heartbeats of life through the eyes of eleven-year-old Annie. With a new baby on the way, a forgetful grandfather, and a moody friend, Annie's life is undergoing changes, as is the apple that her art assignment requires her to draw each day for 100 days.

Giovanni, Nikki, editor. *Hip Hop Speaks to Children: A Celebration of Poetry with a Beat.* Illustrated by Kristen Balouch. Naperville, IL: Sourcebooks, 2008. 72p. ISBN 978-1-40221-048-8. Grades: 4–8.

Packed with a lively, eclectic anthology of fifty-one poems by forty-two poets, this book is a treasure trove to be returned to throughout the school year. The poems reflect the African-American oral tradition and some of them are performed on the accompanying CD.

Greenberg, Jan, editor. *Side by Side: New Poems Inspired by Art from Around the World.* New York: Abrams, 2008. 88p. ISBN 978-0-8109-9471-3. Grades: 6 and up.

This global collection of art, poetry, cultures, and traditions would be equally at home in art, language arts, foreign language, and social studies classes. Thirty-three pieces of art were the inspiration for the accompanying poems. Poems written in languages other than English share the pages with their translations. The book concludes with biographical notes about the artist and the poets, a world map, and an index. Notable Book for a Global Society, 2009.

Roessel, David, and Arnold Rampersad, editors. *Langston Hughes.* Illustrated by Benny Andrews. Monterey, CA: Sterling Publishing, 2006. 48p. ISBN 978-1-40271-845-8. Grades: 6 and up.

This anthology contains twenty-six of Hughes' best-known poems. Andrews' vibrant collage and oil paintings beautifully depict the emotions and stories in the poems. The book includes a detailed introduction, a biography, definitions for unfamiliar words, and background information about each poem. From the Poetry for Young People series. Coretta Scott King Illustrator Award Honor Book, 2007.

Explorations

1. While reading *Rhyming Dust Bunnies* (Thomas, 2009), have the students act out the story.
2. After reading *The Disappearing Alphabet* (Wilbur, 2001) aloud, have the students think of words that would either mean nothing or simply be different from the original without particular letters of the alphabet. Challenge older students to share their examples in rhyme form.
3. *Hummingbird Nest: A Journal of Poems* (George, 2004) and *Heartbeat* (Creech, 2004) can be used as inspiration for students to write their own poems about something they have an opportunity to observe over time, perhaps a class pet. Encourage them to write the poems from different points of view.
4. Select one of the themes from *Read a Rhyme, Write a Rhyme* (Prelutsky, 2005) and read the poems aloud to the students. If possible, project the poems using a document camera. Then, using one of the poemstarts, model for the students how to write poems by writing one as a class. The students will gladly offer suggestions when you get stuck. Allow the students time to write their own poems using the poemstarts.
5. The final poem in *What Is Goodbye?* (Grimes, 2004) is a poem for two voices. Pair the students and have them practice reading the poem together. Then, give the partners time to present to their classmates. The students do not need to memorize the poem, but they do need time to practice.
6. Introduce the students to one of the poetic forms in *A Kick in the Head: An Everyday Guide to Poetic Forms* (Janeczko, 2005). Project the poem with a document camera and explore its structure to help the students understand the form. Then, write a class poem using the form. Encourage the students to try writing poems that match the forms on their own. Remind them that the rules to the form can be broken.
7. Before reading *Zorgamazoo* (Weston, 2008) introduce the book's characters to the students using the Zorgamazoo website at www.zorgamazoo.com/. The website also contains a link to the author's blog that houses audio files of him reading selected chapters.
8. As you read aloud selections from *Langston Hughes* (Roessel and Rampersad, 2006), share with the students how Hughes' life is reflected in his poems. Helping the students make connections between Hughes' life and his poems will

help them understand that when they write, they should write about things that they know.

STORYTELLERS AND WRITERS

Reading about storytellers and writers helps students gather ideas to improve their own writing. In the books that follow, students learn how writers gather ideas for their stories from their lives and their surroundings. The fanciful creatures in Dr. Seuss's books came from his rich imagination fueled by frequent trips to the zoo to observe the animals and a mother who read to him at bedtime. In these books, students learn that writing requires reading, observing life, participating in activities, and reflecting on what has happened. These books can also serve as mentor texts as students write their autobiographies.

Book and Media Choices

Hillenbrand, Will. *Louie!* New York: Penguin, 2009. Unp. ISBN 978-0-399-24707-1. Grades: K–3.

Loosely based on the life of Ludwig Bemelmans, creator of the Madeline stories, the porcine main character in this book loves to draw and he loves to listen to his mother's stories of her Parisian school days. Louie gets in trouble in school for drawing when he is supposed to be studying; however, with the support of adults who understand his passion for drawing, his career flourishes. This book would be a useful addition to an author study of Bemelmans' work.

Krull, Kathleen. *The Boy on Fairfield Street: How Ted Geisel Grew Up to Become Dr. Seuss.* Illustrated by Steve Johnson and Lou Francher. Decorative illustrations by Dr. Seuss. New York: Random House, 2004. Unp. ISBN 978-0-375-92298-5. Grades: K–4.

Having a father who ran the zoo meant that Dr. Seuss got to spend a great deal of time at the zoo. A mother who read to him each evening meant his head was filled with words and images. In school, his drawings broke the rules and earned him a warning from his teacher that he would never be successful at art. However, his fanciful stories filled with illustrations of imaginative creatures made him successful and they continue to capture the hearts and minds of children. A list of Seuss's books and bibliographic information conclude the book.

Gonzalez, Lucia M. *The Storyteller's Candle.* Illustrated by Lulu Delacre. Unp. ISBN 978-0-89239-222-3. Grades: 1–4.

Set in 1929, this story introduces New York City's first Puerto Rican librarian, Pura Belpré. Two Puerto Rican cousins meet her when she visits their school, lights her storyteller's candle, and draws them in with her bilingual stories. She invites the children and the community to the library to celebrate Three Kings' Day. The text is in both English and Spanish. Pura Belpré Author Honor Book, 2009. Pura Belpré Illustrator Honor Book, 2009.

Dray, Philip. *Yours for Justice, Ida B. Wells: The Daring Life of a Crusading Journalist*. Illustrated by Stephen Alcorn. Atlanta, GA: Peachtree Publishers, 2008. 48p. ISBN 978-1-56145-417-4. Grades: 1–5.

Teacher, journalist, and crusader Ida B. Wells courageously spent her life speaking out against and writing about injustice, particularly lynching. Eloquent text and stylized illustrations portray the self-assured, striking crusader and her work. Notes on her life, photographs, information on lynching, a timeline, and a bibliography conclude the book.

Brown, Monica. *My Name Is Gabito: The Life of Gabriel García Márquez/Me llamo Gabito: la vida de Gabriel García Márquez*. Illustrated by Raul Colón. Flagstaff, AZ: Rising Moon, 2007. Unp. ISBN 978-0-87358-934-5. Grades: 2–4.

This picture book biography of Columbian writer Márquez shows readers how events and memories from his childhood provided inspiration for his writing. Surrounded by poverty, he imagined a world filled with wondrous things and created stories from his imaginings. His life and imaginings are captured in the rich, evocative illustrations. A note at the end of the book provides additional information on his life and work. Pura Belpré Honor Book for Illustration, 2008.

Winter, Jonah. *Gertrude Is Gertrude Is Gertrude Is Gertrude*. Illustrated by Calef Brown. New York: Simon and Schuster, 2009. 40p. ISBN 978-1-41694-088-3. Grades: 2–5.

Lively, repetitive text accompanied by rich, colorful, creative illustrations makes this an excellent choice for reading aloud. The text mimics Gertrude Stein's writing style and makes a fun mentor text for students' own writing.

Yolen, Jane. *My Uncle Emily*. Illustrated by Nancy Carpenter. New York: Penguin, 2009. Unp. ISBN 978-0-399-24005-8. Grades: 2–5.

Uncle Emily was the family's name for Emily Dickinson. This fictionalized account of a real event in her life features her young nephew, Gib, who took one of the poems she gave him to school. Dickinson, while reclusive, was noted for a fondness for children, and the book highlights that fondness. Watercolor and ink illustrations capture the period and provide the historical setting for the story. An author's note concludes the book.

Bingham, Jane. *Roald Dahl*. Portsmouth, NH: Heinemann, 2009. Unp. ISBN 978-1-41093-405-5. Grades: 3–5.

The life of popular author Dahl is not explored in detail, but the book does provide information about how events in his life appear in his books. Photographs, still shots from his movies, and activities engage readers as they learn about him. A timeline is included. From the Culture in Action series.

Bryant, Jennifer. *A River of Words: The Story of William Carlos Williams.* Illustrated by Melissa Sweet. Grand Rapids, MI: Eerdmans Books for Young Readers, 2008. Unp. ISBN 978-0-8028-5302-8. Grades: 3–6.

As a young boy Williams began writing poetry, but knew it would not pay his bills. He studied to be a doctor and throughout his life captured moments on scraps of paper that he crafted into poems whenever he found a few minutes. Williams' poems fill the end pages and provide additional glimpses into his life. The book concludes with a timeline, an author's note, an illustrator's note, and resources for learning more. Caldecott Medal Honor Book, 2009. Charlotte Zolotow Honor Book, 2009.

Scieszka, Jon. *Knucklehead: Tall Tales and Mostly True Stories about Growing Up Scieszka.* New York: Viking, 2008. 106p. ISBN 978-0-670-01106-3. Grades: 4–7.

Growing up in a family of six boys gave Scieszka lots of amusing memories to share with his fans, who will instantly recognize his writing style. Readers learn that his childhood escapades and adventures provide him with a wealth of ideas to include in his writing. Lots of family snapshots and clip art illustrate this autobiography, which concludes with an index.

Hjordis, Varmer. *Hans Christian Andersen: His Fairy Tale Life.* Translated by Tiina Nunnally. Illustrated by Lillian Brogger. Toronto, ON, Canada: Groundwood, 2005. 111p. ISBN 978-0-88899-690-9. Grades: 5–8.

Originally published in Denmark, this illustrated biography captures Andersen's humor and energy. As they read, students discover how events and people in his life appeared in his stories. The colorful illustrations with their rich detailed backgrounds capture the fanciful scenes that reflect his life and his tales. ALSC Notable Children's Book, 2006.

Engle, Margarita. *The Poet Slave of Cuba: A Biography of Juan Francisco Manzano.* Illustrated by Sean Qualls. New York: Henry Holt, 2006. 183p. ISBN 978-0-8050-7706-3. Grades: 7 and up.

This biography in verse is a gripping account of a life lived in slavery filled with cruelty and prejudice. Manzano's story is told through the eyes of those who knew him and through his own eyes. Because he was a slave his talents with words and art had to be kept hidden from all but a few. Pura Belpré Medal Winner for Narrative, 2008.

Explorations

1. Before reading *The Boy on Fairfield Street: How Ted Geisel Grew Up to Become Dr. Seuss* (Krull, 2004), read aloud some of Dr. Seuss's books. Then, place them in a reading corner for students to return to after you read the book.
2. Before reading *My Name Is Gabito: The Life of Gabriel García Márquez* (Brown, 2007), ask the students to listen carefully and note how Gabito's life forms the basis for his stories. After reading the book discuss with the students examples of how events in his life appeared in his stories. Next, have the students talk about

ideas for stories based on their lives and then give them time to write their stories and to share them with their classmates.

3. *My Uncle Emily* (Yolen, 2009) is a wonderful introduction to Emily Dickinson. After reading the book to the students, share with them some of Emily Dickinson's other poems, which can be found at www.poemhunter.com.
4. While previewing *A River of Words: The Story of William Carlos Williams* (Bryant, 2008) with the students point out that the collage illustrations contain an assortment of pieces of paper on which Williams jotted down his thoughts. These thoughts later became inspirations for his poems. Encourage the students to jot down their thoughts in their writing notebooks to use as inspiration during writing workshop.
5. After reading *A River of Words: The Story of William Carlos Williams* (Bryant, 2008), return to the book to remind the students that Williams became frustrated trying to write poems that had a set beat and rhymed. When he began writing free verse, his words flowed. This will help children understand that their poetry does not have to follow a set pattern and does not have to rhyme.
6. *Knucklehead: Tall Tales and Mostly True Stories about Growing Up Scieszka* (Scieszka, 2008) is a terrific model for students to use to write their own autobiographies. After reading one of the tales have the students discuss what they like about it and why it makes them laugh. Then, have one of the students share a memory and have the other students offer suggestions on how to write about the memory. This modeling helps all of the students get ideas for their autobiographies.

TEACHER RESOURCES

Many of the teacher resources in this section can be used throughout the curriculum as teachers and librarians seek a variety of ways to extend the books they use with children. The professional organizations and websites that follow contain resources that teachers can easily adapt for use in their own classrooms.

Book and Media Choices

Bookflix. [Online]. New York: Scholastic, 2009. Grades: P–3.

Pairing Weston Woods video storybooks with Scholastic's nonfiction e-books creates an online resource that enhances reading skills, deepens students' knowledge, and reinforces understanding. A free trial of the site is available.

Culham, Ruth, and Raymond Coutu. *Using Picture Books to Teach Writing with the Traits, K-2*. New York: Scholastic, 2008. 112p. ISBN 978-0-545-02511-9. Grades: K–2.

An annotated bibliography and lesson plans for the traits make this a valuable resource for teachers who recognize the benefits of providing students with mentor texts for their writing. References and indexes conclude the book.

Olness, Rebecca. *Using Literature to Enhance Writing Instruction: A Guide for K–5 Teachers.* Newark, DE: International Reading Association, 2005. 204p. ISBN 978-0-87207-560-3. Grades: K–5.

Olness presents a practical, hands-on guide for using literature as models for students' writing based on the Six Trait Analytical Writing Model. The book includes sample lesson plans, checklists, references, and an index.

Dorfman, Lynne R., and Rose Cappelli. *Mentor Texts: Teaching Writing through Children's Literature, K–6.* Portland, ME: Stenhouse Publishers, 2007. 314p. ISBN 978-1-57110-433-5. Grades: K–6.

Dorfman and Cappelli show how children's literature can provide ideas and inspiration for young writers. Examining children's literature to discover how the author crafted the work provides a model for students as they write their own stories. A list of mentor texts with suggested teaching ideas is included.

Ehmann, Susan, and Kellyann Gayer. *I Can Write Like That! A Guide to Mentor Texts and Craft Studies for Writers' Workshop, K–6.* Newark, DE: International Reading Association, 2009. 176p. ISBN 978-0-87207-708-9. Grades: K–6.

Combining their love of children's literature and their passion for writing, the authors have compiled a collection of books and ideas for showing students how to use texts as models for their own writing.

Fuhrken, Charles. *What Every Elementary Teacher Needs to Know about Reading Tests.* Portland, ME: Stenhouse, 2009. 264p. ISBN 978-1-57110-764-0. Grades: K–6.

Fuhrken drew upon his years spent as a test writer to compile this informative book for teachers about how reading tests are created and how teachers can prepare students to take reading tests. A preview of the book and a study guide are available on the publisher's website at www.stenhouse.com.

Dorfman, Lynne, and Rose Cappelli. *Nonfiction Mentor Texts: Teaching Informational Writing through Children's Literature, K–8.* Portland, ME: Stenhouse, 2009. 304p. ISBN 978-1-57110-496-0. Grades: K–8.

Teaching children how to write information texts can be a challenge; however, these authors simplify the task by showing teachers how to use mentor texts as guides for student writers. A preview of the book is available on the publisher's website at www.stenhouse.com.

Matthew, Kathryn I. *Developing Better Readers and Writers Using Caldecott Books.* New York: Neal-Schuman Publishers, 2006. 256p. ISBN 978-1-55570-557-2. Grades: K–8.

Help students understand the connection between reading and writing by sharing these award-winning books with them. After reading the books with the children, model for them how to use the books as mentor texts for writing. Included are plot summaries for the books, prereading activities, postreading activities, writing activities, and ideas for writing conferences. Noted in the activities are the connections to the English Language Arts and Information Literacy standards.

Lowe, Joy L., and Kathryn I. Matthew. *Puppet Magic*. New York: Neal-Schuman Publishers, 2008. 173p. ISBN 978-1-55570-599-2. Grades: K–8.

Storytelling and puppet shows help develop students oral language and listening skills. This book offers a fun way to develop these essential skills. Using either purchased puppets or puppets created with the patterns in the book, teachers, librarians, and students enjoy retelling favorite tales or writing their own scripts for puppet shows.

Patterson, Kathy. *Real Life Literacy: Classroom Tools That Promote Real-World Reading and Writing*. Portland, ME: Stenhouse, 2006. 128p. ISBN 978-1-55138-204-3. Grades: K–12.

Messages, labels, bus schedules, and checks all require students to be able to read and write. This practical guide helps teachers make connections between the reading and writing students do in the classroom and the reading and writing they do outside of school.

Herrington, Anne, Kevin Hodgson, and Charles Moran, editors. *Teaching the New Writing: Technology, Change, and Assessment in the Twenty-First Century Classroom*. New York: Teachers College Press, 2009. 228p. ISBN 978-0-8077-4964-7. Grades: K and up.

In this book are teachers' stories of how they have incorporated twenty-first-century writing techniques into their classrooms. There are examples of how to use blogs, wikis, podcasts, electronic poetry, and other media to transform students into digital writers. The book concludes with references and an index.

Latrobe, Kathy H., Carolyn S. Brodie, and Maureen White. *The Children's Literature Dictionary: Definitions, Resources, and Learning Activities*. New York: Neal-Schuman, 2002. 282p. ISBN 978-1-55570-424-7. Grades: K and up.

The definitions in this dictionary are accompanied by examples and activities for exploring the terms with students. Not only is this a reference source, it is also a teaching resource. Bibliographical references, appendixes, and an index conclude the book.

Silvey, Anita, editor. *The Essential Guide to Children's Books and Their Creators*. Boston: Houghton Mifflin, 2002. 542p. ISBN 978-0-618-19083-6. Grades: K and up.

Her own quest for a reference book on children's literature led former Horn Book editor Anita Silvey to write this volume that is filled with biographical information on authors and illustrators and critiques of some of their works. The inclusion of authors' and illustrators' comments on their works adds to the usefulness of this resource for author and illustrator studies.

Johnson, Paul. *Get Writing! Creative Book-Making Projects for Children.* London, England: Pembroke, 2005. 64p. ISBN 978-1-55138-201-2. Grades: 1–5.

Each section of this book introduces a basic book form, such as a pop-up book, a shape book, a zigzag book, or a flap book, and then gives examples of different ways the design can be used for a variety of writing projects. Johnson gives detailed advice on how to plan each project, how to draft the text, and how to construct the book.

Angelillo, Janet. *Writing about Reading: From Book Talk to Literary Essays, Grades 3–8.* Portsmouth, NH: Heinemann, 2003. 149p. ISBN 978-0-325-00578-2. Grades: 3–8.

Angelillo suggests reading aloud to students every day and, most important, talking to them about the books. Early in the school year the students form partnerships for talking about the books they are reading and they use notebooks to take notes on what they are reading and notes on their conversations about the books. These conversations and notes are then used as they write about what they have read. The book concludes with a bibliography and a list of recommended children's books.

Bentley, Nancy. *Don't Be a Copycat! Write a Great Report without Plagiarizing.* Berkeley Heights, NJ: Enslow, 2008. 64p. ISBN 978-0-7660-2860-9. Grades: 3–8.

The author presents clear and concise information about how to research and write a report. The history of copyright and how to avoid plagiarism helps students understand this important lesson. A bibliography and an index conclude the book.

Chin, Beverly Ann, editor. *The Dictionary of Characters in Children's Literature.* New York: Franklin Watts, 2002. 128p. ISBN 978-0-531-11984-6. Grades: 3–8.

Characters from traditional literature and contemporary literature as well as characters from other times and places are explored. Author anecdotes add rich details that foster understanding their characters. The book includes notes on how to use the book, a list of characters, a bibliography, and an index.

Culham, Ruth. *The Traits of Writing: A Big Classroom Reference Guide.* New York: Scholastic, 2006. 27p. ISBN 978-0-439-79420-6. Grades: 3 and up.

The six traits of writing—ideas, organization, voice, word choice, sentence fluency, and conventions—are explained. Writing samples showcasing the traits and a scoring rubric make this a practical reference book. Back matter includes bibliographic references and an index.

Culham, Ruth. *Using Picture Books to Teach Writing with the Traits.* New York: Scholastic, 2004. 144p. ISBN 978-0-439-55687-3. Grades: 3 and up.

An annotated bibliography and lesson plans for the writing traits, organization, sentence fluency, voice, presentation, word choice, and ideas provide a useful resource for teachers searching for mentor texts for students' writing. References and indexes conclude the book.

Fletcher, Ralph J. *Boy Writers: Reclaiming Their Voices*. Portland, ME: Stenhouse, 2006. 190p. ISBN 978-1-57110-425-0. Grades: 3 and up.

This noted author and father of four sons offers teachers ideas for engaging male students in a writing workshop. The crucial component is allowing males to choose topics of interest to them, topics that may not be of interest to their female teachers. Filled with anecdotes, writing samples, and practical suggestions, this book is an invaluable resource for educators. A personal note, appendixes, and an index conclude the book. This book is also available on CD.

Professional Organizations

International Reading Association (IRA)
PO Box 8139
Newark, DE 19714-8139
800-336-7323
www.reading.org

Journals: *The Reading Teacher*, *Journal of Adolescent and Adult Literacy*, *Reading Research Quarterly*, *Lectura y Vida*

National Council of Teachers of English (NCTE)
1111 W. Kenyon Road
Urbana, IL 61801-1096
271-328-3870
877-369-6283
www.ncte.org

Journals: *Language Arts, English Journal, Research in the Teaching of English, Primary Voices, Voices from the Middle, Talking Points*

National Reading Conference (NRC)
7044 South 13th Street
Oak Creek, WI 53154
414-980-4924
www.nrconline.org

Journal: *Journal of Literacy Research*

Teachers of English to Speakers of Other Languages (TESOL)
1925 Ballenger Avenue, Suite 550
Alexandria, VA 22314-6820
888-547-3369
www.tesol.org
Journals: *TESOL Journal*, *TESOL Quarterly*, *Essential Teacher*

Internet Sites

A to Z Teacher Stuff
atozteacherstuff.com/stuff

The teacher stuff on this site includes a variety of resources and lesson plans. Resources include links to education sites for teachers, a discussion forum, articles, and units. The site is easy to navigate and includes a search engine.

Between the Lions
pbskids.org/lions/

This award-winning site features games, stories, video clips, and parents' and teachers' resources that promote the literacy growth and development of students ages four to seven. This is a companion site to the Emmy Award-winning PBS program.

The Big6: Information and Technology Skills for Student Achievement
www.big6.com

Ideas and resources for teaching information literacy and problem solving can be found on the Big6 site. Big6 stands for (1) task definition; (2) information-seeking strategies; (3) location and access; (4) use of information; (5) synthesis; and (6) evaluation.

The Children's Literature Web Guide
www.ucalgary.ca/~dKBrown/

It seems as though anything you would expect to find on a children and young adult's website is on this one. There are discussion boards, links to book awards, links to teaching ideas for children's books, resources for teachers, parents, and storytellers, research guides, and even a web-traveler's toolkit.

Disney Educational Productions
disney.go.com/create/#/create/

Click the writer link in order to launch Comic Creator, an easy-to-use online comic book tool. Even reluctant writers are eager to create their own comic strips when they discover that they can include popular Disney characters.

EDSITEment: Literature and Language Arts
edsitement.neh.gov/tab_lesson.asp?subjectArea=4

Sponsored by the National Endowment for the Arts, Thinkfinity.org, and Verizon, the literature and language arts portion of the website includes a searchable database of lesson plans and websites for all grades. This is an outstanding resource.

Gaggle.Net
www.gaggle.net

Designed for students from eight to eighteen, this is an easy-to-use web-based e-mail. Teachers receive master accounts and then create student accounts, which they can monitor. The accounts include address books and allow students to send attachments.

Inkless Tales
www.inklesstales.com
This is an entertaining and educational sampling of stories, crafts, games, and poetry for young children. It is attractive and easy to navigate and also includes children's book reviews and other "cool links" for kids. There are also simple suggestions as to how children can write their own poetry.

Inspiration Software, Inc.
www.inspiration.com
Inspiration and its version for young children, Kidspiration, have been joined by Webspiration, an online collaborative visual thinking and outlining tool. This collection of tools allows students to think visually, to collaborate, and to share knowledge.

International Debate Education Association
www.idebate.org
Having students participate in debates is a great way to develop oral speaking skills and to develop critical thinking. The website houses a collection of teaching tools, including debate formats and debate exercises. There is also information on starting a debate club.

National Writing Project
www.nwp.org
This organization focuses on improving the writing of teachers and their students. There are resources for teachers and information about how to connect with teachers in your area who share a common passion for writing.

Play Kids' Games
www.playkidsgames.com
Features of this site include online games for children from prekindergarten through middle school. Alphabet games, vocabulary games, and memory games can help to build students language arts skills. The site also includes mathematics and geography games.

PoemHunter.com
www.poemhunter.com
This database contains information on poets, poems, song lyrics, quotations, and poetry e-books. It is a place to find poems by a favorite poet or to find poems about a particular topic.

ReadWriteThink
www.readwritethink.org
Sponsored by the International Reading Association and the National Council of Teachers of English, this site contains a searchable database of lesson plans, standards, web resources, and student materials.

Starfall
www.starfall.com
This is a free website that helps teach children to read as well as to speak and listen. There are short stories that concentrate on a vowel or blend sound. By clicking on a word, help is given. This is primarily designed for first grade but can also be used for prekindergarten, kindergarten, and second grade.

Storyline Online
www.storylineonline.net
This site has actors reading favorite storybooks. Students can watch the video and listen to the story with or without captions. On-screen suggestions for activities for responding to the story are included as is a downloadable activity guide. The site is sponsored by the Screen Actors Guild Foundation.

Wikispaces
www.wikispaces.com
Create a free wiki for students to use to write collaboratively or to review books they have read. For a fee, there are secure wikis available for K–12 educators to use with their students.

REFERENCES

Arnold, Ted. 1997. *Parts*. New York: Penguin.

Arnold, Ted. 2001. *More Parts*. New York: Penguin.

Bott, Christie. 2002. "Zines—The Ultimate Creative Writing Project." *English Journal* 92, no. 2 (November): 27–33.

Cohen, Barbara. 2004. "The Zine Project: Writing with a Personal Perspective." *Language Arts* 82, no. 2 (November): 129–139.

Cronin, Doreen. 2005. *Diary of a Spider*. New York: HarperCollins.

Cronin, Doreen. 2007. *Diary of a Fly*. New York: HarperCollins.

Grimes, Nikki. 2000. "The Power of Poetry." *Book Links* 9, no. 4 (March): 32–36.

Headley, Kathy N., and Pamela J. Dunston. 2000. "Teachers' Choices Books and Comprehension Strategies as Transaction Tools." *The Reading Teacher* 54, no. 3 (November): 260–268.

Heller, Ruth. 1991. *Kites Sail High: A Book about Verbs*. New York: Penguin.

Heller, Ruth. 1998. *Behind the Mask: A Book about Prepositions*. New York: Penguin.

Heller, Ruth. 1998. *Many Luscious Lollipops: A Book about Adjectives*. New York: Penguin.

Kissel, Brian, and Karen Wood. 2008. "Side Trip: The Pearls and Perils of Spell-Checkers." *Voices from the Middle* 15, no. 3 (March): 31–32.

National Council of Teachers of English. 1986. *Standards for English Language Arts*. [Online]. Urbana, IL: National Council of Teachers of English. Available: www.ncte

.org/standards (accessed March 8, 2010). Standards for the English Language Arts, by the International Reading Association and the National Council of Teachers of English, © 1996 by the International Reading Association and the National Council of Teachers of English. Reprinted with permission.

Sturtevant, Katherine. 2000. *At the Sign of the Star*. New York: Farrar, Straus and Giroux.

Teague, Mark. 2004. *Detective LaRue: Letters from the Investigation*. New York: Scholastic.

Teague, Mark. 2008. *LaRue for Mayor: Letters from the Campaign Trail*. New York: Scholastic.

Wheeler, Rebecca S., and Rachel Swords. 2006. *Code-Switching: Teaching Standard English in Urban Classrooms.* Urbana, IL: National Council of Teachers of English.

Wilde, Sandra. 2008. "'My Kids Can't Spell and I Don't Want to Deal with It': Spelling in Middle School." *Voices from the Middle* 15, no. 3 (March): 10–15.

Chapter 4

Social Studies

Social studies prepares students to be informed citizens who understand that their actions impact the public good and who realize that they are members of a culturally diverse, interdependent universe. However, mandated high stakes tests at the federal and state level that focus on language arts, mathematics, and science have left little time in the school day for teaching social studies (McGuire, 2007; Olwell and Raphael, 2006; Vogler and Virtue, 2006). One way to include social studies in the curriculum is to integrate it into the reading textbooks, which may improve students' reading skills but does not engender thoughtful learning about civic responsibility (McGuire, 2007). The reading textbook selections may not provide the opportunities for the thoughtful study of social studies, but trade books such as the ones included in the Notable Social Studies Trade Books for Young People do. The National Council for the Social Studies (NCSS) appoints a committee that selects the notable books, many of which are included in this chapter.

The National Council for the Social Studies developed *Curriculum Standards for Social Studies* (NCSS, 1994) that establish guidelines for curriculum development. The social studies standards are divided into thematic strands based on what should be in social studies programs. Social studies programs should include experiences that provide for the study of the following:

1. Culture
2. Time, continuity, and change
3. People, places, and environments
4. Individual development and identity
5. Individuals, groups, and institutions
6. Power, authority, and governance
7. Production, distribution, and consumption
8. Science, technology, and society
9. Global connections
10. Civic ideals and practices

Learning social studies through the pages of trade books, viewing videos, listening to audio files, and participating in software simulations enables students to make connections between their personal lives and the lives of those they encounter in their social studies explorations. The words, images, and sounds capture the readers' attention and imagination as they learn what it means to be citizens of the world. Included in this chapter are trade books and media to enhance the teaching of social studies. Sections in this chapter include American history; government; economics; people, places, and culture; geography; general history; and biographies. The chapter closes with reference books and teacher resources.

AMERICAN HISTORY

This section of the chapter is divided into important time periods in American history. These time periods include: The New World 1530–1760, Struggle for Freedom 1761–1790, A New Nation 1791–1840, A Nation Divided 1841–1865, A Changing Nation 1866–1914, Troubled Times 1915–1945, and A World Power 1946–2010. The time periods are each introduced with a brief description. The study of American history encompasses the second social studies strand, which includes time, continuity, and change. Students come to appreciate and understand that individuals view events from different perspectives and that perspectives change over time. They discover that by studying the past they are better prepared to make informed decisions about the present. Studying American history also provides students with information on how structures of power, authority, and governance impact their lives, which is strand six, and strand nine, which focuses on global connections.

The books and media below offer fascinating details about events, institutions, and individuals in America's past. The books and media offer more in-depth information than the broad surveys of time periods found in textbooks. The authors and creators of the following listed materials have a passionate interest in their topics, which is evident in their works.

The New World 1530–1760

During this time period, ancient peoples and European adventurers explored the Americas, the thirteen original colonies were founded, and colonists arrived in the New World for economic and religious reasons. The colonists endured harsh conditions, but survived with the help of the Native Americans, who joined them in a harvest celebration, our present-day Thanksgiving.

Book and Media Choices

Harness, Cheryl. *Our Colonial Year*. New York: Simon and Schuster, 2005. Unp. ISBN 978-0-689-83479-0. Grades: P–2.

Month by month and colony by colony, young readers discover life during colonial times as they read about the chores and pastimes of colonial children. Historically accurate, detailed illustrations accompany the poetic text.

Isaacs, Sally Senzell. *Life in a Colonial Town.* Chicago: Heinemann, 2001. 32p. ISBN 978-1-57572-312-9. Grades: 1–3.

In two-page chapters complete with colorful drawings, photographs, and reproductions, readers discover life in the original colonies. The book concludes with a glossary, a bibliography, and an index. From the Picture the Past series.

Kamma, Anne. *If You Were at . . . the First Thanksgiving.* Illustrated by Bert Dodson. New York: Scholastic, 2001. 64p. ISBN 978-0-439-10566-8. Grades: 2–4.

With questions such as "Who had to clean the dishes?" this informative book uses a question-and-answer format to teach students about the first Thanksgiving. A series of questions and answers even reveal what the real menu would have been for the first Thanksgiving. From the If You . . . series.

Quasha, Jennifer. *Jamestown: Hands-on Projects about One of America's First Communities.* New York: Rosen, 2001. 24p. ISBN 978-0-8239-5701-9. Grades: 2–4.

This introduction to Jamestown includes eight projects with step-by-step instructions. For example, there are instructions for making a hornbook and a topographical map. A glossary, a list of websites, and an index conclude the book. From the Great Social Studies Projects series.

Furbee, Mary R. *Outrageous Women of Colonial America.* Hoboken, NJ: Wiley, 2001. 118p. ISBN 978-0-471-38299-7. Grades: 3–6.

Abigail Adams, Phillis Wheatley, Betsy Ross, and Peggy Shippen Arnold are some of the outrageous women featured in this book. The women's exploits are described in colorful, yet thought-provoking language. They were spies, soldiers, scouts, and slaves. Black-and-white illustrations, maps, and reproductions enhance the stories. The book includes suggested readings, a timeline, and the names of four other Colonial women for students to research. From the Outrageous Women series.

Platt, Richard. *Pirate Diary: The Journal of Jake Carpenter.* Illustrated by Chris Riddell. Cambridge, MA: Candlewick, 2005. 64p. ISBN 978-0-7636-2865-9. Grades: 3–6.

Based on the real adventures of sailors who became pirates in order to escape mistreatment by merchant ship captains, this fictional tale recounts ten-year-old Jake Carpenter's adventures. In 1716, Jake left his home in North Carolina with dreams of becoming a sailor; instead he ended up a pirate. A readers' note, a combination glossary and index, and a bibliography are included.

Yero, Judith Lloyd. *The Mayflower Compact.* Des Moines, IA: National Geographic, 2006. 40p. ISBN 978-0-7922-5892-6. Grades: 3–8.

This document of fewer than 200 words gave the Pilgrims rules to guide their lives in the New World. It also became the foundation for America's democracy. The book includes the full text of the document, prints, photographs, a glossary, and an index. From the American Document Series. Notable Social Studies Trade Book for Young People, 2007.

Freedman, Russell. *Who Was First? Discovering the Americas.* New York: Clarion, 2007. 88p. ISBN 978-0-618-66391-0. Grades: 5–9.

North America and South America have been discovered and settled more than once. Reproductions, charts, maps, and artifacts tell the stories of Vikings, Chinese sailors, Native Americans, and prehistoric adventurers who have all discovered the Americas. Chapter notes, a selected bibliography, and an index conclude the book. Notable Social Studies Trade Book for Young People, 2008.

Wulffson, Don L. *Before Columbus: Early Voyages to the Americas.* Minneapolis, MN: Lerner, 2008. 128p. ISBN 978-0-8225-5978-8. Grades: 5–9.

Combining facts and speculations, Wulffson presents intriguing information about early explorers of the Americas from Phoenicians to Romans to Chinese to Vikings to Columbus. Photographs, maps, sidebars, and illustrations illuminate the details of these early voyages. An introduction, source notes, a selected bibliography, resources for learning more, and an index are included.

Carbone, Elisa. *Blood on the River: James Town 1607.* New York: Penguin, 2006. 237p. ISBN 978-0-670-06060-3. Grades: 6–8.

Orphan Samuel Collier had to fend for himself at an early age, so he learned to fight in order to survive, and he developed a strong, independent spirit. His determination to live served him well when he was transported to James Town as Captain John Smith's page. However, he had to learn to temper his strong, independent spirit and to realize that in the New World survival depended on cooperation. Notable Social Studies Trade Book for Young People, 2007.

Walker, Sally M. *Written in Bone: Buried Lives of Jamestown and Colonial Maryland.* New York: Lerner, 2009. 144p. ISBN 978-0-8225-7135-3. Grades: 6–9.

Walker takes readers along as she joins forensic anthropologists excavating the graves of colonial leaders, indentured servants, and African slaves. She meticulously explains how the anthropologists draw conclusions from the human remains and artifacts they uncover. The book concludes with source notes, bibliographic references, a timeline, resources for learning more, and an index. From the Exceptional Social Studies Titles for Intermediate Grades series.

Sixteenth- and Seventeenth-Century Turning Points in U.S. History. DVD. New York: Ambrose Video, 2008. 200 min. Grades: 6 and up.

Using a variety of presentation techniques, this two-disc series chronicles the settling of the New World from 1502 to the end of the seventeenth century. Both well-known and lesser-known leaders come alive through artwork and video re-creations. A preview of the video is available on the company's website at www.ambrosevideo.com.

Explorations

1. *Life in a Colonial Town* (Isaacs, 2001) readily lends itself to a lesson on comparing and contrasting, as students immediately discover differences in their life and the lives of the people in the colonial town.
2. The question-and-answer format in *If You Were at . . . the First Thanksgiving* (Kamma, 2001) is a useful tool for reading and remembering. As you share the book with students, discuss the format with them. Then, as you read other books with the students help them formulate questions to answer as you read.
3. Before reading *Blood on the River: James Town 1607* (Carbone, 2006), introduce the students to www.virtualjamestown.org. Perusing the site index is a great way to get started learning about Jamestown and to find materials to meet the diverse needs and interests of students. For example, the images of artifacts introduce students to realia of the period and help to build their background knowledge.
4. While reading *Blood on the River: James Town 1607* (Carbone, 2006), explore www.history.com/minisites/jamestownanniversary/ as this interactive website will enhance students' understanding of the book. The site contains videos and graphics depicting life in James Town.
5. After reading *Blood on the River: James Town 1607* (Carbone, 2006), use a projection system to show the students the lists of colonists and their occupations that are on the website www.virtualjamestown.org. These lists are sure to spark a discussion on the usefulness of some of the occupations such as gentlemen and perfumer.
6. After reading *Written in Bone: Buried Lives of Jamestown and Colonial Maryland* (Walker, 2009) students can participate in unraveling the Secret in the Cellar webcomic at anthropology.si.edu/writteninbone/comic/. The Webcomic was developed in conjunction with the Written in Bone exhibit at the Smithsonian Museum of Natural History.
7. After reading *Written in Bone: Buried Lives of Jamestown and Colonial Maryland* (Walker, 2009) students can examine forensic case files at anthropology.si.edu/writteninbone/forensic_files.html in order to learn more about how archaeological investigations uncover skeleton's stories.

Struggle for Freedom 1761–1790

Around the world Spain, France, and England were competing for land during the 1700s. As the traders and settlers from the thirteen American colonies moved westward they began to encroach on the Indians' lands and on land claimed by the French. In 1754, skirmishes between France and Britain broke out in the Ohio River Valley. These skirmishes marked the beginning of the French and Indian War that lasted for nine years. At the end of the war, England needed to raise money to repay the money borrowed to finance the war. England looked to the thirteen American colonies and began imposing taxes. The colonists did not believe that the British had the right to tax them and began protesting. As part of this protest, the colonists drafted the Declaration of Independence declaring themselves free of English rule. However, England was not willing to give up the colonies without a fight and so England and the colonies were soon embroiled in the Revolutionary War.

Book and Media Choices

Edwards, Pamela Duncan. *Boston Tea Party*. Illustrated by Henry Cole. New York: Penguin, 2001. Unp. ISBN 978-0-399-23357-9. Grades: 1–3.

This cumulative narrative tale, a lively imitation of "The House That Jack Built," has young readers chiming in as the story is read. To add to the fun, a band of lively, knowledgeable mice scamper across the bottom of the pages adding their own special commentary as the story unfolds. From picking tea in India to the tea tax to the Boston Tea Party to the revolution, this is a concise rendering of an important event in American history. The book ends with a mice-enhanced timeline of events that begins in 1763 with the end of the French and Indian War and ends in 1783 with the signing of the Treaty of Paris.

Krensky, Stephen. *Dangerous Crossing: The Revolutionary Voyage of John Quincy Adams*. Illustrated by Greg Harlin. New York: Penguin, 2005. Unp. ISBN 978-0-525-46966-7. Grades: 3–5.

When John Adams set out to secure European support for the Revolutionary War, his ten-year-old son Johnny Adams accompanied him. The eventful voyage is told through the eyes of young Johnny interspersed with quotes from John Adams' diary. Watercolor illustrations depict the clothing of the times and life aboard the ship. A map at the beginning of the book charts their journey across the sea and an author's note at the end gives additional information about John Adams and John Quincy Adams. Notable Social Studies Trade Book for Young People, 2006.

Schanzer, Rosalyn. *George vs. George: The American Revolution as Seen from Both Sides*. Des Moines, IA: National Geographic, 2004. 60p. ISBN 978-0-7922-7349-3. Grades: 3–7.

Schanzer introduces George Washington and King George III, notes that there are two sides to every disagreement, and then presents both men's views on government, taxation, the Boston Tea Party, and many of the Revolutionary War battles. Quotes from both the men and their contemporaries coupled with detailed research make this an interesting and very useful book for social studies classes. Orbis Pictus Honor Book, 2005.

Freedman, Russell. *Washington at Valley Forge*. New York: Holiday House, 2008. 100p. ISBN 978-0-8234-2069-8. Grades: 4–8.

Washington credited the success of the American Revolution to the soldiers encamped at Valley Forge during the winter of 1777 to 1778. Freezing cold, starvation, disease, and a lack of warm clothing were the unbearable conditions that the Continental Army endured. Freedman tells not only Washington's story, but also the story of some of the individual soldiers who were camped with him. Maps, quotations, a timeline, a bibliographic essay, and an index are included. Notable Social Studies Trade Book for Young People, 2009. Orbis Pictus Honor Book, 2009.

Fritz, Jean. *Six Revolutionary War Figures.* DVD. New York: Weston Woods, 2007. 16 min. ISBN 978-0-545-02764-9. Grades: 5–8.

Jean Fritz narrates this video based on her well-known books on Paul Revere, King George, Benjamin Franklin, Patrick Henry, Samuel Adams, and John Hancock. The narration is accompanied by music by the Colonial Williamsburg Fife and Drum Corps.

The Revolutionary War (1776–1783). Wynnewood, PA: Schlessinger Media, 2004. 23 min. ISBN 978-1-41710-184-9. Grades: 5–8.

With the Declaration of Independence, the colonies made it known that they were ready to form a new nation. The video includes viewpoints from both sides of the ocean. The audio is in both English and Spanish and a teacher's guide is available. From the American Revolution for Students DVD series.

Yero, Judith Lloyd. *The Declaration of Independence.* Des Moines, IA: National Geographic, 2006. 40p. ISBN 978-0-7922-5396-2. Grades: 6–8.

Events leading up to the Declaration of Independence give students the background they need to understand the impact of this document. Information is also included about the unfinished business of the document, including slavery and women's rights. The book includes the full text of the document, prints, and photographs. From the American Document Series. Notable Social Studies Trade Book for Young People, 2007.

Allen, Thomas B. *George Washington, Spymaster: How the Americans Outspied the British and Won the Revolutionary War.* Illustrated by Cheryl Harness. Des Moines, IA: National Geographic, 2004. 192p. ISBN 978-1-42630-041-7. Grades: 6–9.

Archival art, pen-and-ink sketches, and Washington's secret codebook accompany this riveting account of espionage during the Revolutionary War. Washington, Benjamin Franklin (who was in Paris), Benedict Arnold, and covert women were all involved in spying on the British. A bibliography and an index are included.

Bober, Natalie S. *Countdown to Independence: A Revolution of Ideas in England and Her Colonies, 1760–1776.* New York: Antheneum, 2001. 342p. ISBN 978-1-41696-392-9. Grades: 7 and up.

Bober presents an objective examination of issues leading up to the American Revolution from the perspectives of individuals on both sides of the Atlantic. Quotes from the main characters, anecdotes, photographs, and illustrations complement the well-researched, readable text that examines a crucial time in American history. Included are an author's note, a chronology, lists of the main characters, reference notes, a bibliography, and an index.

Explorations

1. *Boston Tea Party* (Edwards, 2001) can easily be turned into a choral reading. Participating in choral reading helps students become fluent readers while they develop their oral speaking skills.
2. After reading *Dangerous Crossing: The Revolutionary Voyage of John Quincy Adams* (Krensky, 2005) the students can view some of John Adams' diaries on the Massachusetts Historical Society website at www.masshist.org/digitaladams/aea/diary/. Clicking on the link that lists the diaries by date, students can learn about his preparations for his journey including the fact that he had guineas sewn into the garment to hide them in case he was captured at sea. Unfortunately, the garment was stolen on the road between Bourdeaux and Paris.
3. *George vs. George: The American Revolution as Seen from Both Sides* (Schanzer, 2004) is a great way to involve students in debates. Using this book as a model, students can examine other issues in their social studies class from more than one perspective.
4. *Washington at Valley Forge* (Freedman, 2008) includes quotations from the participants and reproductions of engravings, drawings, and paintings. Use a document camera to project them for the students and engage them in focusing on what can be learned from the quotes and illustrations.
5. The codebook in *George Washington, Spymaster: How the Americans Outspied the British and Won the Revolutionary War* (Allen, 2004) may be just the thing to motivate reluctant writers. As they read the book, they can use the code to jot down notes about their reading and then exchange their notes with partners to decipher.

A New Nation 1791–1840

In 1789, George Washington was sworn in as the first president of the United States. He faced the monumental task of establishing a strong government to lead the new nation. His leadership established precedents for governing the nation that are followed to this day. For example, Washington established the precedent of each president serving only two terms in office. This period in American history was characterized by westward expansion and before it ended America extended from the Atlantic Ocean to the Pacific Ocean. It was also during this period that northern states developed industry and established trade routes and southern states developed large farms. The Indian Removal Act of 1830 forced Native Americans onto reservations and homesteaders carved the Indians' lands into farms.

Book and Media Choices

Cotten, Cynthia. *Abbie in Stitches*. Illustrated by Beth Peck. New York: Farrar, Straus and Giroux, 2006. Unp. ISBN 978-0-374-30004-3. Grades: P–2.

Abbie would rather be reading than stitching. But in the 1800s, proper young ladies learned to stitch samplers. Resigned to the fact that she had to create a sampler, hers included a book and the words "I would rather read." For her persistence in finishing the sampler, her mother presented her with a copy of *Gulliver's Travels*. An author's note explains that the story was written after she read about a sampler created by a young woman whose sampler proclaimed that she hated stitching and loved to read. Notable Social Studies Trade Book for Young People, 2007.

Kay, Verla. *Rough, Tough Charley*. Illustrated by Adam Gustavson. New York: Ten Speed, 2007. Unp. ISBN 978-1-58246-184-7. Grades: K–3.

In a time when women were not allowed to vote and were thought to be the weaker sex, one woman lived her life as a man, Charley Parkhurst. This real-life renowned stagecoach driver's secret was not revealed until her death, and in this book her secret is not revealed until the end of the rhyming text. Realistic oil paintings depict the excitement and adventure of her life. Notable Social Studies Trade Book for Young People, 2008.

Broyles, Anne. *Priscilla and the Hollyhocks*. Illustrated by Anna Alter. Watertown, MA: Charlesbridge, 2008. Unp. ISBN 978-1-57091-675-5. Grades: 2–4.

This book tells the story of a young slave girl, Priscilla, whose mother is sold. Priscilla gathers solace from the patch of hollyhocks her mother planted. At the death of her master she is sold to a Cherokee plantation owner and eventually ends up on the "Trail of Tears." A businessman, Silkwood, rescues her and sets her free, raising her as one of his own children. An author's note adds additional details about the real Priscilla and the hollyhocks she grew. Notable Social Studies Trade Book for Young People, 2009.

Lawlor, Laurie. *The School at Crooked Creek*. New York: Holiday House, 2004. 83p. ISBN 978-0-8234-1812-1. Grades: 2–5.

Set in Indiana in the 1820s, six-year-old Beansie does not want to brave the snow, the woods, the wild animals, and the "Injuns" to walk a mile to school. Details about life on a homestead coupled with familiar childhood fears and triumphs will engage young readers as they learn about this time in American history.

Maestro, Betsy. *A New Nation: The United States, 1783–1815*. Illustrated by Giulio Maestro. New York: HarperCollins, 2009. 64p. ISBN 978-0-688-16015-9. Grades: 3–6.

The struggles and triumphs of the new nation are chronicled in detailed watercolor illustrations and maps along with narrative text that lends itself to reading aloud. Quotations, tables of dates, and an index conclude the book.

Blumberg, Rhonda. *York's Adventures with Lewis and Clark: An African-American's Part in the Great Expedition.* New York: HarperCollins, 2004. 88p. ISBN 978-0-06-009113-2. Grades: 4–8.

York was Clark's slave and his invaluable assistance to the expedition is the focus of this book. His strength, agility, and hunting abilities earned him respect and acceptance during the expedition; however, when they returned he was once again treated as a slave. He did not receive the double pay and the acreage that other members of the expedition were awarded. Maps, portraits, sketches, quotes, and photographs help to document his story. Bibliographic references and an index conclude the book. Orbis Pictus Award, 2005.

Silate, Jennifer. *The Calhoun-Randolph Debate on the Eve of the War of 1812: A Primary Source Investigation.* New York: Rosen, 2005. 64p. ISBN 978-1-40420-150-7. Grades: 5–8.

Using primary source documents including maps, photographs, letters, and speeches, Silate explains the opposing viewpoints of congressmen John Calhoun and John Randolph as the nation headed into the War of 1812. References and an index conclude the book. From the Great Historic Debates and Speeches.

Stewart, Mark. *The Indian Removal Act: Forced Relocation.* Mankato, MN: Compass Point, 2007. 96p. ISBN 978-0-7565-2452-4. Grades: 6–8.

The Indian Removal Act of 1830 forced Native Americans to give up their lands and march 800 miles westward. The journey along the Trail of Tears, through the fall and winter of 1838, resulted in many deaths due to disease, exposure to the elements, and exhaustion. Photographs, maps, portraits, and documents enhance the well-organized text that contains a great deal of information. Included in the book are a timeline, a glossary, source notes, bibliographies, and an index. This book is available as an e-book. From the Snapshots in History series.

Jurmain, Suzanne. *The Forbidden Schoolhouse: The True and Dramatic Story of Prudence Crandall and Her Students.* Boston, MA: Houghton Mifflin, 2005. 160p. ISBN 978-0-618-47302-1. Grades: 6 and up.

When Prudence Crandall decided to admit African-American young women to her private academy, the white citizens of Canterbury, Connecticut, protested. They dumped manure down her well, they had her arrested, and they convinced the state legislature to pass a law making it illegal for African Americans from other states to attend the school. Photographs accompany this fast-paced story of the clash between individuals and institutions. The book concludes with an author's note, an epilogue, an appendix, notes, a bibliography, and an index. Notable Social Studies Trade Book for Young People, 2006.

Nineteenth-Century Turning Points in U.S. History. DVD. New York: Ambrose Video, 2002. 200 min. Grades: 7 and up.

In the nineteenth century, the United States expanded from sixteen states to forty-five states and grew to be an industrial power. The four DVDs in this set tell the story using reenactments, journal readings, narration, paintings, and drawings. A preview of the video is available on the company's website at www.ambrosevideo.com and downloadable documents are available to supplement the information in the video.

Explorations

1. Before reading *Abbie in Stitches* (Cotten, 2006) ask the students to share things their parents require them to do that they would prefer not to do. Record their ideas on the board and then have them discuss why they think their parents make them do things they do not want to do.
2. Before reading *Rough, Tough Charley* (Kay, 2007), share the action packed realistic illustrations with the students and have them make predictions about the story.
3. After reading *Rough, Tough Charley* (Kay, 2007), engage the students in a discussion of why Charley lived her life as a man. Then, have them talk about careers that are available to women in the present time.
4. Additional information and resources for learning about *The Indian Removal Act: Forced Relocation* (Stewart, 2007) can be found on the National Park Service Trail of Tears website at www.nps.gov/trte/index.htm.
5. On the Connecticut Commission on Culture and Tourism website at www.cultureandtourism.org is a link to the Prudence Crandall museum. Summaries of her three trials are posted there and can be downloaded for the students to read. After reading through the summaries, engage students in a discussion of the summaries. NCSS standard five examines the intersection of individuals, groups, and institutions, which can be addressed in this discussion.

A Nation Divided 1841–1865

This time period in American history was one of great unrest as Americans fought for equal rights for its citizens. In America, abolitionists worked to free slaves, women sought basic rights, and reformers tried to improve schools and prisons. There was also unrest in Texas, as Texans fought Mexico for their independence. In 1861, the Civil War began and for four long years Northern states and Southern states were locked in a bitter battle over slavery.

Book and Media Choices

Woodruff, Elvira. *Small Beauties: The Journey of Darcy Heart O'Hara.* Illustrated by Adam Rex. New York: Alfred A. Knopf, 2006. Unp. ISBN 978-0-375-82686-3. Grades: P–5.

Born in Ireland during the 1800s, Darcy was a noticer and a collector of small beauties, such as pebbles, flowers, and butterfly wings. Forced to emigrate from

Ireland, Darcy's family travels to America. Sitting in a cramped city cellar, Darcy brings out her small beauties and comforts her homesick family. The last beauty she shows them is a piece of slate from the family's hearthstone. An author's note at the end of the book reveals that Henry Ford's grandparents left Ireland in 1847 and when he went back to visit Ireland he shipped home a hearthstone from his grandparent's cottage. Notable Social Studies Trade Book for Young People, 2007.

Fuchs, Bernie. *Ride Like the Wind: A Tale of the Pony Express.* New York: Scholastic, 2004. Unp. ISBN 978-0-439-26645-1. Grades: K–4.

Mark Twain's account of seeing a Pony Express rider and a storyteller's note at the beginning of the book provide background information that helps young readers understand this fictional account of a young rider riding like the wind to deliver the mail. The book concludes with additional information about the Pony Express.

Woodson, Jacqueline. *Show Way.* Illustrated by Hudson Talbott. New York: Putnam, 2005. Unp. ISBN 978-0-399-23749-2. Grades: K–5.

Woodson shares her own story of how her culture helped to shape her life in this picture book account of how African-American women's quilt creations pointed the way to freedom. Newbery Medal Honor Book, 2006. ALSC Notable Children's Book, 2006.

Fletcher, Susan. *Dadblamed Union Army Cow.* Illustrated by Kimberly Bulcken Root. Unp. ISBN 978-0-7636-2263-3. Grades: 2–5.

During the Civil War, the Fifty-Ninth Regiment of Indiana Volunteers was accompanied by a cow, which refused to stay behind when her owner joined the Union Army. Lyrical text and expressive, humorous illustrations make this an engaging book. An author's note reveals that the book is based on newspaper stories. Notable Social Studies Trade Book for Young People, 2008.

Levine, Ellen. *Henry's Freedom Box.* Illustrated by Kadir Nelson. New York: Scholastic, 2007. Unp. ISBN 978-0-439-77733-9. Grades: 2–5.

Based on the true story of Henry "Box" Brown, this compelling story tells how he escaped to freedom by shipping himself north in a wooden crate. Pencil, watercolor, and oil illustrations depict the sorrow, suspense, and joy of Henry's journey. Caldecott Medal Honor Book, 2008. Notable Social Studies Trade Book for Young People, 2008.

Ichord, Loretta Frances. *Skillet Bread, Sourdough, and Vinegar Pie: Cooking in Pioneer Days.* Illustrated by Jan Davey Ellis. Brookfield, CT: Millbrook Press, 2003. 64p. ISBN 978-0-7613-1864-4. Grades: 3–5.

Imagine trying to store food without a refrigerator. This book explains how pioneers preserved and stored their food, but it does not stop there, as it also discusses how to make a campfire, tells what cowboys ate on the trail, and describes the influences of different ethnic groups on the foods that the pioneers ate. Each chapter ends with a recipe or two. Includes an appendix, source notes, bibliography, and an index. Notable Social Studies Trade Book for Young People, 2004.

Oregon Trail, Fifth Edition. Win. Hiawatha, IA: Broderbund Software, 2008. Grades: 3–5.

Players join pioneers as they travel the Oregon Trail in this challenging simulation that involves decision making, team building, and problem solving. Survival is not certain and players quickly learn that the wrong decision leads to disaster.

McComb, Marianne. *The Emancipation Proclamation*. Des Moines, IA: National Geographic, 2006. 40p. ISBN 978-0-7922-7936-5. Grades: 3–8.

Readers learn how the differences in the economies of the northern and southern states impacted their stands on slavery and that Lincoln's signing of the document hastened the Civil War. The book includes the full text of the document, prints, and photographs. From the American Document Series. Notable Social Studies Trade Book for Young People, 2007.

Curtis, Christopher Paul. *Elijah of Buxton*. New York: Scholastic, 2007. 341p. ISBN 978-0-439-02344-3. Grades: 3–8.

Eleven-year-old Elijah was the first child born free in the settlement of Buxton, a Canadian haven for escaped slaves. When a preacher steals the money that was being saved to free a family of slaves, Elijah sets out with Mr. Leroy to recover the money. Along the way Mr. Leroy dies, but Elijah continues on and witnesses first-hand the horror of slavery. This is a gripping tale with a powerful ending. An author's note about Buxton concludes the book. Coretta Scott King Author Award Winner, 2008. Newbery Medal Honor Book, 2008. Notable Social Studies Trade Book for Young People, 2007.

Murphy, Jim. *Desperate Journey*. New York: Scholastic, 2006. 256p. ISBN 978-043907806-1. Grades: 5–8.

Travel the Erie Canal with Maggie Haggerty as she takes responsibility for delivering a shipment after her father and uncle are arrested for assault. If the shipment is not in Buffalo on time, the family will lose their boat. At the end of the book is a map of the Erie Canal, information about the canal, and a glossary. Notable Social Studies Trade Book for Young People, 2007.

Denenberg, Barry. *Lincoln Shot: A President's Life Remembered*. Illustrated by Christopher Bing. New York: Macmillan, 2008. 40p. ISBN 978-0-312-37013-8. Grades: 5 and up.

Designed to resemble a nineteenth-century tabloid, this oversized edition of *The National News* looks back on Lincoln's life one year after his death. Yellowed pages, vintage photographs, period advertisements, and stories of Lincoln's career and personal life make this an engrossing book. Incorporated into the book is a history of the Civil War. NCTE Notable Children's Book in the Language Arts, 2009.

Lewis, J. Patrick. *The Brothers' War: Civil War Voices in Verse.* Photographs by Civil War photographers. Des Moines, IA: National Geographic, 2007. Unp. ISBN 978-1-42630-037-0. Grades: 6–9.

Moving poems matched with Civil War photographs tell the horror of this war from both sides and present the very human side of war. A table of contents, a timeline, a map, author's notes on the poems, a bibliography, and notes on the photographs are included. This book is available on CD. Notable Social Studies Trade Book for Young People, 2008.

Nelson, Marilyn. *Fortune's Bones: The Manumission Requiem.* Notes and annotations by Pamela Espeland. Asheville, NC: Front Street, 2004. 32p. ISBN 978-1-932425-12-3. Grades: 6 and up.

Poetry, photos, reproductions, notes, and annotations tell the story of how the bones of a slave named Fortune came to be displayed in the Mattatuck Museum in Waterbury, Connecticut. When Fortune died, his physician owner preserved his bones in order to study the human skeleton. Nelson celebrates Fortune's life with this series of poems. Coretta Scott King Author Award Honor Book, 2005.

Walker, Sally M. *Secrets of a Civil War Submarine: Solving the Mysteries of the H.L. Hunley.* Minneapolis, MN: Lerner, 2005. 112p. ISBN 978-1-57505-830-6. Grades: 6 and up.

A mystery from the Civil War unfolds in this fascinating book about Horace L. Hunley's submarine that was designed to sink enemy ships. On its one and only mission, it sunk the USS Housatonic. Unfortunately, the submarine never returned from its mission. The first part of the book describes the construction of the submarine and the second part of the book focuses on locating and recovering the submarine. This book is also available on a CD that includes photographs, maps, and illustrations from the book. Robert F. Sibert Informational Book Medal Winner, 2006.

Worth, Richard. *The Slave Trade in America: Cruel Commerce.* Berkeley Heights, NJ: Enslow, 2004. 128p. ISBN 978-0-7660-2151-8. Grades: 6 and up.

This book focuses on the slave trade during the 1600s and the 1700s. Personal narratives, primary source document excerpts, and illustrations add impact to the readable text that informs without overwhelming readers. A timeline, chapter notes, a glossary, resources for learning more, and an index conclude the book. From the Slavery in American History series.

Explorations

1. Before reading *Ride Like the Wind: A Tale of the Pony Express* (Fuchs, 2004) show the students the video tour of the Pony Express Museum at www.ponyexpress.org/,

as this video provides the students with background knowledge to facilitate their understanding of the Pony Express.

2. Adding food to a lesson always motivates students and *Skillet Bread, Sourdough, and Vinegar Pie: Cooking in Pioneer Days* (Ichord, 2003) combines pioneer recipes and learning. This book also lends itself to having students make comparisons between food preparation and food storage then and now.
3. Before reading *Elijah of Buxton* (Curtis, 2007) have the students visit the Buxton National Historic Site and Museum at www.buxtonmuseum.com/index.html to learn about the history of the settlement.
4. Before reading *Desperate Journey* (Murphy, 2006) have the students listen to the podcast available on the Scholastic website at bookwizard.scholastic.com/tbw/viewWorkDetail.do?workId=4454&. A lesson plan for the book is also available on this website.
5. Before reading *Desperate Journey* (Murphy, 2006) have the students read the material at the end of the book and conduct additional research on the Erie Canal. Building their prior knowledge about the Erie Canal will help them understand the story.
6. Using *Lincoln Shot: A President's Life Remembered* (Denenberg, 2008) as a model and a software-publishing program, students can create their own version of a newspaper based on another president of the United States or a noted personage in history.
7. The pairing of poems and photographs in *The Brothers' War: Civil War Voices in Verse* (Lewis, 2007) make excellent models for students' writing. Students can write their own poems to accompany the photographs or search for other photographs from the Civil War to write poems about.
8. After reading *Fortune's Bones: The Manumission Requiem* (Nelson, 2004), have the students visit the Mattatuck Museum at www.fortunestory.org/fortune/ to learn more about Fortune and the debate concerning whether his bones should be interred. After the students have examined the issue from both sides, they can debate the fate of Fortune's bones. As they research Fortune's life the students can create a blog to share and organize their thoughts at www.blogger.com.
9. Students interested in learning more about the *Secrets of a Civil War Submarine: Solving the Mysteries of the H.L. Hunley* (Walker, 2005) can be directed to the Friends of the Hunley website at www.hunley.org.

A Changing Nation 1866–1914

After the Civil War, Americans began moving westward in great numbers, agriculture flourished, the transcontinental railroad was completed, and rapid industrialization occurred. As Americans moved west, immigrants from other lands arrived and settled in eastern cities. The immigrants lived in tenements in the cities and were exploited by the industrial barons.

Book and Media Choices

Hopkinson, Deborah. *Stagecoach Sal: Inspired by a True Tale.* Illustrated by Carson Ellis. New York: Hyperion, 2009. Unp. ISBN 978-1-42311-149-8. Grades: 1–3.

Based on the real-life adventures of Delia Haskett Rawson, who at fourteen began driving stagecoaches and delivering mail, this rollicking tale tells of her encounter with the bandit Poetic Pete. Hopkinson's version of the story has Sal singing Pete to sleep as she delivers him to jail in the next town. A biography of Rawson, the first woman stagecoach driver, concludes the book.

Roop, Peter, and Connie Roop. *Louisiana Purchase.* Illustrated by Sally Wern Comport. New York: Simon and Schuster, 2004. 84p. ISBN 978-0-689-86443-8. Grades: 3–5.

Background on the events leading up to the Louisiana Purchase, information on the purchase, events happening just after the purchase, and biographical sketches of important people are all included in this concise history. A map, resources for learning more, the first page of the treaty, a glossary, a timeline, and an index are included. From the Milestone Book series.

Nelson, Vaunda Micheaux. *Bad News for Outlaws: The Remarkable Life of Bass Reeves, Deputy U.S. Marshall.* Illustrated by R. Gregory Christie. Minneapolis, MN: Lerner, 2009. 40p. ISBN 978-0-8225-6764-6. Grades: 3–6.

From slave to lawman in the Old West, Reeves, was known for always getting his man. His ability to communicate with the Native Americans, his knowledge of the Indian territory, and his skills with a firearm combined to make him a legendary lawmaker who protected the rights of settlers.

Sandler, Martin W. *Island of Hope: The Story of Ellis Island and the Journey to America.* New York: Scholastic, 2004. 144p. ISBN 978-0-439-53082-8. Grades: 4 and up.

Using primary source documents including memoirs, photographs, interviews, and oral histories, Sandler lets the immigrants tell their own stories. The fascinating details of the story of Ellis Island are interspersed with sidebars containing the personal stories of immigrants such as Golda Meier, former Israel Prime Minister, and Isaac Bashevis Singer, an award-winning author.

Winthrop, Elizabeth. *Counting on Grace.* Illustrated by Patience Brewster. New York: Random House, 2006. 232p. ISBN 978-0-385-90878-8. Grades: 5–8.

A Lewis Hine photograph of a child working in a Vermont cotton mill led to this historical fiction work about child labor. Winthrop explores the issue of child labor in America in 1910 through the eyes of a young immigrant girl, Grace Forcier. Notable Social Studies Trade Book for Young People, 2007.

Haddix, Margaret. *Uprising.* New York: Simon and Schuster, 2007. 346p. ISBN 978-1-41691-171-5. Grades: 6–8.

This historical novel, based on the tragic fire at the Triangle Shirtwaist Factory, explores the power of factory owners and the plight of immigrants who worked and died in American sweatshops. This poignant story is told from the viewpoints of three young girls, only one of whom survives the fire. The book concludes with an afterword. Notable Social Studies Trade Book for Young People, 2008.

Nelson, Scott Reynolds, with Marc Aronson. *Ain't Nothing but a Man: My Quest to Find the Real John Henry.* Des Moines, IA: National Geographic, 2008. 64p. ISBN 978-1-42630-001-1. Grades: 6–9.

As he searched for the real John Henry, historian Nelson uncovered stories about the African-American prisoners, who helped build railroads through the South. Readers follow along as he describes his research process and how he used primary and secondary sources. Appendixes include background information, different versions of the song, a map of the Chesapeake and Ohio railroad line, information on how to be a historian, and resources for learning more. ALSC Notable Children's Book, 2009.

Gourley, Catherine. *Gibson Girls and Suffragists: Perceptions of Women from 1900 to 1918.* Minneapolis, MN: Lerner, 2008. 144p. ISBN 978-0-8225-7150-6. Grades: 7 and up.

This chronologically organized book is filled with photographs and reproductions of magazine, radio, and television advertisements that vividly portray stereotypical feminine roles. The book includes an author's note, a prologue, an epilogue, resources for learning more, and an index. From the Images and Issues of Women in the Twentieth Century series. Notable Social Studies Trade Book for Young People, 2008.

Explorations

1. Prior to reading *Stagecoach Sal: Inspired by a True Tale* (Hopkinson, 2009) share images on the Wells Fargo History website with the students to build their background knowledge. The website can be accessed at www.wellsfargohistory.com/stagecoach/index.html.
2. While reading *Island of Hope: The Story of Ellis Island and the Journey to America* (Sandler, 2004) have the student visit The Statue of Liberty—Ellis Island Foundation at www.ellisisland.org/.
3. While reading *Ain't Nothing but a Man: My Quest to Find the Real John Henry* (Nelson, 2008), visit The John and Ruby Lomax 1939 Southern States Recording Trip website at memory.loc.gov/ammem/lohtml/ to access recordings of the song "John Henry."

Troubled Times 1915–1945

Two world wars and the Great Depression marked this time period in history. In 1917, Americans were brought into World War I and following the war Americans' lives began to change. Prohibition made it illegal to make or sell liquor. Women gained the right to vote. Movies and jazz became part of the culture of the nation. Then, the nation's prosperity began to falter and in the summer of 1929 the stock market crashed and the nation was plunged into the Great Depression. These hard times were followed by World War II, which America joined in 1941 after the bombing of Pearl Harbor. The books in this section provide opportunities for students to learn about this time in American history from multiple sources and multiple perspectives.

Book and Media Choices

Woodson, Jacqueline. *Coming on Home Soon.* Illustrated by E.B. Lewis. New York: Putnam, 2004. Unp. ISBN 978-0-399-23748-5. Grades: K–3.

When Mama travels to Chicago to work cleaning railroad cars, Grandma and Ada Ruth take comfort in knowing that she will be "coming on home soon." Money is scarce and with the men off fighting in a war, Mama can make money to send home by traveling north to work. Rich watercolor paintings and sparse lyrical text convey the evocative story, which ends with a wordless illustration of Mama walking through the snow toward the house.

Hopkinson, Deborah. *Sky Boys: How They Built the Empire State Building.* Illustrated by James E. Ransome. New York: Random House, 2006. 44p. ISBN 978-0-375-93610-4. Grades: K–4.

A young boy and his father provide an eyewitness account of the construction of the Empire State Building by the Sky Boys, whose assembly-line construction technique was a sight to behold. Lyrical prose, stunning oil paintings, and an endnote make this an exciting tale of hope in the midst of the Depression. Vintage photographs of the construction fill the endpapers. ALSC Notable Children's Book, 2007.

Borden, Louise. *The Journey That Saved Curious George: The True Wartime Escape of Margaret and H. A. Rey.* Illustrated by Allan Drummond. Boston, MA: Houghton Mifflin, 2005. 80p. ISBN 978-0-61833924-2. Grades: 3–8.

Students with fond memories of Curious George will be able to make personal connections to this harrowing story of how the Reys escaped from Europe during World War II. Photographs, documents, illustrations from Rey's books, a partial bibliography, and author notes are included. Notable Social Studies Trade Book for Young People, 2006.

Freedman, Russell. *Children of the Great Depression.* Boston, MA: Houghton Mifflin, 2005. 118p. ISBN 978-0-618-44630-8. Grades: 4–8.

In this photo essay accompanied by quotes and comparisons, Freedman depicts the harsh realities of the Great Depression from the perspective of children. The children are not without hope and that is evident in their quotes. Chapters in the book include information on the causes of the Depression and the daily lives of the children as they tried to continue to attend school, to help support their families, and to find small pleasures where they could. Source notes, a bibliography, and an index are included. Orbis Pictus Award, 2006.

Larson, Kirby. *Hattie Big Sky*. New York: Random House, 2006. 289p. ISBN 978-0-385-90332-5. Grades: 5–8.

Set in 1918 on a desolate Montana homestead, the mistrust of German Americans engendered during World War I impacts orphan Hattie Brooks as she works her uncle's claim. Just like the heroine in this book, Larson's great-grandmother worked a Montana homestead alone. The hardships of frontier life and the impact of a distant war are described in rich figurative language that captures the sights and sounds of the times. This book is also available on CD. Newbery Medal Honor Book, 2007.

Oppenheim, Joanne. *Dear Miss Breed: True Stories of the Japanese American Incarceration during World War II and a Librarian Who Made a Difference*. New York: Scholastic, 2006. 287p. ISBN 978-0-439-56992-7. Grades: 6 and up.

When Clara Breed's young Japanese-American patrons were forced from their homes and relocated to internment camps, she corresponded with them, advocated for their release, and sent them books and other treats. Historical documents, photographs, and interviews tell the stories of these intertwined lives and the story of this grave injustice. Included are a foreword, an afterword, an appendix, notes, a bibliography, and an index. NCSS Carter G. Woodson Secondary Level Award Winner, 2007.

Sullivan, Edward T. *The Ultimate Weapon: The Race to Develop the Atomic Bomb*. New York: Holiday House, 2007. Unp. ISBN 978-0-8234-1855-8. Grades: 6 and up.

In this succinct volume, Sullivan explores the science and the personal stories behind the Manhattan Project. Black-and-white photographs, maps, and diagrams help to explain the significance of the development of the atomic bomb. Back matter includes a postscript, an appendix, a chronology, notes, a bibliography, suggestions for further reading, websites, and an index. Outstanding Science Trade Book for Students K–12, 2008. Notable Social Studies Trade Book for Young People, 2008.

Explorations

1. After reading *Coming on Home Soon* (Woodson, 2004) use a document camera to project the text for the students to see. Point out to them how Woodson uses italics rather than punctuation marks to show the dialogue. This technique is a useful way to teach students how to include dialogue in their writing, as they are able to focus on writing the dialogue rather than putting in punctuation marks. Students who compose on the computer can easily italicize their dialogue and students who compose on paper can underline their dialogue. Once students have mastered adding dialogue to their writing, they are then ready to learn how to add the punctuation marks.

2. Before reading *The Journey That Saved Curious George: The True Wartime Escape of Margaret and H. A. Rey* (Borden, 2005), read one of Rey's Curious George books to the students.
3. As you read *The Journey That Saved Curious George: The True Wartime Escape of Margaret and H. A. Rey* (Borden, 2005) have the students create a flowchart showing the Reys' escape route. Once the students complete their flowcharts allow them time to discuss the interactions between individuals, groups, and institutions that impacted the Reys' escape.
4. As students are reading *Hattie Big Sky* (Larson, 2006) have them record examples of the figurative language in the book in their writing notebooks. As they discuss the book with their classmates, ask them to share the examples of figurative language that they noted. Then, ask them for ideas on how they can incorporate figurative language in their own writing.
5. After reading *Hattie Big Sky* (Larson, 2006) help students make connections to the discrimination faced by the German-American immigrants during World War I to the discrimination faced by American immigrants during other wars.
6. Before reading *Dear Miss Breed: True Stories of the Japanese American Incarceration during World War II and a Librarian Who Made a Difference* (Oppenheim, 2006), have the students visit the Clara Breed Collection of the Japanese-American National Museum at www.janm.org/collections/clara-breed-collection/ to explore some of the primary source documents, such as letters and home videos that were used in the research for this book.

A World Power 1946–2010

This time period was marked by growth in the American economy and conflict with foreign nations. By 1947, the peaceful coexistence between nations ended as communism spread throughout Eastern Europe and the Cold War began. Americans fought in the Korean Conflict, the Vietnam War, and the Persian Gulf War. From 1955 to 1965, the Civil Rights Movement swept the land resulting in the Civil Rights Act of 1964 and the Voting Rights Act of 1965, which guarantee basic civil rights to all Americans. On September 11, 2001, the Twin Towers in New York City fell when terrorists hijacked planes and deliberately crashed into them. American conflict continues with the 2001 invasion of Afghanistan and the 2003 invasion of Iraq.

Book and Media Choices

Farris, Christine King. *My Brother Martin: A Sister Remembers Growing Up with the Rev. Martin Luther King.* Illustrated by Chris Soentpiet. New York: Simon and Schuster, 2003. Unp. ISBN 978-0-689-84387-7. Grades: K–4.

As they listen to this book being read aloud students relate to young Martin, who enjoyed playing jokes and hearing family stories. The racial discrimination he faced and his strong family background set him on a peaceful course to ensure freedom. A poem, an afterword, and an illustrator's note conclude the book. International Reading Association Teachers' Choice, 2004.

Farris, Christine King. *March On! The Day My Brother Martin Changed the World.* DVD. New York: Weston Woods, 2008. 20 min. ISBN 978-0-545-10645-0. Grades: 2–5.

Farris offers a unique look at the events that led up to her brother's historic speech. Clips from MLK's speech, crowd noises, and audio clips of Mahalia Jackson's song enhance this stirring video based on Farris' book by the same title. Includes a teacher's guide. ALA Andrew Carnegie Medal for Excellence in Children's Video, 2009.

Judge, Lita. *One Thousand Tracings: Healing the Wounds of World War II.* New York: Hyperion, 2007. Unp. ISBN 978-1-42310-008-9. Grades: 2–5.

Judge tells the story of how her grandmother and mother sent care packages to Europeans after World War II. Families desperately in need of shoes sent tracings of their feet, which were matched to shoes that Judge's family collected. Watercolor illustrations and collage illustrations of the letters, photographs, and tracings draw readers into this compelling story. ALSC Notable Children's Book, 2008.

Borden, Louise. *Across the Blue Pacific: A World War II Story.* Illustrated by Robert Andrew Parker. Boston, MA: Houghton Mifflin, 2006. 48p. ISBN 978-0618-33922-8. Grades: 3–5.

World War II is seen through the eyes of a schoolgirl whose neighbor is serving in the Navy. The peace of the neighborhood is shattered when a few days before Christmas they learn that his submarine is missing. Slowly life returns to normal and the war ends, but the memory of the young sailor lingers. An author's note explains that her uncle died when the USS Albacore sank in the Sea of Japan. Notable Social Studies Trade Book for Young People, 2007.

Weatherford, Carole Boston. *Dear Mr. Rosenwald.* Illustrated by R. Gregory Christie. New York: Scholastic, 2006. Unp. ISBN 978-0-439-49522-6. Grades: 3–5.

Ovella is overjoyed when she learns that her decrepit one-room school is going to be replaced by a new school. Julius Rosenwald, president of Sears, Roebuck, and Company, is donating some of the money for the new school. The community will also have to contribute money and to build the school. Free-verse poems tell the story of the community's efforts to provide a school for the African-American children. The book concludes with an author's note about Julius Rosenwald's donations that helped build schools for African Americans in the rural south. Notable Social Studies Trade Book for Young People, 2007.

Winter, Jeanette. *The Librarian of Basra: A True Story from Iraq.* New York: Harcourt, 2005. Unp. ISBN 978-0-15-205445-8. Grades: 3–5.

Hiding 30,000 books to save them from destruction during the Iraq War took one very determined librarian, Alia Muhammad Baker, and lots of friends. These book lovers hid this valuable collection in their homes and their restaurants. Seventy percent of the library collection was safe when the library was destroyed. Notable Social Studies Trade Book for Young People, 2006.

Fradin, Dennis B. *September 11, 2001*. Tarrytown, NY: Marshall Cavendish, 2010. 47p. ISBN 978-0-7614-4259-2. Grades: 3–6.

This brief introduction to the terrorist attacks on September 11 includes events prior to the attack, information on how the attacks were carried out, and the resulting wars. The book includes bibliographic references, a timeline, and an index.

Sís, Peter. *The Wall: Growing Up Behind the Iron Curtain*. New York: Farrar, Straus and Giroux, 2007. 56p. ISBN 978-0-374-34701-7. Grades: 3–8.

This compelling narrative recounts Sís' life growing up in Communist Czechoslovakia and his escape to America as the Iron Curtain crumbled. His memories are interwoven with history, making this a book to explore on many levels and one to revisit. Illustrations, photographs, journal entries, and compelling text portray the drama of his life and realization of his dream of creative freedom. Robert F. Sibert Informational Book Medal Award Winner, 2008. Caldecott Medal Honor Book, 2008.

Morrison, Toni. *Remember: The Journey to School Integration*. Boston: Houghton Mifflin, 2004. 78p. ISBN 978-0-618-39740-2. Grades: 4–8.

Powerful black-and-white photographs with thought-provoking captions ask readers to remember this journey as a way to develop understanding. An introduction sets the stage for viewing and reading. The book concludes with a dedication to the four girls who died in the Birmingham church bombing on September 15, 1963, a chronology of key events in integration history, and notes about the photographs. Coretta Scott King Author Award Winner, 2005.

Schroeder, Peter W. *Six Million Paper Clips: The Making of a Children's Holocaust Memorial*. Minneapolis, MN: Kar-Ben, 2004. 64p. ISBN 978-1-58013-169-8. Grades: 4–8.

Faced with the challenge of teaching diversity in a middle school with a very homogenous population, it was decided that the curriculum should focus on the Holocaust. To help the students grasp the concept of the eleven million deaths, they began collecting paper clips—one for each of the deceased. As paper clips began coming in from around the world, two German newspaper correspondents based in the United States worked with them to establish a Holocaust Memorial at the school.

Bolden, Tonya. *M.L.K.: Journey of a King*. New York: Abrams, 2007. 128p. ISBN 978-0-8109-5476-2. Grades: 5–8.

This biography of Martin Luther King Jr. is also the story of the Civil Rights Movement. Included in the book are quotes from Martin Luther King Jr. that reveal his passion and commitment to peace and justice. Photographs, a bibliography, a timeline, and an index are included. Orbis Pictus Award, 2008.

Freedman, Jeri. *America Debates Privacy versus Security.* New York: Rosen, 2008. 64p. ISBN 978-1-40421-929-8. Grades: 5–8.

This story begins with September 11, 2001. Since that fateful day, surveillance of Americans has increased, and has impacted their right to privacy. Color photographs and text boxes contain additional information for students to consider. A timeline, a glossary, resources for learning more, a bibliography, and an index conclude the book. From the America Debates series.

Holm, Jennifer. *Penny from Heaven.* New York: Random House, 2006. 274p. ISBN 978-0-375-93687-6. Grades: 5–8.

Readers are transported to New Jersey in the summer of 1953, where eleven-year-old Penny lives with her overprotective mother and her maternal grandparents. Penny learns that her father, an Italian-American immigrant, died in an American internment camp and his death is the reason that her mother is estranged from his family. As Penny recovers from an accident, she reconnects her mother with her father's family. The book is filled with historical details and concludes with an author's note and photographs. This book is available on CD. Newbery Medal Honor Book, 2007.

Kadohata, Cynthia. *Cracker! The Best Dog in Vietnam.* New York: Antheneum, 2007. 312p. ISBN 978-1-41690-637-7. Grades: 5–8.

Cracker and her handler, Rick, train and then serve in Vietnam as part of a military canine unit searching for booby traps. Their adventure-packed story portrays the trusting relationship of a dog and owner when surrounded by danger and uncertainty. Notable Social Studies Trade Book for Young People, 2008.

Kuhn, Betsy. *The Race for Space: The United States and the Soviet Union Compete for the New Frontier.* Breckenridge, CO: Twenty-First Century Books, 2007. 112p. ISBN 978-0-8225-5984-9. Grades: 5–8.

The Soviet Union's launch of Sputnik propelled the United States into a race to put a man on the moon. Kuhn explores the impact of this race on the government, politics, culture, and the arts. Quotes, anecdotes, and black-and-white photographs help to connect this story to American history. Back matter includes source notes, a bibliography, a timeline, and excerpts from transcripts of the first lunar landing. From the People's History series. Notable Social Studies Trade Book for Young People, 2007.

Zwier, Lawrence J., and Matthew Scott Weltig. *The Persian Gulf and Iraqi Wars.* Minneapolis, MN: Lerner, 2005. 96p. ISBN 978-0-8225-0848-9. Grades: 5–8.

The book explores the history of the region and Iraq's wars with the United States, Iran, and Kuwait. The roles of soldiers, key leaders, women, and minorities are explored in this concise volume. A timeline, a glossary, a who's who list, a bibliography, resources for learning more, and an index are included. Notable Social Studies Trade Book for Young People, 2005.

McWhorter, Diane. *A Dream of Freedom: The Civil Rights Movement from 1954 to 1968.* New York: Scholastic, 2004. 160p. ISBN 978-0-439-57678-9. Grades: 5–9.

McWhorter introduces the Civil Rights Movement by beginning with her own upbringing as the child of a segregationist in Birmingham, Alabama. Captioned photographs and informative text boxes highlight the events portrayed in this compelling account of a tumultuous time in history that shaped Americans' lives. The book concludes with a bibliography, resources for learning more, and an index. ALSC Notable Children's Book, 2005.

Karwoski, Gail Langer. *Tsunami: The True Story of an April Fool's Day Disaster.* Illustrated by John MacDonald. Plain City, OH: Darby Creek, 2006. 64p. ISBN 978-1-58196-044-0. Grades: 6–8.

In Hawaii on April 1, 1946, the seawater retreated and revealed the ocean floor. Students and teachers raced to gather the sea's treasures. Then, disaster struck as a tremendous wall of water came crashing down, sweeping away people and buildings in its path. Photographs, diagrams, and maps help to tell the story of this disaster and how scientists are working to provide advance warning for tsunamis. The book concludes with an extensive listing of resources for further learning including books, websites, videos, and articles. Notable Social Studies Trade Book for Young People, 2007.

Kadohata, Cynthia. *Kira-Kira.* New York: Simon and Schuster, 2004. 244p. ISBN 978-0-689-85639-6. Grades: 6 and up.

A vivid, tense family drama unfolds as Katie Takeshima encounters the prejudice of being a Japanese-American in the 1950s, struggles with her sister's death, and witnesses the toll of the long hours her parents spend working in a poultry factory. Newbery Medal Winner, 2005.

Explorations

1. After reading *My Brother Martin: A Sister Remembers Growing Up with the Rev. Martin Luther King* (Farris, 2003) share the poem at the end of the book. Then, have the students recite the poem as a choral reading.
2. After reading *My Brother Martin: A Sister Remembers Growing Up with the Rev. Martin Luther King* (Farris, 2003) have the students visit Chris Sonetpiet's website (www.soentpiet.com/martin.htm) to read about the painting process he used to create the illustrations.
3. Students who want to learn more about the Civil Rights Movement can visit The Martin Luther King Jr. Research and Education Institute online at mlk-kpp01 .stanford.edu/. The site houses primary and secondary sources including King's speeches and sermons.

4. After reading *Across the Blue Pacific: A World War II Story* (Borden, 2006) have the students locate the places mentioned in the book on a large world map. Then, have the students share where their friends and relatives who are in the armed services are stationed. Mark the locations on the map.
5. After reading and discussing *Dear Mr. Rosenwald* (Weatherford, 2006) ask the students why they think Mr. Rosenwald required that the community donate some of the money for the school and required that the community build the school.
6. After reading and discussing *Remember: The Journey to School Integration* (Morrison, 2004), invite the students to work with a partner to write captions for the pictures in the book that do not have captions. Encourage them to use the captions in the book as models for their own writing.
7. A teacher's guide and an audio recording are two resources available for teaching *The Wall: Growing Up Behind the Iron Curtain* (Sís, 2007). They can be downloaded from Sís' website at www.petersis.com/content/wall_fr.html.
8. After reading *Six Million Paper Clips: The Making of a Children's Holocaust Memorial* (Schroeder, 2004), show the students *Paper Clip* (Fab, 2006), a documentary of this story. A DVD of this documentary can be purchased from Virgil Films at www.virgilfilmsent.com/.
9. After discussing *America Debates Privacy versus Security* (Freedman, 2008), use the questions at the end of the book to engage the students in additional research on the topic. After they have completed their research, allow them time to continue to discuss the issues or hold a debate.
10. Before reading *The Race for Space: The United States and the Soviet Union Compete for the New Frontier* (Kuhn, 2007) have the students listen to some of the transmissions from the Apollo 11 mission at www.nasa.gov/mission_pages/apollo/40th/a11_audio_highlights.html.
11. After reading *Tsunami: The True Story of an April Fool's Day Disaster* (Karwoski, 2006) share the Wave That Shook the World website with students at www.pbs.org/wgbh/nova/tsunami/anatomy.html. Click "Launch Interactive" to view graphics and videos that explain how tsunamis develop and travel.

GOVERNMENT

America's founding fathers immediately realized the need to establish a government and to formulate laws. A written constitution was needed to protect the rights of citizens and to limit the power of the national government. The Constitution they created spells out the powers of the federal government. In order to keep the federal government from becoming too strong the Constitution provided for the separation of powers by setting up three branches of government. The collection of materials in this section provides fascinating insights into the history of the American government.

The study of government encompasses strand six, which focuses on structures of power, authority, and governance as students examine their rights and responsibilities as citizens. This strand involves giving students opportunities to develop an understanding of how people develop and alter structures of power, authority, and governance. By studying the functions and the structure of government students develop an understanding of the power and authority vested in these institutions. They study the conflicts between nations and groups in order to develop civic competence. Students learn what happens when the rights of individuals intersect with the rights of the majority. They learn about fairness and justice and rights and responsibilities.

Books in this section also address strand ten, which includes civic ideals and practices. Within this strand students examine civic ideals and civic responsibilities as they develop an understanding of what it means to be a citizen and to fully participate in society. By examining civic ideals and practices across time, students prepare to make the decisions that enable them to make positive choices in order to make a difference in society.

Book and Media Choices

Allen, Kathy. *The U.S. Constitution.* Mankato, MN: Capstone, 2007. 24p. ISBN 978-0-7368-9594-1. Grades: K–2.

This very basic introduction to the Constitution explains how it established the United States government and that later the Bill of Rights was added. The book includes a glossary, books for reading more, and an index. A website at the end of the book is a useful teacher resource. A bilingual version of this book is also available.

Catrow, David. *We the Kids: The Preamble to the Constitution of the United States.* New York: Penguin, 2002. Unp. ISBN 978-0-8037-2553-9. Grades: K–5.

This humorous, illustrated version of the preamble introduces this important document to younger students. For older students, the introduction and the glossary at the beginning of the book offer additional information that helps them understand and discuss the document and its meaning.

Kennedy, Edward E. *My Senator and Me: A Dog's Eye View of Washington, DC.* Illustrated by David Small. New York: Scholastic, 2006. 56p. ISBN 978-0-439-65077-9. Grades: 3–5.

Readers tag along as Senator Kennedy's dog, Splash, shows them what a day on Capital Hill involves. As Senator Kennedy notes at the beginning of the book, it was written to give students a glimpse into public service and the workings of Congress. The book concludes with a brief biography of Senator Kennedy, a brief biography of Splash, and information on how a bill becomes a law. Notable Social Studies Trade Book for Young People, 2007.

Robb, Don. *This Is America: The American Spirit in Places and People.* Illustrated by Joy Pratt. Watertown, MA: Charlesbridge, 2005. 32p. ISBN 978-1-57091-604-5. Grades: 3–5.

Not only does this book capture the American spirit in text and illustrations, it also gives examples of the ideas and beliefs that make up that indefatigable spirit. For example, on the two-page spread on "Courage" there are short descriptions of Fort Sumter, Ivy Green, Helen Keller's Home, Christa McAuliffe, and the Vietnam Veterans Memorial. This would also be a good book to share with middle school English language learners who may find these complex concepts difficult to grasp. Notable Social Studies Trade Book for Young People, 2006.

Finkelman, Paul. *The Constitution.* Des Moines, IA: National Geographic, 2006. 48p. ISBN 978-0-7922-7975-4. Grades: 3–8.

Biographical sidebars introduce the founding fathers to young readers, as they join them at the Constitutional Convention. The book includes the full text of the document, prints, photographs, a glossary, and an index. From the American Document Series. Notable Social Studies Trade Book for Young People, 2007.

Yero, Judith Lloyd. *The Bill of Rights.* Des Moines, IA: National Geographic, 2006. 40p. ISBN 978-0-7922-5396-2. Grades: 3–8.

These first ten amendments to the Constitution guarantee citizens' basic human rights, and Yero places them in the context of young readers' lives. The book includes the full text of the document, prints, and photographs. From the American Document Series. Notable Social Studies Trade Book for Young People, 2007.

Morris-Lipsman, Arlene. *Presidential Races: The Battle for Power in the United States.* Breckenridge, CO: Twenty-First Century Books, 2008. 112p. ISBN 978-0-8225-6783-7. Grades: 6–8.

Imagine winning a presidential election without launching an expensive, time-consuming campaign. In this chronicle of presidential campaigns, students learn George Washington's campaign was very different from current campaigns. Photographs and political cartoons help tell the stories of presidential campaigns in the United States. Resources for learning more and a chart of election results conclude the book. From the People's History series. Notable Social Studies Trade Book for Young People, 2008.

Explorations

1. Before reading *The U.S. Constitution* (Allen, 2007) introduce the words in the glossary and help the students pronounce them. The large print and short sentences make this a book that some young students will be able to read on their own. To help them with the pronunciation of unknown words have the students use www.dictionary.com.

2. After reading *The U.S. Constitution* (Allen, 2007) return to the text to discuss the words in the glossary in the context of the text.
3. In the introduction to *We the Kids: The Preamble to the Constitution of the United States* (Catrow, 2002), David Catrow describes what the real constitution looks like. Access the image of the Constitution at www.usconstitution.net/constpix.html to share with the students.
4. While reading *We the Kids: The Preamble to the Constitution of the United States* (Catrow, 2002), pause on each page to allow the students time to examine the illustrations and discuss whether they help the students understand the words.
5. *This Is America: The American Spirit in Places and People* (Robb, 2005) uses text, examples, and illustrations to explain concepts including liberty, equality, pioneer spirit, and diversity. Some of these concepts are difficult for native English speakers to grasp, but they are even more difficult for English language learners to understand. Share one term at a time with the students and then invite them to give examples from their own lives to help them define the terms. Consider putting the terms on the classroom word wall.
6. While reading *Presidential Races: The Battle for Power in the United States* (Morris-Lipsman, 2008), have students discuss the impact of national and international issues on the presidential races.

ECONOMICS

Books in this section encompass strand seven—production, distribution, and consumption—and strand eight—science, technology, and society. Strand seven encompasses the study of how societies arrange for the production, distribution, and consumption of goods and services. As students examine the decisions they make as consumers they learn about consumption and the impact their decisions have on others. They explore how the distribution of resources impacts not only the United States' economy but also economies around the world. Strand eight requires students to examine societal issues related to science and technology, such as the evolution of technology and its impact on society. Students also explore the relationships between human values, technology, and behaviors. For example, in the books annotated below students learn about technologies that provide early warnings for disasters and they discover how people respond to these early warnings.

Book and Media Choices

Demarest, Chris L. *Hurricane Hunters! Riders on the Storm.* New York: Simon & Schuster Children's Publishing, 2006. 40p. ISBN 978-0-689-86168-0. Grades: K–2.

Climb on board the WC-130 Hercules and join its six-person crew as the plane flies into the eye of a hurricane. These daring hurricane hunters collect data that are used to predict the size of the storm and where it is expected to make landfall. The book begins with a cutaway diagram of the interior of the WC-130 and ends with an author's note containing additional information on the hurricane hunters and their work. Notable Social Studies Trade Book for Young People, 2007.

Agee, Jon. *Nothing.* New York: Hyperion, 2007. Unp. ISBN 978-0-7868-3694-9. Grades: K–3.

Suzie Gump is rich enough to buy anything she wants, and when Otis has nothing to sell her she insists on buying nothing. Soon the entire town wants to buy nothing. This tongue-in-cheek tale spoofs fads and the furious quests to get the latest fad items. ALSC Notable Children's Book, 2008.

Peterson, Chris. *Clarabelle: Making Milk and So Much More.* Photographs by David R. Lunquist. Honesdale, PA: Boyds Mills, 2007. Unp. ISBN 978-1-59078-310-8. Grades: 2–4.

The daily life on a Wisconsin dairy farm shows the interconnection of production and consumption as Clarabelle produces both milk and manure. Readers learn where the milk on their cereal comes from and that methane from the manure powers an electrical generator. NCTE Orbis Pictus Recommended Book, 2008.

Marrin, Albert. *Oh, Rats! The Story of Rats and People.* New York: Penguin Young Readers, 2006. 48p. ISBN 978-0-525-47762-4. Grades: 3–5.

Not for the squeamish, this book presents a detailed look at how rats have impacted society throughout time. Rats are noted for being nuisances and pests but they have also been essential to human survival. For example, rats swarming on a ship's deck or leaping overboard were a sure indicator that the ship had sprung a leak. The book is filled with fascinating facts about rats, sidebars that contain additional information, and a bibliography that includes information about rats in literature. Notable Social Studies Trade Book for Young People, 2007. Outstanding Science Trade Book for Students K–12, 2007.

Paulsen, Gary. *Lawn Boy.* New York: Random House, 2007. 96p. ISBN 978-0-385-90923-5. Grades: 3–8.

The birthday gift of a riding lawn mower sets a twelve-year-old boy on the road to financial independence. Investing his earnings from his lawn-mowing enterprise results in the young entrepreneur having more money than his parents. As the hilarious story develops, it teaches economic principles. Notable Social Studies Trade Book for Young People, 2008.

Hopkinson, Deborah. *Up Before Daybreak: Cotton and People in America.* New York: Scholastic, 2006. 120p. ISBN 978-0-439-63901-9. Grades: 4–8.

From slaves on plantations to millworkers in textile factories, Hopkins traces the history of cotton and its impact on American lives and the economy. Photographs, documents, and illustrations enhance the story and draw readers into this fascinating story. Bibliographic references, endnotes, and an index conclude the book. ALSC Notable Children's Book, 2007.

Explorations

1. Learn more about the *Hurricane Hunters* (The Fifty-third Weather Reconnaissance Squadron) on their website at www.huricanehunters.com.
2. After reading *Lawn Boy* (Paulsen, 2007) have students access Lemonade Stand at www.lemonadegame.com/ and play the online version of the computer game. This online simulation gives students experiences with supply and demand. In addition, this version of Lemonade Stand allows students to compete with kids across the nation.

PEOPLE, PLACES, AND CULTURE

Books and media about children from different cultures and ethnic backgrounds foster understanding of those cultures and ethnic backgrounds. The materials in this section offer students opportunities to learn about others and help them understand others' perspectives. While studying about the lives of other children, students discover similarities and differences between their lives. These discoveries help students appreciate their own lives as well as the lives of others. Sharing books about other cultures encourages children to move beyond their own world as they come to understand cultures that are different from their own. Discussions about the text and careful examinations of the illustrations help children comprehend the concepts. During discussions teachers can encourage children to share information about their own cultures, which fosters understanding and acceptance from their classmates.

Strand nine requires an understanding of global connections among societies. In this strand students confront the reality of global connections and interdependence as they discover how the diverse world societies impact one another. They analyze the tensions that occur as national interests confront global interests on issues of health care, human rights, the environment, and economic development. Examining the issues involved in global connections is not enough; students need to discuss and initiate action plans to address these issues. Materials in this section help students to understand different cultures and provide students with multiple perspectives for viewing their world.

Book and Media Choices

Muth, Jon J. *Zen Shorts*. New York: Scholastic, 2005. 40p. ISBN 978-0-439-33911-7. Grades: P–3.

Stillwater, a panda, shares Zen stories with three children. Not only is this an introduction to Zen principles, it also shares stories of forgiveness, acceptance, and generosity that are easily understood. These gentle stories enable readers to make connections between their own lives and the lives of the characters, and in the process they learn about universal human kindness. An author's note about Zen concludes the book. Notable Social Studies Trade Book for Young People, 2006.

Foreman, Michael. *Mia's Story: A Sketchbook of Hopes and Dreams.* Cambridge, MA: Candlewick, 2006. Unp. ISBN 978-0-7636-3063-8. Grades: P–5.

In the Andes Mountains of Chilé, Forman encountered Manuel who recycled and sold trash from a city dump. Manuel and his fellow villagers inspired this book about taking care of our planet and dreaming of a better life. The story focuses on Manuel's daughter Mia's contributions to the family dream of owning a home. Notable Social Studies Trade Book for Young People, 2007.

Sheth, Kashmira. *My Dadima Wears a Sari.* Illustrated by Yoshiko Jaeggi. Atlanta, GA: Peachtree, 2007. Unp. ISBN 978-1-56145-392-4. Grades: K–3.

Rupa's grandmother explains the advantages of wearing a sari, such as using the end for a fan and using it as an umbrella in an unexpected storm. An author's note with instructions for tying a sari concludes the book. Notable Social Studies Trade Book for Young People, 2008.

Cruise, Robin. *Little Mama Forgets.* Illustrated by Stacey Dressen-McQueen. New York: Farrar, Straus and Giroux, 2006. 40p. ISBN 978-0-374-34610-3. Grades: K–5.

Little Mama is Lucy's beloved grandmother who might forget how to tie her shoes, but she remembers how to button her dancing shoes to twirl across the floor with Lucy. Within the embrace of a loving family and under the watchful eyes of a doting granddaughter, the forgetful Little Mama lives with the family where she participates in family activities and shares stories of her life in Mexico. Notable Social Studies Trade Book for Young People, 2007.

Morris, Ann. *Grandma Esther Remembers: A Jewish-American Family Story.* Photographs and illustrations by Peter Linenthal. Minneapolis, MN: Lerner, 2002. 32p. ISBN 978-0-7613-2318-1. Grades: 1–4.

As Pamela and Allison spend time with their grandmother, they learn about their family history and their culture. Photographs, some from family albums, help to tell the story of Grandmother Esther's escape from Russia during World War II and her immigration to America. From the What Was It Like, Grandma? series.

Coy, John. *Around the World.* Illustrated by Antonio Reonegro and Tom Lynch. New York: Lee and Low, 2005. Unp. ISBN 978-1-58430-244-5. Grades: 1–4.

Travel the globe as a game of street basketball moves from country to country with the turn of a page. As the game travels, the names of the children change, their looks change, and their surroundings change, but through it all the moves on the court are the same. Energetic pictures, brief text boxes, and dialogue bubbles with a cartoon format entice students to explore this book. The book ends with instructions for playing the basketball game "Around the World."

Ruurs, Margriet. *My Librarian Is a Camel: How Books Are Brought to Children Around the World.* Honesdale, PA: Boyds Mills, 2005. Unp. ISBN 978-1-59078-093-0. Grades: 3–5.

Camels, elephants, and boats deliver books to people in remote areas of the globe. Full-color photographs, some taken by the librarians themselves, give students a glimpse into the lives of children around the world. Small fact boxes contain information about each of the thirteen countries whose unusual, mobile libraries are featured in the book.

Frazier, Sundee Tucker. *Brendan Buckley's Universe and Everything in It*. New York: Random House, 2007, 198p. ISBN 978-0-385-73439-4. Grades: 4–6.

Biracial ten-year-old Brendan's interest in rocks and minerals draws him to a mineral show at the mall where he strikes up a conversation with an older man, who happens to be the white grandfather he has never met. Brendan's parents are against him getting to know his grandfather, Ed, as it was his bigotry that divided the family. Notable Social Studies Trade Book for Young People, 2008.

Halls, Kelly Milner. *Mysteries of the Mummy Kids*. Plain City, OH: Darby Creek, 2007. 72p. ISBN 978-1-58196-059-4. Grades: 4–8.

A compelling photograph of a child mummy on the cover entices readers into this fascinating book that explores the mysteries of mummies from around the world. Photographs, interviews with scientists, maps, and well-researched text tell the stories of these ancient citizens. The book is divided into sections including South American Mysteries, Mysterious Mummies of Egypt, Kid Mummies of Europe and Asia, and Kid Mummy Mysteries from North America. A listing of museums that house mummies, a glossary, and an index are included. The extensive bibliography includes articles, videos, audio files, and websites.

Jaramillo, Ann. *La Linea*. New Milford, CT: Roaring Brook, 2006. 144p. ISBN 978-1-5964-3154-6. Grades: 6 and up.

Miguel's perilous journey across the border to reunite with his parents in California is complicated by the fact that his sister, Elena, follows him. In this fast-paced, realistic story the siblings encounter robbery, violence, and an unrelenting desert. An epilogue describes their adult lives. Spanish words, phrases, and culture are interwoven into the text. An author's note explains that even though the book is fiction it is based on actual events. Notable Social Studies Trade Book for Young People, 2007.

Explorations

1. After reading and discussing *Zen Shorts* (Muth, 2005) ask the students to share stories of their own about others' kindnesses toward them. On the overhead or chart paper write a short paragraph about a time when someone was kind to you. Then, have the students return to their seats to write about acts of kindness.
2. Use the illustrations with their short descriptive sentences in *Mia's Story: A Sketchbook of Hopes and Dreams* (Foreman, 2006) as models for young students' writing. English language learners and students with exceptionalities will also

benefit from being able to tell their stories in pictures accompanied by short sentences.

3. *Grandma Esther Remembers: A Jewish-American Family Story* (Morris, 2002) introduces student to researching and writing their own family stories. The book concludes with ideas for conducting interviews, creating family albums, and making a family tree.
4. After reading *Around the World* (Coy, 2005), review the directions for playing "Around the World" with the students, then take them outside to play the game.
5. After reading *Mysteries of the Mummy Kids* (Halls, 2007) older students who want to learn more about mummies can explore multimedia resources at www.pbs .org/wgbh/nova/bog. They can watch a preview of the video "The Perfect Corpse" and listen to Seamus Heaney's poem, "The Tollund Man," about the most famous bog body of all. As with all websites, be sure to preview this one before sharing it with students, as it contains explicit material about mummification.

GEOGRAPHY

Social studies content strands three, eight, and nine help students understand the importance of geography as they learn about their world. Strand three focuses on students' understanding of the relationships between people and their environments. Strand eight introduces students to the impact of technology on their lives. Strand nine requires an understanding of global connections among societies. Through books and media in this section students journey across the United States, journey to other continents, and explore the polar regions.

Book and Media Choices

Our World: A Child's First Picture Atlas. Des Moines, IA: National Geographic, 2006. 32p. ISBN 978-0-7922-7576-3. Grades: K–2.

Prints, photographs, maps, and simple text help young readers understand their world. The four oceans, the seven continents, and the major countries of the world are introduced in this oversized colorful book. The book includes information on ethnic groups, foods, and animals. Notable Social Studies Trade Book for Young People, 2007.

Pattison, Darcy. *The Journey of Oliver K. Woodman.* Illustrated by Joe Cepeda. DVD. Guilford, CT: Nutmeg Media, 2005. 14 min. ISBN 978-0-9772338-3-0. Grades: K–3.

When Tameka's Uncle Ray cannot travel from South Carolina to visit her in California, he sends a hinged wooden man, Oliver K. Woodman, hitchhiking across America to visit her. This video is based on the book by the same name. Includes a teacher's guide. ALA Notable Children's Video, 2006.

Shulevitz, Uri. *How I Learned Geography*. New York: Farrar, Straus and Giroux, 2008. Unp. ISBN 978-0-374-33499-4. Grades: K–3.

During World War II, Shulevitz and his family fled Poland to the Soviet Union. Returning from a daily search for food, his father brings home not food, but a map of the world. Shulevitz spent days traveling the world in his mind as he stared at the map hanging on the wall. An author's note on his life and the map concludes the book. Caldecott Medal Honor Book, 2009.

Hopkinson, Deborah. *Apples to Oregon: Being the (Slightly) True Narrative of How a Brave Pioneer Father Brought Apples, Peaches, Pears, Plums, Grapes, and Cherries (and Children) Across the Plains*. Illustrated by Nancy Carpenter. New York: Simon and Schuster, 2004. Unp. ISBN 978-0-689-84769-1. Grades: K–4.

In this delightful tall tale, Delicious narrates her family's trip from Iowa to Oregon in the 1800s. Since Daddy could not bear to leave behind his fruit trees, he packs them up along with his wife and eight children. Working together, the family saves the trees from a variety of hazards and their ingenious efforts are revealed in the humorous illustrations. A map of the family's journey is on the endpaper and an author's note tells that the book is based on Henderson Luelling, who delivered fruit trees to Oregon.

Lehman, Barbara. *The Red Book*. Boston, MA: Houghton Mifflin, 2004. Unp. ISBN 978-0-618-42858-8. Grades: K–6.

When a young girl opens the red book she plucked from a snowbank, a series of pictures reveal a young boy on a beach picking up a red book buried in the sand. The pictures in his book reveal the girl who has been looking at him in her book. She buys a bouquet of helium balloons and floats off to join him. This wordless picture book with its series of pictures invites readers to imagine the wondrous journeys they can enjoy within the pages of books. Caldecott Medal Honor Book, 2005.

Priceman, Marjorie. *How to Make a Cherry Pie and See the U.S.A.* New York: Alfred A. Knopf, 2008. Unp. ISBN 978-0-375-81255-2. Grades: 1–4.

What does it take to make a cherry pie? Travel the United States with a spunky young baker as she gathers natural resources to make her pie. The book concludes with a Fourth of July parade celebrating the states she visited in her travels. A map of the United States covers the end papers and a recipe for cherry pie is included at the front of the book. This book is a follow-up to *How to Make an Apple Pie and See the World* (Priceman, 1994).

Patent, Dorothy Hinshaw. *When the Wolves Returned: Restoring Nature's Balance in Yellowstone*. Photographs by Dan Hartman and Cassie Hartman. New York: Walker, 2008. 39p. ISBN 978-0-8027-9687-5. Grades: 2–5.

Written on two levels—one a read-aloud narrative and the other detailed, explanatory text—the story unfolds the impact of the U.S. government's extermination of the wolves in Yellowstone Park. National Park Service images and photographs by the Hartmans help to explain how the extermination upset the park's delicate food chain and how the restoration of the wolves restored the balance. NCTE Orbis Pictus Honor Book, 2009.

Siebert, Diane. *Tour America: A Journey Through Poems and Art*. Illustrated by Stephen T. Johnson. San Francisco, CA: Chronicle Books, 2006. 64p. ISBN 978-0-8118-5056-8. Grades: 3–5.

Ten years of travel throughout the United States enabled Siebert to capture scenic American treasures in poetry that reflects the distinctive mood of each site. Each poem sings the praises of a unique treasure, such as the Gateway Arch, the Golden Gate Bridge, and the Everglades. Additional information is contained in a text box along with small outline maps of the states in the poem and the mainland United States. Luminous illustrations in a variety of mediums depict each of the sites and are listed at the end of the book. Notable Social Studies Trade Book for Young People, 2007.

Shoveller, Herb. *Ryan and Jimmy: And the Well in Africa That Brought Them Together*. Tonawanda, NY: Kids Can Press, 2006. 56p. ISBN 978-1-55337-967-6. Grades: 3–6.

When first grader Ryan Hreljac learned that much of the world did not have safe drinking water he began raising money to pay for a well. His campaign led to a trip to Agweo Village, Uganda, for the unveiling of the well and to a lifelong friendship with orphan Akana Jimmy who now lives with Ryan and his family. Notable Social Studies Trade Book for Young People, 2007.

***Mapmaker's Toolkit*. Mac/Win. Watertown, MA: Tom Snyder Productions, 2003. ISBN 978-1-59009-020-6. Grades: 4–12.**

With this software students can create and interpret a variety of different kinds of maps. Included in the software are libraries of maps and map symbols. There are approximately forty-eight theme maps showing precipitation, temperature, population density, and vegetation. Technology and Learning Award of Excellence, 2003.

Lourie, Peter. *Arctic Thaw: The People of the Whale in a Changing Climate*. Honesdale, PA: Boyds Mills, 2007. 48p. ISBN 978-1-59078-436-5. Grades: 4 and up.

Lourie traveled to Barrow on the North Slope of Alaska to observe the impact of global warming on the whale-hunting Inupiaq Eskimos. He lived with scientists at the Barrow Arctic Science Consortium, as they conducted experiments to help them understand the causes and impact of global warming. He left Barrow committed to making changes in his own life that will help to slow down global warming. An arctic map, graphs, intriguing color photographs, and color charts help readers relate to the lives of the Inupiaq. A glossary, ideas for fighting global climate change, websites, suggested readings, and an index conclude the book. Society of School Librarians International Honor Book, 2007.

Atkins, Jeannine. *How High Can We Climb? The Story of Women Explorers.* Illustrated by Dusan Petricic. New York: Farrar, Straus and Giroux, 2005. 224p. ISBN 978-0-374-33503-8. Grades: 5–8.

The twelve intrepid explorers profiled in this book refused to believe that they could not accomplish their dreams to explore the environment. From mountaintops, to the depths of the ocean, and to the ends of the earth these women traveled and uncovered the earth's stories. Their accomplishments span 240 years from 1766 to 2001. The book concludes with an author's note, selected books, and websites as well as an index. Notable Social Studies Trade Book for Young People, 2006.

Gilley, Jeremy. *Peace One Day: The Making of World Peace Day.* Illustrated by Karen Blessen. New York: G. P. Putnam's Sons, 2005. 48p. ISBN 978-0-399-24330-1. Grades: 5–8.

Doubtful that one person could make a difference, Gilley decided to try to establish a world peace day. With a cameraman by his side he crossed the globe, talking about his ideas with heads of state, the Dalai Lama, and United Nations Secretary-General Kofi Annan. His efforts resulted in September 21 being declared UN International Day of Peace. Notable Social Studies Trade Book for Young People, 2006.

Ashabranner, Brent K. *The Washington Monument: A Beacon for America.* Photographs by Jennifer Ashabranner. Brookfield, CT: Millbrook Press, 2002. 64p. ISBN 978-0-7613-1524-7. Grades: 5–8.

In 1783, the Continental Congress passed a resolution to build a monument to honor George Washington. That monument was not dedicated until February 21, 1885. The 102-year story of the construction of the Washington Monument includes debates about the location, the design, the construction, and the financing. Included are an introduction, information about the Washington Monument, a bibliography, and an index. This book is available as an e-book.

Revkin, Andrew C. *The North Pole Was Here: Puzzles and Perils at the Top of the World.* Boston: Houghton Mifflin, 2006. 128p. ISBN 978-0-753-45993-5. Grades: 6–8.

Award-winning environmental reporter Andrew Revkin chronicles his expedition at the North Pole where an international band of scientists are studying the warming of the Arctic. Revkin tells not only his own story of adventure, but also tells of past explorations and the intrepid adventurers who have gone before him. Readers discover how their actions and the actions of others on this planet impact the North Pole. A table of contents, an index, photographs, diagrams, illustrations, source notes, a list of *The New York Times* articles for further reading, and a metric conversion chart encompass a wide array of additional resources to enhance a study of the North Pole. Notable Social Studies Trade Book for Young People, 2007.

Explorations

1. The father in *Apples to Oregon: Being the (Slightly) True Narrative of How a Brave Pioneer Father Brought Apples, Peaches, Pears, Plums, Grapes, and Cherries (and Children) Across the Plains* (Hopkinson, 2004) was based on Henderson Luelling. He was not only a key figure in the Pacific fruit industry, he was also active in the Underground Railroad when he lived in Iowa. To learn more about him, students can visit the Aboard the Underground Railroad website at www.nps.gov/history/nr/travel/underground/ia3.htm.
2. While reading *How to Make a Cherry Pie and See the U.S.A.* (Priceman, 2008), stop as the states are visited to have the students locate the states on a map.
3. After reading *When the Wolves Returned: Restoring Nature's Balance in Yellowstone* (Patent, 2008) use the last page in the book, "The Wolf Effect," to review the delicate balance between the plants and animals in Yellowstone.
4. Before reading *Tour America: A Journey Through Poems and Art* (Siebert, 2006) have the students brainstorm a list of treasures in their state. After reading the book provide the students time to do research on the state's treasures and then use the poems in the book as models for writing their own poems.
5. After reading *Ryan and Jimmy: And the Well in Africa That Brought Them Together* (Shoveller, 2006), students can visit WaterCan at www.watercan.com/ to learn what they can do to help provide clean drinking water to children around the world.
6. Before reading *Arctic Thaw: The People of the Whale in a Changing Climate* (Lourie, 2007) show students the Barrow Arctic Science Consortium website at www.arcticscience.org. A link on the left side of the page provides information on the importance of studying the Arctic.
7. After reading *Arctic Thaw: The People of the Whale in a Changing Climate* (Lourie, 2007) or *The North Pole Was Here: Puzzles and Perils at the Top of the World* (Revkin, 2006) have the children work in groups to make a list of things that kids can do to make a difference. They can gather ideas from the back of Lourie's book and at websites such as www.epa.gov/globalwarming/kids/difference.html or www.sierraclub.org/globalwarming. Then have the students develop and implement an action plan for making a difference.
8. After reading about Ann Bancroft and Liv Arnesen's expeditions in *How High Can We Climb? The Story of Women Explorers* (Atkins, 2005) explore their website at www.yourexpedition.com to learn about their latest adventures and to post a message on their blog. Clicking the education tab on the website reveals resources for teachers.
9. Prior to reading *Peace One Day: The Making of World Peace Day* (Gilley, 2005) introduce the book to the children by showing them some of the video clips at www.peaceoneday.org.

10. After reading *Peace One Day: The Making of World Peace Day* (Gilley, 2005) have the students work in groups to talk about different ways they can celebrate peace on September 21.

GENERAL HISTORY

Books and media in this section span more than one time period in history and encompass both American history and world history. The books include tantalizing tidbits of history, journeys to freedom that span the globe, children's roles in history, and Native Americans' history.

Book and Media Choices

Armstrong, Jennifer. *The American Story: 100 True Tales from American History.* Illustrated by Roger Roth. New York: Alfred A. Knopf, 2006. 368p. ISBN 978-0-375-91256-6. Grades: 3–5.

Arranged in chronological order, these short stories span the years 1565 to 2000. American history is filled with stories about individuals, groups, and institutions that sometimes clash but also tie us together. The story arcs at the end of the book make connections between the stories based on themes such as communication, Native Americans, and religion. In addition to the story arcs the book contains a table of contents, an introduction, an index, and a bibliography. Notable Social Studies Trade Book for Young People, 2007.

King, David C. *DK Smithsonian Children's Encyclopedia of American History.* 160p. New York: DK Publishing, 2003. ISBN 978-0-7894-8330-0. Grades: 3–8.

This is a concise overview of the major events in American history. It is organized chronologically and combines photographs, illustrations, and easy-to-understand text. Notable Social Studies Trade Book for Young People, 2004.

Dreary, Terry. *The Wicked History of the World: History with the Nasty Bits Left In!* Illustrated by Martin Brown. New York: Scholastic, 2006. 93p. ISBN 978-0-439-87786-2. Grades: 4–7.

Fifty of the worst villains and their cruel deeds are chronicled in this nonfiction text that is sure to have reluctant readers interested in learning more. An epilogue concludes the book and challenges readers to consider the lessons to be gleaned from the stories. Notable Social Studies Trade Book for Young People, 2007.

Buckley, Susan Washburn, and Elspeth Leacock. *Journeys for Freedom: A New Look at America's Story.* Illustrated by Rodica Prato. Boston, MA: Houghton Mifflin, 2006. 48p. ISBN 978-0-618-22323-7. Grades: 4–8.

Historical facts, maps, and detailed illustrations tell the story of twenty journeys undertaken to escape slavery and oppression. The *Amistad* revolt, César Chávez's work, and the "lost boys" of Sudan are some of the events chronicled in the two-page spreads. Maps, fact boxes, and brief descriptions of the journeys complete with numbers matched to the maps guide students as they read these remarkable stories. This book is also available on CD. Notable Social Studies Trade Book for Young People, 2007.

Buckley, Susan Washburn, and Elspeth Leacock. *Kids Make History: A New Look at America's Story*. Illustrated by Randy Jones. Boston, MA: Houghton Mifflin, 2006. 48p. ISBN 978-0-618-22329-9. Grades: 4–8.

Examine American history from 1607 to 2001 through the eyes of twenty remarkable kids in two-page spreads filled with detailed watercolor illustrations and brief essays. Contained in the essays are quotes from the children, noted in double quotation marks, and imagined dialogue, noted in single quotation marks. The illustrations contain small, red, numbered boxes that are matched to the text. A table of contents, authors' notes, and an index are included. This book is also available on CD.

Hakim, Joy. *A History of US*. New York: Oxford University, 2006. 11 vol. ISBN 978-0-19-532727-4. Grades: 5–8.

This eleven-volume set covers American history from the first inhabitants to the twenty-first century. Diagrams, reproductions, photographs, maps, sidebars, and text boxes enhance the very readable text that appeals to readers young and old. Bibliographic references, a sourcebook, and an index are included.

Decisions, Decisions 5.0 Series. Mac/Win. Watertown, MA: Tom Snyder Productions, 2003. Grades: 5–10.

The role-playing simulations in this software series require students to research historical events covering topics such as building a nation, colonization, immigration, prejudice, and the Cold War. Students use a five-step model to gather information, analyze the information, and make informed decisions. Each program in the series includes a teacher's guide with lesson plans.

A History of American Indian Achievement. DVD. New York: Ambrose Video, 2008. 4 hr. Grades: 7 and up.

This four-disc set explores the Native Americans' culture, history, survival, architecture, and resistance to the westward expansion. Extras included on the DVD are printable graphics, a teacher's guide, quizzes, images, timeline, and maps. Spanish subtitles are included and the video is close-captioned. A preview of the video is available on the company's website at www.ambrosevideo.com.

Explorations

1. *Journeys for Freedom: A New Look at America's Story* (Buckley and Leacock, 2006) can be used as the starting point for students to discover and to write about their own families' journeys to America.

2. After reading *The Wicked History of the World: History with the Nasty Bits Left In!* (Dreary, 2006) have the students work as partners to learn more about one of the villains mentioned in the book. They can post the information they learn on a class blog and then use the blog to discuss what lessons can be learned from the villains and their impact on society.
3. After reading *Kids Make History: A New Look at America's Story* (Buckley and Leacock, 2006), students who want to learn more about these remarkable children can start with the references noted at the end of the book.

BIOGRAPHIES

These biographies tell the stories of people who have made positive impacts on society. Their stories reveal much about the times in which they lived, which helps students understand the impact of society and institutions on their lives. This understanding can provide them with inspiration and courage as they confront challenges in their own lives. In addition, biographies show students that one person can make a difference in their world.

As students study about the lives of famous people, their study reflects content strands three, four, and five. Strand three deals with students' understanding of the relationships between people and their environments. Strand four addresses how individual development and identity is impacted by culture, groups, and institutional influences. Strand five focuses on the interactions among individuals, groups, and institutions. The words and actions of the individuals in these biographies have made a difference in society.

Book and Media Choices

Capaldi, Gina. *A Boy Named Beckoning: The True Story of Dr. Carlos Montezuma, Native American Hero*. Minneapolis, MN: Lerner, 2008. Unp. ISBN 978-0-8225-7644-0. Grades: 2–5.

As a young boy, Yavapai Indian Wassaja was kidnapped and sold to Carlo Gentile, a photographer. Renamed Carlos Montezuma, he grew up to become a doctor and an advocate for the rights of Native Americans. The well-researched biography is based on a letter Montezuma wrote about his life. Included are an author's note, an epilogue, photographs, supplemental information, resources for learning more, and a detailed bibliography. Notable Social Studies Trade Book for Young People, 2009.

Smith, Lane. *John, Paul, George, and Ben*. DVD. New York: Weston Woods, 2007. 13 min. ISBN 978-0-439-02752-7. Grades: 2–5.

This riotous animated video is a mixture of fiction and nonfiction based on Smith's book by the same title. The early lives of five founding fathers—John Hancock, Paul Revere, George Washington, Benjamin Franklin, and Thomas Jefferson—are portrayed in humorous, exaggerated pen-and-ink animations. Narrated by James Earl Jones. ALA Notable Children's Video, 2008.

Lasky, Kathryn. *John Muir: America's First Environmentalist.* Illustrated by Stan Fellows. Cambridge, MA: Candlewick, 2006. 48p. ISBN 978-0-7636-1957-2. Grades: 3–5.

John Muir was passionate about the wilderness and he spent his life exploring it and recording what he saw in his notebook. His words spring from the pages of the book in quotes from his diaries. He witnessed the destruction of the wilderness and formed the Sierra Club to establish a conservation policy to preserve the wilderness. The book includes a table of contents, epilogue, bibliography, and information about the Sierra Club. Notable Social Studies Trade Book for Young People, 2007.

Lewis, J. Patrick. *Heroes and She-roes: Poems of Amazing and Everyday Heroes.* Illustrated by Jim Cooke. New York: Penguin, 2005. 40p. ISBN 978-0-8037-2925-4. Grades: 3–5.

From an elementary teacher to Lady Godiva to César Chávez to Joan of Arc, these poems celebrate individuals who gave of themselves to help others. Following each poem is a brief biographical note about the person. An author's note concludes with information on Lewis' African-American school janitor, who was a hero because of what he did for others. Notable Social Studies Trade Book for Young People, 2006.

McCully, Emily Arnold. *Marvelous Mattie: How Margaret E. Knight Became an Inventor.* New York: Farrar, Straus and Giroux, 2006. 32p. ISBN 978-0-374810-6. Grades: 3–5.

In the 1800s, some thought that women were not capable of inventing anything; however, Margaret E. Knight—Mattie—did not know that. Her father died when she was a young child and she inherited his toolbox. With the toolbox and a notebook, Mattie designed and then created her inventions. She is best known for inventing a machine to create flat-bottom paper bags. Soft watercolors and pen-and-ink drawings draw readers into this story about a remarkable woman. Sketches of some of Mattie's inventions are located at the bottom of some of the pages. The book concludes with an author's note that provides additional information about Margaret E. Knight and a brief bibliography. Notable Social Studies Trade Book for Young People, 2007.

Krull, Kathleen. *Harvesting Hope: The Story of César Chávez.* Illustrated by Yuyi Morales. San Diego: Harcourt, 2003. Unp. ISBN 978-0-15-201437-7. Grades: 3–6.

When Chávez's family lost their ranch, they became migrant workers. The harsh conditions of migrant workers' lives and the racism they encountered resulted in Chávez's nonviolent protests that ultimately led to improved conditions for migrant workers. Lush illustrations with their intense colors reflect the emotions portrayed in this moving story. ALA Notable Children's Book, 2004. NCSS Carter G. Woodson Elementary Level Honor Book, 2008.

Rappaport, Doreen. *Abe's Honest Words: The Life of Abraham Lincoln.* Illustrated by Kadir Nelson. New York: Hyperion, 2008. 44p. ISBN 978-1-42310-408-7. Grades: 3–6.

Lincoln's words punctuate the concise text, which is set off by luminous illustrations. A chronology of Lincoln's life, resources for learning more, and the Gettysburg Address conclude the book. IRA Teachers' Choice Award, 2009.

Rappaport, Doreen. *Eleanor, Quiet No More: The Life of Eleanor Roosevelt.* Illustrated by Gary Kelley. New York: Hyperion, 2009. 48p. ISBN 978-0-7868-5141-6. Grades: 3–8.

Eleanor Roosevelt's own words, evocative illustrations, and inspiring text tell the story of a first lady who made a difference during a troubled time in American history. Author and illustrator notes conclude the book.

Bolden, Tonya. *George Washington Carver.* New York: Harry Abrams, 2008. 40p. ISBN 978-0-8109-9366-2. Grades: 4–7.

Born in slavery and raised on a farm by the German couple that owned his mother, Carver developed a passion for nature. He devoted his life to making people aware of the treasures of nature and taught people how to cultivate plants that benefited the earth and people on the earth. Photographs and some of Carver's own illustrations help tell the story of this remarkable scientist. This book was published in association with the Field Museum of Chicago. An afterword, notes, and selected sources conclude the book. The "George Washington Carver Tech DVD," part of the Modern Marvels series, is available through the History Channel Store at www.history.com.

Giblin, James Cross. *The Many Rides of Paul Revere.* New York: Scholastic, 2007. 85p. ISBN 978-0-439-57290-3. Grades: 4–7.

While most famously remembered for his rides, Paul Revere was a man of many talents including silversmith, engraver, printer, and dentist, among others. His many contributions to the Revolution are described with interesting details highlighted by photographs of artifacts and important historical sites, maps, and documents. Included is the text of Henry Wadsworth Longfellow's poem "Paul Revere's Ride," and Giblin notes where the poem deviates from known facts. A bibliography, timeline, and index conclude the book.

Timmesh, Catherine. *Madam President.* Illustrated by Douglas B. Jones. Boston, MA: Houghton Mifflin, 2008. 80p. ISBN 978-0-618-39666-5. Grades: 4–7.

Originally published in 2004, this new version of the book includes updates on the accomplishments of Hillary Clinton, Nancy Pelosi, and Condoleezza Rice. Brief biographies of twenty-three influential women in politics provide inspiration for young women. Back matter includes a timeline and a bibliography.

Bausum, Ann. *Our Country's First Ladies.* Des Moines, IA: National Geographic, 2007. 127p. ISBN 978-1-42630-006-6. Grades: 4–8.

Forty-four first ladies are profiled in this book, which includes informative text, a portrait, quotes, fact boxes of personal data, and interesting anecdotes. The book includes a bibliography and an index. Notable Social Studies Trade Book for Young People, 2008.

Bausum, Ann. *Our Country's Presidents: All You Need to Know about the Presidents from George Washington to Barack Obama.* Des Moines, IA: National Geographic, 2009. 215p. ISBN 978-1-42630-376-0. Grades: 5–8.

For each president Bausum provides factual information, anecdotes, and a reproduction of his official portrait. Included are eighteen essays related to the presidency including one on the Electoral College, a bibliography, a filmography, and an index.

Colman, Penny. *Adventurous Women: Eight True Stories about Women Who Made a Difference.* New York: Holt, 2006. 186p. ISBN 978-0-8050-7744-5. Grades: 5–8.

Women featured in this collective biography include Louise Boyd, Mary Gibson Henry, Juana Briones, Alice Hamilton, Mary McLeod Bethune, Katherine Wormeley, Biddy Mason, and Peggy Hull. These short biographies showcase several unfamiliar women who dared to live their lives with passion and adventure. The book concludes with resources for learning more, an author's note, and an index.

Harness, Cheryl. *The Adventurous Life of Myles Standish and the Amazing-but-True Survival Story of the Plymouth Colony.* Des Moines, IA: National Geographic, 2006. 144p. ISBN 978-0-7922-5919-0. Grades: 5–8.

The narrative account of Miles Standish's life portrays him as a hothead, but also an effective leader who was instrumental in the survival of the Plymouth Colony. The book concludes with a bibliography, lists of Mayflower passengers, and resources for learning more. From the Cheryl Harness Histories series. Notable Social Studies Trade Book for Young People, 2007.

Harness, Cheryl. *The Remarkable, Rough-Riding Life of Theodore Roosevelt and the Rise of the Empire America.* Des Moines, IA: National Geographic, 2007. 144p. ISBN 978-1-42630-009-7. Grades: 5–8.

This biography captures Roosevelt's enthusiasm with lively writing, quotes, and black-and-white illustrations. A biography, a timeline, and an index are included. From the Cheryl Harness Histories series. Notable Social Studies Trade Book for Young People, 2008.

Taylor, Sarah Steward. *Amelia Earhart: This Broad Ocean.* Illustrated by Ben Towle. New York: Hyperion, 2010. 96p. ISBN 978-1-42311-337-9. Grades: 5–8.

When young Grace encounters Amelia Earhart, she sets out to learn more about this intrepid aviator whose exploits led the way for generations of female aviators. Astronaut Eileen Collins' introduction to this graphic biography tells how Earhart's life inspired her.

Explorations

1. After reading *A Boy Named Beckoning: The True Story of Dr. Carlos Montezuma, Native American Hero* (Capaldi, 2006), have the students visit the Yavapai-Apache Nation website (www.yavapai-apache.org/) to learn more about Dr. Montezuma's culture and history.
2. Students can respond to the book *Heroes and She-roes: Poems of Amazing and Everyday Heroes* (Lewis, 2005) by brainstorming a list of heroes they know and then picking one as the subject for a poem. Model for the students how to write their poem using one of the poems in the book as a starting point. Call the students' attention to the fact that some of the poems rhyme and are written in stanzas and some are free verse and do not rhyme.
3. Prior to reading *Marvelous Mattie: How Margaret E. Knight Became an Inventor* (McCully, 2006) discuss the word inventor with the students. Then, show them the line drawings of Mattie's inventions at the bottom of the pages in the book.
4. After reading *John Muir: America's First Environmentalist* (Lasky, 2006) visit the John Muir exhibit at www.sierraclub.org/john_muir_exhibit/ and explore the chronology of his life.
5. Before reading *Abe's Honest Words: The Life of Abraham Lincoln* (Rappaport, 2008), share the illustrations with the students and ask them what they can learn about Lincoln's life from the illustrations.
6. After reading *Amelia Earhart: This Broad Ocean* (Taylor, 2010) share some of Earhart's quotes with the students to spark a discussion about this remarkable woman's spirit. Quotes can be found at www.ameliaearhart.com/about/quotes.html.

TEACHER RESOURCES

This section contains resources for teaching social studies. These resources include books and media, contact information for professional organizations, and Internet sites.

Book and Media Choices

Berson, Michael, Barbara C. Cruz, James A. Duplass, and J. Howard Johnston. *Social Studies on the Internet*, Third Edition. Upper Saddle River, NJ: Pearson, 2007. 154p. ISBN 978-0-13-238319-6. Grades: K–8.

This book contains an annotated collection of websites that correspond to the NCSS social studies standards. There are websites for asking experts, locating e-mail pals, primary source documents, simulations, and virtual field trips to name a few. It also contains an introduction to using the Internet including safety issues and resources for teaching social studies to diverse student populations.

Thornton, Stephen J. *Teaching Social Studies That Matters: Curriculum for Active Learning*. New York: Teachers College, 2005. 127p. ISBN 978-0-8077-4522-9. Grades: K–8.

Thornton views teachers as the "gatekeepers" of the social studies curriculum and he offers ideas for teachers as they develop a vision for their teaching. He recognizes that teachers have the power to build a strong social studies curriculum and to motivate children to learn.

Matthew, Kathryn I., and Joy L. Lowe. *Guide to Celebrations and Holidays Around the World: The Best Books, Media, and Multicultural Learning Activities*. New York: Neal-Schuman Publishers, 2006. 452p. ISBN 978-1-55570-479-7. Grades: K–8.

Explore the cultures of the world through their celebrations and holidays while exploring children's literature. Arranged by season and by month, this book offers a yearlong celebration of cultural diversity. Book annotations are accompanied by learning activities that help students make connections between their holidays and holidays around the world.

Berdan, Kristina, Ian Boulton, Elyse Eidman-Aadahl, Jennie Fleming, Launie Gardner, Iana Rogers, and Asali Solomon, editors. *Writing for a Change: Boosting Literacy and Learning through Social Action*. San Francisco, CA: Jossey-Bass, 2006. 165p. ISBN 978-0-7879-8657-5. Grades: 5–8.

Reading through these stories of how social action projects engaged students in their learning provides teachers with the information they need to explore social action projects with their students. These problem-solving projects can be used to focus the social studies curriculum on authentic opportunities to become productive citizens.

Professional Organizations

National Council on Economic Education
1140 Avenue of the Americas
New York, NY 10036
212-730-7007 or 1-800-338-1192 (Phone)
212-730-1793 (Fax)
sales@ncee.net
www.ncee.net

National Council for Geographic Education
1710 16th St., NW
Washington, DC 20009
202-360-4237
ncge@ncge.org
ncge.org

National Council for the Social Studies
8555 Sixteenth Street
Silver Spring, MD 20910
301-588-1800 (Phone)
301-588-2049 (Fax)
www.socialstudies.org

Internet Sites

American Memory: Historical Collections for the National Digital Library
memory.loc.gov

The collections, which include documents, photographs, maps, films, and audio recordings of the Library of Congress are only a click away at this site. There are learning pages for students and teachers, lesson plans, and media analysis tools.

Ben's Guide to Government for Kids
bensguide.gpo.gov

Materials on this site are grouped according to grade levels and include materials for parents and teachers. Information is included on the site's namesake, Benjamin Franklin.

EconEdLink
www.econedlink.org

The purpose of this site is to provide materials to ensure that students in kindergarten through twelfth grade develop an understanding of economic principles. This site includes lesson plans, information on current events, a catalog of publications, and links to other useful sites.

Mr. Dowling's Electronic Passport
www.mrdowling.com

This award-winning site has an impressive collection of information and links related to social studies and history. A great deal of the information is text-based and written for students in sixth grade and up.

National Geographic
www.nationalgeographic.com

On this site are videos, activities, games, and stories to actively involve students. Also included are links to click to learn more about animals and about people and places. The link to "My Page" allows children to set up their own pages on the National Geographic Server. An e-mail is sent to the parents or guardians to let them know the children have created their own pages.

The History Channel
www.historychannel.com

Video clips, article, speeches, and "This Day in History" brings history to your classroom computers. Under the "Classroom" link are study guides, speech archives, and resources created by teachers and other classroom-tested materials.

UNICEF– Voices of Youth
www.unicef.org/voy/
Sponsored by the United Nations International Children's Emergency Fund (UNICEF) the Voices of Youth website encourages students to learn about issues and crises facing children around the globe. Games, videos, audio files, news, and events can be found on the site.

REFERENCES

McGuire, Margit E. 2007. "What Happened to Social Studies? The Disappearing Curriculum." *Phi Delta Kappan* 88, no. 8 (April): 620–624.

National Council for the Social Studies. 1994. *Expectations of Excellence. Curriculum Standards for Social Studies*. [Online]. Washington, DC: National Council for the Social Studies. Available: www.socialstudies.org/standards/strands (accessed March 8, 2010). Curriculum Standards for Social Studies (c) 1994 National Council for the Social Studies.

Olwell, Russell, and Nicole Raphael. 2006. "The Problems of Elementary Social Studies: Are Curricular and Assessment Sprawl to Blame?" *The Social Studies* 97, no. 5 (September/October): 222–224.

Priceman, Marjorie. 1994. *How to Make an Apple Pie and See the World*. New York: Alfred Knopf.

Vogler, Kenneth E., and David Virtue. 2006. "'Just the Facts, Ma'am': Teaching Social Studies in the Era of Standards and High-Stakes Testing." *The Social Studies* 98, no. 2 (March): 54–58.

Chapter 5

Health

Reading and responding to books about health issues helps children learn not only the importance of being healthy but also how to take responsibility for their own health and well-being. For children to reach their full potential, they need these developmental assets: positive peer influence, cultural competence, restraint, self-esteem, achievement motivation, and values (Scales, 2000). Further, he contends that while schools cannot by themselves be responsible for students' developmental assets, they can build on these developmental assets through health education. As teachers and librarians read aloud and discuss books that promote healthy behaviors, they demonstrate that maintaining good health is important and they establish open lines of communication with students who may not be in healthy environments.

The Joint Committee on National School Health Education Standards (2007) developed the *National Health Education Standards: Achieving Excellence*. These standards describe what children should know to secure their own health as well as the health of their family and their community. The standards are organized in grade level bands: P–2, 3–5, 6–8, and 9–12. Accompanying the standards are performance indicators to assist teachers and librarians as they share books and develop lessons to teach children the importance of maintaining healthy lifestyles and to aid in developing assessments to determine the students' knowledge and skills.

STANDARD 1: Students will comprehend concepts related to health promotion and disease prevention to enhance health.

STANDARD 2: Students will analyze the influence of family, peers, culture, media, technology, and other factors on health behaviors.

STANDARD 3: Students will demonstrate the ability to access valid information and products and services to enhance health.

STANDARD 4: Students will demonstrate the ability to use interpersonal communication skills to enhance health and avoid or reduce health risks.

STANDARD 5: Students will demonstrate the ability to use decision-making skills to enhance health.

STANDARD 6: Students will demonstrate the ability to use goal-setting skills to enhance health.

STANDARD 7: Students will demonstrate the ability to practice health-enhancing behaviors and avoid or reduce health risks.

STANDARD 8: Students will demonstrate the ability to advocate for personal, family, and community health.

Books in this chapter provide students with resources and information on taking responsibility for their actions to enable them to develop healthy lifestyles that will last a lifetime. The chapter has three main sections: (1) healthy behaviors; (2) families; and (3) growth and development. Subsections under health behaviors are hygiene, safety, illnesses and disabilities, and nutrition. Under families the subsections include family constellations, divorce and separation, adoption and foster care, and homelessness. Subsections under growth and development include birth and growth, feelings, friendship, self-esteem, manners, and aging and death. The concluding section contains resources for teachers.

HEALTHY BEHAVIORS

Books and media on hygiene, safety, illnesses, disabilities, and nutrition help children learn the importance of being responsible for their own well-being and to learn empathy for those who are ill or have disabilities. It is important for children to establish healthy habits and routines, as these behaviors will impact them throughout their lives.

Hygiene

Books in this section help students learn to take care of themselves. Cleanliness, tooth care, and getting enough sleep are explored in the books that follow. Standard two includes the impact of culture and families on healthy behaviors and books in this section examine cultural aspects of tooth loss and sleep behaviors.

Book and Media Choices

DeGezelle, Terri. *Taking Care of My Hair.* Mankato, MN: 2006. 24p. ISBN 0-7368-4261-6. Grades: P–2.

Basic facts about taking care of hair are presented in full-page, color photographs and short sentences in large font. This is a great book to first share with students and then let them read it on their own. A code for accessing www.facthound.com is included. This website contains additional age-appropriate information. Back matter includes a glossary, resources for learning more, and an index. From the Pebble Plus Keeping Healthy series.

DeGezelle, Terri. *Taking Care of My Skin.* Mankato, MN: 2006. 24p. ISBN 0-7368-4263-2. Grades: P–2.

Basic facts about taking care of skin are presented in three chapters focusing on how amazing skin is, what it does, and how to take care of it. There are full-page, color photographs and short sentences in large font. A code for accessing www .facthound.com is included. This website contains additional age-appropriate information. Back matter includes a glossary, resources for learning more, and an index. From the Pebble Plus Keeping Healthy series.

Fox, Ella. *Ella Kazoo Will Not Brush Her Hair.* Illustrated by Jennifer Piecas. New York: Walker, 2010. Unp. ISBN 978-0-8027-8836-8. Grades: P–2.

Determined not to brush her hair, Ella hides her brush. As her unruly hair grows, it envelops everything it encounters including clothes, household items, her dog, and her mother. Bouncy rhymes filled with descriptive language and comical, cartoon illustrations tell the cautionary tale that concludes with a much-needed haircut.

Shannon, Terry Miller, and Timothy Warner. *Tub Toys.* Illustrated by Lee Calderon. Berkeley, CA: Ten Speed Press, 2002. Unp. ISBN 978-1-58246-066-6. Grades: P–2.

Bath time requires all the toys in the toy box and reluctant bathers relate to this bath-time tale. Computer-generated artwork lends itself to the morphing of the characters and the toys.

Keller, Laurie. *Open Wide: Tooth School Inside.* 18 min. DVD. Norwalk, CT: Weston Woods, 2006. ISBN 978-0-439-84916-6. Grades: P–3.

Based on Keller's book by the same name, this video enrolls readers in a school where the pupils are teeth. This is an entertaining way to learn about teeth, how to care for teeth, and how dentists help keep teeth healthy. A study guide is included. ALSC Notable Children's Video, 2007.

Pinkney, Andrea Davis. *Sleeping Cutie.* Illustrated by Brian Pinkney. New York: Harcourt, 2004. Unp. ISBN 978-0-15-202544-1. Grades: K–2.

Desperate to get Cutie to sleep at night, her parents buy her a talking stuffed Night Owl guaranteed to make her fall asleep at night. Once Mom and Dad leave the room the owl comes to life and transports Cutie to Dreamland Nightclub where the dancing and antics wear her out. Watercolor and pen-and-ink illustrations convey the musical rollicking nighttime scene.

Diakite, Penda. *I Lost My Tooth in Africa.* Illustrated by Baba Wague Diakite. New York: Scholastic Press, 2006. Unp. ISBN 978-0-439-66226-0. Grades: K–4.

On a visit to family in Bamako, Mali, Amina loses her tooth and the African tooth fairy brings her two chickens. The book is filled with the sights and customs of Africa enveloped in the embrace of a loving family. The book concludes with a glossary, a song, and a recipe for African onion sauce. ALSC Notable Children's Book, 2007.

Miller, Edward, III. *The Tooth Book: A Guide to Healthy Teeth and Gums.* New York: Holiday House, 2008. Unp. ISBN 978-0-8234-2092-6. Grades: K–4.

From the tooth timeline to the tooth cutaway to the information, this book is a concise guide to taking care of teeth. There is a two-page spread on tooth first aid covering toothaches, knocked-out teeth, broken teeth, and bleeding gums. The colorful cartoon-like drawings laced with snippets of text contain important information about tooth care.

Lauber, Patricia. *What You Never Knew about Beds, Bedrooms, and Pajamas.* Illustrated by John Manders. New York: Simon and Schuster, 2006. 32p. ISBN 978-0-689-85211-4. Grades: 2–4.

An important component of staying healthy is getting enough sleep. Here is a fascinating look at the history of beds, bedrooms, and pajamas, which is a great way to introduce the universal subject of sleep. The book concludes with a bibliography and an artist's note. From the Around the House History series.

Stauffacher, Sue. *Donutheart.* New York: Random House, 2006. 200p. ISBN 978-0-375-93275-5. Grades: 6–8.

Sixth grader Franklin Delano Donutheart is completely immersed in his own problems—limbs that are growing at different lengths, germs that are hiding everywhere, and safety issues that seem to bother no one but him. He does not quite grasp his mother's preoccupation with her boyfriend and her preoccupation with his classmate Sarah Kervick who lives with her father. In this sequel to *Donuthead* (Stauffacher, 2003), Franklin overcomes his fear of germs to rescue Sarah from her aunt. Readers come to recognize, as does Franklin, that his growing concern for others results in him being less concerned about himself.

Explorations

1. Before reading *Ella Kazoo Will Not Brush Her Hair* (Fox, 2010) have children share their experiences with brushing their hair as many of them will be able to relate to Ella's dislike of hair brushing.
2. During writing workshop share with students how Fox used her own child's refusal to brush her hair as inspiration for *Ella Kazoo Will Not Brush Her Hair*. Next, ask the students about things they do not like to do, for example, brushing their teeth or taking a bath. Then, model for the students how to use one of their ideas as the basis for a story.
3. Bring a funnel to class and before reading *Tub Toys* (Shannon and Warner, 2002) ask the children to brainstorm all the things they can do with a funnel. Then, show them the double-page spread in the book where the bather uses his imagination to find a variety of uses for a funnel. Compare the students' list to the uses depicted in the illustration.
4. Preview the video *Open Wide: Tooth School Inside* (Keller, 2006) and decide on two places that you will stop the video and discuss it with the students rather than watching it all the way through. Stopping to discuss the video will help focus students' attention and foster retention of the content.
5. After reading *I Lost My Tooth in Africa* (Diakite, 2006) have the students discuss their experiences with the tooth fairy compared to Amina's experiences. Then,

have them talk about similarities and differences between their houses and families and Amina's.

6. Before reading *What You Never Knew about Beds, Bedrooms, and Pajamas* (Lauber, 2006) tell the students that as you read, you will stop periodically to have them discuss the similarities and differences between their beds, bedrooms, and pajamas and the ones in the book. As you read stop and give the students opportunities to make comparisons.

Safety

Sharing books with students about safety at home, at school, and in their neighborhoods teaches students about avoiding risky behaviors and staying safe. However, modeling safe behaviors is perhaps more important than talking about safe behaviors. Morrongiello, Corbett, and Belissimo (2008) found that children whose parents modeled appropriate safety behaviors were more likely to report that they would practice safety as adults. It is interesting to note that the children's present safety habits coincided with what their parents told them to do even if the parents do not behave as they required their children to behave. So for safety lessons to have the greatest impact it is important that adults model appropriate behaviors, not just talk about them. This section addresses standard five regarding the use of decision-making skills to enhance health and safety.

Book and Media Choices

Cuyler, Margery. *Stop, Drop, and Roll.* Illustrated by Arthur Howard. New York: Simon and Schuster, 2001. Unp. ISBN 978-0-689-84355-6. Grades: P–2.

Jessica, the worrywart, discovers during Fire Prevention Week that there is much to worry about. She enlists the aid of her parents as they make sure their house is safe. However, her worries continue as she cannot seem to remember the correct order for the words in "Stop, Drop, and Roll." As children laugh at Jessica's antics, they also learn about fire safety. This book is also available on DVD.

Pancella, Peggy. *Home Safety.* Chicago, IL: Heinemann, 2005. 32p. ISBN 978-1-40344-932-0. Grades: P–3.

Color photographs and simple text explain to young readers how to be safe at home in short two-page chapters. This practical introduction to safety at home also includes a chapter on making a home safety plan. The book includes a table of contents, a list of safety tips, a glossary, and an index. From the Be Safe! series.

Raatma, Lucia. *Safety in Your Neighborhood.* Chanhassen, MN: The Child's World, 2005. 32p. ISBN 978-1-59296-240-2. Grades 4–7.

From reporting burned-out street lights to getting to know your neighbors to not opening the door to strangers, the brief chapters in this book provide a wealth of information about staying safe. The colorful photographs and double-spaced text with keywords in blue font make the information in the book easily accessible to young readers. A glossary, resources for learning more, and an index conclude the book. From the Living Well series.

Raatma, Lucia. *Safety Around Strangers*. Chanhassen, MN: The Child's World, 2005. 32p. ISBN 978-1-59296-244-0. Grades 4–7.

The book starts with a scenario of a child's encounter with a stranger in the park. The succeeding chapters define strangers; discuss strangers in the neighborhood, on the phone, on the Internet and at school. Readers are told to discuss strangers with their parents and to establish a family code word, for parents to share only with people they know in case of an emergency. A glossary, resources for learning more, and an index conclude the book. From the Living Well series.

Howitt, Mary Botham. *The Spider and the Fly*. Illustrated by Tony DiTerlizzi. New York: Simon and Schuster, 2002. Unp. ISBN 978-0-689-85289-3. Grades: 4 and up.

In this timeless classic, a hapless flapper fly is cajoled with flattery to enter the dapper spider's abode where she quickly becomes his dinner. Howitt wrote this poem for her own children to teach them to be wary of flattery. DiTerlizzi's spooky black-and-white illustrations contain hints about the fate in store for the fly. The book concludes with a warning letter from the spider, information about the author, and information about the illustrator. Caldecott Medal Honor Book, 2003.

Explorations

1. Before reading *Stop, Drop, and Roll* (Cuyler, 2001) ask the students what they think "stop, drop, and roll" means. Students who are familiar with the term can demonstrate for their classmates what it means. After reading the book give all the students a chance to practice this life-saving technique.
2. After reading *Home Safety* (Pancella, 2005) have students draw a floor plan of their home. Then, have them take the floor plan home and work with their parents to devise an escape plan.
3. Since many children spend time alone at home create an emergency phone list to send home with them. At the top of the list put 911 followed by the numbers for the local police and fire department along with the phone number for the school. Include blank spaces for their parents to include their work phone numbers, a neighbor's phone number, and phone numbers for doctors.
4. Using a computer and projection system visit the Home Safety Council website at homesafetycouncil.org and tour the MySafeHome so students can learn more about how to be safe in their homes.
5. Prior to reading *Safety in Your Neighborhood* (Raatma, 2005) have students brainstorm on the topics covered in the chapter. Place four pieces of chart paper on the walls around the classrooms. At the top of each page write one of the following phrases: know your neighbors, strangers on the street, someone at the door, and ways to keep the neighborhood safe. Then, after reading the book, have the

students add information they learned to the chart paper. Invite students to talk about what they think was the most interesting or important thing they learned.

6. At the end of *Safety Around Strangers* (Raatma, 2005) there are suggestions for helping keep friends safe. One of the suggestions is to role-play an encounter with a stranger. Provide the students with an opportunity to role-play using the scenarios discussed in the book, such as a stranger trying to lure a child into a car.
7. After reading *The Spider and the Fly* (Howitt, 2002) share the spider's warning letter with the students. Have the students discuss snares that they have been warned to avoid. Then, have them use the spider's letter as a model to write their own warning letter.

Illnesses and Disabilities

Books in this section provide information on illnesses and disabilities that students might encounter in their own families or in their classrooms. There are books about the impact of an illness or a disability on families and resources for helping family members and friends. These stories have the potential to help children develop empathy and understanding for their friends and classmates with disabilities (Kurtis and Gavigan, 2008). Rather than being the focus of nonfiction books, Matthew and Clow (2007) advocate for the casual inclusion of disabled characters in fiction books. Further, they contend that just as children from diverse ethnicities are a natural feature of books, disabled children should also be included. Books in this section address standard seven on practicing health-enhancing behaviors and avoiding risks and standard eight on advocating for health.

Book and Media Choices

Thompson, Lauren. *Ballerina Dreams: A True Story.* Photographs by James Estrin. New York: Feiwel and Friends, 2007. Unp. ISBN 978-0-312-37029-9. Grades: K–2.

Dressed in tutus, tights, tiaras, and ballet slippers, five determined young ballerinas with muscle disorders danced in front of the footlights for a very special dance recital. The dedication and pride of their ballet teacher, Joann Ferrara, their on-stage helpers, their parents, and the ballerinas shine through in the color photographs that accompany the text. ALSC Notable Children's Book, 2008.

Dwight, Laura. *Brothers and Sisters.* New York: Star Bright Books, 2005. Unp. ISBN 978-1-887734-80-6. Grades: K–3.

Clear, crisp photographs of multiethnic siblings, some with disabilities, are interspersed with short blocks of text. Readers quickly learn that these sibling relationships are much like their own: sometimes they get along and sometimes they do not. The children's disabilities are explained as are the accommodations they need each day. Sometimes the children manage on their own and sometimes they need help from a sibling. The book ends with a glossary that defines each physical disability: congenital amputation, Asperger's syndrome, blindness, Down syndrome, deafness and hearing impairment, and cerebral palsy.

Golding, Theresa Martin. *Abby's Asthma and the Big Race.* Illustrated by Margeaux Lucas. Morton Grove, IL: Albert Whitman, 2009. Unp. ISBN 978-0-8075-0465-9. Grades: K–3.

Abby wants to run in the big race, but her asthma makes it difficult to run. While her classmates tease her and her father discourages her, her doctor encourages her to run the race. With help from a health club trainer, she not only runs the race, she wins it. An endnote offers information about asthma and exercise.

Heelan, Jamee Riggio. *Can You Hear a Rainbow? The Story of a Deaf Boy Named Chris.* Illustrated by Nicola Simmonds. Atlanta: Peachtree, 2002. Unp. ISBN 978-1-56145-268-2. Grades: K–3.

Deaf from birth, Chris has never heard his parents' voices or an alarm clock, or a rainbow. The book explains the accommodations that help Chris including sign language, lip reading, and a vibrating alarm clock. The book makes the point that some things like rainbows need not be heard to be enjoyed. From A Rehabilitation Institute of Chicago Learning Book series.

Burstein, John. *Staying Well.* Photographs by Chris Pinchbeck. Illustrations by Ben McGinnis. Milwaukee, WI: Gareth Stevens, 2007. 32p. ISBN 978-0-8368-7744-1. Grades: 2–4.

From earaches to tummy aches to measles to asthma to diabetes, this book contains succinct information on a variety of ailments. Colorful photographs and cutaway diagrams expand on the text. The "Something to Think About" text boxes encourage students to reflect on what they read. Back matter includes a glossary, resources for learning more, and an index. From the Slim Goodbody's Good Health Guides series.

O'Neal, Claire. *The Influenza Pandemic of 1918.* Hockessin, DE: Mitchell Lane, 2008. 32p. ISBN 978-1-58415-569-0. Grades: 3–6.

This book provides the basic facts about the Spanish flu pandemic. Photographs and large type draw in beginning and reluctant readers. The five brief chapters begin with the personal story of a cook on a military base stricken by the flu and the book ends with the caution that it is only a matter of time before another pandemic strikes. Words in bold, some with pronunciation keys, are defined in the glossary. A chronology, resources for learning more, and an index are also included. From A Robbie Reader series.

Lord, Cynthia. *Rules.* New York: Scholastic, 2006. 200p. ISBN 978-0-439-44382-1. Grades: 4–7.

Twelve-year-old Catherine is embarrassed by her autistic younger brother, David, and uncomfortable with her relationship with fourteen-year-old paraplegic, Jason.

To help David negotiate the world and to keep him from embarrassing her, she makes up rules for him to follow. Each chapter title is one of the rules, such as "If it fits in your mouth, it's food." Newbery Medal Honor Book, 2007.

Gray, Susan H. *Living with Cerebral Palsy*. Chanhassen, MN: The Child's World, 2003. 32p. ISBN 978-1-56766-101-9. Grades: 5–8.

This concise look at cerebral palsy has double-spaced text and colorful photographs of multiethnic children living with cerebral palsy. Share this book with children to show them that with help from their classmates these children can participate in a variety of activities. Back matter includes a glossary, resources for learning more, an index, and information about what it means to have cerebral palsy and how to offer help.

Dying to Be Thin. DVD. Boston: WGBH, 2004. 60 min. ISBN 978-1-59375-168-5. Grades: 5 and up.

Susan Sarandon narrates this documentary on the complex causes and treatments for eating disorders. Viewers meet young women who have sought treatment for these potentially life-threatening disorders.

Moss, Jenny. *Winnie's War*. New York: Walker, 2009. 178p. ISBN 978-0-8027-9819-0. Grades: 6–8.

When soldiers returning from the war bring the Spanish flu back with them, no one is safe from it. Winnie takes it upon herself to keep her family safe from the flu, but a younger sister and her best friend succumb to the disease.

Huffing: The Latest Facts about Inhalant Abuse. DVD. Mount Kisco, NY: Human Relations Media. 20 min. 978-1-55548-007-3. Grades: 6–9.

Abusers, parents, and friends tell their personal stories of the dangers and tragedies of huffing inhalants, which are substances found in every house. The eyewitness accounts and dire warnings can be used for discussion starters about this less recognized danger. Includes a teacher resource guide. ALSC Notable Children's Video, 2008.

Shivack, Nadia. *Inside Out: Portrait of an Eating Disorder*. New York: Simon and Schuster, 2007. 64p. ISBN 978-0-689-85216-9. Grades: 6 and up.

Shivack's sketches on paper napkins while she was in treatment for her eating disorder formed the basis for this graphic novel about her struggles. Statistics and facts are interspersed with the drawings and the book concludes with resources for learning more. The book ends on a hopeful note as Shivack recounts how she continues on the road to recovery. Notable Social Studies Trade Book for Young People, 2008.

Orr, Tamra. *When the Mirror Lies: Anorexia, Bulimia, and Other Eating Disorders*. DVD. New York: Franklin Watts, 2007. 144p. ISBN 978-0-531-16791-5. Grades: 7–10.

Case studies of both males and females struggling with eating disorders help readers understand the impact on not just the young people suffering with the diseases but also their families. The facts are presented in a readable format and the photographs, lists, text boxes, and pull quotes hold the readers' attention. The book concludes with a checklist for determining if readers have a problem and advice on what to do to help themselves. A glossary, resources for learning more including websites and toll-free phone numbers, source notes, and an index conclude the book.

Gay, Kathlyn, and Sean McGarrahan. *Epilepsy: The Ultimate Teen Guide.* Lanham, MD: Scarecrow, 2002. 103p. ISBN 978-0-8108-4339-4. Grades: 7 and up.

Pythagoras, Edgar Allan Poe, and Danny Glover are just some of the famous people with the brain disorder epilepsy. Beginning with an explanation of epilepsy, the book tells the history of epilepsy and then provides information on diagnosis, treatment, and living with epilepsy. The book concludes with an appendix, chapter notes, a glossary, resources for learning more, and an index. From the It Happened to Me series.

Gay, Kathlyn. *Am I Fat? The Obesity Issue for Teens.* Berkeley Heights, NJ: Enslow, 2006. 112p. ISBN 978-0-7660-2527-1. Grades: 7 and up.

Obesity, eating disorders, and the dangers of dieting and weight-loss surgery are explained in the first six chapters. The concluding two chapters discuss research on obesity and suggestions for developing a healthy lifestyle, including video games that get young people up and moving. Back matter includes chapter notes, a glossary, resources for learning more, and an index. From the Issues in Focus Today series.

Pharm Parties: A Lethal Mix. DVD. Mount Kisco, NY: Human Relations Media, 2009. DVD. 24 min. Grades: 7 and up.

Throwing prescription and over-the-counter drugs into a bowl creates a potent trail mix that is served to friends at pharm parties. Stories from survivors and stories from family members of those who did not survive a pharm party make riveting viewing. Health care professionals share their personal stories of the tragedies they have witnessed. Includes a teacher resource guide. An ALSC Notable Children's Video, 2009.

Rebman, Renée C. *Addictions and Risky Behaviors: Cutting, Bingeing, Snorting, and Other Dangers.* Berkeley Heights, NJ: Enslow, 2006. 104p. ISBN 978-0-7660-2165-5. Grades: 7 and up.

Drug addiction, alcoholism, inhalant abuse, smoking, eating disorders, self-mutilation, and Internet addiction claim the lives of teenagers at alarming rates. Separate chapters describe these risky behaviors and feature the stories of teens who have experienced the devastating impact these behaviors inflict on the teens, their families, and their friends. Back matter includes chapter notes, a glossary, resources for learning more, and an index. From the Issues in Focus Today series.

Explorations

1. *Can You Hear a Rainbow? The Story of a Deaf Boy Named Chris* (Heelan, 2002) has a compare/contrast format. As children read the book have them record the differences and similarities in a Venn diagram.

2. After reading *The Influenza Pandemic of 1918* (O'Neal, 2008) students can access a letter from a doctor at Camp Devens, Massachusetts, for a first-person account of the impact of the flu. The letter can be found at www.pbs.org/wgbh/amex/influenza/sfeature/devens.html. Students who are familiar with e-mailing and text messaging can revise the letter as it might look as an e-mail message or as a text message. This site has additional information and a link for purchasing the film *Influenza 1918*.
3. Pair *The Influenza Pandemic of 1918* (O'Neal, 2008) with *Winnie's War* (Moss, 2009) and help the students compare and contrast the way the information about influenza was presented in the two books.
4. Before reading *Living with Cerebral Palsy* (Gray, 2003) ask the students to take note of the ways the children's classmates help them participate in activities. After reading the book, have the students brainstorm a list of ways they can help people with disabilities.

Nutrition

Eating the right foods is one component of staying healthy, as food is fuel for the body and gives it the energy to move and grow. Maintaining good nutrition while they are growing impacts students' health for the rest of their lives. Knowing what foods they need to eat helps students make wise choices at mealtime and snack time. Since adults are the ones making food purchases in the home, it is important to share nutrition information with them so that students receive consistent messages (Blom-Hoffman et al., 2008). One way to do this is by sending books and activities about proper nutrition home with students to share with adults in their homes. Books, media, and activities in this section relate to standard six regarding using goal-setting skills to enhance health.

Book and Media Choices

Leedy, Loreen. *The Edible Pyramid: Good Eating Every Day*, Revised Edition. New York: Holiday House, 2007. Unp. ISBN 978-0-8234-2074-2. Grades: P–3.

First published in 1994, the book has been revised to include the redesigned food pyramid. Each section of the pyramid is explained and double-page spreads show examples of foods in that section. The foods are labeled, making this a useful book for teaching students the names of a variety of foods. Portion equivalents are provided and the book makes the point that the right amount of food depends on your size. The book concludes by explaining that the stairs going up the left side of the pyramid serve as a reminder to exercise each day.

Freese, Joan. *Tables and Graphs of Healthy Things*. New York: Gareth Stevens, 2008. 24p. ISBN 978-0-8368-8471-5. Grades: K–2.

Large print on a white background, colorful photographs, and clear easy-to-read tables and graphs introduce students to math and nutrition concepts. A glossary concludes the book. From the Math in Our World series.

Gibbons, Gail. *The Vegetables We Eat*. New York: Holiday House, 2007. Unp. ISBN 978-0-8234-2001-8. Grades: K–3.

Red peppers, yellow corn, green peas, and orange carrots provide a kaleidoscope of colorful vegetables that just might tempt young readers to try them. Even picky eaters might be convinced to add vegetables to their diets if they grow them in their own garden; the book includes basic information on growing them. The book concludes with some veggie trivia.

Miller, Edward. *The Monster Health Book: A Guide to Eating Healthy, Being Active, and Feeling Great for Monsters and Kids*. New York: Holiday House, 2008. 40p. ISBN 0-8234-1958-8. Grades: 1–5.

A bright, colorful table of contents written on a milk carton and an assortment of foods immediately engages readers and has them eagerly turning pages. The book contains a kaleidoscope of facts on healthy eating, exercise, sleep, self-esteem, and addictive habits accompanied by a large, friendly, green monster. The book concludes with a terrific collection of websites for learning more about staying healthy.

Burstein, John. *Eating Right*. Photographs by Chris Pinchbeck. Illustrations by Ben McGinnis. Milwaukee, WI: Gareth Stevens, 2007. 32p. ISBN 978-0-8368-7740-3. Grades: 2–4.

The thirteen chapters are comprised of two-page spreads with a repetitious format that helps readers comprehend the text. "Something to Think About" text boxes encourage students to reflect on what they read and to make connections to their eating habits. Back matter includes a glossary, resources for learning more, and an index. From the Slim Goodbody's Good Health Guides series.

Ruffin, Frances E. *Kitchen Smarts: Food Safety and Kitchen Equipment*. New York: Rosen, 2005. 48p. ISBN 978-1-40420-301-3. Grades: 5–8.

Chapters include information on the importance of maintaining clean and safe kitchens, food poisoning, and determining the shelf life of pantry foodstuffs. Included in the book are photographs of multiethnic families cooking together in the kitchen. A glossary, resources for learning, a bibliography, and an index conclude the book.

Ballard, Carol. *Food for Feeling Healthy*. Chicago, IL: Heinemann Library, 2006. 56p. ISBN 978-1-40348-571-7. Grades: 6–9.

This concise text is filled with nutrition information supplemented by color photographs, interesting text boxes, charts, and diagrams and is a good starting place for learning about nutrition. The book not only explains the Nutrition Facts label found on packaged food; it also explains the information about Daily Values of foods. At the end of the book are recipes, a weeklong menu, a glossary, resources for finding out more, and an index. From the Making Healthy Food Choices series.

Morris, Neil. *Food for Sports*. Chicago, IL: Heinemann Library, 2006. 56p. ISBN 978-1-40348-571-7. Grades: 6–10.

Students interested in improving their sports performance discover the importance of eating the right foods in this easy-to-understand book. Informative text boxes throughout the book contain useful information. For example, one demonstrates the impact of carbohydrates on endurance and another explains the difference in types of sports drinks. The book concludes with ideas for healthy eating, recipes, a glossary, resources for finding out more, and an index. From the Making Healthy Food Choices series.

Shryer, Donna. *Body Fuel: A Guide to Good Nutrition*. Tarrytown, NY: Marshall Cavendish, 2008. 139p. ISBN 978-0-7614-2552-6. Grades: 7–10.

Carbohydrates, fiber, fat, protein, and water are just some of the topics explored in this book. Color photographs, diagrams, and text boxes supplement the informative text. For example, one text box has a Nutrition Facts label and it explains why the labels are important and how to use them. Appendixes, notes, a glossary, resources for learning more, and an index conclude the book. From the Food and Fitness series.

Explorations

1. After reading *Eating Right* (Burstein, 2007) have students visit the Team Nutrition website at teamnutrition.usda.gov/Resources/mypyramidblastoff.html to learn more about the food pyramid by playing the interactive game, MyPyramid Blast Off.
2. Before reading *Eating Right* (Burstein, 2007) visit www.slimgoodbody.com to locate activities for your students to help them remember the information presented in the book.
3. After reading *Kitchen Smarts: Food Safety and Kitchen Equipment* (Ruffin, 2005) have the students examine a selection of pantry foodstuffs that you have brought in so that they can practice determining the expiration dates on the foods. If they cannot determine the expiration dates allow them time to research the manufacturers' websites to determine if the information is available there. Mealtime.org (www.mealtime.org/) offers a chart to help decipher the expiration codes on canned foods.
4. Ask the students to collect nutrition fact labels from the processed foods their families eat or visit the manufacturers' websites and print out nutrition fact labels to share with your students. After reading *Food for Feeling Healthy* (Ballard, 2006) or *Body Fuel: A Guide to Good Nutrition* (Shryer, 2008) have the students use the information in the book to help them read and understand the labels. Then, have each student select one nutrition fact label to talk about with a partner. Then, have the students write down what they learned from their label.

5. Using the nutrition fact labels for similar products from different manufacturers, have the students compare the calories, fat, cholesterol, sodium, carbohydrates, and protein. Then, have them create oral presentations on their findings to share with their classmates.

FAMILIES

This portion of the chapter includes sections on family constellations, divorce, adoption and foster care, and homelessness. Exploring single-parent families, divorced families, families with aging grandparents, and homeless families in books provides opportunities for children to explore and discuss these issues from different points of view. By evaluating the characters' actions they gain insight into their own actions when faced with similar situations. After reading these books students need opportunities to make connections between the characters in the books and their own lives. Books, media, and activities in this section help students use interpersonal communication skills to enhance their personal health, which corresponds to standard six.

Family Constellations

Reading books about different family constellations ensures that children find families similar to their own between the pages of the books, which enables them to find personal meanings in the text as they make connections between their lives and the lives of the characters. The books in this section reflect a variety of family constellations including two mothers, two fathers, blended families, living with a grandparent, and temporarily absent fathers who are traveling or in prison.

Book and Media Choices

Fearnley, Jan. *Billy Tibbles Moves Out!* New York: HarperCollins, 2004. Unp. ISBN 978-1-42235-557-2. Grades: P–2.

Billy Tibbles likes having his very own bedroom and when his parents decide that it's time for his baby brother to share his room, Billy moves out. When neither the bathroom nor the shed suit him, he returns to the house and discovers that sharing a bedroom with his brother has its advantages. The experiences of this furry feline family resonate with family members both young and old.

Garden, Nancy. *Molly's Family.* Illustrated by Sharon Wooding. New York: Farrar, Straus and Giroux, 2004. Unp. ISBN 978-0-374-35002-4. Grades: P–2.

When kindergartener Molly draws her family with two mommies one of her classmates tells her she cannot have two mommies. Another classmate chimes in that he only has a father and the teacher joins the group to help them understand that you can have two mommies. With support from her teacher and love from her two mommies Molly's picture of her family is hung in the classroom for open house.

Juster, Norton. *The Hello, Goodbye Window.* Illustrated by Chris Raschka. New York: Hyperion, 2005. Unp. ISBN 978-0-7868-0914-1. Grades: P–2.

For a small, biracial girl the kitchen window at her Nanna and Poppy's house is a magical place that reflects the love that envelops her. During the day she peers in to surprise her grandparents and at night she peers out seeing her reflection in the glass. This window is a place to note comings and goings from the security of a warm, cozy kitchen. Simple black lines and colorful squiggles and swirls set just the right tone for this lively tale. Caldecott Medal Winner, 2006.

Kerley, Barbara. *You and Me Together: Moms, Dads, and Kids Around the World.* Washington, DC: National Geographic Society, 2005. Unp. ISBN 978-0-7922-8298-3. Grades: P–2.

Whether they are walking hand in hand, cooking a meal, catching a fish, or playing a tune this book is a celebration of the special bond between moms, dads, and kids. Large color photographs (many spanning two pages) accompanied by simple text feature families from around the world. Information at the end of the book contains a map showing where the photographs were taken, and captioned thumbnail sketches of the photographs in the book fill a two-page spread. The book ends with a note on the children of the world from Marian Wright Edelman, President of the Children's Defense Fund.

Parr, Todd. *The Family Book.* New York: Little, Brown, 2003. Unp. ISBN 978-0-316-73896-5. Grades: P–3.

Family diversity is explored in this colorful book filled with clever illustrations and simple sentences. Families come in different sizes and lots of different combinations: two parents, one parent, parents of the same sex, stepfamilies, adopted children, noisy, messy, and different colors. No matter the combination, families are about love and support.

Richardson, Justin, and Peter Parnell. *And Tango Makes Three.* Illustrated by Henry Cole. New York: Simon and Schuster, 2005. Unp. ISBN 978-0-689-87845-9. Grades: P–3.

Realistic watercolor illustrations in soft blues, grays, and browns depict the penguin daddies, Roy and Silo, and their daughter, Tango. The focus of the story is on the loving family rather than the homosexual relationship. The book is based on a true story and an authors' note at the end of the book invites readers to the New York Central Park Zoo to visit the chinstrap penguins featured in the story. ALA Notable Book, 2006. Notable Social Studies Trade Book for Young People, 2006.

Pelton, Mindy L. *When Dad's at Sea.* Illustrated by Robert Gantt Steele. Morton Grove, IL: Albert Whitman, 2004. Unp. ISBN 0-8075-6339-0. Grades: K–2.

While Emily's dad is away at sea, a paper chain helps her track the days until he returns. The support of her mother and the friendship of another child whose dad is on the same ship help her cope. Children whose parents are members of the

United States Armed Forces relate to this story of a loving family separated by deployment.

Harrington, Janice N. *Roberto Walks Home.* Illustrated by Jody Wheeler. New York: Viking, 2008. Unp. ISBN 978-0-670-06316-1. Grades: K–3.

Roberto sits outside of his school forgotten by his older brother Miguel, who has promised to walk him home from school and to play basketball with him. When he realizes his brother is not coming, Roberto walks home alone and spies Miguel playing basketball with his friends. Safely home, his anger explodes. When Miguel comes home, he apologizes and takes Roberto out to play. The brothers in this story were based on characters created by Ezra Jack Keats.

Newman, Lesléa. *Heather Has Two Mommies* (20th Anniversary Edition). Illustrated by Diana Souza. Los Angeles, CA: Alyson Books, 2009. Unp. ISBN 978-1-59350-136-5. Grades: K–3.

When Heather joins a playgroup, she discovers that not everyone has two mommies like she does. She learns that there are different kinds of families, but the one thing they all have in common is that they share a special love for each other.

Williams, Vera B. *Amber Was Brave, Essie Was Smart: The Story of Amber and Essie Told Here in Poems and Pictures.* New York: HarperCollins, 2001. 57p. ISBN 978-0-06-029460-1. Grades: 1–5.

With Dad in jail and Mom working long hours at minimum wage to support the family, Amber and Essie forge a sisterly bond that helps them through the good times and the bad. The book is composed of free-verse poems that focus on the small moments of their lives. It is illustrated with black-and-white sketches; however, a color sketch starts the book and the end is a collage of color illustrations celebrating Dad's homecoming. ALA Notable Book, 2002.

Mazer, Norma Fox. *Ten Ways to Make My Sister Disappear.* New York: Scholastic, 2007. 148p. ISBN 978-0-439-83983-9. Grades: 4–6.

Frustrated by her older sister's teasing, ten-year-old Sprig makes a list of ways to make her sister disappear. With their father away on business in Afghanistan and an elderly neighbor in need of care, the two sisters' conflicts and collaborations depict a typical and complex sibling relationship with which readers can relate.

Withrow, Sara. *Box Girl.* Toronto, Ontario, CN: Groundwood Books, 2001. 181p. ISBN 978-0-88899-436-3. Grades: 6–8.

Five years ago Gwen's mother left leaving her in the care of her father and his partner, Leon. When postcards begin arriving from her mother promising a reunion, Gwen concocts rituals to ensure the reunion happens. She resists Clara's attempts to become friends because she does not want to reveal her father's lifestyle. However, Gwen comes to learn that Clara has problems of her own and knowing that helps Gwen realize that families are the people who love you and care for you.

Explorations

1. Before reading *Billy Tibbles Moves Out!* (Fearnley, 2004) share the author information on the back book cover flap with the students. Fearnley writes about how the book is based on her own life experiences as the youngest of six children. Then, share the Tibbles family portrait on the back cover and the other family photos on the inside cover.
2. While reading *You and Me Together: Moms, Dads, and Kids Around the World* (Kerley, 2005) pause periodically to have the children make comparisons between activities they do with their parents and the activities of the parents and children in the book.
3. After reading *You and Me Together: Moms, Dads, and Kids Around the World* (Kerley, 2005) use a wall map to help the students locate where the families depicted in the book live. The map at the end of the book will help you find the locations.
4. Before reading *Heather Has Two Mommies* (Newman, 2009) provide the students with drawing paper and crayons and ask them to draw a picture of their families. When they finish their drawings, hang them on the bulletin board.
5. After reading *Amber Was Brave, Essie Was Smart: The Story of Amber and Essie Told Here in Poems and Pictures* (Williams, 2001) focus on one of the poems in the book and examine how it was written. Then have the students write their own small poems about small moments in their families' lives.
6. Use *Roberto Walks Home* (Harrington, 2008), *Amber Was Brave, Essie Was Smart: The Story of Amber and Essie Told Here in Poems and Pictures* (Williams, 2001), or *Ten Ways to Make My Sister Disappear* (Mazer, 2007) to engage students in a discussion on the ups and downs of sibling relationships.
7. Several books in this section lend themselves to having students complete feelings charts to help them relate to the characters and their reactions to events in the story (Yopp and Yopp, 2010). Across the top of the chart list the characters' names and down the left side of the chart list four or five events in the story. Read each event and have the students discuss and then fill in how each character feels about the event.

Divorce and Separation

Books in this section include both fiction and nonfiction selections dealing with the feelings and emotions children experience when their parents divorce. Some of these books provide students with practical suggestions for coping with divorce and the inherent changes in their lives. These books also provide teachers, librarians, and parents with insight into divorce from children's perspectives. Books, media, and activities in this section relate to standard five on using decision-making skills to enhance health.

Book and Media Choices

Coffelt, Nancy. *Fred Stays with Me!* Illustrated by Tricia Tusa. New York: Little, Brown, 2007. Unp. ISBN 0-316-88269-0. Grades: K–3.

As a young girl moves between her mother's house and her father's house, her one constant is her dog, Fred. However, Fred is a troublemaker and causes problems at both houses. When both parents complain and declare that Fred cannot stay with either of them, the young girl proclaims that Fred stays with her. So, working together the parents each find their own solutions to living happily with Fred. ALSC Notable Children's Book, 2008. *Boston Globe*–Horn Book Award for Excellence in Children's Literature Honor Book, 2008.

Amos, Janine. *Divorce.* Illustrated by Gwen Green. Photographs by Angela Hampton. Milwaukee, WI: Gareth Stevens, 2002. 32p. ISBN 0-8368-3090-3. Grades: 1–4.

Interspersed with fictional letters from children coping with divorce is factual information that offers solid advice for discussing divorce with children. The book contains useful ideas for helping children whose parents are getting divorced. From the Separations series.

Bingham, Jane. *Why Do Families Break Up?* Chicago, IL: Raintree, 2005. 48p. ISBN 978-0-7398-6683-2. Grades: 4–8.

Color photographs of multiethnic families, fact boxes, and quotes from adults and children tell readers that these are real people who have survived trying situations. Back matter includes a glossary, resources for learning more, and an index. From the Exploring Tough Issues series.

Smith, Hope Anita. *Keeping the Night Watch.* Illustrated by E. B. Lewis. New York: Henry Holt, 2008. ISBN 978-0-8050-7202-0. Grades: 4 and up.

When Daddy leaves home and after a time returns, the whole family walks on eggshells. In a powerful collection of poems, Smith captures the family's worry, rejection, fear, and distrust as seen through the eyes of the oldest son who, since the father's return, is no longer the "man of the house." Lewis' uncluttered, luminescent watercolors capture the essence of this African-American family's struggles to become whole.

Brown, Susan Taylor. *Hugging the Rock.* Berkeley, CA: Tricyle, 2006. 170p. ISBN 978-1-58246-180-9. Grades: 5–8.

In free-verse poems, Rachel tells the story of her mother's mental illness and abandonment. Rachel and her father develop a loving relationship as they learn to cope with the reality of their lives and come to depend on each other. ALSC Notable Children's Book, 2007.

Roberts, Marion. *Sunny Side Up.* New York: Random House, 2008. 218p. ISBN 978-0-385-73672-5. Grades: 5–8.

In first-person narrative Sunny, age eleven, describes her rapidly changing life as her father and his new wife welcome a baby, her mother's boyfriend and his children move in, and she develops a relationship with her estranged grandmother. When her narrative takes off on tangents, the "Tangent Police" rein her back in and get the story back on track. Lists and small photographs add to the story and focus readers' attention.

Smith, Yeardley. *I, Lorelei.* New York: HarperCollins, 2009. 339p. ISBN 978-0-06-149344-7. Grades: 5–8.

Knowing that one day she will be a famous actress, Lorelei keeps a diary so that her biographers will be sure to have the information they need. Rather than "Dear Diary" she addresses each entry to her recently deceased cat, Mud. Writing helps her explore her feelings about trying out for a school musical, her father's infidelity, and the resulting restructuring of her family. The characters' imperfections reveal their complexities and help readers relate to their problems.

Trueit, Trudi Strain. *Surviving Divorce: Teens Talk about What Hurts and What Helps.* New York: Franklin Watts, 2007. 112p. ISBN 978-0-531-12368-3. Grades: 6 and up.

Interspersed with stories, facts, and photographs is practical advice for children about surviving divorce. Depression, anger, and eating disorders are just some of the ways that divorce impacts teens. The book explores teens' feelings and helps them see that divorce is not their fault. Back matter includes a glossary, resources for learning more, and an index.

Explorations

1. Before reading *Fred Stays with Me!* (Coffelt, 2007) make a list on the board of all the things that Fred does that cause problems. Then, ask the students for suggestions on how to stop Fred from causing problems. After reading the book return to the list and compare the parents' solutions to the ones the students suggested.
2. After reading *Fred Stays with Me!* (Coffelt, 2007) discuss why it was so important for Fred to stay with the little girl.
3. Before reading *Why Do Families Break Up?* (Bingham, 2005) have students read aloud selected quotes in the book. Give the students a chance to practice reading the quotes before they read them for their classmates.
4. After reading *Keeping the Night Watch* (Smith, 2008) have the students discuss why Smith wrote the story as a series of poems. Would it have been more or less effective written as a narrative?
5. Before reading *Keeping the Night Watch* (Smith, 2008) put the students in small groups and let each group select one person in the family that they will become. Then, as you read have the groups listen to the poems from that character's perspective. After reading the book have the groups talk about the events in the story from their character's perspective.

6. Consider reading *Sunny Side Up* (Roberts, 2008) aloud to the students a chapter or two at a time. Project the photographs in the books and ask the students to describe what they see and then write about what they predict will happen in the story based on what they observe in the photographs.

Adoption and Foster Care

Adoption and foster care are not as secretive and mysterious as they once were. The books in this section help students understand that their feelings and questions about adoption and foster care are normal. Reading fiction and nonfiction books about foster care can benefit foster children, foster parents, and caseworkers (Baker, 2007). Further, she notes that within the pages of these books, foster children find characters that they can identify with and learn from as they discover that others in foster care share their feelings. Books, media, and activities in this section help students develop interpersonal communication skills, which relate to standard four, and develop the skills necessary to advocate for personal and family health, which is standard eight.

Book and Media Choices

Parr, Todd. *We Belong Together: A Book about Adoption and Families*. New York: Little, Brown, 2007. Unp. ISBN 978-0-316-01668-1. Grades: P–1.

The repeated refrain "We belong together because . . ." flows through this book as children and adults who need one another form families. The bright, colorful illustrations depict diverse families who come together to share their love and their homes.

Carlson, Nancy L. *My Family Is Forever*. New York: Viking, 2004. Unp. ISBN 978-0-14-240561-1. Grades: K–3.

Based on her friends' adoption of a baby girl from Korea, Carlson shows how families are bound together by love without concern for what you look like or where you were born. Wondering about birth parents, traits shared with adoptive parents, and joyous family celebrations are all part of the life of this loved little girl.

Woodson, Jacqueline. *Locomotion*. New York: Putnam, 2003. 100p. ISBN 978-0-399-23115-5. Grades: 4–6.

Eleven-year-old Lonnie has lost his parents in a fire and is separated from his sister who was placed in a different foster home. He explores his life in free-verse poetry as he tries to make sense of his world and his new family. ALSC Notable Children's Book, 2004.

McDowell, Marilyn Taylor. *Carolina Harmony*. New York: Random House, 2009. 323p. ISBN 978-0-385-90575-6. Grades: 4–7.

When an accident kills Carolina's parents and her younger brother, she is moved in and out of foster care homes. She eventually settles in on Harmony Farm, but resists believing that the family really accepts her as their own. Set in the mountains of North

Carolina in the summer of 1964, the setting and the characters draw readers into this story of foster care, love, and racial prejudice. This book is also available as an e-book.

Giff, Patricia Reilly. *Pictures of Hollis Woods.* New York: Random House, 2002. 166p. ISBN 978-0-385-32655-1. Grades: 5–7.

Abandoned at birth, twelve-year-old Hollis Woods has run away from a series of foster homes. When she is placed with a retired art teacher, her artistic talents bloom and the two form a close bond. Her life is revealed through flashbacks and readers develop an empathy for her as they learn about her past. Newbery Medal Honor Book, 2003. ALSC Notable Children's Book, 2003.

Warren, Andrea. *Escape from Saigon: How a Vietnam War Orphan Became an American Boy.* New York: Farrar, Straus and Giroux, 2004. 110p. ISBN 978-0-374-32224-3. Grades: 5 and up.

Her own experience adopting a Vietnam War orphan led Warren to write this compelling book. She recounts the story of an orphan, Long, who was eight years old when as part of Operation Babylift he was brought to America and adopted. Black-and-white photographs accompany the informative text that echoes the hope of the author that children around the world whose lives are impacted by war will not be forgotten. An afterword, resources for learning more, and an index conclude the book. NCTE Orbus Pictus Recommended Book, 2005.

Explorations

1. Consider doing an author study of Nancy Carlson's books. Her optimistic picture books portray characters who are coping with challenges similar to those of your students. Her website at www.nancycarlson.com has information about the books she has written and illustrated.
2. As you are reading aloud the poems in *Locomotion* (Woodson, 2003) periodically pause and project the poems for students to read for themselves. Then, engage the students in discussions about the author's word choice and the impact of word choice on the emotions the poems convey.
3. Before students read *Pictures of Hollis Woods* (Giff, 2002) discuss the use of flashbacks in the book and why the author used them to tell the story.
4. After reading *Escape from Saigon: How a Vietnam War Orphan Became an American Boy* (Warren, 2004) allow students to explore the website www.vietnambabylift.org/ to learn more about Operation Babylift. The website includes a timeline, photographs, audio files and other resources including personal stories to help students understand the impact of war on innocent children.

Homelessness

Homeless people are seen on the side of the road, living under overpasses, and camping out on city sidewalks. Included in the homeless population are children and their parents. The books in this section enable students to learn about homelessness from the perspective of the homeless and to develop empathy for them as students discover the challenges homeless individuals face as they try to stay fed, warm, and clean. Books and media in this section help students learn how to advocate for the homeless, which encompasses standard eight.

Book and Media Choices

Upjohn, Rebecca. *Lily and the Paper Man.* Illustrated by Renné Benoit. Toronto, Ontario, CN: Second Story, 2007. Unp. ISBN 978-1-897187-19-7. Grades: P–2.

Lily's initial reaction is to run away from the homeless man standing in the snow. However, the image of the man haunts the young girl and with the help of her parents and neighbors she collects warm clothing for him. Colorful, realistic illustrations accompany this heartwarming story that shows readers that everyone, no matter their age, can help someone less fortunate.

Gunning, Monica. *A Shelter in Our Car.* Illustrated by Elaine Pedlar. San Francisco, CA: Children's Book Press, 2004. Unp. ISBN 978-0-89239-189-9. Grades: K–5.

Zettie and her mother are living in their car and washing in a park restroom. Finding a place to park the car each night, having enough food to eat, and taunting classmates are some of the problems Zettie copes with each day. Her mother's love and hope for a better life surround her. Bold colors, thick black lines, and the distorted faces of the characters depict their despair.

Hannah's Story. DVD. Montreal, Quebec, CN: National Film Board of Canada, 2008. 29 min. Grades: 3 and up.

Eleven-year-old Canadian Hannah Taylor encountered a homeless person when she was five. This encounter so troubled her that she set about making a difference in her world by establishing the Ladybug Foundation to increase awareness of homelessness and to provide for the homeless. Hannah's inspirational story leaves viewers with ideas for what they can do to help in their communities. A teaching guide for the film is available on the National Film Board of Canada website at onf-nfb.gc.ca/. ALSC Notable Children's Video, 2009.

O'Connor, Barbara. *How to Steal a Dog.* New York: Farrar, Straus and Giroux, 2007. 170p. ISBN 978-0-374-33497-0. Grades: 4–8.

When her father walks out and her mother does not have enough money to pay the rent, Georgina, her younger brother Toby, and her mother end up living in their car. Her friends reject her and her teachers worry about her. Her mother is working two jobs and still they are living in their car. Realizing that her mother does not seem to be able to make enough money for them to have a house, Georgina decides it is up to her to help. Stealing a dog and then collecting the reward for its safe return might be just the thing to do.

Explorations

1. After reading *A Shelter in Our Car* (Gunning, 2004) revisit the book to find evidence of the loving bond between the mother and the child.
2. In *How to Steal a Dog* (O'Connor, 2007) Georgina makes a list in her notebook of the steps to steal the dog. However, she keeps leaving things off the list, like where to hide a dog if you are living in a car. Her brother points out these things as the plot hatches. Have the students stop as they read the story and look at Georgina's list and see if they can predict the things that are missing before Toby points them out.
3. After reading *How to Steal a Dog* (O'Connor, 2007) have the students discuss ways to help the homeless or what to do if they suspect a friend is going through a difficult time. Return to the book and talk about different ways Luanne Godfrey turned out not to be the best friend Georgina thought her to be. Ask the students to suggest things that Luanne could have done differently.

GROWTH AND DEVELOPMENT

This section includes books on growing up and growing older—from dealing with a new sibling to discovering body parts, and understanding aging. Throughout life, events occur that surprise and delight, such as a new baby and discovering bodily changes. Children's literature serves as an introduction to new events that are taking place in children's lives and serves to reassure them that their reactions and feelings are a normal part of growing up. The books in this section offer opportunities not just to introduce new events but also to discuss them and to respond to them through a variety of activities.

Birth and Growth

Being born and growing up are the most personal topics that children hear and read about. During all stages of life, it is important to be aware of the changes taking place in their bodies and to stay healthy so they can appreciate all that life has to offer. Books, media, and activities in this section relate to standard five, using decision-making skills to enhance their health, and standard six, using goal setting to stay healthy.

Book and Media Choices

Carlson, Nancy. *Get Up and Go!* New York: Viking, 2006. Unp. ISBN 0-670-05981-1. Grades: P–2.

A delightful crew of animal characters shows readers how to get moving and exercise by walking, bike riding, and playing sports. Bright, colorful illustrations of friends and families participating in activities give students ideas for getting up and getting moving.

Paratore, Coleen. *Catching the Sun*. Illustrated by Peter Catalanotto. Watertown, MA: Charlesbridge, 2008. Unp. ISBN 978-1-57091-720-2. Grades: P–2.

On the morning of his fifth birthday Dylan and his pregnant mom steal outside in the cool, dark morning onto the Cape Cod beach to capture the sun. As the sun breaks through he closes his eyes and captures the memories of the first glint of the sun and a very special time with his mother. His life is changing but he will always have the memory of this special time alone with his mother.

Adolf, Jaime. *Small Fry*. Illustrated by Mike Reed. New York: Penguin, 2008. Unp. ISBN 978-0-525-46935-3. Grades: K–3.

Nineteen free-verse poems explore what it means to be a "small fry," such as not being tall enough to go on amusement park rides and wondering about growing tall. However, being small has its advantages and they are also noted in the poems. Lively, colorful illustrations reflect the words and capture the rhythm of the poems.

Silverstein, Alvin. *Growth and Development*. Minneapolis, MN: Twenty-First Century Books, 2008. 112p. ISBN 978-0-8225-6057-9. Grades 4–8.

In seven chapters Silverstein presents a great deal of information about how humans, animals, and plants grow. Photographs, text boxes, and diagrams break up the text and make it more comprehensible. The last chapter focuses on future developments and current research. Back matter includes a glossary, a bibliography, resources for learning more, and an index. From the Science Concepts series.

Explorations

1. Students can easily relate to the poems in *Small Fry* (Adolf, 2008), but Adolf did not write about every experience children have when they are not tall enough. Ask the students to brainstorm a list of things that have happened to them or things they are waiting to do until they grow taller. Then, have the students use the poems in this book as models for writing about their own experiences.
2. After reading *Small Fry* (Adolf, 2008), have the students work together to dramatize some of the poems. Then, have them visit other classrooms to perform.
3. Students can read *Growth and Development* (Silverstein, 2008) with a partner. The students take turns reading short sections of the book. When the reader stops, the listener recounts his understanding of what was read. Then, they swap roles and the reader becomes the listener.

Feelings

Everyone has feelings and children need to know that feelings are normal. They may need help understanding their feelings and learning to deal with them appropriately. In the pages of these books students find children with feelings similar to ones they have experienced and they learn how these children deal with their feelings. Students may benefit from being able to role-play dealing with different feelings.

Book and Media Choices

hooks, bell. *Grump Groan Growl.* Illustrated by Chris Raschka. New York: Hyperion, 2008. Unp. ISBN 978-0-7868-0816-8. Grades: P–1.

Overcome by a bad mood? Rhyming text painted into the illustrations explores that mood and counsels readers to "Just let it slide." The book shows children that bad moods are normal and offers a way to deal with them. The large bold illustrations and the large dark text make this a book for reading aloud and it is one that children will then pick up on their own to revisit.

Rotner, Shelley. *Lots of Feelings.* Brookfield, CT: Millbrook Press, 2003. 24p. ISBN 978-0-7613-2377-8. Grades: P–1.

Angry, loving, surprised, and sleepy faces are just some of the feelings captured in the full-page photographs. Each full-page face is accompanied by two smaller faces and a short phrase or sentence naming the feeling. At the end of the book is a two-page spread of faces depicting lots of different feelings. An author's note with ideas for sharing the book with young readers is included.

Harris, Robie H. *Don't Forget to Come Back!* Illustrated by Harry Bliss. Cambridge, MA: Candlewick, 2004. Unp. ISBN 0-7636-1782-2. Grades: P–2.

When Mommy and Daddy announce they are going out for the evening, their daughter immediately protests being left with a babysitter. When her predictions of impending disasters fail to convince them to stay home, she runs away to the closet but does not stay gone long. Throughout the story the parents continue their preparations and leave when the babysitter arrives. Morning comes with her parents sleeping in their beds. The surprise ending will have everyone giggling.

Jackson, Ellen B. *Sometimes Bad Things Happen.* Brookfield, CT: Millbrook Press, 2002. Unp. ISBN 978-0-7613-2810-0. Grades: P–2.

Full-page color photographs and short, simple sentences let children know that bad things happen, but that good things follow. Parents yell, accidents happen, games get canceled, and other familiar disappointments are noted. Following these incidents are suggestions of what to do to feel better, such as help someone, hug a friend, or sing a song.

Lichtenheld, Tom. *What Are You So Grumpy About?* New York: Little Brown, 2003. Unp. ISBN 0-316-59236-6. Grades: P–2.

Life is full of reasons to be grumpy, from favorite clothes in the laundry to getting underwear for a birthday present to being touched by a sibling. These and other childhood annoyances are explored in hilarious cartoon illustrations and large scrawled fonts. However, a good tickle can turn a mood around and make the grumpies disappear.

Medina, Sarah. *Proud.* Chicago, IL: Heinemann, 2007. 24p. ISBN 978-1-40349-296-8. Grades: P–3.

In nine short chapters readers learn the definition of proud and explore what it means to be proud. The illustrations feature rich colors, strong lines, and multiethnic children. A short quiz, a picture glossary, and an index conclude the book. From the Feelings series.

Wood, Douglas. *The Secret of Saying Thanks.* Illustrated by Greg Shed. New York: Simon and Schuster, 2005. Unp. ISBN 978-0-689-85410-1. Grades: P–3.

Muted oil paintings depict a child and her faithful canine companion as she gives thanks for nature, her home, and her family. The book reveals that the secret to happiness is to take time to notice and to give thanks.

Peterson, Jeanne Whitehouse. *Don't Forget Winona.* Illustrated by Kimberly Bulcken Root. New York: HarperCollins, 2004. Unp. ISBN 0-06-027198-1. Grades: K–4.

Keeping track of a younger sibling is not an easy task and it is even more difficult when a family is relocating to a new home. When the dust storms drove the family from their home in Oklahoma, they traveled Route 66 to a better life in California. More than just the story of westward migration, it is also the story of a loving family who pulls together during difficult times to make a better life for themselves.

Raum, Elizabeth. *New Brothers and Sisters.* Chicago, IL: Heinemann, 2008. 32p. ISBN 978-1-43290-820-1. Grades: 1–3.

This brief chapter book has large text and captioned color photographs offering information on what happens when a new baby arrives. Readers learn that feeling left out is normal and that talking to an adult helps. Back matter includes a glossary, resources for learning more, and an index. From the Tough Topics series.

Becoming an Organized Student. DVD. Mount Kisco, NY: Human Relations Media, 2008. 20 min. ISBN 978-1-55548-597-9. Grades: 5–9.

Disorganized middle schoolers will recognize themselves in the students featured in this film, which offers effective solutions to getting organized. An on-screen quiz gets students involved in viewing the film and making changes to organize their lives. ALSC Notable Children's Video, 2008.

Hyde, Margaret O., and Elizabeth H. Forsyth. *Stress 101: An Overview for Teens.* Minneapolis, MN: Twenty-First Century Books, 2008. 120p. ISBN 978-0-8225-6788-2. Grades: 7–10.

From a description of stress to the impact it has on the body to how to control stress, this book contains useful information for teens in a very readable format. The book makes a very important point about sometimes not being able to control stressors, but being able to control the response to a stressful situation.

Explorations

1. Before reading *Grump Groan Growl* (hooks, 2008) or *What Are You So Grumpy About?* (Lichtenheld, 2003) have the students brainstorm a list of things that make them grumpy and then predict whether or not they are in the book. After reading the book have students use the book as a model to create a sequel to the book, putting in the things that make them grumpy that were left out of the book.
2. After reading *Lots of Feelings* (Rotner, 2003) take digital photographs of the students making different faces for different feelings. Then, compare the students' faces to the faces in the book to identify different emotions.
3. After reading *Don't Forget to Come Back!* (Harris, 2004) discuss the cause-and-effect pattern in the story. For the youngest students this might simply be asking them what happened when the little girl's parents tell her they are going out for the evening.
4. After reading *Sometimes Bad Things Happen* (Jackson, 2002) have the students talk about what they can do to help someone feel better after something bad happens. You might begin the discussion by asking them what makes them feel better after something bad happens.
5. While *Sometimes Bad Things Happen* (Jackson, 2002) is for younger students, it could also be read aloud to older students in order to start a discussion of appropriate ways to behave when bad things happen.
6. After reading *Don't Forget Winona* (Peterson, 2004), ask the students what they think is the worst thing about moving and the best thing about moving. Telling the best thing last helps ensure that the sharing ends on an upbeat note.
7. Before reading *Stress 101: An Overview for Teens* (Hyde and Forsyth, 2008) make a list of stressors and then a list of things they do to relieve stress. After reading the book, add to the lists. Leave the lists up and encourage students to add to them throughout the school year.
8. While *Stress 101: An Overview for Teens* (Hyde and Forsyth, 2008) is for older students, teachers can have younger students practice body scanning and the quieting reflex. Before handing out tests give the students time to try one of these relaxation techniques.

Friendship

One of the first experiences children have outside of the family is making friends. The many facets of friendship are examined in these books, including how to make friends, what it means to be a friend, and the value of friends. Reading these books provides children with opportunities to learn friendship skills that they can role-play with their classmates. Throughout their lives they will be able to use these interpersonal skills.

Book and Media Choices

Chodos-Irvine, Margaret. *Best Best Friends.* New York: Harcourt, 2006. Unp. ISBN 978-0-15-205694-0. Grades: P–1.

Set in a preschool classroom, this story of two best friends whose argument explodes into "YOU ARE NOT MY BEST FRIEND!" resonates with preschoolers. They will recognize the familiar backdrop of the classroom and playground depicted in the bright colorful prints. The friends resolve their differences without adult intervention and provide a model for solving differences. ALSC Notable Children's Book, 2007.

Chaconas, Dori. *Cork and Fuzz: Short and Tall.* Illustrated by Lisa McCue. New York: Viking, 2006. 32p. ISBN 978-0-670-05985-0. Grades: P–2.

Muscrat Cork is older and possum Fuzz is taller. When Cork decides that since he is older he should be taller, the friends try a variety of ways to make it happen and in the end decide they can be friends just the way they are. This short chapter book is just right for beginning readers. From the Viking Easy-to-Read series. ALSC Notable Children's Book, 2007.

Ormerod, Jan. *Emily and Albert.* Illustrated by David Slonim. San Francisco, CA: Chronicle Books, 2004. Unp. ISBN 978-0-8118-3615-9. Grades: P–2.

Emily, an ostrich, and Albert, an elephant, are the best of friends, so Albert just goes along as Emily decides what is best for both of them. Younger readers will enjoy the delightful story and astute readers will recognize that while Emily and Albert have their differences, what matters most is their friendship. The five short chapters include lively illustrations that hold the details of this special relationship.

Willems, Mo. *I Am Going!* New York: Hyperion, 2010. Unp. ISBN 978-1-42311-990-6. Grades: P–2.

Gerald and Piggie are the best of friends. When Piggie announces, "I am going!" he ruins Gerald's day and sends him into a tizzy. The cartoon illustrations and the spare capitalized text depict Gerald's anguish. All ends well, when Gerald realizes that Piggie is just going to lunch and that lunch is big enough to share.

English, Karen. *Hot Day on Abbott Avenue.* Illustrated by Javaka Steptoe. New York: Clarion, 2004. Unp. ISBN 978-0-395-98527-4. Grades: P–3.

Best friends Kishi and Renée are mad at each other and the tension between them heats up in the hot summer sun. But just as best friends do, they forgive each other and join together for jump rope—double dutch. Textured cut paper collage illustrations accented with found objects fill the pages. ALSC Notable Children's Book, 2005.

Frazee, Marla. *A Couple of Boys Have the Best Week Ever.* Orlando, FL: Harcourt, 2008. Unp. ISBN 978-0-15-206020-6. Grades: K–3.

A weeklong celebration of friendship is chronicled in favorite childhood activities when two boys spend the week at one boy's grandparents' beach house. By day they attend nature camp, which is shown on the end pages of the book. The real fun is in the illustrations where it is revealed that quiet meditation is actually video games and the popcorn party comes complete with snoring grandparents. The detailed cartoon illustrations capture a very special friendship. Caldecott Medal Honor Book, 2009. ALSC Notable Children's Book, 2009. *Boston Globe*–Horn Book Award for Excellence in Children's Literature Honor Book, 2008.

Varon, Sara. *Robot Dreams*. New York: Roaring Brook, 2007. 205p. ISBN 978-1-59643-108-9. Grades: 3 and up.

This almost-wordless graphic novel depicts the friendship between a dog and his mail-order robot. When a day at the beach leaves the robot rusty and immobile, the dog, uncertain as to how to help, leaves his friend behind. While dog and robot do not end up back together again, the book has a satisfying ending. The cartoon artwork with its muted earth-tone colors sets the tone for this story of friendship and loss. ALSC Notable Children's Book, 2008.

Perkins, Lynne Rae. *Criss Cross*. New York: HarperCollins, 2005. 337p. ISBN 978-0-06-009273-3. Grades: 6–9.

Set in a small town in the 1970s, this sequel to *All Alone in the Universe* (Perkins, 2005) follows three friends, Debbie, Hector, and Lenny, as their lives intertwine through the spring and summer. The text blends together a narrative replete with figurative language, poems, photographs, and dialogue. Newbery Medal Winner, 2006.

Explorations

1. After reading *Best Best Friends* (Chodos-Irvine, 2006) invite the students to talk about how the girls resolved their differences.
2. After reading *Hot Day on Abbott Avenue* (English, 2004) have the students discuss what friendship means and why it is good to have friends. Then, have them do a five-minute quickwrite on friendship. As the students are writing, write along with them. When the students are finished ask for volunteers to share what they have written. If students are not willing to share what they have written, then share your writing with them.
3. While reading *A Couple of Boys Have the Best Week Ever* (Frazee, 2008) pause to have the students record the actions and feelings in the book that indicate the boys are best friends.
4. After reading *A Couple of Boys Have the Best Week Ever* (Frazee, 2008) have the students complete a chart comparing the similarities and differences between the two boys in the book and their personal friends.
5. Stop about halfway through *Robot Dreams* (Varon, 2007) and have the students predict how the story will end. When you finish reading the book ask the students why they think Varon chose the ending she did.

6. While students are reading *Criss Cross* (Perkins, 2005) have them note how the author weaves together different writing formats in the book including narrative, poems, dialogue, and questions and answers. During writing workshop encourage the students to blend together one or two different formats in their writing.

Self-Esteem

Sharing books that contain positive gender role models and are quality literature can help build positive self-esteem in children. Students' engagement and personal responses to books are important if they are to benefit from books.

Book and Media Choices

Otoshi, Kathryn. *One*. San Rafael, CA: KO Kids Books, 2008. Unp. ISBN 978-0-9723946-4-2. Grades: P–K.

Using bright, round splashes of primary colors and the numbers one to seven, Otoshi tells a powerful, simple story about standing up to a bully. It just takes one to stand up to a bully and when the others follow along the bully backs down. Then, they invite the bully to be friends. E.B. White Read Aloud Honor Book, 2009.

Helakoski, Leslie. *Woolbur*. Illustrated by Lee Harper. New York: HarperCollins, 2008. Unp. ISBN 978-0-06-084726-5. Grades: P–1.

Woolbur is a sheep like no other and that is fine by him. Unfortunately, his parents think he needs to act like the other sheep even though Grandpa reassures them that Woolbur is fine just as he is. By the end of the book Woolbur convinces the other sheep that perhaps they should be more like him. This book is available on DVD.

D'Amico, Carmela, and Steven D'Amico. *Ella the Elegant Elephant*. DVD. Homes, NY: Spoken Arts, 2006. 11 min. ISBN 978-0-8045-8044-1. Grades: K–3.

Based on the book by the same name, this video features a familiar tale of the new child at school being the target of a bully. Starting a new school is never easy and Ella dons her grandmother's "good luck hat" for reassurance. At first the hat is ridiculed but when it helps Ella rescue the bully, everyone wants a hat like Ella's. ALSC Notable Children's Video, 2006.

Cannon, Janell. *Crickwing*. New York: Harcourt, 2000. Unp. ISBN 978-0-15-201790-3. Grades: 1–4.

A cockroach with a crooked wing, who just happens to like sculpting his food into animals before he devours it, is picked on by larger animals. He then in turn begins to bully the leaf-cutting ants, who capture him and plan to turn him over to the army ants. But the leaf-cutting ants cannot leave him to be shredded by the army ants. In turn he helps them trick the army ants into leaving them alone. The book concludes with information on cockroaches, leaf-cutting ants, and army ants.

Let's Get Real. DVD. Harriman, NY: New Day Films, 2003. 35 min. ISBN 978-1-57448-116-7. Grades: 6–8.

Middle school students speak about the name-calling and bullying that they endure. Heard too are the voices of those who pick on other students and the voices of those who intervene. Bonus features include an interview with the director, and a curriculum guide is available. ALSC Notable Children's Video, 2005.

Jessup, Maggie. *Just Yell Fire: Empowering Girls to Protect Themselves.* DVD. Vancouver, WA: Just Yell Fire, 2008. 45 min. Grades: 6 and up.

What started out as Dallas Jessup's school project has resulted in a nonprofit organization to protect teenage girls from assault. This film empowers young girls to avoid dangerous situations and to protect themselves if they are attacked. The film is available for downloading at www.justyellfire.com, and it is available on DVD. ALSC Notable Children's Video Winner, 2008.

Explorations

1. After reading *One* (Otoshi, 2008) or *Crickwing* (Cannon, 2000) help the students recognize the bullying that happened in the story. Then, help them decide on a plan of action when they are the target of bullying, being sure to help them understand that frequently adult intervention is needed.
2. After reading *Ella the Elegant Elephant* (D'Amico and D'Amico, 2006) ask the students to share their experiences about attending a new school. Ask them what others could have done to make the day easier for them. Then, have them develop a plan to help new students get acquainted with their school.
3. While watching *Let's Get Real*, stop it every ten minutes and have the students take two or three minutes to write down their reactions to what they have seen. As the students write take this opportunity to write down your own reflections. When teachers write with students they provide powerful models for the students. At the end of the film have the students share their reflections and also share your reflections.
4. After watching *Let's Get Real*, provide the students with opportunities to role-play dealing with bullies.

Manners

Good manners require showing others common courtesies; in other words, treating them respectfully. Sharing books about manners and offering students opportunities to practice good manners facilitates the creation of a classroom environment conducive to learning and provides students with essential life skills. Using humor and common sense, the books in this section provide examples of appropriate manners to use in a variety of social situations.

Book and Media Choices

Willems, Mo. *Time to Say "Please"!* New York: Hyperion, 2005. Unp. ISBN 978-0-7868-5293-2. Grades: P–3.

Clever cartoon illustrations with round-faced children and zany mice holding word balloons make the point that "please" is a very important word to know and to use. There are lots of reasons given for using "please" and "sorry," with "thank you" and "excuse me" thrown in for good measure.

DeGezelle, Terri. *Manners at a Friend's Home.* Mankato, MN: Capstone, 2005. 24p. ISBN 0-7368-2643-2. Grades: K–2.

Colorful photographs and simple sentences explain how to make introductions, how to share, how to be polite, and what to do when it is time to go home, along with other appropriate behaviors. The book concludes a glossary, resources for learning more, and an index.

Katz, Alan. *Are You Quite Polite? Silly Dilly Manners Songs.* Illustrated by David Catrow. New York: Simon and Schuster, 2006. Unp. ISBN 978-0-689-86970-9. Grades: K–3.

Colorful cartoon characters show readers how to be polite and how to be not so polite. The delightful rhyming text can be sung to the tunes of familiar songs. Fights with siblings, birthday party manners, writing thank-you notes, and table manners are just some of the etiquette topics that are explored with comic twists.

Keller, Laurie. *Do Unto Otters: A Book about Manners.* New York: Henry Holt, 2007. Unp. ISBN 978-0-8050-7996-8. Grades: K–3.

From the title pun to the frenetic illustrations of eye-popping rabbits and otters, this is a charming look at how to get along with others or otters. Readers see how the golden rule guides them as they cooperate, share, play fair, and apologize in their interactions with others. Along the way they can learn to say "please," "thank you," and "excuse me" in five languages including Pig Latin. The video version of this book produced by Weston Woods is an ALSC Notable Children's Video, 2009.

Marciano, John Bemelmans. *Madeline Says Merci: The-Always-Be-Polite Book.* New York: Viking, 2001. Unp. ISBN 978-0-670-03505-2. Grades: K–3.

Ludwig Bemelmans' beloved characters live on in this book on manners written by his grandson. There are five sections to the book including saying hello, please and thank you, kindness and consideration, sorry, and goodnight. Simple text and charming pictures provide easy-to-follow basic directions for being polite.

Post, Peggy, and Cindy Post Senning. *Emily's Everyday Manners.* Illustrated by Steve Bjorkman. New York: HarperCollins, 2006. Unp. ISBN 978-0-06-076177-6. Grades: K–3.

Lively, colored illustrations show Emily and Ethan using good manners at school, at home, and in the president's office. Dos and don'ts tucked into the lefthand corners of some pages add emphasis to the manners lessons. The book concludes with an afterword offering advice for adults to help children develop good manners.

Senning, Cindy Post, and Peggy Post. *Emily's Sharing and Caring Book.* Illustrated by Leo Landry. New York: HarperCollins, 2008. Unp. ISBN 978-0-06-111698-8. Grades: K–3.

Large print and short sentences make this a book that children can read on their own after loving adults read it with them and discuss the concepts of sharing and caring. The book concludes with a letter to parents offering advice on helping children develop sharing and caring habits.

Huget, Jennifer LaRue. *Thanks a Lot, Emily Post!* Illustrated by Alexandra Boiger. New York: Random House, 2009. Unp. ISBN 978-0-375-83853-8. Grades: K–3.

Emily Post's first etiquette book came out in the 1920s and when the mother in this story brings the book home and insists her children follow the rules, they resist. Since Mother cannot be deterred, the children insist that Mother also has to follow the rules. In the end, Mother sends the book packing. Watercolor illustrations filled with slapstick comedy depict the chaos that reigns in the household. An endnote provides additional information about Emily Post.

Explorations

1. After reading *Time to Say "Please"!* (Willems, 2005) have the students role-play situations so they can practice saying "please," "thank you," and "sorry."
2. After reading *Manners at a Friend's Home* (DeGezelle, 2005) have the students participate in the activity in the back of the book, Hands On: Introductions. The students sit in a circle and introduce themselves by saying their names and something they like.
3. Have the students sing along to *Are You Quite Polite?: Silly Dilly Manners Songs* (Katz, 2006).
4. After reading *Are You Quite Polite? Silly Dilly Manners Songs* (Katz, 2006) project some of the verses for the students to see and ask them to point out the rhyming words. Then, model for them how to write a verse about manners for behaving in the movies, on the school bus, in the bathroom, or while waiting in line. Give the students time to write their own silly songs. Writing in rhyme is not always easy and to avoid forced rhymes just have the students focus on the writing rather than the rhyming.
5. After reading *Emily's Sharing and Caring Book* (Post and Senning, 2008) have the students work in groups to make lists of things they can do to make others feel good and to show that they care. Combine the students' lists and hang them in the classroom. Periodically review the lists with the students.
6. The Emily Post Institute website at www.emilypost.com has resources including videos for teaching proper etiquette.

Aging and Death

Sharing books that have realistic portrayals of older adults helps children overcome the media stereotypes of how older adults look and act. Through books children can explore what it means to age and they can make connections between the older adults in their lives and the characters in the books. Books such as the ones in this section help children see the importance of intergenerational relationships in their lives and the benefits of being loved and cherished by older adults. Older adults and grandparents, in books as in life, may be the ones to talk to children about not only aging but about death. Grandparents encountered within the pages of books share their thoughts about and experiences with death as well as share with the children lasting memories and legacies that will sustain them (Corr, 2003/2004a).

Books about death help children explore the emotional impact of losing a loved one and in some books the cultural and mourning rituals, as well as spiritual beliefs surrounding passing from life (Poling and Hupp, 2008). The loved one who dies might be a pet, who has given unconditional love. With the death of a pet children learn about death, grieving, and coping (Corr, 2003/2004b). Conflicting emotions exhibited by characters in realistic fiction books dealing with death add depth and dimension to the characters that enable students to identify with them. Hunt (2006) notes that grieving children have an innate ability to connect with stories that reflect their experiences with death. Further, she contends that they need to have opportunities to explore a variety of texts and if needed have the texts read to them again and again. Teachers and librarians may feel unprepared to discuss death with children and may need assistance from school district support personnel, such as counselors.

Book and Media Choices

Goldman, Linda. *Children Also Grieve: Talking about Death and Healing.* Philadelphia, PA: Jessica Kingsley, 2006. Unp. ISBN 978-1-84310-808-5. Grades: P–1.

Told from the point of view of the family dog, this book explores how the family members react differently to Grandfather's death. The book includes fill-in-the-blank sentences and opportunities to draw pictures to explore death and grief. A glossary of words related to death is included. The book ends with an extensive note for adults to help children deal with grief.

Krishnaswami, Uma. *Remembering Grandpa.* Illustrated by Layne Johnson. Honesdale, PA: Boyds Mills, 2007. Unp. ISBN 978-1-59078-424-2. Grades: K–3.

When Grandpa's death brings sadness to Grandma, Daysha sets out to capture memories of him in order to cheer up Grandma. Towing her wagon, she visits places he loved and gathers flowers, rocks, leaves, a snakeskin, and other reminders of her grandpa. On top of the pile she sets his guitar and invites Grandma to remember the happy times. Pastel illustrations depict the wondrous desert world.

Moore-Mallinos, Jennifer. *I Remember*. Illustrated by Marta Fabrega. Hauppauge, NY: Barrons Educational Series, 2005. Unp. ISBN 978-0-7641-3274-2. Grades: K–3.

Rich, full-page pastel illustrations tell the loving story of a faithful companion, Jake, as he grows from a puppy to an adult dog and eventually dies. The boy remembers all of the fun they had together and even though he has a new puppy, he still remembers Jake.

Creech, Sharon. *Love That Dog*. New York: HarperCollins, 2001. 128p. ISBN 9–78-0-06-029287-4. Grades: 3–6.

For every child who has struggled to write poetry and for every teacher who has struggled to teach children to write poetry, this book holds answers and ideas. First find a topic the writer cares deeply about; in this case it is the death of a faithful canine companion. As the boy's poetry writing develops, the story of the loss of his dog unfolds. It is a moving story that shows that with time comes healing.

Henkes, Kevin. *Bird Lake Moon*. New York: HarperCollins, 2008. 179p. ISBN 978-0-06-147076-9. Grades: 4–7.

Summer on the lake brings two boys together in unexpected ways. Spencer and his family have returned to the lake where his older brother died at the age of four. Mitch is at the lake with his mother staying with his grandparents while his parents are making plans for their divorce. Their lives briefly intertwine as they both confront the losses in their lives. This book is also available on CD.

Nicholls, Sally. *Ways to Live Forever*. New York: Arthur A. Levine Books, 2008. 212p. ISBN 978-0-545-06948-9. Grades: 4–7.

Eleven-year-old Sam McQueen is dying of lymphoblastic leukemia and uses writing to help him make sense of his life and death. As his parents try to deal with his impending death, his younger sister tries to understand the changes in the family, and his best friend and cancer victim, Felix dies. Sam makes a list of things to do before he dies and then sets out to do them. He copes with his eventual demise with questions, humor, and grace. Notable Children's Book, 2009.

Spinelli, Jerry. *Eggs*. New York: Little, Brown, 2007. 220p. ISBN 978-0-316-16646-1. Grades: 4–8.

Thirteen-year-old Primrose moves into an abandoned van in order to get away from her fortune-telling mother. Nine-year-old David has moved in with his grandmother after his mother's tragic death. Primrose's father has never been part of her life and David's father is a traveling salesman. The two children squabble like siblings as they come to depend on each other as they cope with the death and desertion each has felt. This book is also available as an e-book.

Tolan, Stephanie S. *Listen!* New York: HarperCollins, 2006. 197p. ISBN 978-0-06-057936-4. Grades: 4–8.

The death of her mother, a car wreck that leaves her with a slow-to-heal leg injury, and a father who spends more time at his office than at home are all devastating blows to twelve-year-old Charley. To strengthen her leg she takes long walks, careful to avoid the woods that remind her of her nature-photographer mother, until the day that she encounters a stray dog who needs food and a loving home. The two develop a strong bond that heals them both.

Kids Talkin' about Death. DVD. Montreal, Quebec, CN: National Film Board of Canada, 2005. 20 min. Grades: 5–8.

An interviewer asks children about death and their candid, insightful comments provide the context for starting a discussion about a difficult topic. Through this documentary children develop an understanding of how death is an important part of life. A study guide is available. A preview of the film is available at www.ipexview.com/solution/videos/National_Film_Board_of_Canada/Kids_Talkin_about_death/44/. ALSC Notable Children's Video, 2006.

Peacock, Carol Antoinette. *Death and Dying*. New York: Franklin Watts, 2004. 80p. ISBN 978-0-531-12370-6. Grades: 5–8.

"Grief is unique," readers are reassured in the first chapter that also defines grief and briefly describes three levels of grief including physical, emotional, and behavioral. The focus of the book is coping with grief with the final chapter giving ideas for moving on. The book concludes with a glossary, resources for learning more, and an index.

Almond, David. *The Savage*. Illustrated by Dave McKean. Somerville, MA: Candlewick, 2008. 79p. ISBN 978-0-7636-3932-7. Grades: 5–9.

His father's death and being picked on by the town bully, Hooper, lead Blue to create a graphic novel about a savage boy. One night the savage visits Hooper and the lines between fantasy and reality blur. The book exposes Blue's powerful, raw emotions and in the climax readers come to understand how expressing the powerful emotions tempers them. Children's Choices, 2009.

Kennedy, Richard. *Come Again in Spring*. DVD. Montreal, Quebec, CN: National Film Board of Canada, 2006. 12 min. ISBN 1-800-542-2164. Grades: 6 and up.

This quiet animated film based on a story by Richard Kennedy looks at the cycle of life as an old man bargains with Death so that he can feed his birds come springtime. While the book is out of print, the film is available at www.onf-nfb.gc.ca/. ALSC Notable Children's Video, 2009.

Explorations

1. After reading *Remembering Grandpa* (Krishnaswami, 2007), have the students share happy memories of their family members.
2. After reading *I Remember* (Moore-Mallinos, 2005), return to the book and have the students create a list of the changes Jake undergoes as he grows older. Then, have them talk about the changes in their own lives as they grow older.
3. After reading *Love That Dog* (Creech, 2001), have the students use the book as a model to craft their own poems about a beloved pet.

4. Before students begin reading *Eggs* (Spinelli, 2007), put two shoe boxes in the classroom, one with Primrose written on the top and one with David written on the top. As the students read the book ask them to put in the box small objects or to draw pictures of the objects that help others understand the characters. For example, a small model of a van or a picture of a van could go in the box to represent Primrose's home. When students finish reading the story, have them pull the objects out of the box and use them to review the story.
5. After watching *Kids' Talkin' about Death*, provide the students with time to talk about how death is an important part of life. The school counselor can offer ideas for conducting the discussion.
6. *Death and Dying* (Peacock, 2004) suggests different ways to deal with grief, including writing in a journal. Students who may not feel comfortable talking about their grief may welcome the opportunity to write about their feelings.

TEACHER RESOURCES

This section includes books, professional organizations, and Internet sites filled with useful resources for teaching health related topics.

Book and Media Choices

Petty, Karen. *Deployment: Strategies for Working with Kids in Military Families.* St. Paul, MN: Redleaf, 2009. 186p. ISBN 978-1-933653-74-7. Grades: K–6.

From what to expect from children when a parent is deployed to how to help their families, this concise guide is filled with practical ideas. The book concludes with resources including helpful children's books, websites, a glossary, and references. A sample chapter and table of contents can be downloaded from the publisher's website at www.redleafpress.org.

Cox, Adam J. *Boys of Few Words: Raising Our Sons to Communicate and Connect.* New York: Guilford, 2006. 337p. ISBN 978-1-59385-218-4. Grades: K–8.

The communication divide, especially challenging boys, and how to make lasting differences are the sections in this book. Because boys spend so much of their time in school the book includes ideas for teachers. Back matter includes an epilogue, resources, a bibliography, and an index.

DesMaisons, Kathleen. *Little Sugar Addicts: End the Mood Swings, Meltdowns, Tantrums, and Low Self-Esteem in Your Child Today.* New York: Three Rivers, 2004. 274p. ISBN 978-1-40005-164-9. Grades: K–8.

While teachers do not have control over what children eat at home or in the school cafeteria, this book provides the information they need to teach students about making wise food choices. Recipes, resources, a bibliography, and an index are included.

Okie, Susan. *Fed Up! Winning the War Against Childhood Obesity.* Washington, DC: Joseph Henry, 2005. 322p. ISBN 978-0-309-09310-1. Grades: K–8.

"The Fattest Generation" is the title of the first chapter in the book and it begins with the story of an overweight youngster. This book includes interviews with children, teens, and their parents and facts about childhood obesity. Being overweight impacts not only health but also self-esteem. Okie includes suggestions on how to find help for overweight children. Back matter includes resources, notes, and an index.

Popkin, Barry. *The World Is Fat: The Fads, Trends, Policies, and Products That Are Fattening the Human Race.* New York: Penguin, 2009. 229p. ISBN 978-1-58333-313-6. Grades: K–8.

The obesity epidemic is worldwide and the reasons why become evident as Popkin profiles the lifestyles of two American families, one Mexican family, and one Indian family. The book begins with a history of the modern diet, explores the changes in lifestyles and diets over the years, and ends with suggestions for change. Sources and references as well as an index conclude the book.

Thomas-Presswood, Tania N., and Donald Presswood. *Meeting the Needs of Students and Families from Poverty: A Handbook for School and Mental Health Professionals.* Baltimore, MD: Brookes, 2008. 234p. ISBN 978-1-55766-867-7. Grades: K–12.

Part one focuses on understanding poverty and part two focuses on working with children and families. This is a practical guide that examines the challenges of teaching students from poverty and offers strategies to improve their academic achievement. The book concludes with references and an index.

Professional Organizations

American School Health Association
7263 State Route 43
PO Box 708
Kent, OH 44240
330-678-1601 (Phone)
330-678-4526 (Fax)
www.ashaweb.org
Journal: *Journal of School Health*

School Health Education and Services
American Public Health Association
800 I Street, NW
Washington, DC 20001-3710
202-777-APHA (Phone)
202-777-2534 (Fax)
www.apha.org/membergroups/sections/aphasections/schoolhealth/

Internet Sites

American Dental Association
www.ada.org

Games, videos, career information, and curriculum materials are all available on this site. ADA Dental Minutes are short, informative videos on a variety of dental health topics that can easily be slipped into classroom lessons.

American Dietetic Association
www.eatright.org

This website is the place to find extensive information on food and nutrition. There are publications, movies, and tip sheets for developing healthy eating habits.

American Heart Association
www.americanheart.org

On this website are links to information to help prevent heart disease. Tips on making fast food friendlier and tips on how to get nonathletic kids moving can also be found on the site.

American Red Cross
www.redcross.org

The site has tools for teachers and parents to use to teach children about preparing for natural disasters and fire safety.

BAM! Body and Mind
www.bam.gov

Sponsored by the Department of Health and Human Services Centers for Disease Control, this site has information on diseases, nutrition, physical activity, the body, and life. This interactive site houses games and quizzes to get students thinking and learning. For example, Ad Decoder is a game that involves students in deciphering the messages in advertisements.

Centers for Disease Control and Prevention
www.cdc.gov

Online health information is available here on topics including diseases and conditions; healthy living; emergency preparedness and response; injury, violence, and safety; environmental health, travelers health; life stages and populations; and workplace safety and health. Podcasts, videos, widgets, and gadgets are available to enable viewers to track the latest information on health issues including food product recalls.

Food and Drug Administration
www.fda.gov

A link for kids provides access to songs, quizzes, interactive games, and crossword puzzles to help children learn about health and safety. There is also information on careers in health and safety.

GriefNet
www.griefnet.org
Support for those dealing with grief, major loss, and death can be found in this Internet community. There are support groups for adults and kids. Kidsaid is linked from this website and it connects grieving kids of similar ages through e-mail exchanges. This group also provides support to veterans and their families who are recovering from posttraumatic stress.

It's My Life
www.pbskids.org/itsmylife/
For students there is information on dealing with friends, family, school, body, emotions, and money. There are games, videos, and advice. The link for teachers includes lesson plans on health-related topics including bullies, drug abuse, smoking, and time management.

Kids Health
www.kidshealth.org
This website has three sections: parents, kids, and teens. There are movies, games, a dictionary of medical terms, information on feelings, and ideas for staying healthy. A Spanish version of the site is available.

National Aging Information Center
www.nih.gov/nia/
There are publications in English and Spanish on a variety of age-related topics. There is also information on research and clinical trials. One section of the site is dedicated to Alzheimer's disease.

National Association for Anorexia Nervosa and Associated Eating Disorders, Inc.
www.anad.org
This group takes an active role in advocating for those with eating disorders. The site contains links to support groups and links to treatment facilities. Also available are guidelines for schools and a booklet with information about how to help a friend with an eating disorder.

National Eating Disorders Association, Inc.
www.nationaleatingdisorders.org
This organization provides help for individuals and families who are dealing with eating disorders. The website contains information on what coaches and educators can do to help children and an educator's toolkit can be downloaded from the website. There is a "Get Help Today" link that includes a toll-free number to call (800-931-2237), a survival guide, insurance information, and other immediately available resources. A Spanish version of the website is available.

Teen Health and Wellness
teenhealthandwellness.com

This award-winning online database houses a collection of resources for learning about diseases, drugs, nutrition, fitness, mental health, and other topics of interest to teens. A free thirty-day trial to the database is available and additions to the site can be followed on Twitter.

United States Department of Agriculture
www.usda.gov

This site can be browsed by topics including educators and students, consumers, and parents and caregivers. There are links related to food, nutrition, dietary health, food safety, careers, recreational activities, and resources for kids. A Spanish version of the website is available.

REFERENCES

Baker, A. J. L. 2007. "Fostering Stories: Why Caseworkers, Foster Parents, and Foster Children Should Read Stories about Being in Foster Care." *The American Journal of Family Therapy* 35, no. 2 (March/April): 151–165.

Blom-Hoffman, Jessica, Kaila R. Wilcox, Liam Dunn, Stephen S. Leff, and Thomas J. Power. 2008. "Family Involvement in School-Based Health Promotion: Bringing Nutrition Information Home." *School Psychology Review* 37, no. 4, 567–577.

Corr, Charles A. 2003/2004a. "Grandparents in Death-Related Literature for Children." *Omega: Journal of Death and Dying* 48, no. 4, 383–397.

Corr, Charles A. 2003/2004b. "Pet Loss in Death-Related Literature for Children." *Omega: Journal of Death and Dying* 48, no. 4, 399–414.

Hunt, Kathy. 2006. "'Do You Know Harry Potter? Well, He Is an Orphan': Every Bereaved Child Matters." *Pastoral Care in Education* 24, no. 2 (June): 39–44.

Joint Committee on National School Health Education Standards. 2007. *National Health Education Standards: Achieving Excellence*. Atlanta, GA: American Cancer Society.

Kurtis, Stephanie A., and Karen W. Gavigan. 2008. "Understanding (Dis)abilities through Children's Literature." *Education Libraries: Children's Resources* 31, no. 3 (Spring): 23–31.

Matthew, Nicole, and Susan Clow. 2007. "Putting Disabled Children in the Picture: Promoting Inclusive Children's Books and Media." *International Journal of Early Childhood* 39, no. 2 (Fall): 65–78.

Morrongiello, Barbara A., Michael Corbett, and Alexandra Bellissimo. 2008. "'Do as I say, not as I do': Family Influences on Children's Safety and Risk Behaviors." *Health Psychology* 27, no. 4 (July): 498–503.

Poling, Devereaux A., and Julie M. Hupp. 2008. "Death Sentences: A Content Analysis of Children's Death Literature." *The Journal of Genetic Psychology* 169, no. 2 (June): 165–176.

Scales, Peter C. 2000. "Building Students' Developmental Assets to Promote Health and School Success." *The Clearing House* 74, no. 2 (November/December): 84–88.

Stauffer, Sue. 2003. *Donuthead*. New York: Random House.

Yopp, Ruth Helen, and Hallie Kay Yopp. 2010. *Literature-Based Reading Activities*, Fifth Edition. Boston: Allyn and Bacon.

Chapter 6

Sports, Recreation, and Dance

Participating in sports, recreational activities, and dance requires students to move and to be physically active. Physical activity is important because when combined with proper nutrition children are more likely to lead healthy, productive lives. While the benefits of physical activity are widely recognized, an analysis of worldwide data indicates high rates of sedentary lifestyles in children and in adults, and these rates continue to increase (Knuth and Hallal, 2009). Batch (2005) recommends that children and adolescents participate in a variety of physical activities every day and that they participate in vigorous physical activity at least three times a week. To get children involved in physical activity, Gilbert (2006) suggests capitalizing on their natural affinity to play and have fun by involving them in physical activities that they enjoy. Rather than seeing physical activity as something that has to be done, she suggests ideas for getting students to view it as something they get to do. To help achieve this goal, this chapter includes books and media that encourage children to have fun as they participate in physical activities, including games, organized sports, and dance.

The National Association for Sport and Physical Education (NASPE, 2004) and the American Alliance for Health Physical Education Recreation and Dance (AAHPERD) revisited and reviewed the previous Content Standards for Physical Education to address current concerns and to clarify what physically educated students should know and be able to demonstrate. These standards include benchmarks to assess students' competency in movement forms, ability to maintain a physically active lifestyle, and an understanding of the importance of physical activity. These standards state that a physically educated person:

Has learned skills necessary to perform a variety of physical activities

1. Is physically fit;
2. Does participate regularly in physical activity;
3. Knows the implications of and the benefits from involvement in physical activities; and
4. Values physical activity and its contribution to a healthful lifestyle in order to pursue a lifetime of healthful physical activity.

The following are the content standards:

1. Demonstrates competency in motor skills and movement patterns needed to perform a variety of physical activities.
2. Demonstrates understanding of movement concepts, principles, strategies, and tactics as they apply to the learning and performance of physical activities.
3. Participates regularly in physical activity.
4. Achieves and maintains a health-enhancing level of physical fitness.
5. Exhibits responsible personal and social behavior that respects self and others in physical activity settings.
6. Values physical activity for health, enjoyment, challenge, self-expression, and/or social interaction.

Dance enables children to explore their body movements and to discover the creative potential dance offers them to express their emotions through movement. As they move, students develop an awareness and appreciation of their bodies. Developing an appreciation of their bodies helps to promote positive self-esteem.

The National Dance Association (NDA, 1994), a member of the AAHPERD, developed the following content standards:

- Identifying and demonstrating movement elements and skills in performing dance;
- Understanding choreographic principles, processes, and structures;
- Understanding dance as a way to create and communicate meaning;
- Applying and demonstrating critical and creative thinking skills in dance;
- Demonstrating and understanding dance in various cultures and historical periods;
- Making connections between dance and healthful living; and
- Making connections between dance and other disciplines.

The content standards for physical education and for dance serve as guidelines for teachers as they develop their classroom curriculum. Sections in this chapter include physical fitness and recreation, sports, athletes, dance, dancers, and teacher resources.

PHYSICAL FITNESS AND RECREATION

Regular physical activity provides health benefits to all students, including those with disabilities. In order to benefit from physical activity students need to be up and moving, and having fun is always an inducement to participate. Hence, the books and media in this section focus on recreational activities requiring students to get up, to get moving, and to most of all have fun. They can imitate animal movements, turn themselves into letters, Double Dutch jump rope, skip, hop, or act out a baseball poem. As students participate in these activities, they are developing motor skills, which addresses content standard two. Books and media in this section also help students develop an understanding that physical activity provides opportunities for enjoyment, challenge, self-expression, and social interaction, which address content standard seven.

Book and Media Choices

Bluemie, Elizabeth. *How Do You Wokka-Wokka?* Illustrated by Randy Cecil. Unp. ISBN 978-0-7636-3228-1. Grades: P–1.

Everyone has a unique way to wokka-wokka and this lively book shows just some of the movements that go with the catchy beat of the rhyming text. Young readers get to join in the fun by creating their own unique ways to wokka-wokka.

Jenkins, Steve, and Robin Page. *Move!* Boston, MA: Houghton Mifflin, 2006. Unp. ISBN 978-0-618-64637-1. Grades: P–1.

Animals slither, swim, slide, float, waddle, and fly, and so does the text in the bold, colorful mixed-media collage illustrations in this book. Additional information about the animals is appended, which makes this book a useful addition to the science curriculum.

Ajmera, Maya. *Come Out and Play*. Watertown, MA: Charlesbridge, 2001. Unp. ISBN 978-1-57091-385-3. Grades: P–1.

Children around the world play outdoors, and while "playing in water" for some may be a sprinkler on the lawn for others it might be a body of water. Large font and colorful photographs depict children playing in different countries. The universality of play is explained in Kermit the Frog's foreword and the endnotes summarize how imagination and friendship are important components of play.

O'Connor, Jane. *Ready, Set, Skip!* Illustrated by Ann James. New York: Viking, 2007. Unp. ISBN 978-0-670-06216-4. Grades: P–1.

The young heroine in this story can do many things well including slurping, burping, and hopping, but she cannot skip. Building on what she can do—hop—her mother demonstrates that skipping is hopping on one foot and then the other. The exuberant illustrations show a determined child learning to skip. Simple, rhyming text carries the story along and adds to the fun of reading and listening and mimicking the actions of the small girl.

Rissman, Rebecca. *Shapes in Sports*. Chicago, IL: Heinemann, 2009. Unp. ISBN 978-1-43292-170-5. Grades: P–1.

This introductory book uses colorful sports photographs to teach seven different shapes. Baseball, kayaking, cycling, and soccer are some of the sports included in the photographs. Each photograph asks a question whose answer is revealed when the page is turned. From the Spot the Shape series.

Willems, Mo. *Are You Ready to Play Outside?* White Plains, NY: Hyperion, 2008. Unp. ISBN 978-1-42311-347-8. Grades: P–2.

Piggie and his elephant friend, Gerald, are heading outdoors to run, skip, and jump when rain begins falling. When they see two worms enjoying the rain, they decide to make the best of the rainy day. ALSC Notable Children's Book, 2009. Theodor Seuss Geisel Award Winner, 2009.

Adler, David A. *Cam Jansen and the Sports Day Mysteries: A Super Special.* New York: Penguin, 2009. 118p. ISBN 978-0-670-01163-6. Grades: K–3.

On Sports and Good Nutrition Day fifth grader Cam Jansen solves three mysteries: the backwards race mystery, the soccer game mystery, and the baseball glove mystery. The combination of sports and mysteries will appeal to young fans of this intriguing series. At the end of the book are Cam Jansen memory games. From the Cam Jansen Adventure series.

The Human Alphabet. Photographed by John Kane. New York: Roaring Brook, 2005. Unp. ISBN 978-1-59643-066-2. Grades: K–4.

The Pilobolus Dance Company forms the letters of the alphabet and accompanying each letter is a human formation of a word starting with the letter. The answers to the human word formations are found at the end of the book. Students will be fascinated by the twisted shapes of the human letters and will be eager to imitate them.

Lowry, Lois. *Crow Call.* Illustrated by Bagram Ibatoulline. New York: Scholastic, 2009. Unp. ISBN 978-0-545-03035-9. Grades: K–4.

Based on an incident in Lowry's life, this is a heartwarming story of a young girl and her father reconnecting after he returns from war. One crisp autumn morning, they set out to hunt crows that are eating the farmers' crops. Intrigued by his daughter's crow-calling ability and the large number of crows she attracts, he watches in admiration, not raising his gun. The muted photorealistic illustrations capture the autumn morning and this special father-daughter moment.

Prelutsky, Jack. *Good Sports: Rhymes about Running, Jumping, Throwing, and More.* Illustrated by Chris Raschka. New York: HarperCollins, 2007. 40p. ISBN 978-0-375-83700-5. Grades: K–5.

Watercolor and ink illustrations capture the action, excitement, joy, and despair of the sporting events described in the poems. Basketball, gymnastics, baseball, and karate are among the sports explored in the poems. These energetic poems are perfect for reading aloud and performing. ALSC Notable Children's Book, 2008.

Katz, Alan. *Going, Going, Gone! And Other Silly Dilly Sports Songs.* Illustrated by David Catrow. New York: Simon and Schuster, 2009. Unp. ISBN 978-1-41690-696-4. Grades: 1–3.

The songs in this collection skewer baseball, football, fishing, archery, and other sports. The words are new, but the tunes are old favorites, such as "Ring around the

Rosie." The illustrations are filled with silly caricatures that add visual humor to the lively tunes.

Polacco, Patricia. *Rotten Richie and the Ultimate Dare*. New York: Penguin, 2006. Unp. ISBN 978-0-399-24531-2. Grades: 1–4.

Sibling rivalry sets Trish and Richie off to prove whose hobby is the most difficult, hockey or ballet. Trish plays in a hockey game and Richie dances in a ballet recital and the siblings gain new respect for each other and their talents. The book is based on Polacco's arguments with her brother over whose hobby was the most challenging and the endpapers feature pictures of Polacco and her brother interspersed with characters from the book.

Chryssicas, Mary Kaye. *I Love Yoga*. Photographs by Angela Coppola. New York: DK, 2005. 47p. ISBN 978-0-7566-1400-3. Grades: 2–5.

Full-page color photographs of children in soothing pastel clothing demonstrating yoga poses draw young readers into this book. The introductory chapters describe the equipment and explain yoga's benefits, including stress relief. The book concludes with a glossary and an index.

Loy, Jessica. *Follow the Trail: A Young Person's Guide to the Great Outdoors*. New York: Henry Holt, 2003. 48p. ISBN 978-0-8050-6195-6. Grades: 3–6.

Sisters Emma and Lydia take three friends with them on a camping trip in this beginner's guide to camping. Information on planning, packing, safety, campfires, weather, and outdoor activities is included. Color photographs of the children camping, diagrams, and text boxes supplement the informative text. Sources and resources conclude the book.

Platt, Richard. *They Played What? The Weird History of Sports and Recreation*. Lanham, MD: Cooper Square, 2007. 48p. ISBN 978-1-58728-585-1. Grades: 3–6.

This journey through history examines weird, absurd, and quite normal sports and recreational endeavors. From war games to Eastern arts to snail races to the circus to dance, there is something here for everyone to enjoy reading about and this is a great book for luring in reluctant readers.

Thayer, Ernest L. *Casey at the Bat: A Ballad of the Republic Sung in the Year 1888*. Illustrated by Christopher Bing. New York: Chronicle, 2000. Unp. ISBN 978-1-929766-00-0. Grades: 3–6.

Thayer's classic poem about Casey and the Mudville Nine is set within a scrapbook filled with newspaper clippings, advertisements, tickets, photographs, and other baseball memorabilia. The collage illustrations draw readers in again and again to search for all of the baseball mementos they contain. Caldecott Medal Honor Book, 2001.

Lupica, Mike. *The Big Field.* New York: Penguin, 2008. 243p. ISBN 978-0-399-24625-8. Grades: 5–8.

In this action-packed, nail-biter story, fourteen-year-old Hutch's American League baseball team makes it to the Florida State championship series. The journey is not without conflict, as he loses his shortstop position to the fiercely competitive Darryl and he struggles to connect with his distant father, a former baseball star. This book is available on CD. Children's Choices, 2009.

Paulsen, Gary. *How Angel Peterson Got His Name: And Other Outrageous Tales about Extreme Sports.* New York: Random House, 2003. 111p. ISBN 978-0-440-22935-3. Grades: 5–8.

Wrestling with a live bear to impress a girl and snow skiing while tethered to a speeding car are two of the extreme sports tales Paulsen recounts from his teenage years growing up in Minnesota. While the audience is teenage boys, audiences of all ages enjoy these stories. This book is also available as an e-book.

Spicer, Doreen, Regina Hicks, and Karin Gist. *Jump In!* DVD. Burbank, CA: Walt Disney Home Entertainment, 2007. 85 min. ISBN 978-0-7888-7296-9. Grades: 5–8.

In this made-for-television movie, Izzy Daniels decides that rather than follow his father's dream of becoming a boxer, he is going to follow his own dream and join his neighbor's Double Dutch jump rope team. Andrew Carnegie Medal Winner, 2008.

Paulsen, Gary. *Brian's Hunt.* New York: Random House, 2003. 103p. ISBN 978-0-385-74647-2. Grades: 6–10.

Fans of Brian Robeson, from *Hatchet* and its sequels, have a chance to revisit the Canadian north woods. Brian returns to the island home of his friends and discovers that a bear has killed them. As Brian hunts for the bear, the bear hunts Brian. The book is based on true events and concludes with cautions about encounters with real bears.

Explorations

1. While reading *Move!* (Jenkins and Page, 2006), have the students imitate the animal movements in the book and then teach them the words to describe the movements. For older students, this book is a wonderful way to introduce action verbs.
2. After reading *Are You Ready to Play Outside?* (Willems, 2008) take the students outside and let them act out the story by running, skipping, and jumping.
3. Use a document camera to project the illustrations in the memory games at the back of *Cam Jansen and the Sports Day Mysteries: A Super Special* (Adler, 2009). Then, have the students work with a partner or in small groups to answer the questions about the illustrations. Afterward, provide the students with time to create their own memory games using illustrations in other books or reproductions of works of art found in online museum collections.
4. Use poems from *Good Sports: Rhymes about Running, Jumping, Throwing, and More* (Prelutsky, 2007) as models for students to write poems about their own

experiences with sports. Students may prefer to first draw a picture about their favorite sport and then use the picture as inspiration to write their poem. Tux Paint (www.tuxpaint.org/) is a free, open source drawing software that students can use to draw their sports pictures.

5. After reading *Good Sports: Rhymes about Running, Jumping, Throwing, and More* (Prelutsky, 2007), have the students pick poems to act out with partners or in small groups.
6. Students who enjoyed *Rotten Richie and the Ultimate Dare* (Polacco, 2006) and are interested in reading other books by Polacco can learn about other books on her website located at www.patriciapolacco.com/index.htm.
7. *Follow the Trail: A Young Person's Guide to the Great Outdoors* (Loy, 2003) includes diagrams and instructions for tying four different knots. Place the book and some one-foot lengths of rope in an easily accessible spot in the classroom or library so the children can practice tying the knots.
8. With copies of the poem and some props, students can act out *Casey at the Bat: A Ballad of the Republic Sung in the Year 1888* (Thayer, 2000) or use the poem for a choral reading. The choral reading can be recorded using Audacity software to create a podcast.
9. *How Angel Peterson Got His Name: And Other Outrageous Tales about Extreme Sports* (Paulsen, 2003) contains stories for reading aloud and for discussing. Once students become acquainted with the stories, they will be clamoring to take the book home for leisure reading.

SPORTS

The books in this section encompass a variety of sports and help to address the physical education content standards. By participating in sports children learn sportsmanship and the importance of teamwork, which addresses content standard five, demonstrating responsible personal and social behavior in physical activity settings. Learning to play different sports and games provides students with ways to spend their leisure time throughout their lives and promotes the development of a physically active lifestyle, which addresses content standard three. In addition, books on favorite sports may motivate reluctant readers who want to learn to play a particular sport. While not all sports are represented in the books and media that follow, many of them are from a series that have books and videos on a wide variety of sports.

Book and Media Choices

Diehl, David. *Home Run! My Baseball Book*. New York: Lark Books, 2008. Unp. ISBN 978-1-60059-268-3. Grades: P–1.

Written for very young baseball fans, this colorful board book explains in text and illustrations baseball terms such as "pitcher" and "home run."

Diehl, David. *Touchdown! My Football Book.* New York: Lark Books, 2008. Unp. ISBN 978-1-60059-239-3. Grades: P–1.

This board book is for the youngest of football fans. Colorful, energetic illustrations help to explain football terms such as "fumble" and "snap."

Corey, Shana. *Players in Pigtails.* Illustrated by Rebecca Gibbon. New York: Scholastic, 2003. Unp. ISBN 978-0-439-18305-5. Grades: K–4.

While reading the lyrics of "Take Me Out to the Ball Game," Corey discovered that the song was about Katie Casey's love of baseball, and this book tells her story. The endpapers contain the lyrics to "Take Me Out to the Ball Game" and "Victory Song." An author's note contains additional information about the All-American Girls Professional Baseball League. This book is available on CD and DVD.

Crossingham, John. *Lacrosse in Action.* New York: Crabtree, 2003. 32p. ISBN 978-0-7787-0329-7. Grades: 2–4.

Native Americans invented the sport of lacrosse and a brief history of the game is included. This book provides basic information about how the game is played including the equipment and the rules. Color photographs and illustrations. A glossary and an index conclude the book. From the Sports in Action series.

Page, Jason. *Basketball, Soccer, and Other Ball Games.* New York: Crabtree, 2008. Unp. ISBN 978-0-7787-4029-2. Grades: 2–4.

This is a brief look at the ball games played in the 2008 Summer Olympics in Beijing. The brief histories of the game and the fun facts are starting points for further explorations by interested readers. From The Olympic Sports series.

Wingate, Brian. *Football: Rules, Tips, Strategy, and Safety.* New York: Rosen, 2007. 48p. ISBN 978-1-4042-0993-0. Grades: 2–4.

In addition to information on the football rules, tips, and strategies, there is information about football players and football plays. The book concludes with a glossary, resources for learning more, and an index. From the Sports from Coast to Coast series.

Low, Alice. *The Fastest Game on Two Feet: And Other Poems about How Sports Began.* Illustrated by John O'Brien. New York: Holiday House, 2009. 40p. ISBN 978-8-2341-905-0. Grades: 2–5.

Witty poems and clever cartoon illustrations explain the origins of different sports and this collection of poems appeals to sports enthusiasts. At the beginning of each poem is a short paragraph that provides information about how the sports began. An author's note, anecdotes, and a timeline complement the information in the poems.

Walker, Niki, and Sarah Dann. *Badminton in Action.* Illustrated by Katherine Kantor. Photographs by Marc Crabtree. New York: Crabtree, 2003. 32p. ISBN 978-0-7787-0334-1. Grades: 2–5.

The history, equipment, proper techniques, rules, and scorekeeping of badminton are explained in simple text, illustrations, and photographs. A glossary and an index conclude the book. From the Sports in Action series.

Jones, Jen. *Gymnastics Skills: Beginning Tumbling.* Mankato, MN: Capstone, 2007. Unp. ISBN 978- 07368-6470-1. Grades: 2–6.

Colorful action photographs and simple text with step-by-step illustrations introduce gymnastic fundamentals with an emphasis on safety. The book concludes with a glossary, resources for learning more, and a brief index. From the Snap Books series.

Crossingham, John. *In-line Skating in Action.* Illustrated by Bonna Rouse. Photographs by Marc Crabtree. New York: Crabtree, 2003. 32p. ISBN 978-0-7787-0328-0. Grades: 3–5.

Basic movements and techniques of in-line skating along with safety tips are included in these two-page chapters. Color photographs and illustrations enhance the informative text. From the Sports in Action series.

Crossingham, John, and Niki Walker. *Swimming in Action.* Illustrated by Bonna Rouse. New York: Crabtree, 2003. 32p. ISBN 978- 0-7787-0331-0. Grades: 3–5.

Basic information about swimming is covered including floating and some basic strokes. The short two-page chapters complete with photographs and illustrations are easy to read and understand. The section on pool games will be of particular interest to children looking for ideas for summertime fun. A glossary and an index conclude the book. From the Sports in Action series.

Miller, Debbie. *The Great Serum Race: Blazing the Iditarod Trail.* Illustrated by Jon Van Zyle. New York: Walker, 2003. 40p. ISBN 978-1-4178-1562-3. Grades: 3–6.

During the winter of 1925, a diphtheria outbreak in Nome threatened the population and the nearest antitoxin serum was 1,000 miles away in Anchorage. In subzero weather dogsled teams raced to bring the serum back to Nome. Illustrations by the official artist of the Iditarod, Van Zyle, bring the story to life. Bibliographic references and historical notes provide rich details about this dramatic race. NCTE Orbis Pictus Recommended Book, 2003.

Studelska, Jana Voelke. *Archery for Fun!* North Mankato, MN: Capstone, 2008. 48p. ISBN 978-0-7565-3390-8. Grades: 3–6.

From the history of archery to the equipment needed to safety tips, this introductory book provides the basics for students who are interested in learning about this sport. Information on archery competitions and on noted archers is included. A bibliography and an index conclude the book. From the For Fun! Sports series.

Will, Sandra. *Golf for Fun!* North Mankato, MN: Capstone, 2004. 48p. ISBN 978-0-7565-0486-1. Grades: 3–6.

Readers learn the basics of golf including scoring, techniques, rules, and golf etiquette. A bibliography and an index conclude the book. From the For Fun! Sports series.

Calder, Kate. *Horseback Riding in Action.* Illustrated by Bonna Rouse. New York: Crabtree, 2001. 32p. ISBN 978-0-7787-0167-5. Grades: 3–8.

This book is a great choice for introducing horseback riding to the beginner equestrian. Information on caring for horses, needed equipment, and safety requirements are some of the topics covered. Colorful photographs enhance the text. From the Sports in Action series.

Drewett, Jim. *How to Improve at Tennis.* New York: Crabtree, 2008. 48p. ISBN 978-0-7787-3571-7. Grades: 3–8.

Children interested in learning how to improve their tennis game find this book a valuable resource. It includes ideas for improving technique, step-by-step demonstrations, and secrets from professional tennis players. From the How to Improve At series.

Fitzpatrick, Jim. *Skateboarding.* Ann Arbor, MI: Cherry Lake, 2008. 32p. ISBN 978-1-60279-017-9. Grades: 3–8.

Colorful photographs and informative sidebars complement this basic text for beginning skateboarders. Resources for learning more, a glossary, and an index conclude the book. From the Innovation in Sports series.

Gikow, Louise. *Extreme Sports: A Chapter Book.* New York: Children's, 2004. 48p. ISBN 978-0-516-24683-3. Grades: 3–8.

Surfing, skateboarding, snowboarding, and bicycle motocross are the extreme sports covered in this book. Readers are also introduced to athletes who excelled in these sports. Resources for learning more, a glossary, and index conclude the book. From the True Tales Sports series.

Chester, Jonathan. *Young Adventurer's Guide to Everest: From Avalanche to Zopkio.* New York: Random House, 2002. 48p. ISBN 978-1-58246-151-9. Grades: 4–6.

From A to Z, readers discover what it takes to climb Mount Everest. Color photographs put readers on the mountain with the climbers. The splendors, the risks, and the challenges of scaling the Goddess of Mother Earth unfold in the pages of this book. NCTE Orbis Pictus Recommended Book, 2003.

Thomas, Keltie. *How Baseball Works.* Illustrated by Greg Hall. Toronto, Ontario, CN: Maple Leaf, 2004. 64p. ISBN 978-1-894379-60-1. Grades: 4–6.

From what the ball is made of to how to doctor a ball before pitching it, the first chapter sets the stage for this entertaining book. Other chapters focus on topics such as hitting, pitching, and keeping statistics. Simple experiments and brief anecdotes about players add to the fun-to-read text. The book concludes with rules, a glossary, and an index.

Drewett, Jim. *How to Improve at Soccer.* New York: Crabtree, 2008. 48p. ISBN 978-0-7787-3569-4. Grades: 4–8.

Beginning soccer players wanting to improve their game find this a useful resource as it includes not only instructions on skills and practice drills but also has the rules of the game. Photographs and illustrations aid in understanding the text. A glossary and an index conclude the book. From the How to Improve At series.

Jacobs, Greg. *The Everything Kids Football Book: The All-Time Greats, Legendary Teams, Today's Superstars—and Tips on Playing Like a Pro.* Avon, MA: Adams Media, 2008. 138p. ISBN 978-1-59869-565-6. Grades: 4–8.

From facts to stats to puzzles, this is an entertaining look at the history of football including the National Football League and fantasy football and how to play the game. The book also includes reproducible puzzle pages and a glossary. From the Everything Kids series.

Beckham, David. *David Beckham's Soccer Skills.* New York: HarperCollins, 2006. 159p. ISBN 978-0-06-115475-1. Grades: 5–8.

Color photographs and succinct instructions explain soccer techniques. Beckham includes references to his soccer playing both in his youth and as a professional. The information in the book will help young soccer players hone their skills.

Nelson, Kadir. *We Are the Ship: The Story of Negro League Baseball.* New York: Hyperion, 2008. 96p. ISBN 978-1-4379-6953-5. Grades: 5–8.

From 1920 and the formation of the first Negro League to Jackie Robinson joining the all-white baseball league, this narrative tells the history of African-American baseball players who endured hatred and segregation in order to play the game they loved. The stunning artwork showcases these spirited players who were giants in their time. Hank Aaron wrote the foreword to the book. This book is also available on CD. Coretta Scott King Author Award Winner, 2009. NCTE Orbis Pictus Honor Book, 2009.

Play Better Racquetball: Skills and Drills. DVD. Danielson, CT: SportVideos, 2007. 37 min. UPC 189098007891. Grades: 5–8.

The skills and drills demonstrated on this DVD are sure to improve students' racquetball skills to help them develop into consistent players. A preview of this video is available at www.sportvideos.com.

Pollack, Pamela. *Ski! Your Guide to Cross-Country, Downhill, Jumping, Racing, Freestyle, and More.* Washington, DC: National Geographic, 2002. 64p. ISBN 978-0-7922-6738-6. Grades: 5–8.

This guide includes information on the equipment needed, techniques, and tips for different styles of skiing. Sidebars and photographs complement the informative text and make this a useful introduction to the sport. From the Extreme Sports series.

Swoopes on Hoops. DVD. West Long Branch, NJ: SRO Sports Entertainment, 2005. 53 min. ISBN 978-0-7697-7823-5. Grades: 5–8.

Houston Comets basketball star Sheryl Swoopes teaches basic basketball skills including dribbling, passing, catching, layups, and jump shots. This video was originally produced in 1997.

Gola, Mark. *Winning Softball for Girls,* Second Edition. New York: Facts On File, 2008. 224p. ISBN 978-0-8160-7716-8. Grades: 6–8.

In 1996, softball was accepted as an Olympic sport and the number of players increased dramatically. This is a sport that can be played by girls with varying ability levels. The book includes a brief history of the sport and the rules of the game. The book includes photographs, a list of softball organizations, a bibliography, and a detailed index. From the Winning Sports for Girls series.

Summers, David, editor. *The Sports Book.* New York: DK, 2007. 448p. ISBN 978-0-7566-3195-6. Grades: 6 and up.

Information and illustrations on more than 200 sports are included in this informative guide. The rules, winning tips, facts, and statistics are all here. There is also information on the Olympic Games.

Swimming: Techniques in Action. DVD. Wiltshire, England: Crowood Films, 2008. 80 min. ISBN 978-1-84797-008-4. Grades: 6 and up.

Drills, strokes, and racing skills are covered in this film. Techniques for improving these four strokes are included: butterfly, backstroke, breaststroke, and freestyle. A clip from this DVD can be viewed on the Crowood website at www.crowood.com.

Blumenthal, Karen. *Let Me Play: The Story of Title IX: The Law That Changed the Future of Girls in America.* New York: Atheneum, 2005. 152p. ISBN 978-1-4379-6649-7. Grades: 7 and up.

In 1972, Title IX was passed, providing women equal treatment and equal opportunity to play sports. This book follows the creation, revisions, and fights surrounding this important legislation. Photographs and vignettes enhance the story of the passage of this law. The book concludes with information on the changes brought about by this law. NCTE Orbis Pictus Honor Book, 2006.

Explorations

1. After reading *Lacrosse in Action* (Crossingham, 2003), students wanting to learn more about this sport can visit the website of the national organization at www.uslacrosse.org/. The website includes a link to information about lacrosse for youths and a link to the Lacrosse Museum and National Hall of Fame.
2. Create a class wiki pbworks.com/ with one page for each of the ball games discussed in *Basketball, Soccer, and Other Ball Games* (Page, 2008). The students can learn more about the games using the Olympic Movement website at www.olympic.org and then contribute what they learn to the class wiki pages.
3. Students can use the poems in *The Fastest Game on Two Feet: And Other Poems about How Sports Began* (Low, 2009) as models to write their own poems about their favorite sports. Remind the students that their poems do not have to rhyme. Forcing poems to rhyme often results in stilted poems that do not make sense.

4. Video clips and photographs on the Iditarod website at www.iditarod.com/ can be used to introduce *The Great Serum Race: Blazing the Iditarod Trail* (Miller, 2003). After the students read the book, they are eager to return to the site to learn more about this unique event. Under the link "For Teachers" are a variety of resources for teachers and students including a Reader's Theater Play.
5. After reading *We Are the Ship: The Story of Negro League Baseball* (Nelson, 2008), students who are interested in learning more can visit www.infoplease .com/sports and conduct a search on the term "Negro League."
6. Students interested in learning about Title IX will find *Let Me Play: The Story of Title IX: The Law That Changed the Future of Girls in America* (Blumenthal, 2005) a useful resource as well as the Women's Sports Foundation website at www.womenssportsfoundation.org/. The website houses video and audio files and features information on women athletes. Grant and scholarship resources are also on the site.
7. Books in this section can be used to introduce students to the skills, vocabulary, and equipment used in different sports that they play in their physical education classes or sports that they participate in after school. While reluctant readers may not be interested in fiction, they may be interested in reading a book about their favorite sport.

ATHLETES

Athletes in the books and media in this section serve as role models for children because the athletes through hard work and perseverance achieved success in their chosen sports. Reading books and watching videos about athletes helps students appreciate and respect the differences among people, which is addressed in content standard six. Also, students learn that participation in sports involves challenge, self-expression, and social interaction, which are addressed in content standard seven.

Book and Media Choices

Adler, David A. *Campy: The Story of Roy Campanella.* Illustrated by Gordon C. James. New York: Penguin, 2007. Unp. ISBN 978-0-670-06041-2. Grades: P–2.

Roy Campanella started his major league baseball career in the Negro Leagues not long after the Dodgers signed Jackie Robinson. He endured discrimination as the first African-American catcher in the major leagues, but he persisted. His baseball career ended with a car accident that left him a quadriplegic. The remarkable determination that made him an outstanding ball player also made him an inspiration to others with disabilities. Important dates, quotes, and suggested readings conclude the book. Notable Social Studies Trade Book for Young People, 2008.

Deans, Karen. *Playing to Win: The Story of Althea Gibson.* Illustrated by Elbrite Brown. New York: Holiday House, 2007. Unp. ISBN 978-0-8234-1926-5. Grades: K–3.

As a youngster Althea was resilient, rebellious, and full of energy. In her teens, she discovered she had a talent for tennis and so channeled her energy into becoming a top-notch tennis player. The book concludes with a timeline and resources for learning more.

Yolen, Jane. *All Star! Honus Wagner and the Most Famous Baseball Card Ever.* Illustrated by James Burke. New York: Penguin, 2010. Unp. ISBN 978-0-399-24661-6. Grades: K–4.

Born in a Pennsylvania coal-mining town, bow-legged Honus Wagner became one of the greatest shortstops through talent, persistence, and passion. When Honus discovered that his baseball card was being included in packages of cigarettes, he refused permission to continue production of the card, as he did not want to promote smoking to his young fans.

Gerstein, Mordicai. *The Man Who Walked Between the Towers.* New York: Macmillan, 2003. Unp. ISBN 978-0-7613-1791-3. Grades: K–4.

In 1974, during the construction of the World Trade Towers, French trapeze artist Philippe Petit strung a tightrope between the towers and walked the rope high above New York City for forty-five minutes. Breathtaking images from dramatic perspectives including two gatefolds capture the excitement and adventure of his walk. The final pages reference that the Towers no longer stand. Caldecott Medal Winner, 2004. The video based on this picture book won the Andrew Carnegie Medal for Excellence in Children's Video, 2006.

Abraham, Philip. *Extreme Sports Stars.* New York: Children's, 2007. 48p. ISBN 978-0-531-12585-4. Grades: 1–4.

Sports such as skateboarding, BMX riding, and motocross are considered extreme sports, and this book contains brief biographies of champions in each of the sports. The book is an introduction to these sports and sure to have students looking for more books on their favorite extreme sports. From the Sports Stars series.

Bruchac, Joseph. *Jim Thorpe's Bright Path.* Illustrated by S.D. Nelson. New York: Lee and Low, 2004. 40p. ISBN 978-1-58430-166-0. Grades: 1–4.

Known as the "World's Greatest Athlete," Native American Jim Thorpe could chase down a jackrabbit. This is a powerful story of the adversity he overcame to win Olympic gold medals only to have them confiscated and later restored. An author's note, a chronology, and thumbnail photographs conclude the book. NCSS Carter G. Woodson Elementary Level Award Winner Book, 2005.

Winter, Jonah. *You Never Heard of Sandy Koufax?!* Illustrated by Andre Carrilho. New York: Random House, 2009. Unp. ISBN 978-0-375-83738-8. Grades: 1–5.

Narrated by an unnamed teammate, this picture book biography introduces readers to a remarkable athlete who endured anti-Semitism as he pitched his way to the top of the Dodgers' lineup. Carrilho's digitally enhanced illustrations capture the drama and exuberance of the story. A teacher's guide is available on the publisher's website at www.randomhouse.com.

Yoo, Paula. *Sixteen Years in Sixteen Seconds: The Sammy Lee Story.* Illustrated by Dom Lee. New York: Lee and Low, 2005. Unp. ISBN 978-1-58430-247-6. Grades: 2–4.

Imagine diving into a pit of sand in order to practice diving. That's what Korean-American Sammy Lee did since he was only allowed to swim in the neighborhood pool on Wednesdays. In 1948, his determination led him to become the first Asian-American to win an Olympic gold medal. An author's note with additional details about his life concludes the book.

Buckman, Virginia. *Football Stars.* New York: Children's Press, 2007. 49p. ISBN 978-0-531-12586-1. Grades: 2–6.

The football careers of Peyton Manning, Shaun Alexander, LaDainian Tomlinson, and others are discussed briefly in this book. Sidebars with facts about the players and the game are included. The book concludes with a glossary, resources for learning more, and an index. From the High Interest Books: Greatest Sports Heroes series.

Shea, Therese. *Basketball Stars.* New York: Scholastic, 2007. 48p. ISBN 978-0-531-12584-7. Grades: 2–6.

The careers and accomplishments of LeBron James, Tim Duncan, and others are briefly explored in this short book that will spark students' interest and have them eager to read more books about basketball stars. Back matter includes a glossary, resources for learning more, and an index. From the High Interest Books: Greatest Sports Heroes series.

Weatherford, Carole Boston. *Jesse Owens: Fastest Man Alive.* Illustrated by Eric Velasquez. New York: Walker, 2007. Unp. ISBN 978-0-8027-9550-2. Grades: 2–6.

Swiftly moving free verse recounts the story of runner Jesse Owens, who won four gold medals in the 1936 Olympics in Berlin. The text briefly touches on segregation, concentration camps, and Hitler. Biographical information is included at the end of the book.

Collie, Ashley Jude. *Gridiron Greats: 8 of Today's Hottest NFL Stars.* New York: Rosen, 2003. 96p. ISBN 978- 0-8239-3691-5. Grades: 2–8.

Eight football players including Kurt Warner, Drew Bledsoe, and Brett Favre are profiled in this book. The challenges they overcame to become professional football players inspire readers to overcome challenges in their own lives. There is a glossary, a list of resources, and an index. From the Sports Illustrated for Kids Books series.

Weatherford, Carole Boston. *Racing Against the Odds: The Story of Wendell Scott, Stock Car Racing's African American Champion.* Illustrated by Eric A. Velasquez. Tarrytown, NY: Marshall Cavendish, 2009. 40p. ISBN 978-0-7614-5465-6. Grades: 3–5.

In 1963 race car driver Wendell Scott became the first and only African American to win a NASCAR race. However, the racially biased judges declared a white driver the winner. Weatherford tells the story of Scott's passion for speed and the prejudice he endured as he pursued his dreams.

Crowe, Ellie. *Surfer of the Century: The Life of Duke Kahanamoku.* Illustrated by Richard Waldrep. New York: Lee and Low, 2007. 40p. ISBN 978-1-58430-276-6. Grades: 4–7.

Duke not only introduced the world to surfing; he was also a medal-winning Olympic swimmer having participated in four Olympics. With fierce determination he overcame poverty and racism to follow his passion. The blue and beige illustrations of ocean and sand blend together with the text to create a fitting tribute to the State of Hawai'i Ambassador of Aloha. NCSS Carter G. Woodson Elementary Level Honor Book, 2008.

Kent, Deborah. *Athletes with Disabilities.* Danbury, CT: Franklin Watts, 2003. 63p. ISBN 978-0-531-12019-8. Grades: 4–7.

The challenges and triumphs of these athletes with disabilities provide inspiration for readers and foster understanding and acceptance of these champions. Information about the Special Olympics and the Disabilities Act of 1990 is included. Back matter includes a glossary, a timeline, resources for learning more, and an index. From the Watts Library: Disabilities series.

Rappoport, Ken. *Profiles in Sports Courage.* Atlanta, GA: Peachtree, 2006. 151p. ISBN 978-1-56145-368-9. Grades: 4–7.

Twelve athletes from different countries and different sports each having overcome specific challenges are profiled in this collective biography. Athletes profiled in this book include Muhammad Ali, Lance Armstrong, Kerri Strug, and Ekaterina Gordeeva among others. The book includes bibliographic references.

Robinson, Sharon. *Promises to Keep: How Jackie Robinson Changed America.* New York: Scholastic, 2004. 64p. ISBN 978-0-439-42592-6. Grades: 4–7.

Sharon Robinson shares family memories as she chronicles the life of her famous father, baseball legend Jackie Robinson, and his impact on American culture. As America's first African-American Major League Baseball player, his courage, dignity, and character were tested in a segregated society. Personal family photographs and letters reveal a dedicated father who became an inspiration to the nation. The book includes a table of contents and an index.

Stewart, Mark, and Mike Kennedy. *Swish: The Quest for Basketball's Perfect Shot.* Minneapolis, MN: Millbrook Press, 2009. 64p. ISBN 978-0-8225-8752-1. Grades: 4–8.

The book begins with a chapter on basketball history and then moves on to game-winning shots. These famous shots are depicted in action-packed photographs, a brief narrative about the game, and brief profiles of the players. There is a list of resources and an index at the end of the book.

Tosiello, David P. *Michael Phelps: Swimming for Olympic Gold.* Berkeley Heights, NJ: Enslow, 2009. 48p. ISBN 978-0-7660-3591-1. Grades: 5–8.

In the 2008 Olympic Summer Games in Beijing, Phelps won a record-breaking eight gold medals. While students may be aware of his 2008 performance, they may not know much about his years of practice and his initial struggles with swimming. His parents' divorce and his diagnosis of ADHD will resonate with some readers and provide them with a role model. Back matter includes a glossary, a timeline, bibliographical references, and an index. From the Hot Celebrity Biographies series.

Explorations

1. Before reading *Campy: The Story of Roy Campanella* (Adler, 2007), show the students the video of Roy Campanella on the National Baseball Hall of Fame website at web.baseballhalloffame.org/sightssounds/.
2. After reading *The Man Who Walked Between the Towers* (Gerstein, 2003) show the students a video of Petit's walk available at www.youtube.com, at www.cbsnews.com/videos, and www.pbs.org/wgbh/amex/newyork/sfeature/sf_interviews.html.
3. Introduce and read *Jesse Owens: Fastest Man Alive* (Weatherford, 2007) to the students. Read the book a second time and project the illustrations using a document camera. While you read, pause to show the students how the illustrations can be used to help them understand unfamiliar words in the text.
4. After reading *Jesse Owens: Fastest Man Alive* (Weatherford, 2007) return to the book with the students to make connections between his life and events they have studied in their social studies class. You might begin by focusing on key vocabulary words in the poem that students will need to know in order to understand the events in his life.
5. After reading *Racing Against the Odds: The Story of Wendell Scott, Stock Car Racing's African American Champion* (Weatherford, 2009) students can visit the Legends of NASCAR website (www.legendsofnascar.com/Wendell_Scott.htm) to learn more about Scott. The information includes his racing statistics, photographs of him and his cars, and an interview with his wife, Mary.
6. Before reading *Athletes with Disabilities* (Kent, 2003) search Google images for photographs of athletes with disabilities to share with the students. These photographs will inspire athletes of all ages and abilities.
7. After sharing *Promises to Keep: How Jackie Robinson Changed America* (Robinson, 2004), return to the book to examine the personal letters and family photographs in the book. Have the students share what they learned about Jackie Robinson from the letters and photographs. Caution them about making inferences and remind them to just talk about the facts depicted in the letters and photographs. Then, have them use the facts to make inferences about what they see and to write down the facts that support their inferences.

DANCE

While reading the books in this section or watching the videos, students discover the inherent movement in the act of dancing. While there are particular steps and moves involved in dances such as ballet, hula, or hip-hop, children can also be creative and develop their own moves in response to the sounds and rhythms of the music. Books and media in this section help ensure that students meet the dance content standards one through five as they learn about dance and practice dance steps.

Book and Media Choices

Collins, Pat Lowery. *I Am a Dancer*. Illustrated by Mark Graham. Minneapolis, MN: Lerner, 2008. Unp. ISBN 978-0-8225-6369-3. Grades: P–3.

Moving to the sounds and rhythms of life enables students to dance every day as they move through their world. This joyful poem is filled with the motions of dance, as are the acrylic paintings. The book invites readers to dance to the beat they hear in their heads.

Gauch, Patricia Lee. *Tanya and the Red Shoes*. Illustrated by Satomi Ichikawa. New York: Philomel, 2002. Unp. ISBN 978-0-399-23314-2. Grades: K–3.

The determination and hard work required to become a ballerina, specifically to dance in toe shoes, is the focus of this sixth picture book about Tanya and her dreams. Vibrant watercolor illustrations capture the expressions and fluid movement of the ballerinas.

I Want to Be a Hula Dancer and Wear a Flower Lei! DVD. Makawao, HI: Kuleana Productions, 2003. 60 min. UPC 800007696998. Grades: K–3.

Use this video to introduce children to the traditional Hawaiian dance, the hula, through step-by-step instructions. Directions for three easy dances and how to make a flower lei are included.

Nelson, Marilyn. *Beautiful Ballerina*. Photographs by Susan Kuklin. New York: Scholastic, 2009. Unp. ISBN 978-0-545-08920-3. Grades: K–3.

Photographs of four female ballerinas from the Dance Theatre of Harlem accompany the poetry that celebrates the noble, graceful dancers. The repeated refrain "Beautiful ballerina, you are the dance" beckons children to chime in as the text is read aloud. Notes on the Dance Theatre of Harlem are included and provide the background needed to fully comprehend the poetry.

Boynton, Sandra. *Rhinoceros Tap: Deluxe Illustrated Lyrics Book*. New York: Workman, 2004. 59p. ISBN 978-0-7611-3323-0. Grades: K–4.

Silly songs and tapping feet quickly get students moving as they respond to this illustrated book and its accompanying CD. Sandra Boynton and Michael Ford wrote the music. The book has a table of contents and ends with lyrics and musical notations.

Hip-Hop for Kids: Pop! Lock! and Break. DVD. New York: Jumping Fish Productions, 2004. 60 min. ISBN 978-0-9649828-3-3. Grades: 4–10.

Roger D and children from his dance studio introduce hip-hop moves including popping, breaking, and locking. This fast-paced video challenges students to keep practicing to learn the moves. Included is a bonus feature on proper nutrition. Parents' Choice Award Winner, 2005.

Bingham, Jane. *Ballet.* Chicago, IL: Heinemann, 2009. 48p. ISBN 978-1-43291-374-8. Grades: 5–8.

Photographs, information on famous ballerinas, dance techniques, and career options fill this resourceful book. Also included is information on how ballet connects to cultures around the world. Back matter includes resources for learning more and an index. From the Dance series.

Do You Want to Dance? DVD. West Long Branch, NJ: Kultur Films, 2003. 80 min. ISBN 978-0-7697-2931-2. Grade: 5–8.

The video includes instructions for ballroom, Latin, country and western, wedding, and disco dancing. A clip of the video can be viewed on the company website at www.kulturfilms.com/.

Fitzgerald, Tamsin. *Hip-Hop and Urban Dance.* Chicago, IL: Heinemann, 2009. 48p. ISBN 978-1-43291-378-6. Grades: 5–8.

The history and culture surrounding hip-hop and urban dance are explored as well as dance techniques. Color photographs depicting dancers and their moves accompany the text. A bibliography, glossary, websites, and an index conclude the book. From the Dance series.

McAlpine, Margaret. *Working in Music and Dance.* New York: Gareth Stevens, 2006. 64p. ISBN 978-0-8368-4777-2. Grades: 6 and up.

Color photographs and sidebars complement the informative and interesting text. There is information on the skills and schooling needed for the careers and profiles of those currently working in dance. From the My Future Career series.

Explorations

1. While reading *I Am a Dancer* (Collins, 2008) encourage the students to mimic the movements of the children in the illustrations.
2. While watching *I Want to Be a Hula Dancer and Wear a Flower Lei!*, let the students try to mimic the moves of the dancers. While they may not succeed at getting the moves just right, this will get them out of their desks and moving around.
3. After reading *Beautiful Ballerina* (Nelson, 2009) students who want to learn about the Dance Theatre of Harlem can visit the website at www.dancetheatreofharlem.com/ and a search at www.youtube.com will reveal videos of the dance company.

4. While sharing *Rhinoceros Tap: Deluxe Illustrated Lyrics Book* (Boynton, 2004) play the accompanying CD and encourage children to join in the singing and dancing.
5. Jumping Fish Productions produced *Hip-Hop for Kids: Pop! Lock! And Break* and students can view more videos on the company website at www.hiphop4 kids.net/.
6. Play the bonus feature about proper nutrition on the *Hip-Hop for Kids: Pop! Lock! And Break* DVD to help the students understand that the stamina needed for dancing comes from both practice and proper nutrition.

DANCERS

As students read the biographies of noted dancers they learn about the challenges they faced that required not only hard work and perseverance but also overcoming cultural stereotypes and prejudices. Students relate to the youthful dancer in *A Young Dancer: The Life of an Ailey Student* (Gladstone, 2009) and they discover how important family support was to the success of the dancer. Books and media in this section address content standard three as students discover that dance is a way to create and to communicate meaning. Also, content standard five is addressed as students recognize the place of dance in different cultures.

Book and Media Choices

Dillon, Leo, and Diane Dillon. *Rap a Tap Tap: Here's Bojangles—Think of That!* New York: Scholastic, 2002. Unp. ISBN 978-0-590-47883-0. Grades: P–2.

Legendary dancer "Mr. Bojangles" is profiled in this picture book and perhaps the phrase that best sums up his dancing is "made art with his feet." The rhyming text and the energetic illustrations capture his rhythmic motions. An afterword identifies Bill Robinson as the real Mr. Bojangles and provides more information about his life.

Barasch, Lynne. *Knockin' on Wood: Starring Peg Leg Bates.* New York: Lee and Low Books, 2004. Unp. ISBN 978-1-58430-170-7. Grades: 1–4.

The loss of his leg in a factory accident at the age of twelve did not deter African-American Clayton Banks from pursuing his love of dancing. He was known as Peg Leg Bates. This inspirational book shows that with talent and determination a young person's dreams can be realized. Quotations from Banks conclude the book.

Orgill, Roxane. *Footwork: The Story of Fred and Adel Astaire.* Illustrated by Stephanie Jorisch. Cambridge, MA: Candlewick Press, 2007. Unp. ISBN 978-0-7636-2121-6. Grades: 1–4.

This picture book biography tells the story of siblings Fred and Adel Astaire and their dancing careers. The siblings danced their way from New York to London where Adel married an Englishman and gave up her career. Fred Astaire became one of the most famous dancers of the twentieth century.

Reich, Susanna. *Jose! Born to Dance: The Story of Jose Limon*. Illustrated by Raul Colon. New York: Simon and Schuster, 2004. Unp. ISBN 978-0-689-86576-3. Grades: 2–4.

During the Mexican Revolution, Limon's family fled Mexico for California. He was both a talented painter and a talented dancer. The rhythm and the onomatopoeic phrases throughout the text make this a delightful book to read aloud. The book begins with a glossary of the Spanish terms included in the text and it concludes with biographical information and resources for learning more.

Gladstone, Valerie. *A Young Dancer: The Life of an Ailey Student*. Photographs by Jose Ivey. New York: Henry Holt, 2009. Unp. ISBN 978-0-8050-8233-3. Grades: 3–8.

Thirteen-year-old African-American Iman Bright's life as an Ailey dancer is told in first person accompanied by large, clear color photographs. Her joyful dedication to dance inspires young dancers and makes the book a delight to read. An author's note about the Alvin Ailey American Dance Theater concludes the book.

Siegel, Siena Cherson. *To Dance: A Ballerina's Graphic Novel*. Illustrated by Mark Siegel. New York: Simon and Schuster, 2006. 64p. ISBN 978-0-689-86747-7. Grades: 3–8.

Based on Siegel's life as a ballerina, this graphic novel candidly portraits her love for dancing and the toll it took on her body. Accepted at the American School of Ballet, she performed in ballets by George Ballanchine until an ankle injury ended her career. Watercolor and ink illustrations help to tell her story. Robert F. Sibert Honor Book, 2007.

Abrams, Dennis. *Gregory Hines: Entertainer*. New York: Chelsea House, 2008. 98p. ISBN 978-0-7910-9718-2. Grades: 5–8.

Gregory Hines was a dancer, a singer, and an actor. He started tap-dancing at the age of two and for many years performed with his brother Maurice. The book recounts his struggles and the inspiration he received from other performers. Resources for learning more, a timeline, and an index conclude the book.

Nathan, Amy. *Meet the Dancers: From Ballet, Broadway, and Beyond*. New York: Henry Holt, 2008. 231p. ISBN 978-0-8050-8071-1. Grades: 5–9.

This collective biography contains the stories of sixteen dancers including Gillian Murphy, David Leventhal, and Jamal Story. While each story is unique, they all describe the hard work, the determination, and the family support needed to succeed in this challenging profession. Black-and-white photographs and interesting sidebars complement the interesting text. A glossary, resources for learning more, and an index conclude the book. Notable Social Studies Trade Book for Young People, 2009.

Govenar, Alan. *Stompin' at the Savoy: The Story of Norma Miller*. Illustrated by Martin French. Cambridge, MA: Candlewick Press, 2006. 64p. ISBN 978-0-7636-2244-2. Grades: 6–8.

In the 1920s during the Jazz Age and in the heart of the Harlem Renaissance, Norma Miller was born. In a segregated America she realized her dream of becoming a dancer in the Savoy Ballroom in New York City. The Savoy was not segregated but as a teenager Norma's dancing brought her out into the world beyond the Savoy, where she learned about segregation and racism. Norma Miller told her remarkable story during interviews with Govenar. Notable Social Studies Trade Book for Young People, 2007.

Explorations

1. Pair *Knockin' on Wood: Starring Peg Leg Bates* (Barasch, 2004) with *Athletes with Disabilities* (Kent, 2003), which is in the sports section in this chapter, to start a discussion about being accepting of those with disabilities.
2. Use *Jose! Born to Dance: The Story of Jose Limon* (Reich, 2004) to reinforce for the students how including onomatopoeia in their writing makes it more interesting and lively. Then, have the entire class collaborate to write a short piece that includes onomatopoeia using a projection system or by writing on the chalkboard.
3. Students wanting to learn more about the Ailey Dance Theater featured in *A Young Dancer: The Life of an Ailey Student* (Gladstone, 2009) can visit the website at www.alvinailey.org.
4. After reading *Meet the Dancers: From Ballet, Broadway, and Beyond* (Nathan, 2008), ask the students about connections they can make between their lives and the dancers' lives. Even though the students may not be studying dance they can make connections between the support the dancers need in their lives and the support the students need in their lives.
5. After reading *Stompin' at the Savoy: The Story of Norma Miller* (Govenar, 2006) have the students discuss how living across from the Savoy and being born during segregation impacted Miller's life and shaped her identity. Encourage the students to return to the text to support their statements.

TEACHER RESOURCES

Professional books, professional organizations, and Internet sites in this section support teachers and librarians as they work to ensure that students develop the skills necessary to participate in sports and recreational activities throughout their lives. Many of the resources contain ideas for incorporating physical activities and dance into all the content areas, which become more important as physical education classes are being shortened and eliminated.

Book and Media Choices

Reid, Rob. *Something Happened at the Library: Adding Song and Dance to Children's Story Programs*. Chicago, IL: American Library Association, 2007. 158p. ISBN 978-0-8389-0942-3. Grades: P–K.

Singing and dancing gives active young children a chance to participate in storytime programs. The book is filled with tips, ideas, and strategies as well as eight lesson plans. A bibliography, a discography, and an index conclude the book.

Summerford, Cathie. *Action-Packed Classrooms, K-5: Using Movement to Educate and Invigorate Learners*. Thousand Oaks, CA: Corwin, 2009. 159p. ISBN 978-1-41297-091-4. Grades: K–5.

Including movement in the content area classroom has the potential to enhance students' learning and this book is filled with ideas for getting students moving. A bibliography and an index conclude the book.

Bailey, Guy. *The Physical Educator's Big Book of Sport Lead-Up Games: A Complete K–8 Sourcebook of Team and Lifetime Sport Activities for Skill Development, Fitness and Fun!* Vancouver, WA: Educators Press, 2004. 315p. ISBN 978-0-9669727-5-7. Grades: K–8.

Filled with games and activities, this book is a useful resource for busy educators looking for ideas to get students up and moving. An index concludes the book.

Overby, Lynnette Young. *Interdisciplinary Learning through Dance: 101 Moventures*. Champaign, IL: Human Kinetics, 2005. 303p. ISBN 978-0-7360-4642-8. Grades: K–8.

Dance and movement have the potential to enhance students' learning in the content areas and this book contains lesson plans that foster an interdisciplinary approach to teaching. Included in the book is a music CD and an instructional DVD. A bibliography is included.

Mohnsen, Bonnie S. *Teaching Middle School Physical Education: A Standards-Based Approach for Grades 5-8*. Champaign, IL: Human Kinetics, 2008. 584p. ISBN 978-0-7360-6849-9. Grades: 5–8.

This book offers ideas for teaching physical education by matching the unique needs of middle school students to the activities. A bibliography and an index conclude the book. Additional resources are on the CD included with the book.

Professional Organizations

American Alliance for Health Physical Recreation and Dance
1900 Association Drive
Reston, VA 20191-1598
703-476-3400
www.aahperd.org

Journals: *Journal of Physical Education, Recreation and Dance (JOPERD), Strategies: A Journal for Physical and Sport Educators, American Journal of Health Education*

National Association for Sport and Physical Recreation
1900 Association Drive
Reston, VA 20191-1599
800-213-7193 or 703-476-3400
www.aahperd.org/naspe/
Journals: *Journal of Physical Education, Recreation and Dance (JOPERD), Strategies: A Journal for Physical and Sport Educators*

National Dance Association
1900 Association Drive
Reston, VA 20191-1599
703-476-3464
www.aahperd.org
Journals: *Nu Delta Alpha*

Internet Sites

Information Please Almanac: Sports
www.infoplease.com/sports/
Under the sports link is a sports encyclopedia, biographies, timelines, quizzes, and games. A search engine is available to help students find just what they are looking for. The site is maintained by Pearson Education and contains facts and figures on a variety of topics.

Official Web Site of the Olympic Movement
www.olympic.org
This website includes games, videos, a virtual museum, and other resources for learning about the Olympics. A search engine is available to help users quickly find answers to their questions or to locate information.

PE Central: The Premier Website for Health and Physical Recreation
www.pecentral.org
Started by a professor and his doctoral students at Virginia Tech, this website is filled with resources for K–12 physical educators. There are links to current research, information on best practices, lesson plans, assessment, and a newsletter.

Sports Illustrated for Kids
www.sikids.com
Sports Illustrated For Kids magazine sponsors this website, which includes games, videos, photos, news, and blogs. There is even a comic book builder.

SportVideos.com
www.sportvideos.com

Videos and DVDs on over thirty different sports are available from this company. More than 2,000 titles in the collection ensure that coaches and athletes will be able to find just the right one to learn the skills and techniques they need to succeed in their sports.

REFERENCES

Batch, J. A. 2005. "Benefits of Physical Activity in Obese Adolescents and Children." *Internal Medicine Journal* 25, no. 8 (August): 446.

Gilbert, Jennie A. 2006. "No, You Do Not Have to Run Today, You Get to Run." *Journal of Physical Education Recreation and Dance* 75, no. 6 (August): 25–31.

Knuth, Alan G., and Pedro C. Hallal. 2009. "Temporal Trends in Physical Activity: A Systematic Review." *Journal of Physical Activity and Health* 6, no. 5 (September): 548–570.

National Association for Sport and Physical Education. 2004. *Moving into the Future: National Standards for Physical Education*, Second Edition. Reston, VA: Author.

National Dance Association. 1994. *National Standards for Dance Education*. [Online]. Available: www.aahperd.org/nda/profDevelopment/standards.cfm (accessed December 19, 2009).

Chapter 7

Art

When art teachers, librarians, and content area teachers collaborate, their shared knowledge enhances students' learning and results in dynamic multimodal projects. Teachers know the content, librarians know books that can enhance the content, and art teachers know a variety of techniques for creating memorable works of art to showcase what the students learn. Meagher (2006) offers ideas for cross-curricular projects involving content area curriculum, trade books, and art activities such as quilting and weaving. Combining literature, art activities, and discussion ensures that literature and art become significant in children's lives (Carger, 2004). Sections in this chapter include art appreciation, art in children's literature, creating art, art movements, art and life, artists, and teacher resources.

The *National Standards for Arts Education: Visual Arts* (Music Educators National Conference, 1994) establish a framework for ensuring that students understand and appreciate the visual arts. The standards include:

Content Standard 1: Understanding and applying media, techniques, and processes.
Content Standard 2: Using knowledge of structures and functions.
Content Standard 3: Choosing and evaluating a range of subject matter, symbols, and ideas.
Content Standard 4: Understanding the visual arts in relation to history and cultures.
Content Standard 5: Reflecting upon and assessing the characteristics and merits of their work and the work of others.
Content Standard 6: Making connections between visual arts and other disciplines.

ART APPRECIATION

By examining and discussing art students decide what they like and they develop the skill they need to think critically about art. Exposure to a wide variety of art helps children develop their preferences, make connections between art and their lives, and see the world from the artists' perspectives. As students develop an appreciation of art they recognize that art evokes feelings and they come to see the power of art in their lives. Books, media, and explorations in this section engage students in art experiences that address standards one, two, three, and five.

Book and Media Choices

Gonzalez, Maya Christina. *My Colors, My World/Mis Colores, Mi Mundo*. San Francisco, CA: Children's Book Press, 2007. Unp. ISBN 978-0-89239-221-6. Grades: P–2.

Hidden in the browns and grays of the desert are vibrant colors waiting to be discovered. As Maya searches the desert she finds all the colors of the rainbow. Her quest can inspire young readers to search for all the colors in their lives. The illustrations span the double-page spreads. Beneath the illustration on the left side the text is in English and on the right side the text is in Spanish. A note from the author and a bilingual color glossary conclude the book. Pura Belpré Honor Book for Illustration, 2008.

Micklethwait, Lucy. *I Spy Shapes in Art*. New York: HarperCollins, 2004. Unp. ISBN 978-0-06-073193-9. Grades: P–2.

Fourteen works of art, each containing a shape such as a semicircle, a triangle, or a heart, have young readers searching and often finding more than what they are looking for. An author's note at the beginning of the book encourages adults to have young readers looking for other shapes, focusing on the colors, and making up stories about the pictures. The book concludes with the shapes, a list of the art works, and their locations.

Museum ABC. Boston: Little, Brown, 2002. 60p. ISBN 978-0-316-07170-3. Grades: P–3.

A is for apple, b is for boat, and c is for cat, which is not unusual; however, when the apple, the boat, and the cat are all from paintings in the collection of The Metropolitan Museum of Art, that is unusual. As students learn the letters of the alphabet they are exposed to a variety of works of art and begin to develop an appreciation for art from different time periods, different styles, and different cultures.

Niepold, Mil, and Jeanyves Verdu. *Oooh! Picasso*. Berkeley, CA: Ten Speed Press, 2009. Unp. ISBN 978-1-58246-265-3. Grades: P–4.

Close-up colorful photographs of portions of five of Picasso's sculptures challenge readers to look closely and guess what they are seeing. As readers turn the pages different pieces of the artwork are revealed until in the end the whole sculpture is revealed. Concluding the book is a photograph of Picasso and reproductions of the sculptures with identifying information.

Raczka, Bob. *3-D ABC: A Sculptural Alphabet*. Minneapolis, MN: Millbrook Press, 2008. Unp. ISBN 978-0-7613-9456-3. Grades: P–5.

Spectacular sculptures, one for each letter of the alphabet, fill the pages of the book. Each photograph is accompanied by text explaining how the sculpture relates to the letter. The title of the piece, the name of the artist, and the location of the piece are included. Orbis Pictus Recommended Book, 2008.

Raczka, Bob. *No One Saw: Ordinary Things through the Eyes of an Artist.* Brookfield, CT: Millbrook Press, 2002. 32p. ISBN 978-0-7613-2370-9. Grades: K–4.

The repetitive "No one saw..." introduces children to different artists and their views of the world. For example, Mary Cassatt's intimate views of mothers, Georgia O'Keefe's flower close-ups, and Degas' studies of ballet dancers. Each artist had a way of looking at ordinary objects in unordinary ways and their paintings cause viewers to pause and to see the world from their perspective. At the end of the book young artists are encouraged to draw from their own unique perspectives. A list of the paintings featured in the book and brief biographical notes on the artists conclude the book.

Raczka, Bob. *Art Is...* Brookfield, CT: Millbrook Press, 2003. 32p. ISBN 978-0-7613-2874-2. Grades: K–5.

Reproductions of twenty-seven works of art and rhyming couplets with the repeated "Art is..." delight the eyes and the ears as readers are introduced to works of art that span centuries. For younger readers there is the art and wordplay to enjoy and for older readers there is the opportunity to go beyond the book to discuss "What is art?" Endnotes include thumbnails of the reproductions accompanied by a tiny piece of information about the work or the artist.

Raczka, Bob. *Artful Reading.* Minneapolis, MN: Millbrook Press, 2008. Unp. ISBN 978-0-8225-6754-7. Grades: 1–4.

Reading is important and that message reverberates throughout this artful celebration of reading in magnificent works of art. Each reproduction features someone reading and the subjects range from Cézanne's father to Dürer's apostles to Spitzweg's bookworm. Back matter includes thumbnails of the paintings and information about the artists' own reading and writing lives.

Raffin, Deborah. *Mitzi's World.* Illustrated by Jane Wooster Scott. New York: Abrams, 2009. Unp. ISBN 978-0-8109-8004-4. Grades: 1–4.

Through folk-art-style paintings readers follow Mitzi, a small black and white dog, as she traverses the seasons in quaint villages, farmsteads, and rolling hills. Accompanying each illustration is a list of items to find. As they search, readers are drawn into the images and they begin to develop an appreciation of folk art.

Sturgis, Alexander. *Dan's Angel: A Detective's Guide to the Language of Painting.* La Jolla, CA: Kane/Miller, 2003. Unp. ISBN 978-1-929132-47-8. Grades: 1–4.

With the help of Fra Angelico's Angel Gabriel, Dan discovers iconography and symbolism in twelve great works by artists including de Goya, Picasso, and Botticelli. Gabriel accompanies Dan through the museum showing him how to use the clues in the paintings to uncover their stories.

Cressy, Judith. *Can You Find It?* New York: Harry N. Abrams, 2002. 40p. ISBN 978-0-8109-3279-1. Grades: 2–5.

After playing "Can you find it?" with nineteen reproductions from the Metropolitan Museum of Art, looking at a painting will never be the same. Beside each large colorful reproduction is a list of items to find within it. To find the items requires viewers to focus on the smallest details in the paintings. The book concludes with the answers and a bit of information about the painters and their paintings.

Montanari, Eva. *Chasing Degas*. New York: Abrams, 2009. Unp. ISBN 978-0-8109-3878-6. Grades: 3–5.

When Degas inadvertently picks up a young ballerina's bag instead of his own, the young dancer sets off through the streets of Paris searching for him. On her trek she encounters Impressionist painters and their works, including Monet and Cassatt. An author's note and color reproductions of the artwork introduce readers to the Impressionists.

Johnson, Stephen. *A Is for Art: An Abstract Alphabet*. New York: Simon and Schuster, 2008. 36p. ISBN 978-0-689-86301-1. Grades: 3 and up.

This imaginative trip through the alphabet includes twenty-six paintings, collages, sculptures, and installations created from everyday objects over the course of several years. Most compositions include the letter of the alphabet and each is accompanied by an alliterative caption sure to trip the tongue as they are read. ALA Notable Children's Book, 2009. NCTE Notable Children's Book in the Language Arts, 2009.

Raczka, Bob. *Unlikely Pairs: Fun with Famous Works of Art*. Minneapolis, MN: Millbrook Press, 2006. 32p. ISBN 978-0-7613-2936-7. Grades: 4 and up.

Thirteen "unlikely pairs" of famous paintings entice children to critically examine the works and discover the similarities between them. In this wordless book, the answers lie in the reproductions themselves. However, older students can conduct research to compare and contrast the historical time periods during which the paintings were created. The book ends with thumbnails of the reproductions and very brief artists' biographies.

Wenzel, Angela. *Do You See What I See? The Art of Illusion*. Munich: Prestel, 2001. 29p. ISBN 978-3-7913-2488-3. Grades: 5–8.

Trompe-l'oeil, perspective, and color contrasts are just some of the illusion techniques that cause viewers to pause, to carefully examine, and to question what they are looking at. Works by Escher, Dali, Bridget Riley, and Albers among others are used to explain the illusions. The back flyleaf has additional information about the illustrations in the book.

Armstrong, Jennifer. *Photo by Brady: A Picture of the Civil War*. New York: Simon & Schuster, 2004. 147p. ISBN 978-0-689-85785-0. Grades: 6–9.

Mathew Brady and his crews photographed searing images of the death and the destruction of the Civil War. While the focus of the book is the Civil War, it also includes detailed information on photographic techniques. Studying the black-and-white photographs enables readers to understand the techniques and to learn about the Civil War. Back matter includes notes, a bibliography, picture credits, and an index.

Explorations

1. After reading *Museum ABC* have the students create their own alphabet book using copyright-free images from the Internet. Using a paint program, have the students crop out the parts of the image that they need.
2. Using the cropped images in *Oooh! Picasso* (Niepold and Verdu, 2009) as models for their own cropped images, have the students visit virtual museums to collect digital images of sculptures and paintings. Then, have the students import the images into a paint program and crop them. The cropped images and the full images can be inserted into PowerPoint slide shows to slowly reveal the different parts of the images as the slides change.
3. After reading *Oooh! Picasso* (Niepold and Verdu, 2009) have students take digital pictures of familiar objects in the school such as a water fountain or the door to the classroom. Then, have them crop the images using a photo-editing program such as paint.net (Win) available at www.getpaint.net or Preview (Mac). Print the pictures and post them in the classroom or upload them to the class website so that other students can guess the objects.
4. In *3-D ABC: A Sculptural Alphabet* (Raczka, 2008) there is an overhead shot of a carefully arranged vacuum cleaner and hose. Using that photograph as a model, have the students take digital photographs of objects to represent the letters of the alphabet so they can create their own sculptural alphabet. Use a desktop publishing program to publish their sculptural alphabet. Students can upload their photographs to www.befunky.com to apply different effects.
5. Use *Mitzi's World* (Raffin, 2009) as an introduction to folk art by having students study the paintings as you describe the characteristics of folk art.
6. After reading *Dan's Angel: A Detective's Guide to the Language of Painting* (Sturgis, 2003) have the students each select one of the reproductions to carefully examine. Then, have the students share their ideas about the story within the picture with their classmates. Once they have shared their stories orally, have them write their stories down.
7. Ask the students to pick a pair of artworks from *Unlikely Pairs: Fun with Famous Works of Art* (Raczka, 2006) and then, working with a partner, have them jot down words that connect the two paintings. Then, have the students go to Wordle at wordle.net to enter their words and create a "word cloud" to share with their classmates (Hayes, 2008).
8. The students can take a virtual museum trip to The Metropolitan Museum of Art at www.metmuseum.org/ to search for artworks to combine into their own unlikely pairs. After they have selected the pairs, they can write an explanation of why they selected their pairs.

ART IN CHILDREN'S LITERATURE

In the author's note at the beginning of *Show & Tell: Exploring the Fine Art of Children's Book Illustration*, Evans (2008) reminds readers that picture books are often the first place that children discover art, where they learn about life, and where their imaginations take them on wondrous journeys. Examining the art in picture books provides bilingual/bicultural children opportunities to develop their critical thinking skills as they engage in discussions about the illustrations and bring their own cultural backgrounds into the discussions (Carger, 2004). As children develop an understanding of the visual arts in relation to culture they are addressing standard four. Discussing illustrations and creating art enables students to make connections between the books and their own lives, which addresses content standards one and six.

Book and Media Choices

Aldana, Patricia, editor. *Under the Spell of the Moon: Art for Children from the World's Great Illustrators*. Translated by Stan Dragland. Toronto, Ontario, CN: Groundwood Books, 2004. 80p. ISBN 978-0-88899-559-9. Grades: P and up.

Artists from around the globe have illustrated text they have chosen or written. The text appears in English and in the illustrator's native language. It is a delightful celebration of how literature and art bridge cultures around the world. Katherine Patterson provides a brief foreword that explains the work of the International Board on Books for Young People (IBBY) and its founder, the late Jella Lepman. The book concludes with brief biographies of the artists whose works appear in the book.

Why Did the Chicken Cross the Road? New York: Penguin, 2006. Unp. ISBN 978-0-8037-3094-6. Grades: 1–4.

Fourteen children's book illustrators answer the age-old question with illustrations that span two-page spreads and include very few words. The illustrations are hilarious and they require careful examination in order to capture all of the details. Showcased within the pages of the book are the artists' unique styles, making this a book that older art students appreciate. The last two-page spread asks, "Why did the artist cross the road?" Each of the contributors' chickens responds in word balloons.

Reading Is Fundamental. *The Art of Reading: Forty Illustrators Celebrate RIF's 40th Anniversary*. New York: Dutton, 2005. 96p. ISBN 978-0-525-47484-5. Grades: 3 and up.

Not only does this book celebrate RIF, it also celebrates the power of children's literature to impact lives. Forty illustrators share a book from their childhood with a visual homage and a personal remembrance on the impact of the book.

Selznick, Brian. *The Invention of Hugo Cabret: A Novel in Words and Pictures*. New York: Scholastic, 2007. 534p. ISBN 978-0-439-81378-5. Grades: 4–9.

Selznick artfully weaves mysterious pencil illustrations and suspenseful text into a combination picture book/graphic novel/film. Living within the walls of a Paris train station, a young orphan, Hugo, is secretly maintaining the station's clocks as he tries to fix the automaton his father was working on at the time of his death. Hugo's life intersects with a toymaker and his granddaughter in an intricate plot that keeps readers turning the pages to uncover the connections, but also to reveal the masterful illustrations. The character of the toymaker is based on filmmaker George Melies. An audio version of the book is available. Caldecott Medal Winner, 2008.

Artist to Artist: 23 Major Illustrators Talk about Their Art. New York: Penguin, 2007. 105p. ISBN 978-0-399-24600-5. Grades: 4 and up.

The twenty-three artists featured in this book share brief personal reflections on art in the form of a signed letter, personal photographs, self-portraits, and foldout pages of their artwork, including some of their childhood illustrations. The book begins with a note from Eric Carle in which he acknowledges the teachers and mentors who have encouraged him throughout his life and offers hope that this book will mentor future artists. Profits from the sale of the book benefit the Eric Carle Museum of Picture Book Art

Marcus, Leonard S. *A Caldecott Celebration: Seven Artists and Their Paths to the Caldecott Medal.* New York: Walker, 2008. 55p. ISBN 978-0-8027-9704-9. Grades: 4 and up.

Marcus has profiled one Caldecott artist from each decade that the award has been given. Included in the book are Robert McCloskey, Marcia Brown, Maurice Sendak, William Steig, Chris Van Allsburg, David Weisner, and Mordicai Gerstein, who was added for this updated version of the book. Preliminary drawings and sculptures as well as photos of the authors and other related items make this a fascinating exploration of the artists and their work.

Marcus, Leonard S. *Pass it Down: Five Picture Book Families Make Their Mark.* New York: Walker, 2007. 55p. ISBN 978-0-8027-9600-4. Grades: 4 and up.

Five picture book families (Crews/Jonas, Hurd, Myers, Pickney, and Rockwell) share the stories of how writing and/or illustrating was handed down from parents to children. Family photographs, letters from editors, and samples of their work combined with tantalizing tidbits of information tell the stories of these gifted authors and illustrators whose works are widely known.

Evans, Dilly. *Show & Tell: Exploring the Fine Art of Children's Book Illustration.* San Francisco, CA: Chronicle, 2008. 143p. ISBN 978-0-8118-4971-5. Grades: 7 and up.

From the endpapers that feature covers of the artists' books to the graphic table of contents to the biographies to the analysis of the art in children's books, Evans enlightens and educates readers about the world of picture book art. Noted agent and picture book authority Evans takes readers on an in-depth exploration of the work of twelve artists. An author's note, acknowledgments, and an index are included.

Explorations

1. After reading *Why Did the Chicken Cross the Road?* have the students create their own versions of the answer to the riddle using the illustrators' answers as models for their own.
2. Prior to reading *The Invention of Hugo Cabret: A Novel in Words and Pictures* (Selznick, 2007) have the students visit The Franklin Institute website (www.fi.edu/learn/sci-tech/automaton/automaton.php?cts=instrumentation) to view a video of Brian Selznick and the Maillardet Automaton that was the inspiration for the book.
3. In *A Caldecott Celebration: Seven Artists and Their Paths to the Caldecott Medal* (Marcus, 2008) the author profiles only seven of the artists who have won the Caldecott Medal. Using the information in the book as a model, have the students research and write about other Caldecott Medal winners. Many of the Caldecott artists have websites that students can use as a resource and the artists have done interviews that can be found in magazines and journals.
4. In *Pass it Down: Five Picture Book Families Make Their Mark* (Marcus, 2007) the book ends with only partial lists of the families' books. Ask the students to review the lists and then add their favorites to the lists.
5. After reading *Pass it Down: Five Picture Book Families Make Their Mark* (Marcus, 2007) have the students make a list of the ways the parents helped their children become artists. Then, have the students discuss how their parents help them accomplish their goals.

CREATING ART

Giving children opportunities to create art helps them to understand the time and effort involved in the creative process. Creating art also helps students understand art techniques and terms, which addresses content standards one and two. Liggett (2008) taught students about background, foreground, resist, and mixed media by having students create a detailed work of art based on a book she shared with them. While the book gave the students a shared text to work from, they each created a unique response. The books and computer programs in this section enable students to explore different art techniques as they create their own works of art including painting, sculptures, collages, and graphic novels.

Book and Media Choices

Seeger, Laura Vaccaro. *Lemons Are Not Red.* New York: Roaring Brook, 2004. Unp. ISBN 978-1-59643-008-2. Grades: P–2.

Bright colors, die-cuts, and repetitive text draw readers into this simple concept book that will be a class favorite. Die-cut holes reveal objects in the wrong color, but when the page is turned the objects appear in the correct color.

Wong, Janet S. *The Dumpster Diver*. Illustrated by David Roberts. Cambridge, MA: Candlewick, 2007. Unp. ISBN 978-0-7636-2380-7. Grades: P–2.

Electrician Steve and his band of merry children scour the dumpsters for junk to transform into treasures. The grouch next door voices her disapproval of their exploits, but undaunted Steve and the children continue to recycle the neighborhood cast-offs. After Steve is injured during a dive, they begin knocking on doors asking for discards rather than dumpster diving. Wong based this story on artist Kerry Wade, who creates art from his dumpster-diving expeditions.

Portis, Antoinette. *Not a Box*. New York: HarperCollins, 2006. Unp. ISBN 978-0-06-112323-8. Grades: P–3.

A big-eared imaginative bunny transforms a simple cardboard box into a race car, a mountain, and a burning building among other things. An unseen narrator continues to ask why the rabbit is playing with a box and with each turn of the page the box is transformed. Simple black and red lines depict the bunny and his "not a box." *New York Times* Best Illustrated Children's Book, 2007. Theodor Seuss Geisel Award Honor Book, 2007.

Reynolds, Peter H. *Ish*. DVD. Norwalk, CT: Weston Woods, 2005. 8 min. ISBN 978-0-439-80427-1. Grades: P–4.

When his brother laughs at his artwork, Ramon crumples his drawings and gives up. However, his sister recognizes the possibilities in his artwork and encourages him to continue. The video is based on the book by the same name. Chester Gregory narrates and Joel Goodman has created an original jazz score. ALSC Notable Children's Video, 2006.

Tux Paint. Mac/Win. Davis, CA: New Breed Software, 2008. Grades: P–6.

Tux Paint is a free, open source drawing software that features a variety of drawing tools and is designed for schoolchildren to be able to quickly and easily learn to use. Download the software and documentation at www.tuxpaint.org.

Arnold, Katya. *Elephants Can Paint Too!* New York: Atheneum, 2005. Unp. ISBN 978-0-689-86985-3. Grades: K–2.

Imagine teaching schoolchildren in Brooklyn to paint and teaching elephants in Thailand to paint. That is what artist Katya Arnold does. Colorful two-page spreads display photographs of the children painting next to photographs of the elephants painting. An author's note concludes the book with information on the Asian Elephant Art and Conservation Project and its website, www.elephantart.com. Sales of the elephant's paintings and profits from the book go toward saving the Asian elephants. ALSC Notable Children's Books, 2006.

Emberley, Ed. *Ed Emberley's Drawing Book of Trucks and Trains*. Boston: Little, Brown, 2002. Unp. ISBN 978-0-316-78967-7. Grades: K–3.

Rows and rows and pages and pages of simple drawings fill the book. With simple lines and shapes young artists can easily create their own trucks and trains. Each row is composed of two lines of figures. The top line shows what to draw and the bottom line shows where to put it.

Pericoli, Matteo. *Tomaso and the Missing Line.* New York: Alfred A. Knopf, 2008. Unp. ISBN 978-0-375-94102-3. Grades: K–3.

A missing line from a favorite drawing sets Tomaso off on a journey of discovery searching for the line. With the help of his grandma he finds the line, but not before young readers discover that there are lines everywhere just waiting to be found. Tucked into the black-and-white line drawings are vibrant orange lines making a dog's leash, a cat's tail, and a car's antenna.

Reynolds, Peter H. *The Dot.* Norwalk, CT: Weston Woods, 2004. 9 min. ISBN 978-0-439-73456-1. Grades: K–4.

A caring, concerned teacher encourages Vashti to make a mark and explore the possibilities in her artwork. Narrated by Thora Birch, this video is based on Reynolds' book by the same name. A study guide is available. ALSC Carnegie Medal for Excellence in Children's Video, 2005. ALSC Notable Children's Video, 2005.

Gonyea, Mark. *A Book about Color—A Clear and Simple Guide for Young Artists.* New York: Macmillan, 2010. Unp. ISBN 978-0-8050-9055-0. Grades: K–6.

From learning what primary and secondary colors are to what the colors mean and how colors interact in a composition, this is a simple guide with a big impact.

Animationish. Mac/Win. Boston, MA: Fablevision, 2007. Grades: K and up.

Within minutes children are creating their own animations just for fun or to demonstrate concepts they have learned in content area classes. As students gain confidence and master the animation skills they can move up through three levels of the program. A free demo of the program can be downloaded at www.fablevision.com. Children's Technology Review Editor's Choice Award, 2008.

Teitelbaum, Michael. *Making Comic Books.* Chanhassen, MN: The Child's World, 2007. 32p. ISBN 978-1-59296-733-9. Grades: 2–5.

Three short chapters are packed with information about how a comic book is made. Lots of photographs, illustrations, and text boxes draw readers into the book and the engaging information keeps them reading. Readers are asked questions and invited to make comparisons as they read, which helps keep them focused on the text. A glossary, resources for learning more, and an index conclude the book. From the Reading Rocks! series.

Friedman, Debra. *Picture This: Fun Photography and Crafts.* Tonawanda, NY: Kids Can Press, 2003. 40p. ISBN 978-1-55337-047-5. Grades: 3–5.

This basic introduction to photography teaches students how to take pictures and how to showcase them. Students learn about perspective, light and shadow, framing subjects, and trick photography to name a few. While the book does not have an index it does have a table of contents and a glossary. From the Kids Can Do It series.

Rosinsky, Natalie M. *Write Your Own Graphic Novel.* Minneapolis, MN: Compass Point Books, 2009. 64p. ISBN 978-0-7565-3856-9. Grades: 4–8.

This book has the background information and the step-by-step instructions students need to write their own graphic novel. Included at the back of the book is an ID number that will let young artists access additional information at FactHound. A glossary, resources for learning more, and an index conclude the book. From the Write Your Own series.

Raimondo, Joyce. *Express Yourself! Activities and Adventures in Expressionism.* New York: Watson-Guptil, 2005. 48p. ISBN 978-0-8230-2506-0. Grades: 5–8.

The techniques of Expressionists Munch, van Gogh, Kirchner, Kandinsky, de Kooning, and Pollack provide students with models for making collages, paintings, and prints. A series of questions engage readers in examining and thinking about a reproduction of each artist's work. Step-by-step illustrated instructions invite readers to try the artists' techniques and examples of students' work are included. Brief artists' biographies conclude the book. From the Art Explorers series.

Raimondo, Joyce. *Make It Pop! Activities and Adventures in Pop Art.* New York: Watson-Guptil, 2006. 48p. ISBN 978-0-8230-2507-7. Grades: 5–8.

Cast a hand in plaster, sculpt fake food, create a collage, or paint a cartoon in the Pop Art style of a famous artist using the instructions in this book. Artists showcased in this book include Lichtenstein, Warhol, Rauschenberg, Johns, Oldenburg, and Segal. A brief introduction to Pop Art is followed by information about the work of famous Pop artists, a reproduction of their work and lots of thought-provoking questions about their works. Instructions on how to create Pop Art using the artist's technique and samples of work created by students are included. Brief artists' biographies conclude the book. From the Art Explorers series.

Bang, Molly. *Picture This: How Pictures Work.* New York: NorthSouth Books, 2000. 96p. ISBN 978-1-58717-030-0. Grades: 5 and up.

Geometric shapes represent the characters and the action as they tell the story of "Little Red Riding Hood." Firmly anchored in the story, the abstract shapes allow the reader to explore how the shapes, sizes, and colors in pictures elicit emotions from viewers.

Anime Studio Debut 6. Mac/Win. Aliso Viejo, CA: Smith Micro Software, 2006. Grades: 5 and up.

This 2D animation software allows students to sketch their own graphics, scan graphics, or import graphics including photographs to use to create cartoons, movies, anime, and animations. The software includes tutorials and sample files to enable students to immediately launch their creations. ALA Greater Interactive Software for Kids Winner, 2007.

Explorations

1. While *Not a Box* (Portis, 2006) was written for younger students, it also can be shared with older students. Using a computer paint program such as the one in the accessories folder in MS Windows, have students generate additional ways to transform the box. This activity can also be done with crayons or markers.
2. After reading *Making Comic Books* (Teitelbaum, 2007) create a comic book using an online comic book maker such as ToonDoo at www.toondoo.com. The program is easy to use; however, students will need guidance as they talk about and design their comic strips.
3. In the chapter titled "Step by Step" in *Picture This: Fun Photography and Crafts* (Friedman, 2003) students learn how to tell stories in a series of pictures. The trick is to have the pictures show the sequence so clearly that they do not need words. This will take some practice and the students will need to have the teacher model the process for them.
4. In *Express Yourself!: Activities and Adventures in Expressionism* (Raimondo, 2005) the author suggests that students write a story about why the person in Munch's "The Scream" is screaming. Ask the students to look closely at the painting for clues and then have them talk in small groups about their ideas. Once all the students have ideas for their stories, give them time to write their stories and then share their stories with their classmates.
5. *Make It Pop! Activities and Adventures in Pop Art* (Raimondo, 2006) includes instructions for creating art, such as the plaster hand. The plaster hand sculptures are personalized by putting an object in the hand. Ask the students to put an object in their plaster hand sculpture that tells something about them or something about their culture.
6. After reading *Picture This: How Pictures Work* (Bang, 2000) give the students red, black, and white construction paper and scissors so they can explore Bang's technique.

ART MOVEMENTS

Studying art movements addresses content standard four, understanding the visual arts in relation to history and culture, and addresses content standard five, reflecting upon and assessing the characteristics and merits of their work and the work of others. Many of the books in this section examine only one art movement; however, they belong to series that encompass individual books on many art movements. Look for other books in the series to find books on all of the art movements or look for the books in this section that encompass several art movements. For example, *. . . isms: Understanding Art* (Little, 2004) is a handy pocket guide to a variety of art movements.

Book and Media Choices

Desnoettes, Caroline. *Look Closer: Art Masterpieces through the Ages.* New York: Walker, 2006. 18p. ISBN 978-0-8027-9614-1. Grades: 3–6.

Glossy, creamy card stock sets off the vibrant reproductions featured on the left side of the two-page spreads and means the pages are weighty enough to support two flaps on the right side. Under the first flap are questions and bulleted information and under the second flap is the artist's color palette. The last eighteen pages of the book provide a one-page essay about each painting, placing it in its historic and artistic context.

Langley, Andrew. *Ancient Greece.* Chicago, IL: Raintree, 2005. 48p. ISBN 978-1-41090-517-8. Grades: 4–8.

The history of Greece is examined through the art left behind in the architecture, the pottery, the mosaics, the paintings, the manuscripts, and other artifacts. Colorful, well-organized pages with labeled photographs invite readers into the artwork and into the text. The book concludes with a timeline, a glossary, resources for learning more, and an index. From the History in Art series.

Nilsen, Anna. *Art Auction Mystery.* Boston, MA: Houghton Mifflin, 2005. 48p. ISBN 978-0-7534-5842-6. Grades: 4–8.

Several world-famous masterpieces are going to be auctioned but some of them are fakes. Readers are challenged to find the fakes using the chart and guidelines explained at the beginning of the book. Split pages feature the artworks on the top and the art auction catalog at the bottom. Higher-order thinking skills and mathematics are required to find the fakes. As students solve the mystery they learn about the masterpieces and the artists' style. This book is also available in Spanish.

Salvi, Francesco. *The Impressionists.* Illustrated by L. R. Galante and Andrea Ricciardi. Minneapolis, MN: Oliver, 2008. 64p. ISBN 978-1-934545-03-4. Grades: 5–8.

Each chapter is a double-page spread with the theme of the chapter introduced in the top left corner. Captioned photographs, reproductions, and illustrations that expand on the theme fill the pages. The book concludes with a timeline, glossary, websites, a list of works included, and an index. From the Art Masters series.

Gunderson, Jessica. *Realism.* Mankato, MN: Creative Education, 2009. 48p. ISBN 978-1-58341-612-9. Grades: 5 and up.

As the Industrial Revolution spread across the world impacting politics and economics, it also impacted the art world, which turned its focus to real people and current events. With the introduction of the photographic process, daguerrotype, the art world was dramatically changed. Words in bold appear in the glossary. A timeline, a glossary, a bibliography, and an index conclude the book. From the Movements in Art series.

Gunderson, Jessica. *Romanticism*. Mankato, MN: Creative Education, 2009. 48p. ISBN 978-1-58341-613-6. Grades: 5 and up.

History, inventions, politics, and the artists' lives and their works are interwoven in this introduction to Romanticism. Photographs, reproductions, and illustrations draw readers into the book and the descriptive, informative text holds them. A timeline, a glossary, a bibliography, and an index conclude the book. From the Movements in Art series.

Little, Stephen. *. . . isms: Understanding Art*. New York: Universe, 2004. 159p. ISBN 978-0-7893-1209-9. Grades: 7 and up.

Stash this guide to art history in a pocket and use it as a reference while perusing art museums, suggests the book flap. Students and teachers looking for a quick introduction to art "isms" find this an easy-to-use, well-organized guide. The book is divided into six sections: Renaissance, Baroque and Rococo, the Nineteenth Century, Modernism, Post-Modernism, and Reference. The reference section includes reproductions, key artists, keywords, definitions, key works, and other information.

Explorations

1. The students can use the Timeline of Art History at www.metmuseum.org/toah/ on the website for The Metropolitan Museum of Art to learn more about art movements and to view paintings corresponding to each movement. The timeline can be searched chronologically, geographically, and thematically and features art from around the world.
2. Using iMovie or Microsoft Movie Maker have the students create a video of examples of art from a particular art movement. The students can write the narration to text to accompany the video. A helpful resource for this project is *Video Art for the Classroom* (Szekely and Szekely, 2005), which be found in the teacher resources at the end of this chapter.
3. Put the students on teams and assign each team two or three paintings from *Art Auction Mystery* (Nilsen, 2005) for them to determine whether or not they are forgeries.
4. One of the artists featured in *Romanticism* (Gunderson, 2009) is Eugène Delacroix and the National Museum of Eugène Delacroix is mentioned in the book as a place to visit. While visiting it in person may not be an option, students interested in learning more about this artist and his works can visit the museum online at www.musee-delacroix.fr/en.
5. As the students read about art movements in *. . . isms: Understanding Art* (Little, 2004) encourage them to visit museum websites to find works of art referenced in the book. Then, encourage them to use the information in the book to defend their decisions about why or why not a particular painting belongs to that movement.

ART AND LIFE

Books in this section help students discover how art directly impacts their lives and helps them see that art is part of their lives. Art is intertwined with culture and students may not recognize the artistic elements of a culture, so some of the following books were chosen to help students see art in various cultures. The books also offer students examples of how a passion for art can be turned into a career and how art can be used to express feelings and emotions. Books, media, and explorations in this section enable students to make connections between the visual arts and their lives, which addresses content standard six.

Book and Media Choices

Ajmera, Maya, and John D. Ivanko. *To Be an Artist*. Watertown, MA: Charlesbridge, 2004. Unp. ISBN 978-1-57091-503-1. Grades: K–3.

Through art humans express the wonder and feelings they have for their world and this book is a joyous celebration of that wonder. Color photographs of children around the world depict them creating art through music, dance, paint, and sculpture. The message is clear that art is found in every culture and anyone can be an artist. The last two-page spread in the book is a world map showing the countries represented by the children in the book.

Burton, Marilee Robin. *Artists at Work*. Broomall, PA: Chelsea House, 2003. 24p. ISBN 978-0-7910-7410-7. Grades: 2–4.

Brief profiles of three very different artists offer an introduction to how artists turn their passions into their careers. Showcased in the book are Julie Taymor, producer and costume designer for *The Lion King*; Maya Lin, designer of the Vietnam Veterans Memorial, and Wynton Marsalis, jazz trumpet virtuoso. The book concludes with a glossary, an index, and websites for learning more. From the On the Job series.

Elliott, Zetta. *Bird*. Illustrated by Shadra Strickland. New York: Lee and Low, 2008. Unp. ISBN 978-1-60060-241-2. Grades: 2–5.

Bird is a young African-American boy whose art helps him express his emotions as he struggles with his older brother's drug addiction and death and then his grandfather's death. His grandfather's friend, Uncle Son, provides him with support and reassurance. The poignant story is told in verse. New Voices Honor Award, 2009. ALSC Notable Children's Book, 2009. The Ezra Jack Keats Book Award, 2009.

Arbogast, Joan Marie. *Buildings in Disguise: Architecture That Looks Like Animals, Food, and Other Things*. Honesdale, PA: Boyds Mills, 2004. 48p. ISBN 978-1-59078-099-2. Grades: 2–5.

The introduction explains that mimetic architecture mimics other objects and readers quickly understand the definition, which is framed by photographs of buildings shaped like a duck, a dog, teepees, and an elephant. Past and present photographs of the buildings, statistics, diagrams, and information about their creators and the buildings makes fascinating reading. The book ends with information on the future of mimetic architecture and encourages readers to look for examples in their neighborhoods. On the endpapers is a map showing the locations of the buildings. An epilogue, a bibliography, and an index conclude the book.

Lane, Kimberly. *Come Look with Me: Asian Art*. Watertown, MA: Charlesbridge, 2008. 32p. ISBN 978-1-890674-19-9. Grades: 3–7.

A dozen reproductions of Asian artwork form the basis for an exploration into these ancient cultures. Each reproduction is accompanied by background information and discussion starter questions. The book concludes with additional questions inviting readers to revisit the reproductions. From the Come Look with Me Series.

Bryant, Jennifer. *Pieces of Georgia*. New York: Random House, 2006. 166p. ISBN 978-0-375-83259-8. Grades: 6–9.

The death of thirteen-year-old Georgia's artist mother six years ago, her distant father, her best friend's drug use, and the teasing from schoolmates about her poverty are all recorded in her free-verse journal. An anonymous donor sends her a free membership to the Brandywine River Museum, which offers her the opportunity to connect with the artistic talent of her mother. Slowly, she makes the way out from the depths of despair to reach out to others. IRA Young Adult Choice List, 2008. Notable Trade Book for Social Studies, 2006.

Govenar, Alan B. *Extraordinary Ordinary People: Five American Masters of Traditional Arts*. Cambridge, MA: Candlewick, 2006. 85p. ISBN 978-0-7636-2047-9. Grades: 6 and up.

Each of the extraordinary ordinary people profiled in this book are recipients of the National Endowment for the Arts National Heritage Fellowship award, which is given to an artisan who has mastered a cultural art form. Featured in the book are Qi Shu Fang, who started a Beijing Opera Company in New York City; Ralph Stanley, who builds wooden boats in Maine; Eva Catellanoz, who crafts Mexican Coronas from folded paper and wax flowers in Oregon; Dorothy Trumpold, who weaves rugs in Iowa; and "Tootie" Montana, who made elaborate Mardi Gras Indian costumes in New Orleans. Colorful photographs and intriguing narratives tell the stories of these craftspeople, whose work features cultural traditions.

Lewis, Elizabeth. *Mexican Art and Culture*. Chicago, IL: Raintree, 2004. 56p. ISBN 978-0-7398-6610-8. Grades: 6 and up.

The introduction immerses readers into Mexican history, providing a context for learning about its art and culture. Short chapters filled with colorful photographs, interesting narrative, and informative text boxes showcase how Mexican art is intertwined with the culture. Resources for learning more, a glossary, and an index conclude the book. From the World Art and Culture series.

Explorations

1. After reading *To Be an Artist* (Ajmera and Ivanko, 2004) ask the students to share ways they make art and ways their family members make art.
2. After reading *Buildings in Disguise: Architecture That Looks Like Animals, Food, and Other Things* (Arbogast, 2004) search the Internet to find other examples of mimetic architecture.
3. Many of the questions accompanying the reproductions in *Come Look with Me: Asian Art* (Lane, 2008) lend themselves to multiple paintings, and others can be adapted for different paintings. Have the students find other works of art in books or on the Internet and have them use these questions as models for writing their own questions. Students can work in groups to share their artwork and questions.
4. While reading *Pieces of Georgia* (Bryant, 2006) encourage the students to visit the online collections of the Brandywine River Museum at www.brandywine museum.org/ to look for the paintings Georgia sees.
5. After reading *Pieces of Georgia* (Bryant, 2006) students who want to learn more about her books can visit her website at www.jenbryant.com. The website also contains links to teacher's guides for her books.
6. In *Mexican Art and Culture* (Lewis, 2004) the chapter on jewelry and adornment describes how studying the jewelry and clothing that people wear can reveal information about them. Guide the students as they look at the pictures in the book and record what they can infer about the people. Then, have the students examine what they are wearing and have them write about what their jewelry and clothing tell people about them.
7. Provide the students with books, Internet sites, and other resources for learning about cultural art forms that are indigenous to their state or locale. Encourage them to share the information with their families and see if any of them have skills or knowledge they can share with your students.

ARTISTS

Learning about the lives of artists enables children to better appreciate and understand their art. Many artists depict important people and events in their lives through their work. Carefully looking at artists' works can provide interesting insight into their lives and the historical times in which they lived. Visual arts standard four relates to students' understanding of how history and culture impact the artists' works. By studying about artists and their work, students can learn to make connections between the work and the artists. Studying a body of work by a particular artist enables students to see the changes in the artist's style of work through the years. They can relate these changes in style to changes in the artist's life and society. Learning about the artists' lives and their works also addresses content standards five and six.

Book and Media Choices

Brown, Don. *Mack Made Movies*. DVD. Pine Plains, NY: Live Oak Media, 2008. 14 min. ISBN 978-1-43010-567-1. Grades: K–3.

Based on the book by the same name, this is the story of silent film director Mack Sennett, who brought the world the Keystone Cops, Charlie Chaplin, and Fatty Arbuckle among others. The film includes the option of viewing the text along with the narration. ALA Notable Children's Video Winner, 2009.

Giesecke, Ernestine. *Mary Cassatt*. Des Plaines, IL: Heinemann, 2006. 32p. ISBN 978-1-40348-493-2. Grades: K–3.

Two-page chapters introduce young readers to this American artist and her sensitive portraits of mothers and children. Edgar Degas was a mentor and friend who introduced her to other Impressionists. A timeline of her life, a glossary, resources for learning more, and an index conclude the book.

Browne, Anthony. *The Shape Game*. New York: Farrar, Straus and Giroux, 2003. Unp. ISBN 978-0-374-36764-0. Grades: K–4.

Mom decides that to celebrate her birthday her two sons and husband are going to join her for a visit to London's Tate Britain Gallery. The family's reluctance to spend the day at the museum changes to enthusiasm as Mom invites them to look closely at the paintings and Dad's corny jokes lighten the mood. At first they are outsiders looking in and then they step into the paintings and make personal connections to them. A trip to the museum gift shop where they purchase sketchbooks and markers results in the brothers playing the shape game in which one draws a shape and the other turns the shape into something. Browne closes by noting that he still plays the shape game.

Wallner, Alexandra. *Grandma Moses*. New York: Holiday House, 2004. Unp. ISBN 978-0-8234-1538-0. Grades: K–4.

Throughout her lifetime Anna Mary Robinson, "Grandma Moses," tried to find time to paint, but working, chores, and taking care of her family always prevented her from painting. In 1927, her husband died and her children were grown and so in her late sixties, she finally found time to paint. Her folk art paintings reflected memories from her life and depicted a bygone era. An author's note and a bibliography conclude the book.

Coyne, Jennifer Tarr. *Discovering Women Artists for Children*. West Palm Beach, FL: Lickle, 2005. 32p. ISBN 978-1-890674-08-3. Grades: K–5.

Two-page spreads invite readers to look closely at the full-color reproductions on the left side and to learn more about the artists who created them from the brief biographies on the right side. Also on the right side of each spread are open-ended questions that require readers to use their imaginations and reflect on what each illustration depicts. Twelve women artists are featured, including Sophie

Anderson, Grandma Moses, Faith Ringgold, Georgia O'Keeffe, Frida Kahlo, Artemisia Gentileschi, Louise Nevelson, Mary Cassatt, Jennifer Bartlett, Sofonisba Anguissola, Berthe Morisot, and Sonia Terk Delaunay. From the Come Look with Me Series.

Stone, Tanya Lee. *Sandy's Circus.* Illustrated by Boris Kulikov. New York: Penguin, 2008. Unp. ISBN 978-0-670-06268-3. Grades: 1–4.

This brief picture biography focuses on Alexander Calder's early life and specifically the miniature circus he created from wire, cork, cloth, string, and other objects. The last two-page spread in the book shows Calder seated in a circus ring surrounded by his mobiles. An author's note and a bibliography conclude the book.

Greenberg, Jan, and Sandra Jordan. *Action Jackson.* Illustrated by Robert Andrew Parker. Brookfield, CT: Roaring Brook Press, 2002. Unp. ISBN 978-0-7613-2770-7. Grades: 1–8.

A note at the beginning of the picture book explains that it is an imagined account in May and June of 1950 when Jackson Pollock painted *Lavender Mist.* Lyrical prose and pen-and-watercolor illustrations introduce readers to Pollock's paintings and his creative process. The book concludes with a two-page biography of Pollock including photographs and thumbnail reproductions, notes and sources, and a bibliography.

Rubin, Susan Goldman. *Degas and the Dance: The Painter and the Petits Rats, Perfecting Their Art.* New York: Harry N. Abrams, 2002. 32p. ISBN 978-0-8109-0567-2. Grades: 2–5.

Readers are immersed in a spectacular collection of Degas reproductions as they turn the pages of this book. The paintings and sketches of young ballet dancers fill the pages with barely enough room for captions and narrative. Degas intently studied the dancers in order to portray their hard work and the beauty of ballet. A brief biography of Degas, an author's note, and a bibliography conclude the book.

Winter, Jonah. *Frida.* Illustrated by Ana Juan. New York; Scholastic, 2002. Unp. ISBN 978-0-590-20320-3. Grades: 2–5.

Painting was Frida's refuge from the loneliness and pain that filled her life. This brief picture book biography is accompanied by illustrations filled with Mexican folk art images, such as the ones that surrounded Frida during her lifetime and made their way into her paintings. Back matter includes an author's note and an illustrator's note. ALA Notable Children's Book, 2003.

Venezia, Mike. *Getting to Know the World's Greatest Artists: Andy Warhol.* DVD. Chicago, IL: Getting to Know, 2007. 24 min. Grades: 3–7.

Adapted from Venezia's book, this animated film features Andy Warhol talking about his life and work. Photographs and reproductions help to showcase his art. ALSC Notable Children's Video, 2008.

Venezia, Mike. *Getting to Know the World's Greatest Artists: Mary Cassatt.* DVD. Chicago, IL: Getting to Know, 2008. 24 min. ISBN 1-312-642-5526. Grades: 3–7.

The great American artist Mary Cassatt is portrayed in this animated tale full of humor and irreverence. Viewers learn more about Cassatt's personal life and her influence on the Impressionistic art movement. ALSC Notable Children's Video Winner, 2009.

Whitehead, Kathy. *Art from Her Heart: Folk Artist Clementine Hunter.* Illustrated by Shane W. Evans. New York: G.P. Putnam's Sons, 2008. Unp. ISBN 978-0-399-24219-9. Grades: 4–7.

Hunter painted scenes from her life on a Louisiana plantation using paints left behind by artists visiting the plantation. She became the first African-American woman artist to have her works displayed in a major museum; however, because of segregation laws she was not allowed into the museum to view them. She was slipped in one night after the museum closed to view her works. The book concludes with additional information about Hunter's life and small reproductions of some of her work.

Burleigh, Robert. *Paul Cézanne: A Painter's Journey.* New York: Harry N. Abrams, 2006. 32p. ISBN 978-0-8109-5784-8. Grades: 4–8.

Burleigh does more than just tell the story of Cézanne's life: he invites readers to closely examine the artist's work. Questions interspersed throughout the text cause readers to pause and examine the reproductions with a critical eye. A glossary, a bibliography, a list of places where his paintings hang, and an author's note conclude the book.

Burleigh, Robert. *Toulouse-Lautrec: The Moulin Rouge and the City of Light.* New York: Harry N. Abrams, 2005. 32p. ISBN 978-0-8109-5867-8. Grades: 4–8.

Toulouse-Lautrec's posters and paintings of the Paris nightlife and the circus capture the energy and the lively actions of the dancers and the performers. The text weaves together information about the subjects of the posters and the paintings with information about Lautrec's life. Back matter includes a bibliography and an author's note.

Rubin, Susan Goldman. *Whaam! The Art and Life of Roy Lichtenstein.* New York: Abrams, 2008. 47p. ISBN 978-0-8109-9492-8. Grades: 4–8.

Comic books and newspaper advertisements were a source of inspiration for Lichenstein. To give his paintings a printed, cartoon look he used Benday dots or little printer dots, which became his trademark. While noted for his artwork inspired by comic books, he also created sculptures and landscape art. Back matter includes bibliographical references, discography, filmography, and an index.

Bassil, Andrea. *Vincent van Gogh.* Illustrations by Studio Stalio. Chicago, IL: Gareth Stevens, 2004. 48p. ISBN 978-0-8368-5602-6. Grades: 5–8.

Short bursts of text, reproductions of Van Gogh's works, photographs, and timelines introduce van Gogh and serve as a starting place for students who want to learn more. Few of his paintings sold during his lifetime. He was supported by his brother, Theo, who stood by him as he battled alcoholism, schizophrenia, and epilepsy. He is considered the "Father of Expressionism." A glossary and an index conclude the book. From the Lives of the Artists series.

Lemke, Elisabeth, and Thomas David. *Marc Chagall: What Colour Is Paradise?* Translated by Rosie Jackson. Munich: Prestel, 2000. 28p. ISBN 978-3-7913-2393-0. Grades: 5–8.

Some of Chagall's major paintings reflecting his religious beliefs and his life are woven together with biblical text, biographical facts, information about the paintings, and black-and-white photographs of the artist and his family. The book concludes with additional information about the author and the paintings. From the Adventures in Art series.

Litwin, Laura Baskes. *Diego Rivera: Legendary Mexican Painter.* Berkeley Heights, NJ: Enslow, 2005. 128p. ISBN 978-0-7660-2486-1. Grades: 5–10.

Nonconformist, controversial muralist Rivera led a fascinating life that is explored in this well-written biography. Quotes, photographs, and reproductions of his works enhance the story of his life, including his tumultuous marriage to painter Frida Kahlo. The Virtual Diego Rivera Web Museum at www.diegorivera.com showcases his works and includes videos. A chronology, chapter notes, resources for learning more, and an index conclude the book. From the Latino Biography Library series.

Ellabbad, Mohieddin. *The Illustrator's Notebook.* Toronto, Ontario, CN: Groundwood Books, 2006. 30p. ISBN 978-0-88899-700-5. Grades: 5 and up.

Reading front to back and right to left takes a little getting used to, but that is how books are read in Egypt. This very personal picture book gives readers glimpses of Ellabbad's notebook with the artwork and Arabic text becoming one. The English translation of the text is in the margins. By the end of the book readers have gained insights into another culture and are looking at their world from an artist's perspective.

The Secrets of Da Vinci: The Forbidden Manuscript. Win. Dallas, TX: Tri Synergy/Nobilis, 2006. Grades: 5 and up.

Three years after Da Vinci's death, Valdo has been sent to Manoir du Cloux where Da Vinci died to search for secrets he left behind. The nonlinear adventure has players searching for a secret notebook as they fix various machines and solve puzzles. The setting of Manoir du Cloux is historically accurate and presents a stunning setting for the game. ALSC Notable Computer Software for Children Award, 2007.

Somervill, Barbara A. *Michelangelo: Sculptor and Painter.* Minneapolis, MN: Compass Point Books, 2005. 112p. ISBN 978-0-7565-0814-2. Grades: 6–9.

Reproductions, sketches, photographs, and informative text boxes extend this engaging biography of a sculptor, who was a reluctant painter. Italian Renaissance artist Michelangelo, noted for his sculpture the Pieta, for his statue of David, and for the ceiling frescoes of the Sistine Chapel, also designed buildings. Back matter includes a timeline of his life positioned above a timeline of world events, resources for learning more, a glossary, a bibliography, and an index. From the Signature Lives series.

Spires, Elizabeth. *I Heard God Talking to Me: William Edmondson and His Stone Carvings.* New York: Farrar, Straus and Giroux, 2009. 56p. ISBN 978-0-374-33528-1. Grades: 9–12.

When he was fifty-seven years old, William Edmondson, a Nashville janitor, started sculpting headstones and statues in limestone. He was the first African American to have a solo show at the Museum of Modern Art in New York. Full-page black-and-white photographs of Edmondson and his work accompany the poems Spires wrote using his sculptures as inspiration. Some of the poems incorporate Edmondson's quotes and some of them are written from the sculpture's perspective. A biography of Edmondson concludes the book.

Explorations

1. After reading *Mary Cassatt* (Giesecke, 2006) have the students examine her portraits of mothers and children and ask them to make inferences about the very special bonds between the mothers and children in the portraits. Comparing and contrasting her depictions of mother and children with those of other artists will help students understand why Cassatt is noted for her portraits.
2. The simple rules for playing *The Shape Game* (Browne, 2003) are draw a shape and have a partner turn the shape into something. Browne includes examples on the endpapers of the book. Share the models on the endpapers with the students and then have them play the shape game with a partner using a computer paint program or colored pencils.
3. Before reading *Grandma Moses* (Wallner, 2004) search Google Images at www.images.google.com to find photographs of Grandma Moses and images of some of her artwork to share with the children. Older students might be interested in knowing that her great-grandson, Will Moses, is also a folk artist and they can visit his website at www.willmoses.com.
4. In *Degas and the Dance: The Painter and the Petits Rats, Perfecting Their Art* (Rubin, 2002) the author makes the point that Degas studied the dancers then drew and redrew them. His finished pieces are the result of a great deal of time spent observing and sketching the dancers. Help the students make connections between Degas' studies of the dancers and the way the students learn to accomplish tasks such as riding a bike or writing.
5. Before reading *Frida* (Winter, 2002) use Google Images to find examples of Frida Kahlo's artwork to show the students. Not all of her paintings are suitable for sharing with children, so preview the images.
6. After reading *Paul Cézanne: A Painter's Journey* (Burleigh, 2006) and talking about how he arranged the objects, have the students create their own still life paintings at www.nga.gov/kids/zone/stilllife.htm.

7. While reading *Paul Cézanne: A Painter's Journey* (Burleigh, 2006) have the students create flowcharts showing how his style of painting changed through the years.
8. After reading the first chapter of *Diego Rivera: Legendary Mexican Painter* (Litwin, 2005), have the students discuss how Nelson Rockefeller had Rivera's mural destroyed because it included Vladimir Lenin. More about this incident and a poem by E.B. White can be found at www.diegorivera.com/movies/index.php. Give the students time to discuss who owns the rights to the artist's work—the artist or the person paying for the work.
9. Using the poems in *I Heard God Talking to Me: William Edmondson and His Stone Carvings* (Spires, 2009) as models, have the students select a sculpture from an online collection and then have them write a poem or a narrative inspired by the sculpture.

TEACHER RESOURCES

Art can be integrated across the curriculum and many of the resources listed below help librarians and teachers do just that. The web is a rich source for finding just the right work of art to study or to use to enhance the curriculum.

Book and Media Choices

Danko-McGhee, Kathy, and Ruslan Slutsky. *Impact of Early Art Experiences on Literacy Development*. Reston, VA: National Art Education Association, 2007. 122p. ISBN 978-1-890160-37-1. Grades: K–3.

Art experiences are a vital part of early childhood development and Danko-McGhee and Slutsky explain how to build on those experiences to enhance children's literacy development. The suggested activities develop students' critical thinking skills and their visual perception skills.

Art Museum Image Gallery. [Online]. Bronx, NY: H. W. Wilson, 2009. Grades: K–12.

This online database is available through a licensing agreement. Teachers and students can access more than 62,000 images searching by keyword, artist, title of work, creation year, subject, ownership, type of object, and culture or nationality. It is a tremendous resource for incorporating art into the content area curriculum.

Dorn, Charles M., Stanley S. Madeja, and F. Robert Sabol. *Assessing Expressive Learning: A Practical Guide for Teacher-Directed, Authentic Assessment in K–12 Visual Arts Education*. Philadelphia, PA: Lawrence Erlbaum, 2004. 208p. ISBN 978-0-8058-4524-2. Grades: K–12.

This book shows teachers how to assess K–12 students' creative artwork and to measure development. The book is based on research conducted with seventy art teachers of students in first through twelfth grades.

Hume, Helen D. *The Art Teacher's Book of Lists.* New York: Jossey-Bass, 2003. 432p. ISBN 978-0787974244. Grades: K–12.

The lists in the book help teachers locate information on artists, materials, art history, museums, and more. These lists are a concise compendium of invaluable resources for planning art lessons for K–12 students. For example, there is a list of museums dedicated to the work of a single artist, a list of famous sculptors organized by country, and a list of great architects.

Hurwitz, Al, Stanley S. Madeja, and Eldon Katter. *Pathways to Art Appreciation: A Source Book for Media & Methods.* Reston, VA: National Art Education Association, 2003. 125p. ISBN 1-890160-24-5. Grades: K–12.

No matter the grade level or the content area, art appreciation can be incorporated into the curriculum using the information in this book. The book includes instructional strategies and art activities that enhance students' understanding of the content area curriculum.

Prince, Eileen S. *Art Matters: Strategies, Ideas, and Activities to Strengthen Learning Across the Curriculum.* Chicago, IL: Zephyr Press, 2002. 192p. ISBN 978-1569761298. Grades: K–12.

Part one of the book explains concepts such as aesthetics, symbolism, and research that are common to all of the subject areas. Part two is specific to subject areas including social studies, history, language arts, science, mathematics, and the performing arts. The book concludes with a collection of references and resources and an index.

Stokrocki, Mary, editor. *Interdisciplinary Art Education: Building Bridges to Connect Disciplines and Cultures.* Reston, VA: National Art Education Association, 2005. 243p. ISBN1-890160-31-8. Grades: K–12.

Connecting art education to the content areas is the focus of this book, which combines theory and practice. The examples in the book show how interdisciplinary practices can enhance students' learning and retention of the content area curriculum.

Szekely, George. *How Children Make Art: Lessons in Creativity from Home to School.* Reston, VA: National Art Education Association, 2006. 224p. ISBN 0-8077-4719-X. Grades: K–12.

Children come to school with prior experiences creating art and this book builds on those experiences. Szekely explains how to use these prior experiences to create a meaningful art program for your students.

Szekely, George, and Ilona Szekely, editors. *Video Art for the Classroom.* Reston, VA: National Art Education Association, 2005. 204p. ISBN 1-890160-27-X. Grades: K–12.

Video artists and educators contributed to this anthology of ideas for using video art with K–12 students. The projects span a variety of technology levels and offer instructions for creating animation and for filming documentaries, among others.

Professional Organizations

National Art Education Association
1916 Association Drive
Reston, VA 20191-1590
703-860-8000 (Phone)
703-860-2960 (Fax)
www.naea-reston.org

Journals: *Studies in Art Education: A Journal of Issues and Research*, *Journal of Art Education*

Internet Sites

Artists at Work
www.pbs.org/art21/

This is the website for the PBS series *Art in the Twenty-First Century*, which features artists loosely grouped around themes. To learn more about the series and to receive updates follow the series on Twitter or on Facebook. Lesson plans, glossary, teaching materials, and a space to share students' artwork are available on the website.

Art Teacher on the Net
www.artmuseums.com

Help for classroom art projects is just an e-mail away on this website. "Ask the Art Teacher" provides answers to your questions about art projects. The site includes lesson plans, art lessons, and a place to post students' artwork. The website is extensive and takes some time to explore.

ArtsEdge
artsedge.kennedy-center.org

The National Arts and Education Network is a program of the John F. Kennedy Center for the Performing Arts. The website includes teaching materials, resources for arts education advocacy, and student activities.

Incredible @rt Department
www.Incredibleart.org

Incredible really does describe this site. There are games, activities, videos, career information, lesson plans, and links to other art sites. Learn about news stories and visit art rooms in schools around the world.

Louvre Museum
www.louvre.fr

Take a virtual tour of the Louvre to learn not only about its collections but to also explore the building and its history. Click the "Kaleidoscope" link to see works sorted by themes such as writing, landscape, daily life, and historical figures.

Metropolitan Museum of Art
www.metmuseum.org

Bookmark this website, as you will find yourself returning to it again and again. Explore the museum's collection via the online database or click on the "Explore and Learn" link to discover ways to involve your students in online explorations of art. The "Educational Resources" link includes image resources, teacher resources, online resources, and more. There are podcasts to subscribe to and blogs on current exhibitions.

National Gallery of Art Kids
www.nga.gov/kids/

The Art Zone features interactive art students can make online. While it is a great spot to click and play, it is also a valuable learning resource. Students can create mobiles and still life paintings or explore digital photography and different art forms.

REFERENCES

Carger, Chris Liska. 2004. "Art and Literacy with Bilingual Children." *Language Arts* 81, no. 4 (March): 283–292.

Evans, Dilly. 2008. *Show & Tell: Exploring the Fine Art of Children's Book Illustration*. San Francisco, CA: Chronicle Books.

Hayes, Susan. 2008. "Technology Toolkit: Wordle." *Voices from the Middle* 16, no. 2 (December): 66–68.

Liggett, Katherine. 2008. "Literature in the Art Room: Barn Dance." *Arts and Activities* 144, no. 2 (October): 32–33.

Meagher, Sandy. 2006. "Don't Hesitate, Collaborate." *Teaching Pre K–8* 36, no. 6 (March): 66–67.

Music Educators National Conference. 1994. *National Standards for Arts Education*. Reston, VA: Author. Available: www.menc.org (accessed March 9, 2010). From National Standards for Art Education. Copyright (c) 1994 by Music Educators National Conference (MENC). Used by permission. The complete National Arts Standards and additional materials relating to the Standards are available from MENC: The National Association for Music Education, 1806 Robert Fulton Drive, Reston, VA 20191; www.menc.org.

Chapter 8

Music

Music evokes emotional responses whether listening, singing, or playing an instrument. The emotional responses engender connections to the music and in classrooms these connections have the potential to enhance students' learning. For pre-kindergarten students, experiences with music fosters emergent music literacy and also fosters emergent language literacy (Kenney, 2008; Wiggins, 2007). As children sing they develop an appreciation for the flow and rhythm of language and as they move to the music they learn the stress patterns and inflections in language that they can learn to transfer to reading. Pairing music with children's literature in content area classrooms encourages aesthetic responses, which foster emotional connections to the material that enhances understanding and retention (Paul, 2004). In addition, the rhyme, rhythm, and repetition of the song lyrics provide mnemonic devices that foster retention of key concepts (Palmer and Burroughs, 2002). With MP3 players and the Internet, music is widely accessible and highly portable. Students are listening to music wherever they go and whatever they are doing. Incorporating music into the classroom is a natural extension of students' everyday activities that has the potential to fully engage students in their learning and to motivate them to learn. Sections in this chapter include instruments, singing, creating music, listening and responding to music, understanding music, musicians and composers, and teacher resources. These chapter sections correspond to the content standards delineated below.

In 1994 the National Association for Music Education adopted the following content standards for music:

1. Singing, alone and with others, a varied repertoire of music.
2. Performing on instruments, alone and with others, a varied repertoire of music.
3. Improvising melodies, variations, and accompaniments.
4. Composing and arranging music within specified guidelines.
5. Reading and notating music.
6. Listening to, analyzing, and describing music.
7. Evaluating music and music performances.
8. Understanding relationships between music, the other arts, and disciplines outside the arts.
9. Understanding music in relation to history and culture.

INSTRUMENTS

The books and media in this section provide an introduction to musical instruments both modern and ancient. DVDs and books with CDs such as the ones noted in the following text enable students to hear the instruments as they learn about them. Music education standards addressed in this section include standard two, which involves performing on instruments, and standard six, which has students listening to and analyzing music.

Book and Media Choices

Snicket, Lemony. *The Composer Is Dead.* Illustrated by Carson Ellis. New York: HarperCollins, 2009. Unp. ISBN 978-0-06-123627-3. Grades: K–4.

From the best-selling author of *A Series of Unfortunate Events* comes this suspenseful story about the death of a composer. Through the course of the police inspector's investigation, as each orchestra instrument is interrogated, readers learn about the instruments. Filled with wordplay and personification, the text describes the instruments and their roles in the orchestra. As the plot unfolds, the instruments explain why they could not and would not have murdered the composer. The accompanying CD includes a narration by Lemony Snicket and features the music of Nathaniel Stokey performed by the San Francisco Symphony Orchestra.

Lynch, Wendy. *Keyboards.* Chicago, IL: Heinemann, 2002. 32p. ISBN 978-1-58810-234–8. Grades: 1–4.

This slim volume describes keyboards and tells how they produce sounds. Organs, harmoniums, and other types of keyboards are introduced in text and color photographs. Readers also learn about the types of music created by keyboards. A glossary, resources for learning more, and an index conclude the book. From the Musical Instruments series.

World of Music Discovery: Volume I. DVD. Burbank, CA: Disney Educational Productions, 2005. 71 min. ISBN 978-1-932644-72-2. Grades: 3–6.

Originally produced in 1997, this volume begins with a music overview and then explores the brass family and the string family with animated and live video selections. A teacher's guide and a web link to additional resources are included.

World of Music Discovery: Volume II. DVD. Burbank, CA: Disney Educational Productions, 2005. 96 min. ISBN 978-1-932644-73-9. Grades: 3–6.

This volume begins with a music overview and then explores the voice family, the woodwind family, and the rhythm and percussion families. A teacher's guide and a web link to additional resources are included.

Ardley, Neil. *Music.* New York: DK, 2000. 64p. ISBN 978-0-78945828-5. Grades: 4–8.

From ancient to modern instruments this graphic encyclopedic volume depicts how the instruments are played. It is filled with fascinating facts, color photographs, and concludes with an index. From the Eyewitness Books series.

Helsby, Genevieve, with Marin Alsop. *Those Amazing Musical Instruments! Your Guide to the Orchestra through Sounds and Stories.* Naperville, IL: Sourcebooks, 2007. 176p. ISBN 978-1-40220-825-6. Grades: 4–9.

Conductor Marin Alsop contributed an introductory section to this guide to orchestra instruments. The history, sounds, and stories of the instruments are contained within the pages of this book and the accompanying CD. Each of the musical instrument families is explored in large text and colorful illustrations in separate chapters and readers are prompted to listen to the musical selections on the CD as they read.

Levine, Robert T. *The Story of the Orchestra: Listen While You Learn about the Instruments, the Music and the Composers Who Wrote the Music!* Illustrated by Meredith Hamilton. London: Black Dog, 2001. 96p. ISBN 978-1-57912-148-8. Grades: 5–7.

The first section of the book features composers and the second section features orchestra instruments. Quotes, definitions, illustrations, photographs, text, and the accompanying CD explore the history of the orchestra including the music, the instruments, and the composers. As students read they are directed to listen to musical selections on the CD.

Abbado, Claudio. *The House of Magical Sounds.* DVD. Wynnewood, PA: Library Video, 2007. 50 min. ISBN 978-0-7697-8483-0. Grades: 6 and up.

Based on Claudio Abbado's book, this video combines animation and live rehearsals to introduce students to the orchestra. Abbado's journey from his childhood home to becoming the music director of the Berlin Philharmonic is chronicled in this movie narrated by Raul Julia.

Explorations

1. While reading *The Composer Is Dead* (Snicket, 2009) point out to the students how the characteristics of each instrument are described in the text and how the author includes the definitions of words in the text.
2. After reading *The Composer Is Dead* (Snicket, 2009) return to the text to have the students discuss the wordplay in the book and how to incorporate wordplay in their writing.
3. While students are learning about the musical instruments on *World of Music Discovery: Volume I* and *Volume II* invite them to bring in any musical instruments they play and give a brief demonstration for their classmates.
4. As students are learning about musical instruments from books such as *Those Amazing Musical Instruments! Your Guide to the Orchestra through Sounds and Stories* (Helsby, 2007) and *The Story of the Orchestra: Listen While You Learn about the Instruments, the Music and the Composers Who Wrote the Music!* (Levine, 2001), create a class blog on Class Blogmeister at classblogmeister.com/index.php for the students to share their learning and post their comments.

5. As students are reading *Those Amazing Musical Instruments!: Your Guide to the Orchestra through Sounds and Stories* (Helsby, 2007) they will need a CD player nearby so they can listen to the musical instruments as they read about them.

SINGING

Children begin to sing even before preschool and continue to sing throughout their lives. Both singing and reading require fluency; and the rhythm and the pulse of songs provide students with opportunities to practice fluency (D'Agrosa, 2008). The following books invite students to sing and thus address standard one, singing alone or with others.

Book and Media Choices

Lacoursiere, Patrick. *Dream Songs, Night Songs: From Mali to Louisiana: A Bedtime Story*. Illustrated by Sylvie Bourbonniere. Montreal, Quebec, CN: The Secret Mountain, 2003. Unp. ISBN 978-2-923163-06-2. Grades: P–1.

Around the world children drift off to sleep listening to lullabies. This book and the accompanying CD encapsulate these twilight memories in warm gold and brown two-page illustrations and in brief soothing songs. The one line of text on each page is in English, French, and Spanish. The CD includes the lyrics, the translations, and the illustrations. Parents' Choice Gold Award Winner, 2004.

Fitzgerald, Ella, and Van Alexander. *A-Tisket, A-Tasket*. Illustrated by Ora Eitan. New York: Penguin, 2003. Unp. ISBN 978-0-399-23206-0. Grades: P–2.

Ella Fitzgerald's words turn this nursery rhyme into a celebration of jazz and singing as a little girl grabs a small boy's basket. The lively song accompanied by whimsical mixed-media illustrations has youngsters singing and reading along as the book is read.

Weinstein, Muriel Harris. *When Louis Armstrong Taught Me Scat*. Illustrated by R. Gregory Christie. San Francisco, CA: Chronicle Books, 2008. Unp. ISBN 978-0-8118-5131-2. Grades: P–2.

After an evening of dancing with her mother to Armstrong's scatting, a young girl dreams that he visits and teaches her to scat about bubblegum. The nonsense words are a delight to say and sing, which has young readers joining in forming a lively chorus as the book is read aloud.

Johnson, Paul Brett. *Little Bunny Foo Foo*. New York: Scholastic, 2004. Unp. ISBN 978-0-439-37301-2. Grades: P–4.

Little Bunny Foo Foo's head bopping reaches new levels as he moves beyond field mice to woodchucks, foxes, and bears. The Good Fairy provides the narration of his antics and warns that she will turn him into a goon if his misbehavior continues. The cartoonish, action-packed illustrations enthrall young listeners eager to join in the rousing chorus. The book concludes with the music, the lyrics, and illustrations of the hand motions.

Best of Children's Songs: 40 Well-Known Songs in Easy Arrangement for Piano, Voice and Guitar. London, England: Schott Music, 2007. 88p. ISBN 978-1-902455-83-9. Grades: P and up.

The lyrics for all of the verses of this collection of familiar songs combined with musical arrangements by Barrie Turner make this a useful resource for all grades. There is an index.

Yarrow, Peter, compiler. *The Peter Yarrow Songbook: Let's Sing Together*. Illustrated by Terry Widener. New York: Sterling, 2009. 48p. ISBN 978-1-40275-963-5. Grades: P and up.

"John Jacob Jingleheimer Schmidt" and "My Bonnie Lies Over the Ocean" are just two of the twelve folk songs included in the book and on the accompanying CD. Guitar chords, historical notes, and personal anecdotes are included for each song. From the Peter Yarrow Songbook series.

Cronin, Doreen. *Dooby Dooby Moo*. Illustrated by Betsy Lewin. New York: Simon and Schuster, 2006. Unp. ISBN 978-0-689-84507-9. Grades: K–3.

Farmer Brown's mischievous animals are once again on a mission; this time they are entering a talent show in order to win a trampoline. Each night in the barn the cows and the sheep are practicing songs and the pigs are rehearsing an interpretive dance. When they fail to win the grand prize, duck once again saves the day with his rendition of "Born to Be Wild." The hilarious watercolor illustrations contain punch lines to the text. Duck's prize-winning singing can be heard on the third track of the accompanying CD.

Boynton, Sandra. *Philadelphia Chickens: A Two-Illogical Musical Revue*. Music by Sandra Boynton and Michael Ford. New York: Workman, 2002. 64p. ISBN 978-0-7611-2636-2. Grades: K–4.

Join the chickens in "The Imaginary Musical Revue" and sing along with the accompanying CD. This collection of highly unlikely songs will have students giggling as they sing.

Winans, CeCe. *Colorful World*. Illustrated by Melodee Strong. Oak Park Heights, MN: Maren Green, 2007. Unp. ISBN 978-1-934277-13-3. Grades: K–4.

Winans' upbeat song reminds children that they are each unique and that uniqueness is to be celebrated and appreciated. Children of diverse backgrounds from around the world are depicted in the colorful illustrations. The lyrics to the song are appended and a CD of the song is included.

Weaver, Tesa. *Opera Cat.* Illustrated by Andrea Wesson. New York: Houghton Mifflin, 2002. Unp. ISBN 978-0-618-09635-0. Grades: 2–4.

Every afternoon the maestro visits opera star Madame SoSo's Milan apartment for her lesson. Unbeknownst to them, Madame SoSo's cat, Alma, hidden behind the drapes, is practicing with them. When Madame SoSo contracts laryngitis, Alma comes to the rescue and sings on stage hidden in Madame SoSo's coiffure. The delightful, comic watercolor illustrations introduce readers to Italy, the opera house, and to opera.

Schotter, Roni. *Doo-Wop Pop.* Illustrated by Bryan Collier. New York: HarperCollins, 2008. Unp. ISBN 978-0-06-057968-5. Grades: 2–5.

When five shy children fall under the spell of the school custodian, a former doo-wop singer, they are transformed into doo-wop singers. First, they gather the sounds around them from the footsteps in the halls to the laughter in the walls. Then, they transform the sounds into doo-wop, singing a cappella. Next, they practice their moves. Finally, the self-confident doo-wop singers perform.

Belting, Natalia Marcee, collector. *Whirlwind Is a Spirit Dancing: Poems Based on Traditional American Songs and Stories.* Illustrated by Leo and Diane Dillon. New York: Simon and Schuster, 2006. Unp. ISBN 978-1-59687-173-1. Grades: 3–6.

Based on Native American Indian tribes' traditional songs, this collection of poems is a celebration of the Native American's connections to the environment. Joseph Bruchac wrote the introduction to the book.

Explorations

1. Play one or two songs from the CD accompanying *Dream Songs, Night Songs: From Mali to Louisiana: A Bedtime Story* (Lacoursiere, 2003) to quiet and calm the students when they first come into the library or the classroom.
2. After reading *A-Tisket, A-Tasket* (Fitzgerald and Alexander, 2003) play the song as sung by Ella Fitzgerald. The song is included on her album *A-Tisket A-Tasket* and can be downloaded from www.itunes.com.
3. While third and fourth grade students may think they are too old for *Little Bunny Foo Foo* (Johnson, 2004), many of them will be delighted to revisit the song and learn the narration and hand movements so that they can teach them to younger students in their school. This is a fun way to teach students oral speaking skills.
4. Before reading *Dooby Dooby Moo* (Cronin, 2006) explain to the students that some of the events in the story could really happen while other events could not have happened. As you read pause and ask the students if what you just read could have really happened.
5. Before reading *Opera Cat* (Weaver, 2002) visit the iTunes store at www.itunes.com and download an excerpt from an opera or locate a CD or video of an opera performance.

6. Before reading *Doo-Wop Pop* (Schotter, 2008) share audio clips of doo-wop singers with the students. Clips can be found on Singers.com at www.singers.com/doowop/index.html. After listening to the clips and reading the book provide the students with time to try singing doo-wop.
7. Students can add movements and vocal sounds to the poems in *Whirlwind Is a Spirit Dancing: Poems Based on Traditional American Songs and Stories* (Belting, 2006) to perform for their classmates. In order to perform the poems, the students will need to understand them. After the students select the poems they are going to perform, engage them in discussions of the meanings of the poems and explain any unfamiliar vocabulary words.

CREATING MUSIC

Books and media in this section focus on writing music, singing songs, and playing instruments. *Musician* (Parks, 2004) and *Bravo! Brava! A Night at the Opera: Behind the Scenes with Composers, Cast, and Crew* (Siberell, 2001) take students behind the scenes to explore career opportunities in the music industry. This section includes two pieces of software to help students practice skills they have learned in order to create and to perform music. Music education standards addressed in this section include: standard two, performing on instruments; standard three, improvising melodies, variations, and accompaniments; standard four, composing and arranging music; and standard five, reading and notating music.

Book and Media Choices

Radabaugh, Melinda Beth. *Going to a Concert*. Chicago, IL: Heinemann, 2004. 24p. ISBN 978-140343867-6. Grades: P–1.

Large font and color photographs on each page introduce students to musical performance and the performers. It concludes with a simple quiz, a picture glossary, a note to parents and teachers, and an index. From the First Time series.

Music Ace Maestro: Music Educator's Professional Edition 4.0. Mac/Win. St. Charles, IL: Harmonic Vision, 2007. Grades: 1 and up.

Beginning music students or students interested in reviewing their music knowledge and skills benefit from the lessons and games in this software. Basic music theory and skills such as note reading, listening, and keyboarding are included. Also included is Music Doodle Pad for composing music. ALA Notable Computer Software for Children, 2007.

Parks, Peggy J. *Musician*. Farmington, MI: KidHaven, 2004. 48p. ISBN 978-0-7377-2067-9. Grades: 2–6.

Readers are introduced to the variety of career choices available in the field of music. The informative text is supplemented with color photographs. It concludes with a glossary, resources for learning more, and an index. From the Exploring Career series.

GarageBand. Mac/Win. Cuppertino, CA: Apple Computer, 2009. Grades: 2 and up.
GarageBand offers students lessons for learning to play musical instruments, opportunities to create their own music, or to record a song. This software is often preinstalled on Macintosh computers and can be purchased for Windows computers.

Bryant, Jennifer. *Music for the End of Time*. Illustrated by Beth Peck. Grand Rapids, MI: Eerdmans, 2005. Unp. ISBN 978-0-8028-5229-8. Grades: 3–5.
While a prisoner of war in a German camp during World War II French composer Olivier Messiaen wrote "Quartet for the End of Time," inspired by the song of a nightingale he heard in the prison yard. Messiaen and three other musician prisoners performed the quartet for 5,000 fellow prisoners.

Siberell, Anne. *Bravo! Brava! A Night at the Opera: Behind the Scenes with Composers, Cast, and Crew*. New York: Oxford University Press, 2001. 64p. ISBN 978-0-19-513966-2. Grades: 4–8.
This is an excellent "first" book about opera and what makes it work. There is also a section about the stories of many operas that will be informative to older students as well as younger ones. The book concludes with a glossary, books for further reading, and an index.

Explorations

1. Download the demo version *Music Ace Maestro: Music Educator's Professional Edition 4.0* from www.harmonicvision.com so the students can try it out for themselves.
2. After reading *Musician* (Parks, 2004) have the students read about the life of a particular musician to gain a deeper understanding of what a career as a musician entails. Biographies of musicians are included in a section toward the end of this chapter.
3. Prior to reading *Music for the End of Time* (Bryant, 2005) search the Internet to locate a sample of an audio file of the quartet to play for the students.
4. After reading *Bravo! Brava! A Night at the Opera: Behind the Scenes with Composers, Cast, and Crew* (Siberell, 2001) have the students use Photo Story 3 for Windows to create digital stories about the work of the musicians, conductor, cast, and crew.

LISTENING AND RESPONDING TO MUSIC

Learning to listen and to recognize types of music and musical instruments helps develop students' listening skills. From jazz to reggae to classical to rap, music appeals to listeners of all ages and backgrounds. As students listen to music, they respond to the words and sounds through movement. This combination of words and music blends the phrase structure of the words with the musical phrases and musical melody enhances the natural word inflections (Kenney, 2008). Books and media in this section address standard six, listening to, analyzing, and describing music, and standard seven, evaluating music and music performances.

Book and Media Choices

Teis, Kyra, adapter. *The Magic Flute: An Opera by Mozart.* Long Island City, NY: Star Bright Books, 2008. Unp. ISBN 978-1-59572-058-0. Grades: P–3.

This opera tells the story of how Prince Tamino passes three tests in order to win the hand of the beautiful Pamina. The paint paper collage illustrations in purples and pinks contain ethnically diverse characters. An author's note and extension ideas are included as is a CD containing musical excerpts.

Dillon, Leo, and Diane Dillon. *Jazz on a Saturday Night.* New York: Scholastic, 2007. Unp. ISBN 978-0-59047893-9. Grades: K–4.

This is rhythmic introduction to jazz musicians and the sounds of jazz. A one-page overview sets the stage for transporting readers into the world of jazz and an introduction to jazz greats such as Ella Fitzgerald, Max Roach, Stanley Clark, John Coltrane, Charlie Parker, Thelonius Monk, and Miles Davis. At the end of the book are brief biographical sketches of the musicians featured in the book. The accompanying CD introduces readers to the instruments and the sounds they make. Coretta Scott King Illustrator Award Honor Book, 2008.

Lindeen, Mary. *Cool Classical Music: Create and Appreciate What Makes Music Great!* Edina, MN: ABDO, 2008. 32p. ISBN 978-1-59928-969-4. Grades: 3–7.

In this introduction to classical music readers discover the difference between instrumental music and vocal music. The book also explores timbre, emotion, harmony, and rhythm. From the Cool Music series.

Kenney, Karen Latchana. *Cool Reggae Music: Create and Appreciate What Makes Music Great!* Edina, MN: ABDO, 2008. 32p. ISBN 978-1-59928-973-1. Grades: 3–7.

The unique reggae sound with its soulful, hypnotic quality is explored within the culture in which it was created. Photographs and step-by-step instructions are included for making instruments so students can create their own reggae music. From the Cool Music series.

Lithgow, John. *Carnival of the Animals.* Illustrated by Boris Kulikov. New York: Simon and Schuster, 2004. Unp. ISBN 978-0-689-86721-7. Grades: 4–7.

Left behind in the Natural History Museum after a class trip, a boy dreams that his classmates, friends, and relatives become the museum animals. The rhyming text is based on Camille Saint-Saens' "Carnival of the Animals" composition. The humorous, detailed illustrations of the anthropomorphized animals help tie the story together. Included with the book is a CD narrated by the author and musical passages from the composition.

Lommel, Cookie. *The History of Rap Music.* Philadelphia, PA: Chelsea House, 2001. 120p. ISBN 978-0-7980-5820-6. Grades: 4–8.

While students are probably familiar with rap music, they may not know of its history. From the birth of rap to hip-hop empires, the book explores this popular type of music. From the African-American Achievers series.

Woog, Adam. *The History of American Folk Music.* Farmington Hills, MI: Lucent Books, 2006. 104p. ISBN 978-1-59018-734-0. Grades: 5–8.

Spirituals, the blues, Cajun music, cowboy songs, and country and western are some of the folk music explored in this book. Back matter includes resources for learning more and an index. From the Music Library series.

Myers, Walter Dean. *Blues Journey.* Illustrated by Christopher Myers. New York: Holiday House, 2003. Unp. ISBN 978-0-8234-1545-8. Grades: 5–9.

The call and response poetry in this book sings the blues and makes it come alive for older readers. The blue, black, and brown illustrations depict the racism, the hard luck, and other themes that flow through the blues. An author's note and a glossary provide additional information about the symbolism and the history of blues. This book is available on CD.

Myers, Walter Dean. *Jazz.* Illustrated by Christopher Myers. New York: Holiday House, 2006. Unp. ISBN 978-0-8234-1545-8. Grades: 5–9.

Intense, dark illustrations capture the sounds, rhythms, and moods of jazz, as do the poems that are written in a variety of fonts. The book celebrates the musicians, their music, and their culture. Included are an introduction to jazz, a glossary, and a timeline. This book is available on CD. Coretta Scott King Illustrator Award Honor Book, 2007.

Explorations

1. Before reading *Cool Classical Music: Create and Appreciate What Makes Music Great!* (Lindeen, 2008), download examples of classical music from the Internet or play a selection of classical music from the iTunes library for students.
2. Before reading *Cool Reggae Music: Create and Appreciate What Makes Music Great!* (Kenney, 2008), send notes home with the students asking for donations of items needed to make the musical instruments in the book or post a note in the teacher's lounge asking for donations.
3. While listening to the CD of *Carnival of the Animals* (Lithgow, 2004), periodically stop and discuss with the students how the music is used to depict the various animals (Mizener, 2008).

4. As the students are coming into the classroom and settling down for class, play the CD that accompanies *Jazz on a Saturday Night* (Dillon and Dillon, 2007). After you read the story to the students, play the CD once again.
5. After reading *Jazz on a Saturday Night* (Dillon and Dillon, 2007), have the students work in groups to each define one of these terms: classic jazz, hot jazz, cool jazz, Dixieland, swing, bebop, ragtime, or fusion, using Internet resources or books. Then, have each group share their definitions with their classmates.
6. The poems in *Jazz* (Myers, 2006) are written to be read aloud. Give the students time to work with partners or in small groups to practice reading the poems aloud and to share their performances with their classmates.

UNDERSTANDING MUSIC

Books in this section help students make connections between music and other disciplines. Standard eight, understanding relationships between music, the other arts, and disciplines outside the arts can be addressed by a book such as *Can You Hear It?* (Lach, 2006), which pairs works of art with musical compositions. Standard nine, understanding music in relation to history and culture, can be addressed by helping students make connections between songs and the culture in which they were created. Palmer and Burroughs (2002) suggest pairing children's literature about slavery with African-American spirituals. *Forever Young* (Dylan, 2008) shows students how this song includes references to events and protests during the Vietnam War era. Helping students make these connections fosters understanding and retention of key concepts presented in the content area classroom.

Book and Media Choices

Rodgers, Richard, and Oscar Hammerstein. *My Favorite Things.* Illustrated by Renee Graef. New York: Harper Collins, 2001. Unp. ISBN 978-0-06-443627-4. Grades: P–3.

Soft, pastel illustrations capture the simple pleasures of life, beautifully reflecting the lyrics of this well-known song. The book concludes with the musical arrangement of the song.

Shange, Ntozake. *Ellington Was Not a Street.* DVD. Illustrated by Kadir Nelson. New York: Weston Woods, 2005. 12 min. ISBN 978-0-439-77573-1. Grades: K–6.

The video is based on a book by the same title, which features Shange's poem about the notable African-American men who were visitors in her childhood home. These notable men included Duke Ellington, Paul Robeson, and Dizzy Gillespie among others. Phylicia Rashad narrates the video and Duke Ellington's music accompanies the narration. ALA Notable Children's Video, 2006.

Taylor, Debbie A. *Sweet Music in Harlem.* Illustrated by Frank Morrison. New York: Lee and Low Books, 2004. Unp. ISBN 978-1-58430-165-3. Grades: 1–4.

A fictional picture book follows C. J. searching all over Harlem for his trumpet player uncle's signature beret, which he cannot find. He needs it for a magazine photo shoot. C. J. doesn't find the hat but he finds numerous musician friends who want to be in the picture, too, who follow C. J. back to the site. This make-believe story tells of the source of a popular photograph taken of real musicians in the late 1950s.

Aliki. *Ah, Music!* New York: HarperCollins, 2003. 48p. ISBN 978-0-06-028727-6. Grades: 1–5.

From composers to instruments to artists to performers, Aliki explores music. The book also introduces the history and diversity of music. Although the book does not have an index, it does have a table of contents.

Kenney, Karen Latchana. *Cool Rock Music: Create and Appreciate What Makes Music Great!* Edina, MN: ABDO, 2008. ISBN 978-1-59928-974-8. Grades: 3–6.

This is a basic introduction to rock music and how it influenced the American culture. Photographs, activities, and an index are included. From the Checkerboard How-To Library: Cool Music.

Dylan, Bob. *Forever Young.* Illustrated by Paul Rogers. New York: Simon and Schuster, 2008. Unp. ISBN 978-1-41695-808-6. Grades: 4–8.

The lyrics to Dylan's song by the same title provide the text for the book and the illustrations depict the Vietnam War era and the protests about the war. Thumbnails of the book's illustrations with explanations of the details found in drawings conclude the book. This book would be a useful addition to a study of the Vietnam War.

Lach, William. *Can You Hear It?* New York: Abrams, 2006. 40p. ISBN 978-0-8109-5721-3. Grades: 4–8.

Thirteen reproductions from the collections of The Metropolitan Museum of Art introduce children to music and to art. The book comes with a CD that guides students through the book and connects the artwork to compositions by noted composers. Readers learn about the composers, the artists, and their works.

Handyside, Chris. *Soul and R&B.* Chicago, IL: Heinemann, 2006. 48p. ISBN 978-1-40348-153-5. Grades: 5–8.

The intertwining of soul and rhythm and blues music and American culture is explored in this short book filled with informative text, photographs, and sidebars. The book concludes with a discography, a timeline, a glossary, and an index. From the History of American Music series.

Woodson, Jacqueline. *After Tupac and D Foster.* New York: Penguin, 2008. 153p. ISBN 978-0-399-24654-8. Grades: 6–10.

Set in Queens, New York, in the 1990s, three African-American girls forge a friendship based on their common love of Tupac Shakur's music. His music fills the backdrop of their lives and the book ends with his sudden death, which coincides with D's mother returning to take her out of the foster home where she has been living. This book is available on CD. Newbery Medal Honor Book, 2009. ALA Best Books for Young Adults, 2009.

Giovanni, Nikki. *On My Journey Now: Looking at African-American History through the Spirituals.* New York: Candlewick, 2007. 116p. ISBN 978-0-7636-2885-7. Grades: 6 and up.

The history chronicled in this collection of spirituals is connected to the travails of African Americans. Readers will find this book a starting place to arouse their curiosity and to invite them into further research on African-American history. A bibliography, resources for learning more, a glossary, and an index are included. Notable Social Studies Trade Book for Young People, 2008.

Marsalis, Wynton. *Jazz A-B-Z.* Illustrated by Paul Rogers. New York: Candlewick, 2005. 72p. ISBN 978-0-7636-2135-3. Grades: 7 and up.

This sophisticated alphabet book is for older readers who will appreciate the wordplay, the poems, the language, and the poster art-like illustrations. Each letter of the alphabet is matched to a jazz artist and Marsalis has written a poem that reveals information about the musician and his music. Phil Schaap wrote brief biographies of the musicians. The book concludes with notes on the poetic forms. It could easily be incorporated into English classes, music classes, and American history classes.

Explorations

1. Before reading *My Favorite Things* (Rodgers and Hammerstein, 2001) ask the students if they are familiar with the song or play a recording of the song for them. Sharing the book and the song with the students helps them make connections between singing and reading. Struggling or beginning readers who know the song will be able to read the book.
2. Before reading *Ah, Music!* (Aliki, 2003), use Inspiration software to create a semantic map about music or create one on the chalkboard or document camera. After reading the book, return to the semantic map and have the students add to it and reorganize it based on what they learned from reading the book.
3. After reading *Can You Hear It?* (Lach, 2006) and listening to the CD, challenge the students to create their own matches between works of art and music. The Museum of Modern art at www.moma.org is one source for viewing online artwork and the iTunes library at (www.itunes.com) is one source for music to accompany the works of art.
4. Use *On My Journey Now: Looking at African-American History through the Spirituals* (Giovanni, 2007) to help students make connections between the

stories told in the spirituals and the content they have learned in their social studies classes. The spirituals can help students understand the concepts presented in social studies classes (Miller, 2008).

MUSICIANS AND COMPOSERS

The books in this section include traditional biographies of musicians' and composers' lives. These biographies enable readers to learn about talented musicians and composers as well as about the times and places in which they lived. Books and media in this section support standard nine, which involves an understanding of how history and culture impacts musicians and composers. Although only a very few musicians and composers are included in this section, some of the books are from series that contain additional books about musicians and composers.

Book and Media Choices

Sis, Peter. *Play Mozart, Play!* New York: HarperCollins, 2006. Unp. ISBN 978-0-06-112182-1. Grades: K–3.

This picture book biography introduces young readers to Wolfgang Amadeus Mozart, whose father demanded that he spend many hours each day practicing his music rather than playing. Bright watercolor illustrations portray Mozart and his imaginary friends. The book concludes with a one-page bibliography containing additional details about Mozart's life.

Ryan, Pam Munoz. *When Marian Sang: The True Recital of Marian Anderson, Voice of a Century*. Illustrated by Brian Selznick. New York: Scholastic, 2002. Unp. ISBN 978-0-439-26967-4. Grades: K–5.

On the stage of the Metropolitan Opera House, Marian Anderson's life unfolds in sepia-toned illustrations that capture the emotion and intensity of her life. As a child she sang in the church choir but racial prejudice kept her from attending music school and throughout her life impacted where she was allowed to sing. Eventually, her voice and her persistence carried her over the color barrier and she sang at the Philadelphia Philharmonic Society, Constitution Hall, and the Metropolitan Opera. The book concludes with an author's note, an artist's note, a timeline, and a discography. A Robert F. Sibert Honor Book, 2003.

Troupe, Quincy. *Little Stevie Wonder*. Illustrated by Lisa Cohen. Boston: Houghton Mifflin, 2005. Unp. ISBN 978-0618-34060-6. Grades: 1–4.

This brilliantly illustrated picture book tells in poetry form of the life of Steveland Judkins Morris Hardaway, known professionally as Stevie Wonder. Placed in an incubator after his birth, the oxygen mixture blinded him. At a very early age his musical abilities became apparent to family and friends. He is recognized as one of the world's finest musicians.

Pinkney, Andrea Davis. *Ella Fitzgerald: The Tale of a Vocal Virtuosa.* Illustrated by Brian Pinkney. New York: Hyperion, 2003. Unp. ISBN 978-0-7868-0568-6. Grades: 1–6.

Scat Cat Monroe, a feline in a zoot suit, narrates this picture book biography of Ella Fitzgerald. The book is a lyrical tribute to the "Queen of Scat" with text that sings the rhythms of scat and illustrations filled with vibrant energy. The video of this book narrated by Billy Dee Williams and featuring Ella Fitzgerald's singing was an ALA Notable Children's Video, 2004.

Celenza, Anna Harwell. *The Farewell Symphony.* Illustrated by JoAnn E. Kitchel. Watertown, MA: Charlesbridge, 2000. Unp. ISBN 978-1-57091-406-5. Grades: 2–4.

Based on actual events in Joseph Haydn's life, this story explains how music can capture feelings, thoughts, and emotions, such as sadness and anger. Separated from their families for the summer and into the autumn, Prince Nicholas' musicians' sadness, anger, and longing to see their families was expressed in a new symphony Haydn wrote for the musicians to perform. The moving symphony convinces the prince to return from his summer palace so that his musicians can be reunited with their families. A CD recording accompanies the book.

Mathis, Sharon Bell. *Ray Charles.* Illustrated by George Ford. New York: Lee and Low Books, 2001. Unp. ISBN 978-1-58430-017-5. Grades: 2–5.

By the time he was seven years old, Ray Charles Robinson was completely blind and attending St. Augustine School for the Blind. Of all his classes, the one he loved most was music. He learned to read and write music in Braille and learned to play every musical instrument in the school band. In the early days of his professional career, he decided to shorten his name to Ray Charles so that no one would mix him up with boxer Sugar Ray Robinson. Coretta Scott King Author Award Winner and Coretta Scott King Illustrator Award Winner, 2001.

Stanley, Diane. *Mozart: The Wonder Child: A Puppet Play in Three Acts.* New York: HarperCollins, 2009. Unp. ISBN 978-0-06-072674-4. Grades: 2–5.

While in Austria researching this book, Diane Stanley viewed the famous Salzburg Marionette Theatre and was inspired to produce this biography in the form of a puppet play in three acts. Transcriptions of Mozart's work are included throughout the text. The book concludes with an extensive author's note.

George-Warren, Holly. *Honky-Tonk Heroes and Hillbilly Angels: The Pioneers of Country and Western Music.* Illustrated by Laura Levine. New York: Houghton Mifflin, 2006. Unp. ISBN 978-0-618-19100-0. Grades: 3–5.

The concise introduction describes the history and impact of country and western music, which is followed by two-page spreads containing brief biographies of the entertainers and a one-page portrait. Included in the book are such notables as George Jones, Tammy Wynette, Johnny Cash, the Carter family, Hank Williams, Patsy Cline, and Gene Autry.

Mayer-Skumanz, Lene. *Beethoven*. Illustrated by Winfried Opgenoorth. Translated by Alexis L. Spry. New York: NorthSouth Books, 2007. Unp. ISBN 978-0-7358-2123-1. Grades: 3–6.

Although it may have been speculation, most music critics believe that Beethoven's tragic deafness began with his father's brutal "ear-boxing" when he was a small boy. Beethoven's grandfather and father were musical, though not nearly as spectacular as he was. The book about this incredible composer is softly worked in pastels and is accompanied by a CD containing some of Beethoven's music. From the series A Musical Picture Book.

Gerstein, Mordicai. *What Charlie Heard*. New York: Farrar, Straus and Giroux, 2002. Unp. ISBN 978-0-374-38292-6. Grades: 3–6.

Charles Ives grew up listening to the sounds all around him and he put those sounds into the music he composed. His revolutionary music was largely ignored until he won a Pulitzer Prize for his Third Symphony in 1947. This book is available on CD.

McDonough, Yona Zeldis. *Who Was Louis Armstrong?* Illustrated by John O'Brien. New York: Grosset and Dunlap, 2004. 106p. ISBN 978-0-448-43368-4. Grades: 3–6.

Firing a gun into the air on New Year's Eve landed Armstrong in reform school, where he learned to play musical instruments and perform. Armstrong traveled the world playing jazz and was known as "The King of Jazz." Text boxes scattered throughout the biography provide additional information, such as the definitions of jazz terms and the context for events in Armstrong's life, such as Jim Crow Laws. A timeline and a bibliography conclude the book. From the Who Was series.

Tieck, Sarah. *Taylor Swift*. Edina, MN: ABDO, 2010. Unp. ISBN 978-1-60453-712-3. Grades: 3–6.

This brief biography of country music star Taylor Swift includes information about her childhood and her country music awards. Reluctant readers find the book easy to read and it may encourage them to look for other books and media to learn more about this star. From the Big Buddies Biographies Set 3 series.

Weatherford, Carole Boston. *Before John Was a Jazz Giant: A Song of John Coltrane*. Illustrated by Sean Qualls. New York: Henry Holt, 2008. Unp. ISBN 978-0-8050-7994-4. Grades: 3–6.

"Before John was a jazz giant" begins each stanza in this poem that celebrates Coltrane's childhood. As a child, Coltrane listened and absorbed the sounds and images that surrounded him. He transformed them into musical notes that flowed from his horn. Back matter includes an author's note with additional information about Coltrane's life, a list of CDs for selected listening, and books for further reading. Coretta Scott King Illustrator Award Honor Book, 2009.

Wheeler, Jill C. *Faith Hill.* Edina, MN: ABDO, 2003. 64p. ISBN 978-1-57765-771-2. Grades: 3–6.

This brief biography includes information on her life, her career, and photographs. A glossary and an index conclude the book. From the Star Tracks series.

Bankston, John. *The Life and Times of Franz Peter Schubert.* Hockessin, DE: Mitchell Lane, 2004. 48p. ISBN 978-1-58415-177-7. Grades: 3–8.

At an early age Schubert's musical talent was evident. He died young and after his death his music gained the respect and affection it richly deserved. From the Masters of Music World's Greatest Composers series.

Whiting, Jim. *The Life and Times of Antonio Lucio Vivaldi.* Hockessin, DE: Mitchell Lane, 2005. 48p. ISBN 978-1-58415-241-5. Grades: 3–8.

Vivaldi's love of music and composing interfered with his priestly duties, resulting in him being relieved of his position, which enabled him to devote more time to his music. He is credited with creating the music form, concerto. From the Masters of Music World's Greatest Composers series.

Whiting, Jim. *The Life and Times of Giuseppe Verdi.* Hockessin, DE: Mitchell Lane, 2005. 48p. ISBN 978-1-58415-281-1. Grades: 3–8.

Italian Verdi was not considered a musical genius when he was young as many composers were; however, throughout his life he studied and composed music. His most acclaimed operas include *Rigoletto*, *Otello*, and *Aida*. From the Masters of Music World's Greatest Composers series.

Winter, Jonah. *Dizzy.* Illustrated by Sean Qualls. New York: Arthur A. Levine Books, 2006. Unp. ISBN 978-0-439-50737-0. Grades: 3–8.

John Birks Gillespie was said to have been born with a trumpet in his hands, but the truth is he first fooled around with a piano at a very early age. He picked up a trumpet at the age of thirteen and he was "on his way." This book is written in a very lyrical, poetic fashion and has brilliant yet subdued illustrations. Known for his "shenanigans," his band members began to call him "Dizzy" and the name stuck. From jazz and swing music, he developed his own style and is remembered for being the inventor of "bebop."

Dunham, Montrew. *Mahalia Jackson: Gospel Singer and Civil Rights Champion.* Illustrated by Cathy Morrison. Carmel, IN: Patria, 2003. 106p. ISBN 978-1-882859-38-2. Grades 4–8.

This biographical fiction begins in New Orleans in the early 1900s where Mahalia Jackson was born and ends with her career as a gospel singer. She began singing in the choir of the church where her father was the pastor. From the Young Patriots series.

Bankston, John. *The Life and Times of Duke Ellington.* Hockessin, DE: Mitchell Lane, 2005. 48p. ISBN 978-1-58415-248-4. Grades: 4–8.

When Edward Kennedy Ellington reached fourteen years of age, a friend noticed how well-spoken he was and what a sharp dresser he was and told him he was elegant, like royalty. He called him "Duke," a nickname which followed him the rest of his life. His parents had little formal education and were mostly self-taught. They instilled self-esteem and self-confidence in their son. Duke Ellington's determination, dedication, and work ethic aided him on his musical path. From the Masters of Music: The World's Greatest Composers series.

Galens, Judy. *Queen Latifah.* New York: Thomson Gale, 2007. 104p. ISBN 978-1-59018-930-6. Grades: 4–8.

When Dana Elaine Owens turned eight years old, she began to look for a "new" name. At this time in the United States many African Americans were adopting Muslim names to show their pride in their ancestry. Dana chose "Latifah," which meant "delicate," "sensitive," and "kind." As a teenager she developed a love of "rap" music and added "Queen" as a first name. She achieved fame not only as a "rapper" but also as an actor. Resources for learning more and an index conclude the book. From the People In the News series.

Harrah, Madge. *Blind Boone: Piano Prodigy.* Minneapolis, MN: Carolrhoda, 2004. 129p. ISBN 978-1-57505-057-7. Grades: 4–8.

Few people outside of the music world have ever heard of "Blind Boone," a piano prodigy who played ragtime to classical music. He had an "ear" for music and could play any music he heard including classical music. Born just before the end of the Civil War to a runaway slave, John William Boone became blind at six months of age due to an infection. An author's note, photographs, a chronology, a bibliography, and a list or recordings conclude the book. From the Trailblazer Biographies series.

Uschan, Michael V. *50 Cent.* New York: Thomson Gale, 2008. 104p. ISBN 978-1-4205-0011-0. Grades: 4–8.

Born into poverty, growing up black, and becoming an orphan at an early age, Curtis James Jackson III had a very difficult childhood. Curtis began dealing drugs and was arrested many times, incarcerated, and placed into a very tough rehabilitation program. When he became a father, he realized that he didn't want to rear a baby in the same environment he had grown up in and gave up drugs entirely. He devoted himself to becoming a rap musician. From the People in the News series.

Heos, Bridget. *Jay-Z.* New York: Rosen, 2009. 48p. ISBN 978-1-4358-5052-1. Grades: 5–8.

Jay-Z was named Shawn Carter when he was born in 1969 in Brooklyn, New York. At eleven he became enraptured with "rap" music and began making up rhymes to express in his feelings. As a teenager friends began calling him Jazzy and then Jay-Z. After many problems from drugs to "hustling," he began to achieve a certain amount of fame in selling records and promoting hip-hop music. The book concludes with a timeline, a discography, and a glossary. From The Library of Hip-Hop Biographies.

Freedman, Russell. *The Voice That Challenged a Nation: Marian Anderson and the Struggle for Equal Rights.* New York: Clarion, 2004. 114p. ISBN 978-0-618-15976-5. Grades: 5–9.

This photo-biography celebrates the life of Marian Anderson and her impact on the Civil Rights Movement. Prohibited from singing in Constitution Hall because she was African American, she sang instead on the steps of the Lincoln Memorial before a crowd of 75,000 and a national radio audience, thus sending a message that not all Americans would tolerate racial injustice. References, a discography, and an index conclude the book, which is also available on CD. NCSS Carter G. Woodson Middle Level Award Winner Book, 2005.

Gourse, Leslie. *Sophisticated Ladies: The Great Women of Jazz.* Illustrated by Martin French. New York: Penguin, 2007. 64p. ISBN 978-0-525-47198-1. Grades: 6 and up.

Fourteen women of jazz including Bessie Smith, Ethel Waters, Billie Holiday, Ella Fitzgerald, and Rosemary Clooney among others are profiled in this collective biography. Each of these noted singers made jazz their own by adapting it to their personal style. NCSS Carter G. Woodson Middle Level Honor Book, 2008.

Hampton, Wilborn. *Elvis Presley: A Twentieth-Century Life.* New York: Viking, 2007. 197p. ISBN 978-0-670-06166-2. Grades: 6 and up.

Hampton's admiration for Elvis is evident in this biography written in an easy-to-read style. Elvis' life, his far-reaching impact on the music world, and his impact on American culture are explored in detail, including his drug use and early death. The book contains black-and-white photographs, source notes, a bibliography, and an index. From the Up Close series.

Metzer, Greg. *Rock Band Name Origins: The Stories of 240 Groups and Performers.* Jefferson, NC: McFarland, 2008. 242p. ISBN 978-0-7864-3818-1. Grades: 7 and up.

The origins of the bands' names are fascinating, but equally interesting are the stories about the bands' members, the years the bands performed, and the bands' best-known song and its highest Billboard chart ranking. The book concludes with bibliographical references and index.

Neimark, Anne E. *Johnny Cash: A Twentieth-Century Life.* New York: Viking, 2007. 207p. ISBN 978-0-670-06215-7. Grades: 7 and up.

Born just after the beginning of the Great Depression, Johnny Cash drew on his harsh life experiences for his songwriting and singing. His problems with drugs and alcohol and his temper landed him in jail. He triumphed over his problems to become a music legend known as "The Man in Black." The book includes biographical references and an index.

Explorations

1. After reading *When Marian Sang: The True Recital of Marian Anderson, the Voice of a Century* (Ryan, 2002) have the students create a timeline of her life

using an online tool such as the one at www.teach-nology.com/web_tools/materials/timelines/ or use Timeliner EX software from Tom Snyder Productions to create a timeline of her life. The students will have to conduct additional research on her life to complete the timeline and they can also include information on what was happening in the United States during her lifetime.

2. While reading *Little Stevie Wonder* (Troupe, 2005) have students write down the different instruments (including his voice) that Stevie Wonder learned to play.
3. Listening is an important skill that is not often directly taught in the classroom. After reading *What Charlie Heard* (Gerstein, 2002) use the illustrations in the book as models for the students to create their own sound-filled pictures. Have the students draw a series of pictures while seated in different places such as the classroom, the playground, and the cafeteria. As they draw, have them listen to the sounds around them and include the sounds in their illustrations.
4. The glorious sounds in *What Charlie Heard* (Gerstein, 2002) can be used in the language arts classroom to teach onomatopoeia. Helping students make cross-curricular connections between language arts and music strengthens their learning in both areas.
5. After reading *Before John Was a Jazz Giant: A Song of John Coltrane* (Weatherford, 2008) visit www.johncoltrane.com to view videos of his life and to listen to interviews with him.
6. Prior to reading *Before John Was a Jazz Giant: A Song of John Coltrane* (Weatherford, 2008) Listen to a CD of the John Coltrane Quartet such as *Giant Steps*.
7. Before reading *Dizzy* (Winter, 2006) define the term "shenanigans." During reading have the students note examples of shenanigans in the story.
8. Have the students select a band from *Rock Band Name Origins: The Stories of 240 Groups and Performers* (Metzer, 2008) to create a presentation for their classmates. Encourage them to find out more about the band from other sources and to locate clips of music by the band.

TEACHER RESOURCES

The books, professional organizations, and Internet sites in this section offer educators an array of resources for teaching students to understand and appreciate music. From classical music to rhythm and blues, the resources in this section encompass all types of music.

Book and Media Choices

Nolan, Karin N. *Musi-matics! Music and Arts Integrated Math Enrichment Lessons.* Lanham, MD: Rowman and Littlefield, 2008. 152p. ISBN 978-1-57886-978-7. Grades K–8.

This useful resource contains lesson plans for integrating mathematics and music based on the National Arts Standards.

Sobol, Elise S. *An Attitude and Approach for Teaching Music to Special Learners*, Second Edition. Lanham, MD: Rowman and Littlefield, 2008. 148p. ISBN 978-1-57886-856-8. Grades: K–12.

Music teacher Sobol shares instructional strategies for teaching students with a variety of disabilities and disorders. She includes information on setting up a classroom and classroom management techniques, as well as how to teach musical literacy and critical thinking skills. The book includes a CD.

Bobetsky, Victor V. *The Magic of Middle School Musicals: Inspire Your Students to Learn, Grow, and Succeed*. Lanham, MD: Rowman and Littlefield, 2009. 128p. ISBN 978-1-57886-867-4. Grades 6–8.

Former middle school music teacher Bobetsky offers practical ideas for producing middle school musicals based on his own experiences. Students gain self-confidence and learn to work together as they perform.

Scherer, Barrymore Laurence. *A History of American Classical Music*. Naperville, IL: Sourcebooks, 2007. 247p. ISBN 978-1-40221-067-9. Grades: 6 and up.

From Colonial times to the present, this book explores the history of American classical music in text and audio. In addition to an audio CD, online tracks are available for students to hear and experience classical music.

Lazerine, Cameron, and Devin Lazerine. *Rap-Up: The Ultimate Guide to Hip-Hop and R&B*. New York: Grand Central Publishing, 2008. 335p. ISBN 978-0-446-17820-4.

Told in "street language" by a young man who grew up in the South, this straightforward book would be a good resource for librarians or teachers to get a deeper understanding of this phenomenal event in our culture.

Professional Organizations

American Music Center
322 8th Avenue, Suite 1401
New York, NY 10010
212-366-5260
www.amc.net
Web magazine: *NetMusicBox*

The American Musical Instrument Society
The Guild Associates, Inc.
389 Main Street, Suite 202
Malden, MA 02148
781-397-8870
www.amis.org
Journals: *Journal of the American Musical Instrument Society*, *Newsletter of the American Musical Instrument Society*

The National Association for Music Education
1806 Robert Fulton Drive
Reston, VA 21091
800-336-3768
www.menc.org
Journals: *Music Educators Journal*, *Teaching Music*

National Association of Schools of Music (NASM)
11250 Roger Bacon Drive
Reston, VA 20190-5248
703-437-0700
nasm.arts-accredit.org

Society for American Music
Stephen Foster Memorial
University of Pittsburgh
Pittsburgh, PA 15260
412-624-3031
www.american-music.org
Journal: *Journal of the Society for American Music*

Internet Sites

Alfred Music Publishing
www.alfred.com
Books, CDs, DVDs, sheet music, and software for learning and teaching music are available at this website. The extensive collection of resources on this website is searchable by title, artist, instruments, and product types.

American Music Resource
www.amrhome.net
This text-only reference database contains biographies, lists, and files that can be searched by topic or subject. Some of the resources include Internet links for gathering additional information.

The Children's Group, Inc.
www.childrensgroup.com
Resources, such as DVDs, CDs, and books, for sharing classical music with children are available on this website. The Children's Group is located in Pickering, Ontario, Canada.

Podcast.com
www.podcast.com
Under the education link on this site there is a section for K–12 that includes podcasts and vodcasts covering a variety of topics. The Children's Music Workshop videos include children performing and talking about the instruments they play.

The Secret Mountain
www.lamontagnesecrete.com/eng/index.shtml
Children's books filled with stories and songs accompanied by a CD with recordings of the songs are featured on this website. There are excerpts of the songs available for preview on the website. The stories and songs featured in the books come from various countries and would be terrific additions to social studies classes.

REFERENCES

D'Agrosa, Esther. 2008. "Making Music, Reaching Readers: Making Powerful Connections Possible for Young Students." *General Music Today* 21, no. 2 (Winter): 6–10.

Kenney, Susan H. 2008. "The Power of a Song." *General Music Today* 21, no. 2 (Winter): 35–38.

Miller, Beth Ann. 2008. "A Harmonious Duet: Music and Children's Literature." *General Music Today* 21, no. 2 (Winter): 18–24.

Mizener, Charlotte P. 2008. "Enhancing Language Skills through Music." *General Music Today* 21, no. 2 (Winter): 11–17.

Music Educators National Conference. 1994. *National Standards for Arts Education*. Reston, VA: Author. Available: www.menc.org (accessed March 9, 2010). From *National Standards for Art Education*. Copyright © 1994 by Music Educators National Conference (MENC). Used by permission. The complete National Arts Standards and additional materials relating to the Standards are available from MENC: The National Association for Music Education, 1806 Robert Fulton Drive, Reston, VA 20191; www.menc.org.

Palmer, Jesse, and Susie Burroughs. 2002. "Integrating Children's Literature and Song into the Social Studies Classroom." *Social Studies* 99, no. 3 (March): 73.

Paul, Phyllis M. 2004. "Enhancing Musical Response with Children's Literature." *General Music Today* 17, no. 2 (Winter): 6–16.

Wiggins, Donna Gwyn. 2007. "Pre-K Music and the Emergent Reader: Promoting Literacy in a Music-Enhanced Environment." *Early Childhood Education Journal* 35, no. 1 (August): 55–64.

Teacher Resources

This section contains general teacher resources that are not specific to one subject area. Included in these resources are journals, professional organizations, Internet sites, and media sources such as videos, DVDs, audiocassettes, CDs, and software.

JOURNALS

The following several journals are excellent sources of information on current children's books. Mailing addresses and websites for the journals are provided.

Bookbird: A Journal of International Children's Literature
The Johns Hopkins University Press
2715 North Charles Street
Baltimore, Maryland 21218-4363
419-516-6968
www.press.jhu.edu/journals/bookbird/

The Five Owls
PO Box 235
Marathon, TX 79842
432-386-4257
www.fiveowls.com

The Horn Book Magazine
56 Roland Street, Suite 200
Boston, MA 02129
800-325-1170
www.hbook.com

MultiCultural Review
18213 30th Street
Lutz, FL 33559
800-600-4364
813-264-2772
www.mcreview.com

School Library Journal
360 Park Avenue South
New York, NY 10010-1710
646-746-6759
www.schoollibraryjournal.com

Voice of Youth Advocates—VOYA
Scarecrow Press
4501 Forbes Boulevard., Suite 200
Lanham, MD 20706
888-486-9297
www.voya.com

PROFESSIONAL ORGANIZATIONS

The subject areas represented in the book all have their own professional organizations that support the work of teachers and librarians. Information on these subject organizations is located at the end of each chapter. The professional organizations listed here are ones focusing on other areas of interest to teachers. Information about the organizations and the resources they provide can be obtained by contacting the organizations using the addresses, phone numbers, or websites listed. The organizations have national, regional, state, and local conferences for teachers and librarians. Conferences are an excellent way for teachers to share ideas and to learn new things to enhance their teaching. In addition, many of the organizations publish journals of interest to elementary school teachers and middle school teachers. The names of these journals are included in the information below.

American Library Association
50 East Huron Street
Chicago, IL 60611
www.ala.org
Journals: *Booklist*, *Book Links*, *Journal of Youth Services*, *American Libraries*

Association for the Advancement of Computing in Education
PO Box 1545
Chesapeake, VA 23327-1545
www.aace.org
757-366-5606
Journals: *AACE Journal*, *International Journal on E-Learning (IJEL)—Corporate, Government, Healthcare & Higher Education*, *Journal of Interactive Learning Research (JILR)*

Association for Childhood Education International
17904 Georgia Avenue, Suite 215
Olney, MD 20832
www.acei.org
800-423-3563
Journal: *Journal of Research in Childhood Education*

The Center for Children's Books
501 East Daniel Street MC-493
Champaign, IL 61820-6211
ccb.lis.illinois.edu/
217-244-0324
Journal: *The Bulletin of the Center for Children's Books*

Children's Book Council
12 W. 37th Street, Floor 2
New York, NY 10018
www.cbcbooks.org
212-966-1990

Council for Exceptional Children
1110 North Glebe Road, Suite 300
Arlington, VA 22201
www.cec.sped.org/
888-232-7733
Journals: *Exceptional Children*, *Teaching Exceptional Children*

International Federation of Library Associations and Institutions
P.O. Box 95312
2509 CH The Hague
Netherlands
www.ifla.org
Journal: *IFLA Journal*

International Society for Technology in Education
180 West 8th Avenue, Suite 300
Eugene, OR 97401-2910
www.iste.org
800-336-5191
Journals: *Learning and Leading with Technology*, *Journal of Research on Computing in Education*

National Association for the Education of Young Children
1313 L Street, NW, Suite 500
Washington, DC 20005
www.naeyc.org
202-232-8777
Journals: *Young Children*, *Early Childhood Research Quarterly*

National Association for Gifted Children
1707 L Street, NW, Suite 550
Washington, DC 20036
www.nagc.org
202-785-4268
Journal: *Gifted Child Quarterly*

National Middle School Association
4151 Executive Parkway, Suite 300
Westerville, OH 43081
www.nmsa.org
614-895-4730
Journals: *Middle School Journal*, *Research in Middle Level Education*, *Middle Ground*

INTERNET SITES

Ambrose Video Publishing
www.ambrosevideo.com
Videos on this site are organized according to the following topics: science, history, English, and arts and music. The videos can be ordered on DVDs and some are available via video streaming.

Annenberg Media
www.learner.org
Annenberg Media is part of The Annenberg Foundation, whose mandate is to enhance teaching by providing multimedia resources to aid in the professional development of teachers. Some of the videos on the site are suitable for students. The site includes a search engine.

Ask Kids
www.askkids.com
Designed for children from 6 to 12 years of age, this website contains a search engine that points to appropriate sites for children. Links on the homepage include schoolhouse, movies, games, video, and images.

The Children's Book Council
www.cbcbooks.org
This is a nonprofit trade association of children's book publishers. It is a place to find out about recently published books as well as award-winning books.

Disney Educational Productions
dep.disney.go.com
Multimedia interactive tools for all subject areas and all grade levels are available on this site. DVDs on the site include public performance rights, teacher's guides, and ideas for assessing students' learning.

Educational Freeware
www.educational-freeware.com
Discover free software, learning games, and videos for all grade levels and across the content areas on this website. Some of the software is web-based, some of the software is available for downloading, and some of the software is multilingual.

Great Websites for Kids: Mathematics
www.ala.org/greatsites
The Association for Library Service to Children maintains a searchable collection of websites on a variety of topics including animals, the arts, history and biography, literature and languages, reference desk, mathematics and computers, sciences, and social sciences. The websites are designated as appropriate for prekindergarten through middle school students.

Ink Think Tank
www.inkthinktank.com
Award-winning nonfiction books are just a click away in this searchable database. Registration is required, but it is free. Under the support materials link are articles and books focusing on incorporating nonfiction books in teaching and learning.

Library Video Company
www.libraryvideo.com
Educational videos and audiobooks on a wide variety of topics are available on this site to support content area curriculum. Award-winning Schlessinger Media is a division of this company.

Public Broadcasting System (PBS)
www.pbs.org
The videos and podcasts available on this site can be used to quickly introduce students to new topics or to review familiar topics. There are also links specifically for kids, parents, and teachers. The site does include a search engine to help in locating just the right resources.

Smithsonian Institution
www.si.edu
This website contains links to Smithsonian resources on popular social networking sites such as Twitter, Facebook, and Flickr. There are also RSS feeds, podcasts, and blogs, in addition to online collections to explore and information about the many programs the Smithsonian offers.

Songs for Teaching: Using Music to Promote Learning
www.songsforteaching.com
Discover hand-clapping, toe-tapping songs for teaching across the content areas on this website. Early childhood songs, special education songs, and life skills songs may also be found here. The song lyrics, CDs, DVDs, books, and downloads are available for purchase. Previews are available for some of the songs in MP3 format. Educator resources on the site provide guidance on using songs to teach and a blog is available with ideas for using music in the classroom.

Teachers.net
teachers.net
Blogs, chatboards, and teacher mailrings provide teachers with online opportunities to connect and share ideas. The resources on the site do not stop there; they also include lesson plans, job postings, projects for K–12 students, and articles written by teachers.

Thinkfinity
thinkfinity.org
Sponsored by the Verizon foundation, this website has an impressive collection of consortium partners including ARTSEDGE, EconEdLink, EDSITEment, Illuminations,

Literacy Network, ReadWriteThink, Science NetLinks, Smithsonian's History Explorer, and Xpeditions. The site houses resources for educators, students, parents, and a special section for after-school explorations.

Titlewave
www.titlewave.com
Follett Library Resources sponsors this searchable database of books and much more including digital resources, grants and funding opportunities, book award lists, and behind-the-book interviews.

Tom Snyder Productions
www.tomsnyder.com
Scholastic Corporation is the parent company of this award-winning software company. The software supports learning in science, math, social studies, and reading language arts as well as teacher resources.

Yahoo! Kids
kids.yahoo.com
This site contains a mix of resources for having fun and for learning. Music, jokes, sports, music, games, and a place for asking questions are all available.

MEDIA SOURCES

Annenberg Media
PO Box 55742
Indianapolis, IN 46205-0742
800-532-7637
www.learner.org

itunes
www.apple.com/itunes

Library Video Company
PO Box 580
Wynnewood, PA 19096
800-843-3620
www.libraryvideo.com

Midwest Tapes
6950 Hall Street
PO Box 820
Holland, OH 43528
800-875-2785
www.midwesttapes.com

TeacherTube
www.teachertube.com

Weston Woods
143 Main Street
Norwalk, CT 06851
800-243-5020
teacher.scholastic.com/products/westonwoods/

Author and Illustrator Index

A

B

C

D

E

F

G

H

I

J

K

L

M

N

O

P

S

T

U

V

W

Y

Z

Title Index

A

C

D

E

F

G

H

I

M

N

O

P

Q

R

S

Y

Z

Subject Index

A

B

C

D

E

F

G

N

O

P

R

S

T

U

V

W

X

Y

Z

About the Authors

Kathryn I. Matthew is a former classroom teacher and is a professor at the University of Houston–Clear Lake. She received graduate and undergraduate degrees from the University of New Orleans. She received an EdD in Curriculum and Instruction with an emphasis on technology and reading from the University of Houston. Kathryn and Joy co-authored the *Neal-Schuman Guide to Celebrations and Holidays around the World* and *Puppet Magic*. Kathryn also wrote *Developing Better Readers and Writers Using Caldecott Books*, published by Neal-Schuman. She lives in Sugar Land, Texas, with her husband Chip.

Joy L. Lowe is a former school and public librarian. She taught library science at Louisiana Tech University for 25 years. She received graduate and undergraduate degrees from Centenary College of Louisiana, Louisiana Tech University, and Louisiana State University. She received a PhD in Library and Information Science from the University of North Texas. Kathryn and Joy co-authored the *Neal-Schuman Guide to Celebrations and Holidays around the World* and *Puppet Magic*. Joy lives in Ruston, Louisiana, with her husband, Perry.